T0227435

A FUNCTIONAL START TO COMPUTING WITH
PYTHON

CHAPMAN & HALL/CRC
TEXTBOOKS IN COMPUTING

Series Editors

John Impagliazzo
Professor Emeritus, Hofstra University

Andrew McGettrick
Department of Computer
and Information Sciences
University of Strathclyde

Aims and Scope

This series covers traditional areas of computing, as well as related technical areas, such as software engineering, artificial intelligence, computer engineering, information systems, and information technology. The series will accommodate textbooks for undergraduate and graduate students, generally adhering to worldwide curriculum standards from professional societies. The editors wish to encourage new and imaginative ideas and proposals, and are keen to help and encourage new authors. The editors welcome proposals that: provide groundbreaking and imaginative perspectives on aspects of computing; present topics in a new and exciting context; open up opportunities for emerging areas, such as multi-media, security, and mobile systems; capture new developments and applications in emerging fields of computing; and address topics that provide support for computing, such as mathematics, statistics, life and physical sciences, and business.

Published Titles

Pascal Hitzler, Markus Krötzsch, and Sebastian Rudolph, Foundations of Semantic Web Technologies

Uvais Qidwai and C.H. Chen, Digital Image Processing: An Algorithmic Approach with MATLAB®

Henrik Bærbak Christensen, Flexible, Reliable Software: Using Patterns and Agile Development

John S. Conery, Explorations in Computing: An Introduction to Computer Science

Lisa C. Kaczmarczyk, Computers and Society: Computing for Good

Mark J. Johnson, A Concise Introduction to Programming in Python

Paul Anderson, Web 2.0 and Beyond: Principles and Technologies

Henry M. Walker, The Tao of Computing, Second Edition

Mark C. Lewis, Introduction to the Art of Programming Using Scala

Ted Herman, A Functional Start to Computing with Python

CHAPMAN & HALL/CRC
TEXTBOOKS IN COMPUTING

A FUNCTIONAL START TO COMPUTING WITH

PYTHON

Ted Herman

CRC Press
Taylor & Francis Group
Boca Raton London New York

CRC Press is an imprint of the
Taylor & Francis Group, an **informa** business

A CHAPMAN & HALL BOOK

CRC Press
Taylor & Francis Group
6000 Broken Sound Parkway NW, Suite 300
Boca Raton, FL 33487-2742

First issued in hardback 2017

Version Date: 20130422

ISBN-13: 978-1-4665-0455-4 (pbk)
ISBN-13: 978-1-138-46082-9 (hbk)

Library of Congress Cataloging-in-Publication Data

Herman, Ted, 1952-
    A functional start to computing with Python / author, Ted Herman.
        pages cm. -- (Chapman & Hall/CRC textbooks in computing)
        Summary: "Open source and easy to use, Python offers the availability of exciting libraries of software, application programming interfaces, and even connections to Web services. This textbook uses Python as a working environment to teach the basics of computing for students with no prior programming experience. Unlike similar texts, it organizes topics based on a functional first approach to teaching programming. The book includes case studies of practical problems as well as homework and interactive tools online, such as flashcards"-- Provided by publisher.
        Includes bibliographical references and index.
        ISBN 978-1-4665-0455-4 (pbk.)
        1. Python (Computer program language) I. Title.

QA76.73.P98H47 2013
005.13'3--dc23   2013014251

Visit the Taylor & Francis Web site at
http://www.taylorandfrancis.com

and the CRC Press Web site at
http://www.crcpress.com

Contents

Preface

ACM's 2001 Curriculum Guidelines recognize six directions to introducing computer science: imperative first, objects first, functional first, breadth first, algorithms first, and hardware first. As Python has taken a prominent position as an introductory programming language, the question of how to use it in the functional first direction becomes interesting. Recently, for example, the classic approach of Abelson, Sussman, and Sussman's *Structure and Interpretation of Computer Programs* (McGraw-Hill, 1984), originally targeted to Scheme, has been adapted to Python.

My interest in using Python, yet preferring a functional first approach, is based on observing what beginners find difficult.

> (1) Beginners find assignment to variables troublesome. There is increased cognitive load when distinguishing between a symbol x defined as 3, and later x apparently equaling 103 in the same, brief program. True functional programming avoids this situation. The first half of this book omits all assignment statements, except for one-time definitions of variables in functions. (Incidentally, complaints about Python's dynamic typing become subdued in programs that omit assignment and mutation.)

> (2) Control structures, particularly iteration and exception handling, also confuse beginners. The introduction of control structures is delayed until the second half of the book, which covers imperative programming.

Sticking to life without assignment or loops might seem too constraining to be interesting to students. To be sure, this approach does ask for more patience than a "sink or swim" approach to learning how to program. Fortunately, Python has features that address the functional style. Students usually find working with expressions, manipulating data structures with operators, and simple conditional logic natural enough to be quickly engaged in writing their own functions. String operations of concatenation, slicing, splitting, and joining are appealing material. While the abstractions of more advanced functionals and comprehension syntax are more difficult for beginners, they have the advantage of challenging students who previously have only had exposure to imperative and operational styles of programming.

The second half of the book follows a traditional approach: assignment and iteration ensures that the reader sees the standard notion of imperative loops. Along the way, there is material about common patterns and language idioms, and topics of modules, files, networking, and simple system interfaces that provide motivation. Although discussion of classes and objects is put off until near the end of the book, many of the concepts are implicitly put into action when data types, methods, and variable aliasing are explained. The student is well prepared at the point where object and class terminology appears.

Throughout the book, I have tried to inculcate important concepts of computing along with the specifics of Python. Indeed, if you are looking for a book that teaches just Python as quickly as possible, there are hundreds of texts now on the market. The many boxes and examples stress such things as software engineering motivation, algorithms behind the syntax rules, some advanced functional programming ideas, and there is even a brief exposure to finite state machines.

Early reviewers of the book noted that some decisions will be uncomfortable: working with files and graphics comes late; the many attractive libraries and potential for real-life problem solving is delayed by the functional first approach. For many readers, it may be worth skipping chapters and looking ahead to find these techniques, even if they are not fully understood. The estimated difficulty of the chapters is uneven by design. On a scale from 1 to 8, this graph estimates the technical difficulty of the material from each chapter.

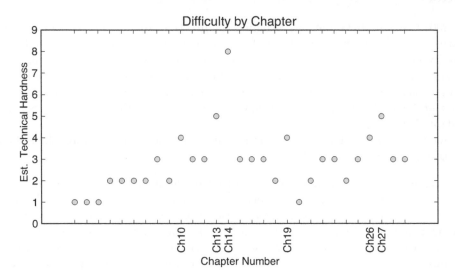

The graph labels more difficult chapters on the x-axis. Chapter 10 describes some of the interesting, but likely unfamiliar ways that Python treats function parameters and arguments. Chapter 13 introduces list comprehensions, followed by Chapter 14 that goes into more advanced functional programming patterns; Chapter 14 could well be skipped by non-avid readers. In the imperative half of the book, Chapter 19, which introduces iteration, again becomes more difficult, and the two later difficult chapters are 26 and 27, because they address exception handling, classes, and objects.

Companion online support for this book is found at `functionalfirstpython.com`, which provides flash cards, a simple interactive Python tracer, software modules, and unit tests (effectively, programming puzzles). Selected exercises in the chapters, annotated with ✰, have answers in the Appendix. In the context of sections of chapters, associated online material is indicated by the arrow/web annotation shown to the right.   ⇨ web

Part I

Motivation and Background

Chapter 1:   Inspirations of Computing

The discovery of music recording was a transformative event in human history. Here was an invention that almost everyone instantly desired. Recorded music can be enjoyed by people who cannot read or write, who cannot themselves play an instrument or sing. It is hard to look back on the first crude recording technologies with their scratchy noises and wobbly playback and understand how people could be satisfied. An amazing accumulation of clever technology has improved the quality of recording and playback to a remarkable extent. Even in the early days, engineers worked hard to reduce noise and ensure good fidelity in reproducing original sound.

In the middle of the last century, magnetic tape became a preferred medium for recording. This medium gives an engineer more options to overcome defects in what has been recorded. A good engineer may be able to cut the tape, splice in part of another recording, and use other tricks of modification. If some piece of equipment fell during a recording session, a recording engineer might even be able to remove the sound of the accident, so the listener would never know. More challenging are live recording sessions in front of an audience. The placement of microphones, the sound levels, and mitigating audience noise become problematic. Another problem during live recording can be that performers (especially in rock venues) might not be able to hear themselves singing; a singer could well miss a note, sing slightly off-key, yet be unaware of the mistake. This leaves the recording engineer with another problem: can the recording be tweaked so that off-key notes are transformed into the proper pitch? It is not so easy. You can speed up the tape to raise the pitch, but that changes the timing. Eventually, with hard work and long hours of trying many things, recording engineers found tricks to overcome the problem of sour notes.

Arguably the discovery with the greatest impact in recent history of recordings is digital technology. By converting the electronic signals from microphones to digital form, the recordings can be stored in highly efficient packages, like MP3s and other compressed formats. Further, the playback and recording devices get smaller and cheaper. Relating back to how engineers improve recording quality, the digital formats can be manipulated in many new ways with far less laborious processes. When this technology first became widespread, recording engineers were somewhat secretive about how they improved recordings. A new technique automated the work of correcting the pitch of a singer. The magic was due to a proprietary product called Auto-Tune. For some years the public was kept in the dark about the existence of Auto-Tune. Then, in 1998, a hit song by Cher exploited and even emphasized the use of Auto-Tune, and it was no secret. What used to be a trick of the trade became widely known to the public.

The story of how Auto-Tune came into existence is one of those surprising sequences of connections that link up, as happens sometimes in the history of innovation. Exploring for oil is now an advanced scientific enterprise, drawing on satellite images, geological research, and measuring seismic reaction to low-frequency vibration in exploratory prospects. The study of vibration is essentially based on acoustic principles, which also apply to the tones of musical instruments. An engineer working at Exxon noticed a connection between the signal processing of sound in oil exploration and the detection of proper pitch in music. Engineering principles used for classifying and removing noise from shock waves during exploratory tests could also be used to reshape sound waves, thus correcting the pitch of off-key notes. This observation eventually resulted, with lots of hard work solving other problems, in Auto-Tune.

After Auto-Tune became more widely known, and accepted by at least some listeners, performers started using it openly, more often, and some would say, more creatively. Rap artist T-Pain used Auto-Tune continuously in performances. Used heavily, Auto-Tune gives the voice clipped sound, with instant transition between notes that can resemble yodeling. The hip-hop group Black Eyed Peas has cultivated this sound, selectively. Other performers came under the influence of the "new sound" of Auto-Tune, to the extent that it became something to emulate even without using Auto-Tune itself. Thus, we have a strange circle of development intertwining technology and popular culture, which appears to be a theme in other areas of modern life.

☆   ☆   ☆

Tracking athletic performance and ranking athletes in different ways has become an industry. It is not just the records of times for track athletes and swimmers, nor are sports fans content with counting strings of victories. Now fantasy sports leagues are million dollar business communities, which track the numbers, events, and achievements of players in new ways. Where did all of this originate? Perhaps the roots go to the motivations of conversation. There is an old saying that all conversation is either bragging, complaining, or gossip (who did what to whom). Whatever the reason, fans of sports follow the tabulations of the teams and their players with enthusiasm.

In America we can credit baseball for the earliest, large scale publication of numbers and records. As early as 1859 journalists started counting various events on the playing field, recording the number of errors, the batting average over the course of a season, and RBI (runs batted in). The event counts, averages, and other numbers became part of the sports news stream, which fans followed, making it easy for them to identify rising stars in baseball. Players with the best records draw an audience. Teams compete to get the best players—team managers also read the papers. The rich teams have sufficient budgets to buy talent from the poorer teams, leading to fame and fortune for players with the best individual statistics. Another way that teams obtain talent is by shrewdly selecting talent, by drafting the right combination of players and cultivating their skills in minor leagues.

The colorful history of baseball and the lore of draft picks, trades, rule changes, and scheduling was for many decades a guild where wisdom was passed down through storytelling. Somewhere during the 1970s, the question of baseball statistics was revisited, questioning whether the right sort of events were being counted. Trade publications began tracking more numbers. Out of the numbers people tried to find correlations between player and team statistics and winning games. The thinking is that if a model can be found which accurately predicts winning on the basis of event counts, like number of walks, number of hits, and so on, then players and managers will know what counts most toward winning games. Even if this prediction is only accurate to a reasonable percentage, it might still win out over the course of a long season.

Two decades later, in the 1990s, a few general managers with some training in scientific methodology proposed taking the statistics further. The conjecture was that the stories passed down among coaches, scouts, and players about talent and strategy were not grounded in statistical knowledge. To test this hypothesis, the manager of the Oakland A's based the selection of players more rigorously and with finer levels of statistics than any team had done before. They were up against a major disadvantage: the budget they had for players was less than a third of the New York Yankees. In spite of being a poor team, the team followed decisions based on a scientific understanding of statistics. The result was surprising. During the 2000–2002 seasons one of the poorest teams in baseball, the Oakland A's, had one of the most successful winning records.[1] A few sports fans are still not satisfied this new approach is valid, pointing out that the A's did not win the World Series

---

[1] Read *Moneyball: The Art of Winning an Unfair Game* by Michael Lewis (W. W. Norton, 2003), for the full story.

(actually, the loss of the Series might be attributed to human error in coaching, which deviated from the strict policy of basing decisions on the statistics). In any case, the success of Oakland caught the attention of other teams, who began emulating statistics-based decision techniques of evaluating players, and copied the new strategies for managing and selecting talent.

If you walk toward the city of Chartres you might see across a flat landscape covered in grain fields a small upright structure in the distance. As you continue walking toward that structure, it begins to rise above the plain and take form. The geometric form becomes clear as spires of the great cathedral are seen in more detail. The view of the cathedral growing up from the plain seems calculated to inspire. The cathedral of Chartres was a pioneering architectural achievement of its time, the construction spanning several centuries. An untold number of anonymous laborers made lasting contributions in building this renowned masterpiece.

What you do not see looking at the cathedral of Chartres or other impressive buildings dating to the time (13th to 16th centuries) is the number of failed attempts at similar construction. Cities competed to have the grandest, tallest, and most impressive churches, however, construction technology coming out of the dark ages was primitive. Many attempts to build tall structures, especially ones that had enough windows to light up the interiors, came to disastrous ends. To be sure, the invention of the flying buttress was a breakthrough in structural engineering, but the knowledge of how to create successful tall cathedrals remained more an informal art than a predictable science.

The human desire to push the envelope of daring architecture continues today. Catalogs of famous buildings of the modern era feature skyscrapers competing for height and for imaginative design. Other dimensions of competition include innovative materials, unusual shapes, hidden perspectives, novel use of lighting, and arranging spaces to evoke certain feelings in a building's occupants. A prominent example is the Guggenheim Museum in Bilbao, often cited for the seemingly random use of curves throughout the edifice. More recent, and on a larger scale, is the Beijing National Stadium, known worldwide from the 2008 Summer Olympics. Sometimes called the "bird's nest," the stadium's construction exposes structural beams that have the appearance, from a distance, of random sticks. In the night, when the stadium's inside is illuminated, a glowing interior can be seen through the lattice of steel beams.

Construction technology, design methods, and mechanical and civil engineering have advanced to the point that creating modern buildings is far more reliable (and safer for construction workers) than were the endeavors of the middle ages. The tension between what an architect can imagine and what can be built has decreased, though building cost remains a concern as it was many centuries ago. Modern civilization can realize architecture that would have been undreamt just a century ago.

What is common to the foregoing stories should come as no surprise, given the title of this book. Each story culminates in technology that depends on software. Andy Hildebrand, working at Exxon with autocorrelation software, created the basic idea for Auto-Tune. Billy Beane, in part exploiting the computer analysis of earlier pioneers of Sabremetrics, led the Oakland A's to winning seasons. Modern, cutting-edge architecture would not be possible without packages like Autodesk's architectural suite of software.

Quietly, computing is fading into the background and fabric of modern society. We take for granted many technologies based on material science, electromagnetic principles, and even social conventions with murky origins. Software and computing is becoming another ubiquitous part of everything. The most common personal computer on the planet is the phone, which typically has well over a million lines of software code.

So how does it all work? At least to some degree, we should be curious and see what is behind the technology. Perhaps with a bit of study, you might even find you can do a bit of programming yourself, and at least have some feel for what is possible, and more important, what are the pitfalls and limitations of software. This book goes beyond simple lessons on traditional programming language topics. The aim is to show that computing has scientific content, and that some design choices are debatable.

Yet, what fundamentally _is_ computing? It seems now to be more than scientific or mathematical calculation. The largest consumers of computing are entertainment and communication industries. In the 1980s, philosopher and scholar Marshall McLuhan reinterpreted human technologies as extensions and amplifications of ourselves. The wheel, in some sense, amplifies the foot—it improves our locomotion. McLuhan saw the computer as a "brain amplifier." In fact, a more accurate view would be to identify computing as an extension of the nervous system. Computing elements are now deeply embedded in aircraft, smart building infrastructure, vehicles, and appliances. Now sensors of all sorts, pressure, vibration, motion, light, and temperature are wired up along with computing elements that sense, route signals, and find patterns of data, as one might expect of an extended nervous system.

As a discipline of study, computing abides by its own precepts and it favors some skills over others. If you ask a professor of law what one learns in law school, the answer might well be "to think like a lawyer"; and to become a psychologist is to learn how to think like a psychologist. So it is with many disciplines, including computing. To gain some inkling of how computing scientists think, you need to learn a bit of programming. In essence, programming is about control. What is being controlled are the flows of data, the state of memory, and possibly the signals leading out to external devices or the signals coming in from sensing components. In some cases, this kind of control can produce music, interactive displays, and guide networked conversations among people. Programming is also a kind of technical self-expression which benefits from creative effort and careful planning. The doorway to learning about programming is to become somewhat fluent in a programming language. The main apparent subject of the remaining chapters is a programming language, Python. It is only one of many computing languages, just as English is only one human language. The real aim of the book is to encourage new ways of thinking about problem solving, ways that even so stupid a device as a computer can perform.

Chapter 2:   Preview of Computing with Python

Many textbooks about programming plunge into the subject with a simple program, say one that prints "Hello" three times. Easy enough in Python, it looks like this:

```
for i in range(3):
    print("Hello")
```

runs with output

```
Hello
Hello
Hello
```

This textbook is different from most other texts: we do not advocate jumping into programming in the usual way. At the end of the chapter, some rationale for the book's approach is explained. The value of the preview here is to show how the "code" for programs can be cryptic, yet parts are understandable. In many cases, the overall logical appearance, and also seeing the result of what a program does when it runs, conveys the general idea. Sometimes it is not that difficult to make a few changes here and there, and quickly modify a program. Many people learn in this way.

Spiral Drawing

Let's draw a spiral, something like what is shown in the shaded box to the left. Of course, it is easy to draw a spiral, but to do it well requires some good drawing skills—or a computer-controlled pen. So, let's think about writing a *program* to draw a spiral.

```
from turtle import *
from math import *
pensize(10)
pencolor("blue")
penup()
goto(20,0)
pendown()
for i in range(1,101):
  newangle = 2 * i * pi / 100
  goto( 20*cos(newangle),
        20*sin(newangle) )
```

Nearly everyone faced with a programming task starts with the same approach: hasn't this been done before? And if not, is there something close to what we want that we can use? These are the same questions that any "maker" asks, whether a carpenter, landscaper, or chef. Turns out, most programming systems do have something for drawing a circle. One such example (easily found through a Web search) is a Python program to draw a circle, seen to the left in small print. It is not important to understand every detail of this program, but it is pretty easy to guess that it means to "draw" with a blue-colored **pen**, and it is using trigonometry to make a circle. The numbers 100 and 101 in the program effectively split the job of drawing a circle into a hundred little drawing steps, each tracing around a circle. When the program runs, it makes a circle something like what you see below. ⇨ web

This "circle" is actually composed of a hundred straight lines. Why not experiment with the program? What would happen if we change the program to only draw through thirty points out of the hundred? Next, the program has been changed, replacing 101 with 30, and you can see the result.

Change 101 to 30 ...

```
from turtle import *
from math import *
pensize(10)
pencolor("blue")
penup()
goto(20,0)
pendown()
for i in range(1,30):
    newangle = 2 * i * pi / 100
    goto( 20*cos(newangle),
     20*sin(newangle) )
```

So reducing the number of lines from 101 to 30 has the expected effect, only a portion of a circle is drawn. Here, in a moment of inspiration, we imagine how to draw a spiral: draw a bit of a circle with a small radius, then continue with a larger radius, and so on. These instructions will "warp" the circle into a spiral. So where is the radius in the program? Is it 2 or 20? (We already know what the role of 100 is.) The hint is that the first **goto** puts the pen at position (20,0), suggesting that the radius is likely 20. The new version of the program changes things by increasing the radius each time a line is drawn.

```
from turtle import *
from math import *
pensize(10)
pencolor("blue")
penup()
radius = 20
goto(radius,0)
pendown()
for i in range(1,30):
    newangle = 2 * i * pi / 100
    goto( radius*cos(newangle),
     radius*sin(newangle) )
    radius = radius + 1
```

You may be able to see how the partial circle has been warped somewhat. But we still do not have a spiral. The problem is that it is only drawing 30 lines, unlike the original hundred. In fact, for a spiral, we need to go around several times, to see the spiral effect. The logic of a hundred lines per 360° sweep around remains, however, the number of tiny lines will increase, say to three hundred. Below, the drawing has been scaled down to fit on the page.

```
from turtle import *
from math import *
pensize(10)
pencolor("blue")
penup()
radius = 20
goto(radius,0)
pendown()
for i in range(1,300):
    newangle = 2 * i * pi / 100
    goto( radius*cos(newangle),
     radius*sin(newangle) )
    radius = radius + 1
```

Reports

Maybe drawing (and especially the trigonometry) are not to your taste, or perhaps the previous example seems too far from practical purposes. Here is a different kind of task, similar things often done in networked businesses. A Web site keeps records of what clients request over the network, in a file that grows throughout each day. Just a few records are shown here (with lots of data suppressed to keep things simple):

```
61.135.249.84 - - [27/May/2011:04:44:36 -0500] "GET / HTTP/1.1" 200 2708 "-"
189.85.128.10 - - [27/May/2011:06:51:59 -0500] "GET /favicon.ico HTTP/1.0" 200 904 "-"
207.46.204.231 - - [27/May/2011:06:59:14 -0500] "GET /robots.txt HTTP/1.1" 404 208 "-"
```

Each record in the file shows a network address (like 207.46.204.231), a date and time of a client request, and other information. The task is to produce a report showing which hours of the day had more than a thousand requests for the Web site.

How might such a report be done? The idea is straightforward: go through all the records, and gradually build up a table of hours and the count of requests for that hour. At the end, just report those hours where the number of requests were more than one thousand. Here is the expression of this idea as a Python program:

```python
import urllib
from pprint import *
webpage = urllib.urlopen("http://acme.br/log/current")
hours = { i:0 for i in range(24) }
for line in webpage:
    fields = line.split()
    timedata = fields[3]
    subfields = timedata.split(':')
    HH = int(subfields[1])
    hours[HH] = hours[HH] + 1
busyhours = { i:hours[i] for i in hours if hours[i]>1000 }
pprint(busyhours)
```

```
{8: 4053,
 9: 1672,
 11: 3150,
 12: 1745,
 14: 1292,
 16: 1102,
 17: 1189,
 19: 1120,
 21: 1358}
```

One can see from the output of this program shown in the shaded box, that peak hours for the Web site were eight and eleven (morning). In the program, the location of the Web site's file of requests is given as a URL, much as browsers use. You can see the URL on the third line of the program. Python's `urllib` library makes it very easy for programs to read Web pages. The program's fourth line creates a table of hours, and the fifth line starts the description of what is done with each line in the file: each record is split up into fields, the hour is extracted and the appropriate table entry is updated. In the final two lines of the program, the hours with counts greater than one thousand are extracted and printed.

Goal

The goal of computer science is to put itself out of business. Rather than instructing a computer with all the individual steps of a task in excruciating detail, we should be able to describe *what we want* instead of *how to do it*. Unfortunately, the current state of affairs is that we are very far away from the computers and software in science fiction movies. The reality is that we often have to resort to providing detailed, step-by-step precise instructions in a program.

There are some signs of hope in computing. For certain kinds of databases, there are natural language interfaces, where we can describe the data needed and the software will figure out how to get it. Similarly, search engines find results based on text queries, sample images, or sounds, without demanding that users write programs. In the realm of software tools, there are some *declarative languages* that avoid details of how computing steps are done. Recently there is renewed interest in *functional languages* (closely related to declarative languages). Some programming difficulties and even bugs can be eliminated using functional languages. However, declarative and functional languages still do require programmers to be precise and think through what they want. The current state of the art remains far from dreams of effortless human-computer interaction.

This text advocates a functional start to learning about computing, even though Python is not a functional language. The learning technique is simply this: we can begin by learning those aspects of Python that are in the spirit of functional languages, and then return to the rest later. This learning technique has advantages:

- ✔ The initial focus on expressions and operations on data is familiar and intuitive to most students. Python's calculator mode encourages experimentation and provides instant feedback.

- ✔ Programs build upon functions and structures of data, so that ways of manipulating data are naturally introduced.

- ✔ The Python language has many standard functional concepts built-in, which other mainstream languages (Java, Javascript, C++) do not have, and this simplifies learning.

There are also some disadvantages:

- ✖ For the impatient, say those who would love to immediately use the `PyGame` environment to design games or tinker with graphics, many of the needed parts of Python are delayed to later chapters. The approach of this book delays gratification.

- ✖ For those who already know another language like Java, the approach of this book does not quickly leverage what they already know.

Chapter 3: General Landscape of Computing Languages

There are people who actually
like programming. I don't understand why they like programming.
— Rasmus Lerdorf, creator of the PHP Programming Language

Jokes do not usually translate well across languages. What is funny in Swahili may not cause any laughter in Greek. Come to think of it, even from one person to the next in English, a joke may not convey humor. Nonetheless, the odds are much worse in getting "funny" to translate between different languages. Why should this be? The answer may depend on the particular joke. Puns are very language specific. Also, there are sometimes cultural bases of jokes which are not part of another language and another culture. And it is not just jokes that translate poorly. Poetry, stories, even proverbs that hold wisdom might not easily be restated in another language and have the same effect. People fluent in several languages sometimes explain that some things are easier to say in one language than another, or that a particular phrase cannot be exactly translated. What accounts for this?

One radical theory holds that languages have some effect on how people think. If this were true, then it might indeed be the case that populations speaking Spanish have a different appreciation for certain phrases than would equivalent groups of English speakers have for the same, translated phrase. Perhaps some languages make it easier to be witty, and maybe other languages promote politeness. There is a name for the theory, the Sapir-Worf Hypothesis. Research on this and similar theories continues. Investigators of such theories agree that no natural language is intrinsically superior to another. However, speakers of one language or another do feel special attachment to their native tongues. It is difficult to find anyone in China who does not feel Chinese is the best language; the same is true in Italy of Italian, and so on.

Programming languages are artificial creations of a few individuals. As with human languages, there are many programming languages. Human languages can be classified into family trees and the evolution of languages can be mapped; the same is roughly true for programming languages. A big difference between these is the reason *why* there are so many languages. For natural languages that humans use, the history of population movement, wars, nations, and trade routes explains the origins of the different languages. The diversity and divergence of programming languages is partly explained by historical factors, but a more fundamental reason for having many programming languages is the need for notation and conventions that are well suited to application needs. Languages for database queries can be streamlined for that purpose, whereas those for robotics are specialized to control mechanics and movement.

Most people acquainted with a personal computer system exhibit the *baby duck syndrome*. Ducklings (and birds generally) bond to the first caregiver they see, usually a parent duck. If the first caregiver is a person, the duckling will bond to that person. The same occurs with people who bond to one kind of computer system, say Windows or Mac, and become fixed on that system as the natural way that computers should be. Similarly, people who learn one programming language well feel it is the best programming language, much as people in Russia might believe that Russian is the best natural language. This kind of bonding can be unfortunate, particularly for readers of this book: the language used here is Python, best known as a scripting language (a language for writing scripts of commands). Python was chosen because it is widely supported in many types of computing platforms, because there is a rich library of available software for Python, and it is well suited to education, with free versions of the language that are easy to install on personal computers. Python is also serious enough to use for practical things. The Google search engine began as a Python program; the popular BitTorrent file sharing software was originally written in Python; web programming kits and game development tools in Python are available. Ultimately, however, Python is just one choice. Other languages like Java, C#, Scheme, Ruby, and C are good choices for learning about programming. The truth is that learning several programming languages is expected of professionals, and it becomes easier to learn another language once you have mastered one of them. There is no "best" programming language.

Background Skills

Many language courses are offered at a university: French, Spanish, Japanese, and other natural languages are typical examples. Methods for learning a natural language can be compared to ways of learning programming languages. Like natural languages, programming languages can take years to fully master; an introductory course only goes so far. Like natural language courses, a beginning class on Python will be somewhat easier to follow for students who have a linguistic aptitude and who have a desire to learn new ways of expression (some memorization and some creativity in combining a language's basic elements). Like learning natural languages, drills and interactive learning sessions are the typical ways of building up skills, and this can sometimes be a time-consuming and frustrating experience. However, unlike learning natural languages, the learning of computing languages requires more appreciation of logical abstractions and precision in how ideas are expressed. At the current state of computing evolution, the computer cannot "guess" what a programmer means (despite science fiction movie portrayals).

Students and teachers have reported that a variety of background skills can be helpful to learning a programming language. Some of these skills are listed here, though previously knowing another programming language is also an obvious advantage (just as knowing some French is a large advantage when taking a French course).

- Knowing how to use a word processor, even if just a simple scratchpad text area for typing, cutting, and pasting, is helpful. Also, being able to use a Web browser and a search engine can be quite useful. For some applications, knowing how to find and launch applications on a windowing desktop is an advantage. Being able to navigate through folders, copy, rename, and move folders and files is necessary in some cases.

- The experience of learning more than one natural language can be good preparation toward learning a programming language. If you are open to new ways of expressing ideas, you might more easily accept different styles of formal computing languages.

- Students who enjoy logical puzzles may have a head start; another asset for learning computer languages is the ability to concentrate on logical games. Proficiency in quick reaction time, first-person shooter games is *not* so helpful.

- Having a good math background is generally helpful, but it is not a sure sign of ability for programming. The chapters that follow only suppose the reader to know basic algebra and arithmetic operations.

- There appears to be some correlation between skill with musical instruments, which require practice, and programming aptitude. Best is the kind of practice incorporating standard music scores and scales, possibly even sight reading.

Learning a Language

There are distinct stages in the progression of language mastery. The initial stage is to learn some vocabulary and basic syntax. The syntax of a language consists of rules on how to combine verbs, nouns, pronouns, articles, and so on, into acceptable phrases and sentences. The learning of syntax and vocabulary can be time-consuming. Exercises of repetition are the usual path to building up memory of vocabulary. The most efficient way to learn a foreign vocabulary is not widely known, but if you have the time and are willing to devote the effort, there are tools to optimize the process (e.g., SuperMemo and similar applications). Computing languages have much smaller vocabularies than natural languages, so memorization is not the biggest challenge for this stage of learning programming.

Another stage in learning a language is the accumulation of idioms and patterns of sentence construction. It turns out that people read and understand text by "chunking," which basically means that groups of words are seen and understood as grouped together as familiar phrases. Programming also depends on familiar patterns and common expressions that programmers tend to repeatedly use. The first phase in this stage is to read and comprehend enough examples so that they become familiar. Mastery only occurs later, when you start writing on your own, using these expressions yourself.

A later stage in learning a language is storytelling. To tell a story, you need to put sentences together coherently. The analog to storytelling in computing languages is problem solving. This is a technical activity which presupposes knowing the vocabulary, syntax, and common expressions of the language.

The chapters of this book organize the material in stages similar to the progression described above. The book's chapters first explain rules of the language and show how to decipher Python programs; later chapters emphasize problem solving and more practical use of the language. This arrangement of the material differs from many modern texts on programming. The current trend is to emphasize writing programs at the outset. The idea of such books is more akin to an immersive experience in learning a foreign language. At the outset, you are surrounded by all kinds of unfamiliar things, but gradually you learn more about the language in all the stages together; vocabulary, syntax, patterns and storytelling, all mixed up. This "sink or swim" approach can be quite effective in a very concentrated environment, however, it can lead to a fragmented and incomplete coverage of the language. The reason this book follows a different order is that the experience of educators teaching computing has exposed certain difficulties students commonly encounter with programming languages. The plan of the book is to delay introducing topics that are obstacles to learning Python; the following paragraphs mention some of the difficulties.

Computing languages fall into two categories, the declarative/descriptive type and the operational/procedural type. The former are languages where you tell the computer what you want, whereas the latter are languages where you tell the computer what to do. The true dream of computing should be to eliminate the latter type. Why should you tell the computer *how* to do something, when the result is the only thing you care about? It would be much better to simply declare what is needed and have the computer figure out how to do it. The current state of the art in computing has not progressed far in declarative languages. The best known examples that are declarative are relational database query languages. Common programming languages are mostly of the procedural type. Students generally find declarative languages simpler and easier to learn than procedural languages. This book attempts to introduce Python by presenting the declarative parts of the language first, to postpone the difficulties of operational reasoning. Even declarative languages may be difficult for students unused to communicating with precision. The danger of a declarative language is the "be careful what you want" phenomenon, where a careless specification might deliver unexpected output.

The experience of education in computing finds two elementary concepts to be typically difficult for students new to computing. First, variable abstraction requires a higher level of reasoning and takes practice getting used to. This book postpones the introduction of variables until later chapters. Second, the sequence of steps controlled by looping and jumping require that a student build a "mental model" of Python's computing behavior. Having a mental model is a road map to understanding and predicting how programs will behave when they run. This aspect of Python is also postponed to later chapters. Rather than introduce these known difficulties early, we examine first a more calculational style of using the language. Fortunately, Python has an interactive "calculator" mode (the REPL, or read-eval-print loop) for experimenting and learning. This mode is the counterpart of having a native speaker to practice with learning a foreign language. Web-accessible versions of Python for beginners are becoming widespread, so beginners can experiment without even having to set up programming environments. Python also has concise notation and enough data operations to do impressive things with expressions, even without variables and controlling sequences of steps.

You think you know when you can learn,
are more sure when you can write,
even more when you can teach,
but certain when you can program.
— Alan Perlis

Chapter 4:   Python Setup

This book, based on the *Python* programming language, is only effective if the reader has ready access to a working computing environment. Many computers come with Python installed, and even when Python is not installed, limited programs can be run using a Web browser. The general philosophy of this book is conservative, avoiding commercial packages and advanced development environments; the reasoning is that the free and basic no-frills Python remains valid even in the more advanced environments.

The Python language is not a native GUI application like games, picture drawing programs, or Web browsers. Python is based on text files which contain lines of commands and definitions needed for making programs. The text files are nothing special: they can be viewed and edited by usual system accessories that are also used to create and edit simple notes. Word processors can also edit Python files, but this is probably not a good idea, since Python does not use paragraphs, special fonts, and formatting. There are some specialized text editors with useful features for Python programming; using one of these is recommended.

Distributions

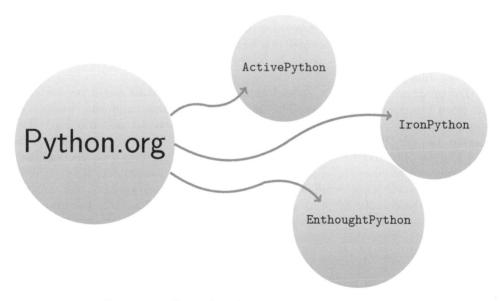

Figure 4.1: Some distributions of Python.

Python itself can be downloaded for free from www.python.org (if it is is not already installed on the computer you use). There are downloadable versions for many operating systems and computer types. There are even ways to install Python on smartphones, but this chapter offers no advice about doing so. When Python is installed, usually there are two ways of running Python programs. One is via a system console. On most Linux/Unix systems, it is as simple as typing in a command on the console and pressing enter to start a Python program. For Windows, an extra step may be needed to set up the "system path" if you would like to run Python from the console. Another way to run Python is via an application called IDLE, which combines an editor with a console so that you can create and modify a program using the editor and run it in another window that IDLE provides.

A number of "distributions" of Python offer some support or bundling advantages. Whereas the official language comes from `python.org`, distributors of the language (some of them commercial) have added value beyond the language: a number of software packages may be preinstalled; better development environments, program debuggers and editors might be included; and there may be connections to operating system features. Figure 4.1 shows the general picture for a few distributions. The figure shows that all distributions start with `python.org`, but then add their own branding. Arrows in the figure indicate that each of the branded distributions copy from the core of the Python language and its libraries, but then add value by some customization, providing additional libraries and tools, and perhaps by offering customer support. Advantages of using these branded distributions are many, but distributions evolve at a different pace from the language and if you learn Python using a customized distribution, it may be more difficult later to use Python in a different setting. This book, therefore, depends only on the vanilla `python.org` distribution.

A few other ways Python programs may run depend on the kind of operating system. Especially for Unix/Linux, Python is called a *scripting* language. You can actually extend the vocabulary of system commands available from a console using Python programs; this kind of new command is a *script*. Again, there is nothing really special about a script, it is just a text file containing Python programming language commands and definitions. It is also possible that a program you write may be launched by clicking on an icon in a folder or on the desktop, but this is a more advanced topic that depends on system details. Another arrangement is to use Python through Web servers and browsers. Web servers can be configured to use Python programs in response to browser requests. The Web server simply looks for a file with a particular name, then runs the Python program in that file, which generates output back to the browser. These are just a few of the ways that a Python program might be run.

For program development, special applications called IDEs might be used. Particularly for more bureaucratic languages like `Java` and `C#` (which emphasize business/enterprise concerns), many consider IDEs to be indispensable. There are now too many IDEs to enumerate, though the most famous ones you might have heard about include Visual Studio and Eclipse. The more advanced IDEs have editors, consoles, tools to organize suites of programs and libraries, automatic spell-checking and auto-completion for partially written phrases (these tools are aware of the programming language syntax), and debugging tools. Except for the complexity of using them—working with some IDEs has been compared to operating the cockpit of a Boeing 747—IDEs can be quite handy. Indeed, some consider IDEs to be the Auto-Tune of programming.

Dialects

It is perhaps a surprise that two native speakers of English may not be able to understand each other. Someone growing up in Baltimore, Maryland may not be able to converse with a native of Kingston, Jamaica, even if they are both speaking English. The problem can be pronunciation, since accents vary depending on location. Nonnative speakers of English might speak a form called "Globish." However the accents may vary, written English is understandable by all, with minor differences in accepted spelling and some vocabulary. Not so simple for Python.

Python is a rapidly evolving language compared to natural human languages. There are several versions with enough differences between them that a Python program written for Version 3.0 probably will not run on a system that only has Version 2.5 installed. The reason for new versions, like the reason for changing rules in sports or passing new laws and regulations, is popular will of the user community who vote on new language features. The trend in new versions is "backward compatibility," meaning that programs written for say Version 2.1 should work on a system running Version 2.6, without needing any modification to the programs. The trend does not always hold. There was a major break in the language syntax going from Version 2 (which means all the versions from 2.0, 2.1, and so on) to Version 3 (including 3.0, 3.1, and so on). For learning about Python this situation is inconvenient, to say the least. If only the whole world switched at once from one version to the next, things would not be so bad. However, it takes time to change existing programs, and it can be dangerous to try this quickly because conversion might introduce bugs.

 The current situation in the software landscape, with respect to Python, is that Version 3 is gradually being installed on many systems, but Version 2 continues to be used as well. Some of the most useful packages constructed with Python still depend on Version 2; nearly all Unix/Linux scripts based on Python use Version 2; many IDEs have not yet caught up with Version 3. Operating systems are flexible enough to allow Version 2 and Version 3 to be installed at the same time, though users may need to call on them by different names. Here are conventions for this and later chapters:

To distinguish between Version 2 and Version 3 (we can forget about antiquated versions like Version 1), the names are Python2 and Python3. In chapters and sections where some language feature is described with different syntax between the versions, we use the symbol shown in the shaded box.

Calculator Mode

```
-bash-3.2$ python
Python 2.4.3 (#1, Jun 11 2009 14:09:37)
[GCC 4.1.2 20080704 (Red Hat 4.1.2-44)] on linux2
Type "help", "copyright", "credits" or "license"
for more information.
>>>
```

The simplest way to experiment with Python is to start an *interactive session*. On a Unix/Linux system or a Mac, this is done by launching a *terminal*, or *console* application, which presents a rectangular area with a command prompt. You can type on the command prompt line, which typically begins with a $, >, or some other symbol, marking the place where you begin typing. The rest of the window shows a history of commands entered and responses from the commands. The command you want to try is simply "python," shown for a Linux system in the shaded box. The response by Python ends with the ">>>" line, which is a prompt from the Python interpreter asking the user (you) to type some Python command and press Enter.

In response to the command python, the system launches an interactive session of Python, sometimes called the *calculator mode* of using Python. Above, you can see that this session uses Python2, specifically Version 2.4.3 (with other technical details we do not care about). The three-line interaction shown to the right is an example of Python calculator mode. Here, 2+2 was evaluated by Python, and the next line shows the result. After the result comes another line, again presenting a prompt, allowing us to try more things.

```
>>> 2+2
4
>>>
```

What about Windows? Under Microsoft Windows, after Python has been installed, the Command Prompt accessory can be launched (found under the Accessories tab). Here is an example showing how that would look:

```
Microsoft Windows [Version 6.1.7600]
Copyright (c) 2009 Microsoft Corporation. All rights reserved.

C:\Users\Bob Zippy>python
Python 2.6.2 (r262:71605, Apr 14 2009, 22:40:02) [MSC v.1500 32 bit (Intel) on win32]
Type "help", "copyright", "credits" or "license" for more information.
>>>
```

The calculator mode works the same under any operating system, once you get to Python's ">>>" prompt.

iPython

```
In [47]: 8.0*2.5
20.0
In [48]:
```

An alternate presentation of Python, known as iPython (also found through Enthought and browser-based pythonanywhere) presents the calculator mode differently. Shown to the left, instead of the ">>>" style of prompt in the basic Python distribution, the interactive mode's prompt in these systems starts with something like "In [47]:" which tells you that this is the 47th prompt in an iPython session. The iPython systems keep track of the history of interactions, allow you to call back earlier things in a session, and even make some system commands available (e.g., listing the contents of directory) while within the iPython session. Generally speaking, the iPython environment combines aspects of an IDE with Python for a sophisticated programming and debugging environment.

Running a Script

```
print ("Hello")
```

Another way to run Python is to use a script. Though a Python script is just a text file, there is a convention about what you name the file. It should be a name ending with ".py" so that applications like IDEs will automatically recognize the file to contain Python language. The next example supposes that hello.py is a text file consisting of one line, as shown to the left. To run the script hello.py we need a terminal (or Command Prompt for Windows). Below this is shown for a Linux terminal on the left and a Windows command prompt on the right. In the example, we see that Python ran the script, which output Hello, and returned control back to the terminal, waiting for another user command. Notice that interacting with a system terminal or command prompt is similar to interacting with Python calculator mode, except that the conversation is with the host operating system, Linux or Windows. Beginning from the terminal or console prompt for a command, the user (you) types python and the name of the script file, and the Python program in file runs, printing output back to the console.

```
-bash-3.2$ python hello.py
Hello
-bash-3.2$
```

```
C:\Users\Bob Zippy>python hello.py
Hello
C:\Users\Bob Zippy>
```

These script examples are missing a crucial detail. The current working directory for the terminal or Command Prompt has to contain the `hello.py` file. For Unix/Linux and Mac, this either means using some "open terminal here" option on a menu, or using `cd` commands to position the session into the correct directory. Under Windows 7, you can hold down shift and right-click on a folder to get an "open command window here" option, for example, for the folder containing `hello.py`.

Microsoft Windows

A few extra notes are helpful to set up Python in Windows, should you need to do that. After you download and install Python, it may be that the command `python` appears to fail. This is most likely because Windows cannot find the `python.exe` program, even though it has been installed. The way to tell Windows about the location of Python is to edit the `Path` environmental variable (not at all obvious). Just how to do this depends on the version of Windows—it is best to use a search engine and look for `edit windows path` along with a keyword about your system version (Windows 7, Windows 8, etc.). Hopefully, you will find some advice on this—if you have no experience in tuning Windows, please seek help in setting things up.

Normally, Python is installed in its own folder, and you will need to find that and add its location to the system path. For example, under Windows 7, you can just type "system path" on the search box, which brings up a System Properties window with an Environmental Variables button; click that and you can scroll through system variables to find `Path`, which you click and then press on an edit button. At the end of the current string of paths (be careful not to change anything already there), add a semicolon and `C:\Python27` or whatever is appropriate for the Python version you installed.

Another useful tool is a Python-friendly editor. For that, `Notepad++` is a good choice. If you launch `Notepad++` and then open a Python script file (or create a new one) there is a menu for language, under which Python and 50 other computer languages appear. Selecting Python adds lots of nice features to help with Python programs.

One frequent source of confusion with Python scripts is the suffix ".py" on the file name. On the Windows desktop or viewing a folder, the suffix is commonly hidden. Some beginners will try to force this by renaming a file, only to have Windows add its own suffix. As a result, one can end up having a `hello.py.py` file. If you are going to be working with scripts, it is a good idea to learn how Windows deals with file types using suffixes, and how to view and change the full file name.

Integrated Development Environments

What are the attractions of Integrated Development Environments (IDEs)? To answer this, let's preview a typical phase of software development. At a certain point in development, the design of a program is finished, but it has not been put into a file; perhaps some small details also need to be further researched. Enter the IDE, viewed as the programmer's helper. Many IDEs have built-in awareness of programming language syntax, knowledge of the (perhaps vast) software libraries available with the language, and even features to automatically detect logical errors in what programs do. Using an IDE, a programmer might see lists of possible completions of words and phrases while typing, similar to auto-completion and spell-checking features of word processors. More than that, different Python keywords may have colors and fonts that make it easier to read and make sense of a program. With sufficient screen area (so-called "desktop real estate"), an IDE may have one window for the program, another for viewing the output of the program when it runs, and a third for debugging information. For debugging, when a Python program stops due to a bug, some IDEs automatically highlight the suspected bug in the editor of the program text.

With all the good things to say about IDEs, there are limitations. For one, many of the intended ways of using Python are not graphical (using windows for output) and IDEs may not be able to run programs for certain environments. If a Python program controls a robot, the commands to turn wheels, lift an object, or inspect a camera image, then that may not work on a desktop IDE. Some aspects of an IDE, which initially seem positive, lose their attractiveness as users become progressively more expert with the language. The auto-completion or suggested options while programming can be distracting; the full-screen view with several windows may be incompatible with the normal mode of typical knowledge workers, who have windows for e-mail, calendar, or other information portals.

The general impression from `python.org`, for whatever reason, is that the job of providing full-featured IDEs is left to some other provider(s). Python's IDLE application is a quite limited IDE compared to the many other competing IDEs now available. Using a search engine or searching directly at `python.org` for IDE leads to many possible choices. It *is* possible to learn Python without an IDE, and this book makes no recommendation about which method of program development to use.

Web Browsers

As a final "platform" for writing and testing Python programs, consider the Web browser. Though current browsers do not directly run Python code, it is possible to connect to a Web site where Python runs, and if the Web server is set up for Python, then in theory you can put a Python program into a form (either by typing or by cut-and-paste from another window), press a button, and have the Web server run the program. This avoids Python setup entirely: in fact, you can write and run Python programs using a tablet, a smartphone, or any similar Web-connected device that has a modern browser. While this idea might seem very easy, be aware of some downsides to working this way. First, if connectivity to the Internet is poor, response time will be slow (similarly, if the server is several time zones away from your device, the round-trip time for signaling over a large distance will cause slow response time). Second, if the same Web server is shared by hundreds to thousands of others, it can bog down under contention, causing unpredictable response time. Third, how do you save your programs to a file for later use? A Web server may or may not allow you to have input files, use advanced library functions or other features that Python has in a fully installed, local system.

In spite of limitations, accessing Python through a Web browser has some excellent benefits. There are Web servers with IDE-like debugging features, code visualization, and tutorial support. Other Web sites may integrate online documentation and "active" textbooks that demonstrate running code immediately in the browser (possibly eReaders will have such a feature soon). Many Web sites supporting Python testing through a browser have appeared recently and more can be expected. It is worth experimenting with at least a few of these.

Part II

Functional-Style Python

Chapter 5:   Types

type
int 1024
bool True
float 0.375E27
string "gate"
tuple (3,4)
list [True,1]
dictionary

Python's Data Types

int, float   ...   42   -21.395   1.0028e-12

character, string   ...   'T'   'storm'

bool   ...   True   False

tuple   ...   (5, 6, True, 'so', 9)

list   ...   ['Take2', 100, 0]

dictionary   ...   { 'ace':12, 'bottom':-3 }

Science is the systematic classification of experience.
— George Henry Lewes

Types are to computing what dimensional units are to physics and chemistry. In physics, units are grams, volts, joules, calories, and degrees, to name a few. In computing there are bits, bytes, terabytes, functions, records, and other nomenclature. Any programming language needs notation and terminology to name the basic units for talking about programs. The choices of such names and units are often hotly debated by the individuals who create and embellish the language. Naming and classification is intrinsic to every specialized discipline, from law to biology to theology. Computing is just another specialized area of study.

Another similarity between physical science and computing is that the units themselves can be a simple sanity check on human reasoning. When solving a problem in physics, a common trick is "dimensional analysis," which is nothing more than making sure that the answer to a problem has the correct measure and that any calculations deriving the answer use units that match and cancel. Of course, the answer could still be wrong due to some mistake, but it is generally helpful to check on units during calculation. Similarly, programs deal with types, and simple checks making sure types match up help prevent bugs from appearing in the software.

The remainder of this chapter tells a little of the story of how types in computer languages have evolved, before going into the Python terminology. After that, Python's most primitive types are introduced, then sequences and dictionaries are explained.

It's All 0 and 1

Nearly all computation is based on electrical signals. It was not always so. A century ago, any computing was done with pencil and paper or in a few cases, mechanically with devices like gears and sliding bars. We use electrical signals because the cost is low, the parts do not wear out, signaling is fast, and the size of components can be reduced to near molecular scale. Typically, voltage is used to distinguish between signals: for instance, two volts might signify the number 1, whereas minus two volts (or maybe zero volts) might signify the number 0. Thus, a common way to measure voltage, for purposes of computing, is a *binary* measurement, symbolically using 0 or 1 to classify voltage. A single item of data, 0 or 1, is called a *bit*; a group of eight bits is a *byte*.

Given that physical quantities like voltage can be measured and expressed with high precision, one question is why we should settle for 0 and 1 when actual voltage values could be 0.00347, 1.21258, 2.19549, and so on. It seems that a more refined way to measure voltage than just a binary classification should be possible. Conceptually, yes, it should be possible to base computing on a richer set of numbers than 0 and 1, however, the cost of more sensitive devices argues for staying with 0 and 1; also, using 0 and 1 simplifies the engineer's job. Further, we have to think of data storage, which often is not electrical. For memory, other physical properties like magnetizing (positive or negative) or crystallizing (oriented or not oriented) have natural binary measures. So, for various reasons of technology, manufacturing cost, and convenience, the binary system of data representation and manipulation is now ubiquitous.

The rules of binary arithmetic are simple, but tedious. We prefer to leave the details of binary to computer engineers, instead focusing on units of data closer to our application purposes: MP3, Web pages, text messages, and the like. Know, however, that all data, at some level, is made up of bits. Engineers have nicely used lots of hidden binary encoding tricks, but the problem they face is daunting: new applications continually get invented faster than computers can be designed and built. We want new applications to run on existing computers. Computer engineers rarely get into the details of application data, preferring to stop their work at giving us a few types of data that are better than binary, yet well short of what rich applications need. The common *native data types* that computers work with are integers, floating point numbers (which approximate real numbers), and characters from limited alphabets. It is left as a task, to computing scientists, software designers, and sometimes students in programming courses, to figure out how to think and use imaginative data units (MP3, Web pages, etc.) when the basic computer only supplies integers, floating point numbers, and characters. In a nutshell, this is one of the basic problems of computing science: take a primitive computing device and convert it into a more intelligent device.

Programming Language Types

Historically, the first method of programming was to directly set *machine language* instructions into computer memory. This tedious job was greatly simplified by the invention of *assembly language*, which enabled programmers to write lists of machine instructions in files. An *assembler* takes such files and converts them into a form suitable to load into memory. In an assembly language, the basic types of data used in the instructions are groups of bits; bytes and "words" are typical names for such groups. A *computer word* is the native machine grouping of bits around which instructions and memory are designed. Computers embedded in cars and appliances may have a word size of eight bits; desktop computers can have a word size of 64 bits.

```
#include <stdio.h>
int main() {
  int i;
  for (i=0; i<10; i++) {
    printf("i=%d\n",i);
  }
  return 0;
}
```

Different vendors offer different assembly languages. In part because of this fact, it is better to use a programming language that works on any kind of computer, regardless of the native word size and regardless of the format of machine language instructions. One prominent solution to this problem is the C programming language. To the left is an example of a C program. The C language is "higher level" than assembly language. Again, a programmer creates a file of instructions, however, the instructions can be more in a free-form style. Further, there are conveniences to avoid having to do bookkeeping arithmetic dealing with memory, concise ways of expressing large lists of instructions in just a few lines of text, and more abstract ways of denoting data. In computing science, *abstraction techniques give us the leverage to amplify human reasoning*. To fully appreciate what that last statement implies, we will need to see many examples, mostly coming later in the book.

```
#define _ F-->OO||F-OO--;
int F=OO,OO=OO;main(){F_OO();
printf("%1.3f\n",4.*-F/OO/OO);}F_OO()
```

These are the first three lines from a C program, the full text of which can be viewed at http://ioccc.org/1988/westley.c The program is a cleverly written, purposefully confusing program submitted to the 1988 Obfuscated C Programming Contest. Such programs *are not* good models for beginners to learn about computing.

Programs written in C can be very efficient, but they can also be quite difficult to understand. A portion of an extreme example is seen on the left. Die-hard fans of the C language admire the way it can so concisely express complicated ideas, however, the other side of the coin is that C programs can become inscrutable.

In the C language, there are essentially three basic data types: integers, floating point numbers, and aggregate structures. The idea of an aggregate structure is to bundle some integers, floating point numbers, and even other aggregates in handy ways. Examples include arrays (which can represent vectors and matrices used for scientific applications) and data records (often used for business applications, where part numbers, stock quantities, and calendar dates can be aggregated into natural data units). Integers are not only used for calculation in C, but are also used to represent alphabetic (a-z, A-Z) characters, and can refer to *locations* in computer memory (*pointers* refer to locations in memory) as well as values stored in memory. Indeed, much of C programming requires that a programmer make a mental image of what computer memory contains and how it is organized, in order to write a program. In this last aspect, C is much like assembler language, requiring us to have some knowledge of the underlying hardware that will run the program.

How does a computer follow the instructions in a C program? First, we need a special tool called a *compiler*. A C compiler takes one or more files containing C language and transforms them into assembly language; then the resulting assembly language is processed by an assembler into machine code, which the computer directly *executes* (follows the machine instructions). Put another way, the compiler's input is C *source code*, and its output is *assembly language*. Some compilers skip the part about assembly language; instead, they directly take C source as input and generate machine code, also called *object code*, as output.

There are many C compilers because there are numerous different computer manufacturers with different standards of memory and calculation styles. This is an unfortunate situation: when we get a new computer, we might need to recompile all of the software using a C compiler suited to the new hardware. Is there some way to avoid this type of dependence on the type of computer? One answer is the concept of a "virtual platform," an imaginary computer. Suppose we have a C compiler that produces object code for an imaginary computer, the MIX 1009 computer. Though nobody has ever built the MIX machine, it is possible to write a software tool called a *virtual machine* (VM) for the MIX. For example, there could be a MIX VM for a smartphone: its input is MIX object code, and what it does it to *emulate* the behavior of the MIX program on the smartphone. In other words, a VM "interprets" the object code for the MIX, using the underlying hardware of the smartphone. For instance, if the MIX object code has an instruction to multiply two numbers, then the VM would need to accomplish that multiplication; in case the smartphone does not have multiplication hardware, the VM would use repeated addition and multiplication tables to get the correct calculation implied for a multiply instruction. Programmers are unaware of the work that a VM has to do in this scenario. They write C programs for the hypothetical MIX machine, and provided that each actual computer has a MIX VM, the object code appears to execute properly on each of them.

The advent of virtual machines has the clear advantage of enabling us to be "platform independent," or "platform agnostic," letting the same programs run on different kinds of computer platforms without needing to rewrite programs or recompile them. But this advantage just scratches the surface of why VMs are so popular as a technique for programming languages. Recall that the subject of this section is programming language types. In contrast to the limited data types offered on real computers, usually just bits and numbers, the imaginary computer for a virtual machine could have all sorts of more user-friendly data types: text, MP3 files, graphical images, and so on. Further, a VM can have features for debugging, networking, and any other reasonable features we dream up.

Three examples of modern programming languages that use virtual machines are `C#`, `Java`, and `Python`. These languages offer basic data types beyond bits and numbers: sequences of text, arrays, and logical values (true and false), as well as integers and floating point numbers. Beyond the basic data types, these languages allow programmers to define their own data types, which puts within reach exotic types of data like MP3 files, graphical images, and so on.

Primitives: Numbers, Characters, Booleans

It is easiest to introduce Python's types in several stages. The simplest and most "primitive" types are numbers, characters, and booleans. Numbers, as defined in mathematics or philosophy, are ideal concepts where the emphasis is on how to formally define them and use them to build theories. Computing is more practical: the way numbers are represented on a screen and entered by keyboard is a foremost concern for programming languages.

105	✔
2 1 4	✘
-2	✔
78409869	✔
7,204	✘
0105	✘

Integers. Integers in Python are just strings of numeric digits (0–9) without punctuation. Implicitly, the notation for integers is decimal (base 10). Perhaps the only surprise is that Python does not permit integer notation for decimal numbers, except for zero, to begin with 0. To the left are some examples of valid (✔) and invalid (✘) decimal integers. The examples show that having embedded spaces, commas, and leading zeros will not work for denoting decimal numbers. (As a preview to more advanced Python, the last two examples will actually give some kind of result in Python, just not what one might expect.)

Floating Point Numbers. Floating point numbers are an approximation to the ideal notion of a real number. The notation for floating point takes its cue from scientific notation, which allows for decimal point and exponent. Like integers, a floating point number is denoted by a string without embedded spaces, using digits (0–9), and possibly a decimal point and possibly an exponent. An exponent is signified by the letter `e` or `E`. Here are some examples, with a third column for valid inputs showing traditional scientific notation:

600.001	✔	6.00001×10^2	`600.00099999999998`
235e8	✔	2.35×10^{10}	`23500000000.0`
−8634.0123E-12	✔	$-8.6340123 \times 10^{-9}$	`8.6340123000000004e-09`
−99999999	✘		

The last line was marked invalid, for a floating point number, because Python considers it to be an integer rather than a floating point number. The fourth column shows Python's approximation for the number when it is input at the keyboard. Why do these approximations deviate from what the numbers obviously represent? That is not an easy question to answer; indeed, a significant part of any course on numerical analysis studies floating point round-off and conversion errors. Nearly all programming languages suffer from imprecision when approximating real numbers, though some hide the imprecision more than others. Fortunately, for nearly all matters in this book, we will not be concerned with calculations involving floating point numbers.

Other Numbers.   Python has many other numeric types and notations for numbers: binary, hexadecimal, octal, fractions, decimal with fixed precision, and more are possible, but we can skip these for now in learning the language. One type worth mentioning, but not covered in this book, is the type for complex numbers. The value $\sqrt{-1}$, denoted by i in mathematics texts, is `0.0+1.0j` in Python.

Characters.   Each key on a keyboard is a character, more or less: some keys control behavior, such as the shift key; and some characters from languages other than English (ö, é, etc.) may not have keys on the keyboard. As a primitive type, characters are those defined in the ASCII standard. The original standard defined characters by a table so that each character corresponded to an arrangement of seven bits. The current ASCII standard assigns eight bits (one byte) to each character. Since the number of possible arrangements of eight bits is 256 (numbers in the range 0 through 255), the ASCII standard could define up to 256 possible characters.

```
>>> ord('k')
107
```

The usual way to denote a character in Python is to surround it by single quotes, such as `'t'`, `'M'`, and so on. This is natural notation for most people, but there are cases of unintuitive characters such as spaces, tabs, newlines, and other *meta-characters*. Using Python interactively, one can ask for the number corresponding to the character, as shown to the left, where we find out that the letter `'k'` is assigned 107 for its value. What would this be in terms of bits? That is a question we almost never need to answer (the answer is given by $107_{10} = 1101011_2$, in case you are curious).

Meta-characters use special notation starting with a backslash: the tab character is denoted by \t. There is also a way to ask the converse question, what is the character corresponding to a particular number, using notation like chr(9), as shown to the right. The attempt chr(300) failed, and Python complained, because ASCII characters are only defined for numbers in the range 0–255. Python's answer to chr(200) looks strange; the reason is that ASCII has not defined any character for the number 200, so Python responds cryptically with notation for the number 200 in hexadecimal (do not worry about what this means). The following table shows a few examples of characters and meta-characters.

```
>>> ord('\t')
9
>>> chr(9)
'\t'
>>> chr(82)
'R'
>>> chr(200)
'\xc8'
>>> chr(300)
ValueError: chr() arg
not in range(256)
```

' '	a single space (blank) character
'a'	lowercase letter a
'A'	upper and lowercase are different characters
'\t'	the tab character
'\n'	the newline character
'\r'	the carriage return character
'.'	period
'/'	forward slash
'#'	pound sign, or hash character
'\\'	the backward slash

The last line of table is a surprise: Python considers the backslash to be a meta-character. The reason is that backslash itself signifies a meta-character, and so the input '\' would confuse Python. To overcome the confusion, we have to denote the backslash character with '\\'. There are a few more cases of confusion when dealing with quotes (' and ") that will be explained later.

Booleans.   Python defines a special primitive type *boolean*. There are only two values in the boolean type, True and False. Unlike English or other natural languages, the meaning of True and the meaning of False do not indicate whether something is a fact or not a fact. The booleans are used to control program behavior, a more advanced topic covered later. The two-valued boolean resembles the binary, low-level way that computers encode information as bits. Indeed, lower level languages like C use 0 for false and 1 for true. For compatibility with older styles of thinking, Python does allow the number 0 to be substituted for False, but it turns out this compromise for "legacy language" programmers can lead to bugs in programs for psychological reasons, when programmers mentally mix up different computer languages. We prefer to use True and False when controlling program behavior.

Sequences: Tuples, Lists, Strings, Dictionaries

Given the primitive Python types of numbers and characters, it makes sense to look at how the primitive types can be bundled into useful aggregations of data. The three *sequence* types introduced in this section are tuples, string, and lists. All of these are sequence types in Python and share some characteristics.

Tuples

Python has special notation for an aggregate of values, using the jargon term *tuple*. A tuple is denoted by putting values in parentheses, separated by commas. Python requires that every tuple except the *empty tuple* have at least one comma. Here are some examples:

`(1,3,5)`	length is 3
`(1,3,5,)`	length is 3
`(False,False,'J',1.5e9)`	length is 4
`(0.001,,True)`	syntax error
`('i','o','w','a',5,2,2,4,2)`	length is 9
`(0)`	not a tuple
`(0,)`	length is 1
`()`	length is 0

The last line shows the special case of the empty tuple. The comment associated with each tuple above is the *length* of the tuple, which is the count of how many items are in the tuple. When the length is 2, we sometimes call the tuple a *pair*, and when the length is 3, the tuple can be called a *triple*. Computer scientists use the term k-tuple to mean a tuple of length k. One last remark about tuples concerns an obscure feature in Python. In selected circumstances, you can use tuples without needing parentheses. Sometimes, Python will just consider `False, 'W', 1.25e4, -351`—without parentheses—to be a tuple (of length 4). The precise rule on when the parentheses are required is complicated, difficult to explain in this chapter. It is always safe to use parentheses, so we prefer to use them in writing tuples.

Lists

Lists are much like tuples, with some small changes in notation. Square brackets enclose the items in a list.

`[1,3,5]`	length is 3
`[1,3,5,]`	length is 3
`[0.001,,True]`	syntax error
`['i','o','w','a',5,2,2,4,2]`	length is 9
`[0]`	length is 1
`[]`	length is 0

Practically the only difference visible between tuples and lists is that a list with a single item can be denoted without using a comma.

Strings

Strings are special types for characters. Though a string typically contains only ASCII characters, they can also have characters from other alphabets for Turkish, Chinese, and so forth. Some examples of strings are:

`'abc'`	length is 3
`'A B'`	length is 3
`'this\tthat'`	length is 9
`"this\tthat"`	length is 9
`'we don't know'`	syntax error
`"we don't know"`	length is 13
`'z'`	length is 1
`' '`	length is 0

The notation for strings gives you several options for saying where a string starts and where it ends. You can use a single quote ('), a double quote ("), or some other advanced techniques to be covered later. Notice the line with the syntax error above. Python got confused by starting a string with a single quote, then trying to include a single quote as part of the string itself. The easy way to avoid this situation is to start and end the string with a double quote, so that when Python encounters the single quote it is a character, rather than a string terminator.

Dictionaries

A useful type that initially seems unintuitive is the *dictionary*. The dictionary type is a simplified form of a database: it associates some data with a lookup value, called a *key*. A dictionary is a list of keys and their associated values. The colon (:) separates the key from its value. The notation is shown by these examples:

```
{7:3.5, 20:-2, 30:True}      three keys
{True:'T'}                   one key
{}                           empty dictionary
{'a':0, 'b':0, 'c':0, 'd':1} four keys
```

Later, in Chapter 15, we see how keys and values in a dictionary can change as a program runs. In Part II of this book, dictionaries do not change: they are only created and used for calculations.

```
>>> {1:2, 1:9, 1:5, 2:10, 1:0}
{1:0, 2:10}
```

In a real database, a key can have only one value with which it associates at any time, though as a database changes, the value may change. Python obeys this property, so dictionaries have only one value per key. You can see this properly in an interactive session with Python, shown to the left: Python took the keyboard input, which seemingly was a dictionary with five key/value items, but then found the key 1 has multiple values—which cannot be allowed. Rather than report an error, Python chose one of the values for 1 and took that. The result is a dictionary with two keys, 1 and 2.

Putting Types Together

With a few exceptions, sequence types and dictionaries can freely use any Python type (even ones not covered so far in these notes) as items, keys, and values. A tuple can contain any type of item:

```
([],'Oak Tree','trail',False)   length is 4
(0,1,{0:'a',1:'b'})             length is 3
((1,2,3),(3,4,5))               length is 2
```

The last line in the list of examples shows that an item of a tuple can itself be a tuple (which, in principle, could contain tuples that contain tuples, and so on). However, the length of, or number of items in a tuple is just determined by counting the items, without regard to their individual lengths, should they happen to be tuples, strings, lists, or dictionaries.

If you have never seen this kind of "type mixing" before, it can initially seem confusing, because of the mixture of symbols possibly close together. It turns out that, except for textbooks and exercises, this sort of notation is not used very often. Yet it is good training to learn how to scan such lines of Python and figure out what is the data type. You should be able to distinguish between correct and incorrect ways of putting together the symbols.

Suppose all the letters, quotes, spaces, colons, and digits are replaced by "o"—so that we just see a string of o's mixed with parentheses, brackets and braces. A result of such replacement might be

> (ooo[oooo{oooo)ooooo}]

There is an error in this line because it starts with a left parenthesis, but does not end with a right parenthesis. An example that does not have an error is

> (ooo(ooo)oooo(oooo)oooo[oooo{oooo(oooo)oooo}oooo]oooooo)

As a mental exercise, you might formulate some way to distinguish between such examples that have errors or are correct. One attempt is just to count the number of each type of symbol: there have to be as many left parenthesis as right parenthesis, and so on. Clearly, this is not enough, since ")ooo(" satisfies that criterion. A more sophisticated rule is needed; Python needs to have such a rule to inspect programs and report errors.

Similar to tuples, lists can mix all types as items.

```
[[False],{False:5,10:"ten"},[(0,),"zero"]]    length is 3
[[1],[1],[1],[2],[2]]                         length is 5
[[1,2,3],(3,4,5))                             length is 2
```

Strings, however, can only contain characters. Dictionaries can mix types, except that keys cannot be lists or dictionaries.

```
{1:(0,True), 'a':[5], False:{False:-1.9}}  ✔
{{3:0,1:2}:'over', -30:'out'}               ✘
{ ('a','b'):0, (False,False,False):[] }     ✔
{ [3,4]:"box", 'e':14 }                      ✘
```

One unfortunate thing about Python is the way it reports errors. For the last example, marked with ✘ to indicate an error, Python reports the error as

```
TypeError: list objects are unhashable
```

which may not be very helpful without understanding deeply many details of the Python language. Thus, it is important to understand the rules for how types can be mixed; if you know the rules yourself, you can generally figure out what is wrong when Python complains, rather than rely on the cryptic way Python tries to tell you the reason for the error.

Type Queries

Python can help you learn about types. Just start an interactive Python session and enter `type(👆)`, replacing "👆" by some text of your choosing. Python should respond with the type of whatever you entered, shown by examples to the right. The commonly seen types are `int`, `float`, `str`, `bool`, `tuple`, `list`, and `dict`. Chapter 6 shows how type queries can be used in programs. The example also demonstrates how you can ask Python to count the number of items in a container, such as list, string,

```
>>> type(-20)
<type 'int'>
>>> type("are")
<type 'str'>
>>> len([False,1.5e12])
2
>>> len("New York")
8
```

tuple, or dictionary. Python's `len` and `type` are just two instances of *built-in functions* in the language (there are many more). Perhaps more interesting than the above are examples that fail, where Python returns some error message. Exercises at the end of this chapter have some incorrect things to try.

⇨ web

Yet More Types

Taxonomy is described sometimes as a science and sometimes as an art, but really it's a battleground.
— Bill Bryson

Python has a few other built-in types not covered in this book, such as `set`, `bytes`, `bytearray`, `complex`, and `frozenset`. (Briefly, the `bytearray` type is mentioned again in Chapter 8.) Further, by including modules from Python's standard library, more types can be accessed, including `Fraction`, `Decimal`, `date`, and `array` types. It is even possible for you to define your own types in Python, a topic touched on much later, in Chapter 27. Below, a bit about the `set` type is discussed.

You may have noticed that some of Python's types are conveniently grouped by having similar properties. Types `int`, `float`, and `complex` are *numeric* types. Types `list`, `tuple`, and `string` are *sequence* types. Another grouping is `list`, `tuple`, and `dict`, each of which can have any other type as an element: this group is sometimes called the *container* group of types. Such a grouping makes it convenient to make statements about Python containers— when we are talking in general about lists, tuples, and dictionaries.

Arrays. For readers familiar with other programming languages like C, Java and the like, two other terms may be known to you: collections and arrays. Python does have collection types, but that is an advanced topic beyond where this book goes. The other term, *array*, is an important point of distinction between Python and some other languages. In Java and C, the language uses an *array* where Python programmers would use a list. The difference between an array and a list is that all the elements of an array need to have the same type. The reason to prefer an array over a list is efficiency: a Java or C compiler can transform source code using arrays into more efficient (faster-running) programs compared to lists. Python also has array types, but they are not covered in this book.

```
set([])
{5}
{"corn","wheat",False}
{0,0,0,17,"end","start","end"}
```

Sets. You can skip reading about Python sets; they are rarely used, but will be of interest to students with some math background. Whereas tuples and lists are ordered containers of items, allowing items to be repeated, sets are unordered containers of distinct items. The older style notation for a set in Python is `set(⊙)`, where "⊙" stands for a Python `list`. For example, `set([2,5])` is a set containing two integer elements, 2 and 5. Newer notation for this (in most recent versions of Python) is the simpler `{2,5}`, which nicely resembles the traditional mathematical notation for sets. On the left are four examples of set notation in Python. The first line defines an empty set (which cannot be denoted with the curly braces). The last line's list contains repeated items; when Python processes this, duplicate items are removed so that the set only contains one copy of each item. Python has facilities in the language to manipulate and combine sets, including operators for union, difference, subset, and intersection.

Terminology Review

Jargon introduced in this chapter includes: bits, bytes, binary, floating point, `type`, `len`, machine language, assembly language, assembler, compiler, computer word, pointer, execute, source code, object code, virtual machine, emulate, character, boolean, `True`, `False`, sequence types, tuple, string, list, dictionary, key.

Exercises

The point of this exercise is just to get some initial experience starting an interactive Python session and trying a few things at the keyboard.

⮕ web

Use Python interactively to determine the type of each line of text below by substituting the line of text for "☕" in `type(☕)`. Some lines have errors (and Python will return an error message). Where appropriate, also try the `len(☕)` on the same text. Use this exercise to learn a few keyboard tricks, such as calling up what you previously typed, editing some characters, and retrying.

1. `(4,44,444,)`

2. `X`

3. `"package pickup at the corner"`

4. `(True,[0],false,[15])`

5. `len("seven")`

6. `{0:(),1:{6:0},5}`

7. `1,True,2`

8. `(18)`

9. `'the\ttournament\nwinner\nis\'`

10. `"what exactly does "status quo" mean?"`

11. `[1008,(19,0,[False,False],"j"]`

12. `type(False)`

13. `9+6e4j`

14. `len`

15. `type`

16. `0b111110111010000101`

Interlude: An Inventory Problem

Like many manufacturing firms, Acme Perfume had its own problems with the supplies of material used to make perfumes. Perfumes are secret mixtures of elemental scents, often based on natural products—these are called the "base notes" for making perfume. Some have intriguing names related to botanical origins, like oakmoss, vetiver, lovage, and costus. Other ingredients are staples of the aroma-chemicals industry, chiefly acetates, esthers, and ketones. In many cases, freshness matters. The odor of a substance may change over time, or be different depending on the year and location where it was obtained. These are challenging to Acme Perfume because customers expect that fragrances for a named perfume will be the same from year to year. If the musk is not stinky in the right way or the lavender is not pungent enough, then the end product could take more labor to produce, because the factory expert (the "nose") will take more time to adjust things, possibly even needing to discard a batch.

One part of the business is to carefully track the supply and current stock of the ingredients. To make things simple, we consider just two facets of the inventory problem here, the ingredients and the suppliers. For each ingredient, suppose we have the substance name, the supplier name, the number of days to expiration, and the quantity in stock. Acme's database should track the status of all ingredients in stock and be updated frequently. Acme sources ingredients from about 20 suppliers; the database should also maintain information about the suppliers, including contact information, e-mails, orders, and billing status. How is all of this information to be organized and represented?

table = greatest invention ever to contain information!

That's right, Acme uses tables. Below are some two-line fragments of what would be Acme's tables of perfume ingredients and suppliers. On the left is part of the table of ingredients; on the right is part of the table of suppliers.

oakmoss28	Botanisco	205
lavender4	Durevelia	834

Botanisco	www.botanisco.co.za	⋯
Olfaktikov	olfaktikov.co.fr	⋯

What Python type can represent such tables? There is no best answer to this question. However, for reasons that make sense in later chapters, a reasonable answer is that each *row* in a table should be a Python `list`. The two rows shown for the ingredients table could thus be

```
["oakmoss28","Botanisco",205],   ["lavender4","Durevelia",834]
```

Similarly, the rows of the suppliers table could also be lists. Another idea might be to arrange the suppliers as a dictionary, like this

```
{ "Botanisco":'www.botanisco.co.za', "Olfaktikov":'olfaktikov.co.fr' }
```

The table of suppliers suggests (the "⋯" in the third column) there could be more information. How would this be accommodated by a dictionary? The trick is to use a list. A revised representation of the suppliers table including phone numbers might be

```
{ "Botanisco":['www.botanisco.co.za',"+44 208.555.1212", etc ] }
```

In practice, this way of showing a dictionary in a textbook is far too lengthy to be practical. Later chapters introduce techniques whereby dictionaries can be created from data in files, where they are conveniently inspected and changed by programs.

which is best, list, tuple, string, or dictionary?

It is a bit early to fully explain the reasons for preferring one type over another, given a choice. Most commonly, the dictionary type is chosen when the intended use is to lookup by a key (i.e., the supplier name). Tuples are often used for data that does not change when a program runs, whereas information in lists can be more dynamic. Later examples, which refer to Acme Perfume, illustrate how Python can work with tables represented by lists and dictionaries.

Chapter 6:   Operators

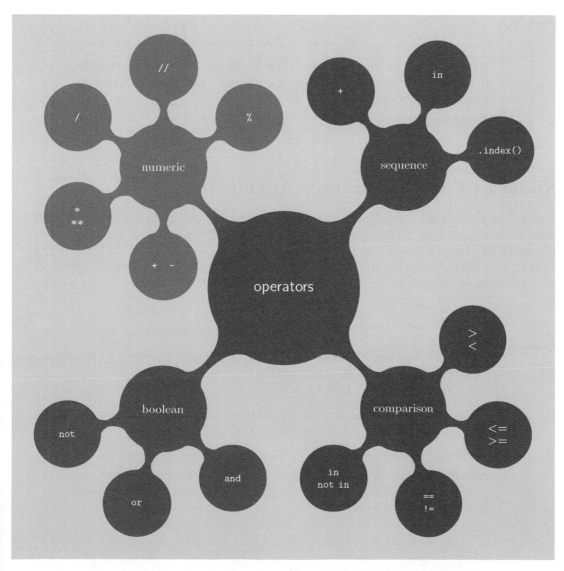

Operators are standing by.
— Anonymous

Calculation consists of reducing expressions to some minimized form. Thus, 100+100 reduces to 200. Computing long ago parted ways with calculations of numerical results. Most of what computers do is search, organize data, find patterns, and sense physical objects. Nevertheless, because most students have learned some algebra, it is reasonable to first introduce Python's numeric operators, and then ease into the less familiar operations.

Unlike low level machine language working with bits, the operators in Python will not work unless types of data are suitable: Python is a *typed* language. Python outputs a `TypeError` message when you try to use an operator on the wrong type of data.

Operators are of two flavors, binary and unary. Binary operators, like * and /, take two *arguments* placed on the left and right sides of the operator. Unary operators have just one argument placed on the right side of the operator.

This chapter starts with familiar numeric operators, then goes on to introduce new ones for boolean and sequence types. After these operators are presented, Chapter 7 shows how operations can be mixed in expressions, and how operator priority helps to resolve ambiguity.

Notation used in this and later chapters is the "➜" symbol, which indicates how Python evaluates an operation or expression, reducing it to an output value.

Example: 100+100   ➜   200.

Numeric: Float and Integer Arithmetic

Numeric operators take integer or floating point arguments and compute a result. Most often, both left and right arguments to an operator have the same numeric type (integer or floating point), but it is possible to mix these as well, putting an integer on the left side and a `float` (floating point) on the right side or the other way around. A few numeric operators are specialized to integers; the section following this one deals with these.

operator	meaning	example
+	addition	`8.03+1.22e3`
-	subtraction	`1723-2521`
*	multiplication	`17*21`
/	division	`6.02e23/10521.0`
**	exponentiation	`144**0.5`

The minus (-) operator uses the same symbol as the negative number sign, and both can be used in a Python operation: 3--10 is calculated to be 13, for example.

Not in Python: Some students who know C, C#, Java or similar languages ask immediately: does Python have the "++" operator or the "--" operator? The answer is no!

The minus operator is also exceptional because it is both a binary and a unary operator. Used as a unary operator, it reverses the sign of its right argument: ---3 is negative 3 because the sign is reversed twice (the third "-" is the sign of the number).

Integer Operators

Division. When Python is presented with the operation 8/3 a choice has to be made. Should the answer be 2.6666666666666665 (the computer approximates fractions) or should the answer be an integer, say 2 or maybe 3? The first answer would be more precise, but it would not be an integer. With operators +, -, and *, an operation on two integers yields an integer. To be consistent, Python should return an integer for division, however, others have a different opinion. This debate was resolved in Python2 in favor of returning an integer whenever two integers are combined by division. Therefore, in Python2, 8/3 is computed to be 2, rounding the true answer down to the nearest integer. Similarly, -8/3 returns -3 by rounding down in Python2.

The debate was not fully settled, however. In Python3 the subject was reconsidered, and a *new operator* // was introduced (actually the // operator is supported in all recent versions of Python2). Here is how it works in Python3:

- 8/3 returns 2.6666666666666665 (which is a floating point number)

- 8//3 returns 2, rounding down to the closest integer value

The general policy that Python3 tried to follow was to be *backward compatible* with Python2, that is, programs written for Python2 should still work, even when processed in the Python3 programming environment. However, the case of the division operator shows that this policy was not strictly followed.

Remainder. Another special integer operator is the division-remainder operator %, which returns the *remainder* from dividing two integers:

8%3	➜	2
8%4	➜	0
9%2	➜	1
-7%4	➜	1
-8%-3	➜	-2

The lines above show examples of what % calculates for different arguments. When the right argument divides evenly (no remainder) into the left argument, then the answer is 0. Otherwise, when the right argument is a positive number, the answer will be some value larger than 0 and less than the right argument. When the right argument is negative, the answer is not so easy to explain; programs almost never use a negative number for the right argument of %, so it is best not to worry about this case (you can safely forget how it works). A handy usage for the % operator is to see if an integer is even or odd. It is even if it is divisible by 2, so x%2 is 0 if x is even and x%2 is 1 if x is odd. It is worth remembering this trick.

Exceptions. Trying to divide an integer by zero, or trying x%0, causes Python to halt computation and output a `ZeroDivisionError` message. Similarly, dividing a floating point number by 0.0 will generate an error. Sometimes floating point operations may produce a result too large or too small for Python to approximate, and you might encounter special values like `inf` or `nan` when this happens. This book does not cover all of what can happen with floating point operators, so you would need to look elsewhere if you are curious about this.

Bit Operations.   Python has the same bit operators that low level languages like C offers (` ˜ >> << & ^ |`), but we skip this topic. Normal programming can do without bit operations, as we hope to concentrate more on useful applications than on low level, machine-oriented topics.

Comparison: Numeric, General, and Type

Comparison operators differ from the standard arithmetic operators because the type of the result is typically different from the arguments: `10>2` ➡ `True`. The result of comparison is a boolean value, either `True` or `False`. The comparison operators are familiar for numeric arguments:

`90<100`	➡	`True`
`100<90`	➡	`False`
`100>90`	➡	`True`
`100>100`	➡	`False`
`100>=100`	➡	`True` (means $\geq$ in math)
`100>=50`	➡	`True`
`100>=200`	➡	`False`
`100<=200`	➡	`True` (means $\leq$ in math)
`100<>200`	➡	`True` (means $\neq$ in math)
`100<>100`	➡	`False`
`100!=200`	➡	`True` (means $\neq$ in math)
`100!=100`	➡	`False`
`100==100`	➡	`True` (means $=$ in math)
`100==200`	➡	`False`

Python also allows a "range test" to determine whether a number lies between two values. Examples of this are

`-200 < 60 < 200.952`	➡	`True`
`1e-4 <= 0.000001 < 8`	➡	`False`

General Comparison

Python allows comparison between other types, boolean and sequence, so long as both arguments to the comparison operator have the same type. Thus, strings can be compared to strings, booleans to booleans, and so on. For booleans, the way this works is simple: if we treat `False` as 0 and `True` as 1, then all of `< > >= <= <> != ==` behave in the expected manner (but, it turns out we never need to compare booleans to each other). String comparison has a more complicated behavior. There are two ways to understand this, an intuitive way and a formal way. The intuition is alphabetic ordering. Think of where a word, say `orbit`, would occur in a dictionary. Would it come before or after the word `ordinary`? Well, both words are in the "o" section of the dictionary, and even the second letter is the same in both words. So we have to look at the third letter to decide: b comes before d in the alphabet, so `orbit` should come before `ordinary` in the dictionary. Put another way, `orbit` has "lower alphabetic ranking" than `ordinary`—so `orbit < ordinary` in some sense.

The preceding seems reasonable to most people, but it leaves lots of questions unanswered. What about capital letters? What about punctuation, blanks, tabs, and other weird things that might be in a string? What if one string is shorter than the other? Worrying about all these special cases, sometimes called *edge cases* or *corner cases*, occupies much of what computer scientists have to manage in order to get correct programs. It is not that difficult because Python and other high level languages can automate the way it works. However, to truly understand how it works, it is revealing to look behind the scenes at how Python does comparison for strings and other sequence types. At the end of this chapter there is a detailed technical explanation of the *algorithm* Python uses for sequence comparison. Most programmers skip over knowing this level of detail, but if you are puzzled by Python's behavior or just curious, you should look at the algorithm.

Type Comparison

Chapter 7 builds on this chapter by combining operators and values into expressions, and introducing the notion of naming a value or the result of calculating a value for an expression. In later chapters, the question arises, what is the Python type of some name? The answer is found by comparing the type of the name to a known type: `type(X)==type(3)` is `True` if X is an integer, but `False` otherwise. For convenience, Python allows you to use `int` in place of `type(3)`, `float` in place of `type(1.8)`, and to use other abbreviations: `bool`, `str`, `list`, `tuple`, `dict`, `type`. Some examples follow, with another type comparison function `instance` in the last few lines.

`type(25)==list`	➜	False
`type(-200)==int`	➜	True
`type(-200)==type(-2e2)`	➜	False
`type("ABC")!=type("XYZ")`	➜	False
`str==type("")`	➜	True
`type([])==type([3,1])`	➜	True
`list!=tuple`	➜	True
`isinstance("hello",str)`	➜	True
`isinstance("1",int)`	➜	False
`isinstance(1e9,float)`	➜	True

The `isinstance` function internally does the type comparison, where the value (or name) is put first and the type is second.

Boolean Operators: And, Or, Not

Python		English
and	*may not mean*	and
or	*may not mean*	or
not	*may not mean*	not

The table above shows the three boolean operators, warning that English usage of the terms could be misleading. Whether they are misleading or not depends on personal background and experience. Lawyers might have a different technical understanding of what English words "and," "or" imply in documents. Some people interpret "or" as being an exclusive

choice, as in *"either this or that."* Python has a technical definition for each operator. The
not operator is unary, and there are just two possibilities:

$$\text{not False} \quad \rightarrow \quad \text{True}$$
$$\text{not True} \quad \rightarrow \quad \text{False}$$

Thus, not is the boolean equivalent of the unary minus operator, for instance: ---3 ➜ -3,
and likewise not not not True ➜ False. The binary operators and and or also have a
limited number of possibilities, shown below:

False and False	➜	False
False and True	➜	False
True and False	➜	False
True and True	➜	True
False or False	➜	False
False or True	➜	True
True or False	➜	True
True or True	➜	True

It is definitely a good idea to memorize the way that Python's boolean operators behave.
In fact, the behavior of these operators is deeply connected with formal logic, a branch of
philosophy.

Sequence Operators: Concatenation and Containment

There are three sequence operators: +, *, and in. The + operator is called the *concatenation*
operator. It takes two sequences of the same type and returns a sequence of that type. Use
the + operator to "glue together" two sequences:

'one' + 'two'	➜	'onetwo'
'' + 'anything'	➜	'anything'
(1,2) + (False,)	➜	(1,2,False)
[7]+["seven","eight"]	➜	[7,"seven","eight"]
['sample']+[]	➜	['sample']
['trace']+['']	➜	['trace','']

Empty sequences (which are '', [], and ()) act like the "zero" of concatenation. The * is
similar to integer multiplication, but using concatenation rather than addition:

4*'E'	➜	'EEEE'
'wow'*2	➜	'wowwow'
0*'object'	➜	''
[False,True]*2	➜	[False,True,False,True]

To use the * operator this way, one argument should be a sequence and the other must be
an integer (negative integers behave like zero).

The in operator resembles a comparison operator because it returns a boolean value.
The left argument of in can be any type and the right argument is a sequence type.

4 in [2,4,6,8]	➜	True
3 in [2,4,6,8]	➜	False
'n' in 'many'	➜	True
'z' in 'sleep'	➜	False
'S' in 'sleep'	➜	False
(1,2) in [0,(1,2),3,4]	➜	True
(3,4) in [0,(1,2),3,4]	➜	False
type(7) in (str,int,float)	➜	True

The `in` operator is sometimes called a *membership*.

But wait, there's more ...

The `in` operator has a special extra feature for strings: it can do a "substring test" for membership.

`'and' in 'candy'`	➜	True
`'sip' in "Mississippi"`	➜	True
`'over' in "ver"`	➜	False
`"will" in "will"`	➜	True
`'45' in '1945-1951'`	➜	True
`"Can" in "cantankerous"`	➜	False
`'' in "anything"`	➜	True

The last line is a special case: the empty string is considered to be contained in every Python string. The membership operation is also valid for sets and dictionaries. For dictionaries, the operation returns `True` if the left argument is a key in the dictionary.

`False in {1:'a',False:0}`	➜	True
`0 in {1:'a',False:0}`	➜	False

Finally, there is a Python operator doing the opposite of `in` (no, it is not called `out`):

$$\texttt{7 not in [1,2,3,4]} \quad ➜ \quad \texttt{True}$$

You can use `not in` anywhere you would use `in` to test nonmembership of the left argument in the sequence or dictionary on the right.

Hidden Operators: Function Application, Indexing, Lookup

Two other operators are unusual because there is no single character or string of characters to represent them. At first sight, these might not even appear to be operators. One has already been introduced, though not as an operator: *function application*. Temporarily, let "✪" be a visible symbol for function application. The expression of applying the *length* function with a string argument could be

$$\texttt{len ✪ "painting"} \quad ➜ \quad 8$$

The ✪ operator takes a function name as the left argument and something else, a *parameter*, that the function uses to find an answer. In fact, Python does not have a symbol ✪ for function application; instead, the notation is:

$$\texttt{len("painting")} \quad ➜ \quad 8$$

Because there is no special symbol, function application is an *implicit operator* (also, it is a binary operator). Later, there will be examples where the right argument to function application looks like a tuple, with multiple items separated by commas.

The other implicit operator is called *indexing*. The left argument is a sequence and the right argument is an integer, for instance

$$\texttt{'oranges' ☕ 3} \quad ➜ \quad \texttt{'n'}$$

where "☕" represents the indexing operator. The right argument, called the *index*, identifies which item of the sequence should be returned, counting left to right, starting from zero. Above, the index for 'o' is 0, for 'r' it is 1, and so on. Of course, Python does not use a "☕" symbol: indexing is an implicit operator. The actual notation is similar to function application, but using brackets rather than parentheses:

$$\text{'oranges'[3]} \quad \rightarrow \quad \text{'n'}$$

A simple way to think of 'oranges'[3] is that it means "skip the first three items and return the next one." Hence, 'oranges'[0] skips no items and returns the first, 'o'.

One feature of Python that is different from other languages is that the index can be a negative integer. When negative, the item to return is found by counting right to left (that is, starting from the end of the sequence and counting backward), with -1 referring to the last item of the sequence. The index value cannot be a floating point number and cannot refer to some position that would be outside of the sequence. Python will output an IndexError message if the index goes "out of bounds" for the sequence.

$$
\begin{array}{lll}
\text{"safe at home"[10]} & \rightarrow & \text{'m'} \\
\text{'reason is why'[13]} & & ✗ \\
[1,3,5,7][-2] & \rightarrow & 5 \\
(\text{False},0,\text{True})[2.0] & & ✗ \\
(\text{"one","two","three","four"})[3] & \rightarrow & \text{'four'} \\
(3,\text{"ready"},[4,5],6)[2] & \rightarrow & [4,5]
\end{array}
$$

The lines with ✗ are cases where the index is out of bounds, killing Python's index operation attempt.

Lookup. Indexing also works for dictionaries, but the value used for the index has to be some key in the dictionary. The index value can thus be any type allowable for a dictionary key (numeric, string, tuple, boolean). If the index given is not in the dictionary, Python will output a KeyError message.

$$
\begin{array}{lll}
\{1:\text{True},\ 2:\text{True},\ 3:\text{True}\}[2] & \rightarrow & \text{True} \\
\{1:\text{True},\ 2:\text{True},\ 3:\text{True}\}[0] & & ✗ \\
\{\text{"Sam"}:61,\ \text{"Chen"}:90,\ \text{"Suzy"}:74\}[\text{"Chen"}] & \rightarrow & 90 \\
\{\text{"Fox"}:-1,\ \text{True}:0,\ 95.5:\text{"x"}\}[\text{True}] & \rightarrow & 0
\end{array}
$$

This type of indexing shows how dictionaries might be used like a database, looking up a value by an associated name. It is up to the programmer to figure out how best to exploit Python's dictionary type.

Why Does Indexing Start with Zero?

Why doesn't `"Vector"[1]` evaluate to `'V'`? After all, "V" is the first character in the string, so shouldn't the number 1 refer to the first character? Over time, this has been a hotly debated question. One reason Python uses 0 instead of 1 as the first index is historical, though there are engineering considerations too. Wikipedia has a description of *zero-based numbering* on this topic, pointing out that other areas of counting may start with zero (for instance, "ground zero" comes to mind). Since computing is all based on bits at the deepest level of data representation, it is worth looking at a simple case and how this influences indexing.

With two bits of information, there are only four possible combinations of bits: 00, 01, 10, and 11. With eight bits, there are $2^3 = 8$ combinations, and generally with any number n of bits, there are 2^n combinations of using 0 and 1. Therefore, in deciding on how to represent integers, it is sensible to let 00 represent zero, 01 to represent 1, 10 to represent 2, and 11 to represent 3—the binary number system (negative integers are another story).

Integers are not only used for arithmetic, but also as a way to refer to different places in computer memory: there is a memory location for 0, a memory location for 1, and so on. To engineers working with memory locations, it is natural to let 0 be the "index" for the first memory location. Languages `C`, `Java`, and related cousins of these all use 0 as the starting index value for data. However, not all language designers made the same choice. There are other computing languages that start with 1; in fact, there is even a computer language which allows the programmer to choose which is the starting value, 0 or 1, to be used when referring to the first item of a sequence.

Example: Suppose memory is a sequence of 8-bit bytes, and the first four bytes look like this:

01011110	11110011	00100001	10011001

The value of memory location zero is `01011110`, which might be expressed in Python-like syntax as `Memory[0]`.

Method Calls

Several modern programming languages offer special syntax for a special type of function application, a *method call* or *method invocation*. To illustrate this feature, some examples follow:

```
'Paris, France'.upper()      →      'PARIS, FRANCE'
'forest'.index('r')          →      2
[4,9,16].index(9)            →      1
```

The effect of **upper** is obvious, it returned the capitalized version of a string. The effect of **index** is a search: it returns the index of a given item in a sequence. How does this syntax for a method call work? The operator here is the period "." It is a binary operator, where the left argument is some Python value and the right argument is a function application. At a deeper level of analysis, there is a more precise explanation of how this works. Suppose, corresponding to **upper** there is a "secret function" named UPPER (different font). Then

'Paris, France'.upper() is equivalent to UPPER('Paris, France')

The UPPER function takes one argument, a string, and returns a capitalized version of the argument. Similarly,

[4,9,16].index(9) is equivalent to INDEX([4,9,16],9)

where INDEX is a function of two arguments, the first being a sequence and the second being an item to find within that sequence. Thus, a method call is really a function call, but with some unusual syntax for the function's arguments.

Why does Python have both functions and method calls? In this chapter, this is not a question we can answer. Later chapters will expose more syntax and justify why method calls are part of the language.

Terminology Review

Jargon introduced in this chapter: binary operators, unary operators, typed language, **TypeError**, argument, parameter, backward compatible, edge cases (corner cases), algorithm, concatenation, membership, function application, implicit operator, indexing, index, method call.

The formula "Two and two make five" is not without its attractions.
— Fyodor Dostoyevsky

Exercises

Evaluate the following lines, trying to predict what Python would return for each use of the operators. To check your work, use Python interactively.

web

1. `type(2>2)`

2. `3-----4`

3. `"Big > small"`

4. `99+'three'`

5. `["A",2]<["A",3]`

6. `20 >= 20`

7. `type(3*"three")`

8. `2**10`

9. `3*len("three")`

10. `'' in "empty"`

11. `"four".index('o')`

12. `"several".index('w')`

13. `{4:1, 3:2, 2:3, 1:4}[2]`

14. `"seven > 5`

15. `8 in {0:1, 1:2, 2:3}`

16. `8 in {0:7, 1:8, 2:9}`

17. `[True,False,True].index(True)`

18. `'timing'[-4]`

19. `'timing'[-4]+'timing'[-2]`

Python's Algorithm for Comparison Want to understand the precise way Python compares sequences? To see how Python internally performs sequence comparison, it is helpful to see its recipe, or *algorithm* for comparing two strings. Suppose the comparison operator is •, standing for < or == (we do this so we do not have to repeat the explanation twice). The algorithm consists of four rules, applied over and over, until an answer is obtained. Before revealing the algorithm, imagine there are two strings, 'hyperbole' and 'hyena' and visualize them using tables:

h	y	p	e	r	b	o	l	e
∧								

h	y	e	n	a
∧				

The ∧ symbol underneath the h in both tables is called a *cursor*, much like what you see on a screen as you type. The significance of the cursor is that the algorithm starts by looking at the first item of both sequences, h in this example. Then it tries to determine whether the answer is `True` or `False` at the cursor's location in both sequences. If the answer is found, the algorithm terminates right away. Otherwise, the algorithm moves each cursor to the right and tries the whole thing over again. For example, if the answer for 'hyperbole' versus 'hyena' is not found on the first try, then the algorithm will try again with

h	y	p	e	r	b	o	l	e
	∧							

h	y	e	n	a
	∧			

Notice how the cursor moved over for both strings. Here are the rules of the algorithm:

1. If both cursors are beyond the end of the strings, then the answer is `True` if • is == and `False` if • is <.

2. If the cursor for the left argument is beyond the end of the string, but the cursor for the right argument is not, then the answer is `False` if • is == and `True` if • is <.

3. If the cursor for the right argument is beyond the end of the string, but the cursor for the left argument is not, then the answer is `False`.

4. If the cursors for both strings are within the strings, let x be the cursor's character for the left argument and let y be the cursor's character for the right argument; now, if $x==y$ → `True`, then move both cursors to the right and retry starting from Rule 1. Otherwise, the result is:

   (a) if • is == the answer is `False`;

   (b) if • is < the answer is the result of comparing `ord`(x) < `ord`(y).

Finally, at rule 4(b) we see the trick of comparing strings which have punctuation, blanks, digits, and so on: it uses `ord` to convert a character into a number, and then falls back to numeric comparison. To illustrate the algorithm consider these examples:

`'a'<'any'`	→	`True`
`'capital'<'cap'`	→	`False`
`'Average'<'and'`	→	`True`

The first line shows the effect of rule 4 and rule 2: the algorithm compares `'a'` to `'a'`, then moves the cursor (rule 4), putting the cursor beyond the end of the left argument. Here, rule 2 determines the answer to be `True`. For the last line, rule 4(b) evaluates `ord('A')<ord('a')`; this turns out to be 65<97, which determines the answer.

Are programmers supposed to know the integers of `ord` for all characters? No, though for alphabetic characters these integers have sensible values, so that comparison of letters follows alphabetic order; perhaps the only thing worth knowing is that any capital letter is considered to be smaller than all the lowercase letters.

Leftover. The algorithm does not say how to handle > <= >= <> != == operators. Rather than explain this here, there is a simpler way to understand these cases by first learning about boolean operators.

Tuples and Lists. Comparison operators also work for the other sequence types, tuples and lists, using essentially the same algorithm that string comparison uses.

   `[True,25,"hello",19,False] < [True,25,"hello",9,False]` → `False`

The reasoning, using rules 1–4, starts with cursors at the beginning of each list. The first, second, and third items of these lists are equal, so rule 4 repeats three times, putting the cursor at 19 for the left argument and at 9 for the third argument. Then the comparison 19<9 determines the answer to be `False`.

Chapter 7:   Expressions

"orange"[(2,9,-2,5)[2]]

10>7 or "m">"b" and True

2**81-3**45

len("vortex")*2%12

(not True, "t", 72/6)[2-4]

"easy" in ("yes ease"*2)

I can calculate the motion of heavenly bodies,
but not the madness of people.
— Isaac Newton

Computing starts to become interesting when operators and types combine to form *expressions*. Throughout science, there are expressions about equalities or inequalities, typically called formulas or equations. Scientific breakthroughs sometimes have concise technical statements expressed by such formulas. Students learn how to calculate with expressions (usually algebraic expressions), but the same general way of manipulating symbols happens with logic, balancing chemical reaction equations, deducing voltages for a circuit, and so on. Every student learns how, with the aid of a calculator, to find the x satisfying $x = 8/(5^2 - 3 \times 7)$. Early on, students learn rules of what to do first, how to proceed from one step to the next, in order to solve such problems. Similarly, programming languages need *syntax rules* that guide interpretation of source code, which is the topic of this chapter. A Python program might contain an expression

```
not True or not False and True
```

Without *syntax rules*, this expression seems ambiguous. Programs can also mix operators and arguments having a variety of types; here, syntax rules (like grammar in English) can improve programming style, so that programs written by one person are more easily understood by someone else.

Sequential Reduction

Let us reconsider, in "slow motion," how an arithmetic expression is reduced to a final answer. The following table shows the original expression and lines that make one simplification to the previous line, until the last line is a single number.

```
1-2-3-4      ➡      -1-3-4
  -1-3-4      ➡      -4-4
    -4-4      ➡      -8
```

The *order of evaluation* for these steps is *left-to-right*, that is, each step calculates the leftmost operation in the expression to get the next line. This is Python's normal way of reducing or *evaluating* expressions. So long as an expression has an operator in it, there is further evaluation work to do. It is easy to change the order of evaluation by inserting parentheses:

```
1-(2-3)-4      ➡      1--1-4
  -1--1-4      ➡      0-4
      0-4      ➡      -4
```

When part of an expression is enclosed in parentheses, Python evaluates that part first, but otherwise the order of evaluation remains left to right. Unfortunately, Python does not show this detailed, sequential reduction of an expression: Python appears to instantly evaluate the expression and return an answer. However, it can sometimes be a useful exercise to manually go through an evaluation one step at a time. You may already suspect that Python has an algorithm for evaluation.

Well-Formed Expressions

Using some "rules of construction," a clear definition of the syntax of expressions emerges. The rules, taken together, define *well-formed expressions*. These are expressions that follow the syntax, but may still be incorrect. The rules define expressions that superficially look reasonable: parentheses match, operators have arguments, and so on. Yet, according to the rules, "9/(3-2-1)" is a well-formed expression, even though Python would output a `ZeroDivisionError` message when trying to evaluate it. This is a general phenomenon of programming languages: so-called *syntax errors* are found by compilers, before the program ever runs; whereas *runtime errors* are discovered later, when the program executes. Think of the well-formed formula rules as a gatekeeper for correct programs. The rules may not find all the bugs, but can find some obvious ones. Another nice property of the syntax rules is that programming language editors (which are essentially word processors specialized to programs) can be aware of the rules, finding errors even as you use the keyboard to write source code. This works somewhat like spell-checkers that watch what you type, suggesting whether or not a word is suspicious according to its dictionary. At the end of this chapter, the rules for well-formed expressions are given along with some examples. You can get some feel for how well-formed expressions work just by studying working programs, so most programmers do not need to memorize such rules.

Parentheses and Priorities

Even when an expression is well-formed and is valid in Python, meaning that it runs without halting and outputting an error message, the result might not be what we expect. The problem is that, without a further kind of rule, there can be some ambiguity about the order of sequentially reducing an expression to a final result. Consider this mixture of string concatenation and indexing:

```
"mobility"+"patterns"[0]
```

Without knowing better, you might think this should reduce to `'m'`, reasoning that evaluation goes left to right, so the intermediate result would be `"mobilitypatterns"[0]`, which returns `'m'`. But, instead, Python returns `"mobilityp"`, because the indexing operation occurred first, before the string concatenation. If you wanted the first order of operations, then you would need to use:

```
("mobility"+"patterns")[0]
```

Using parentheses forces the order of evaluation, so the answer here is `'m'`. What is needed, in order to make Python's evaluation of expressions predictable, is to know about all the exceptions to the normal, left-to-right, evaluation process. Figure 7.1 shows the priority of Python operators, with the highest priority operator at the top of the table.

Examples. As done earlier in the chapter, working through examples sequentially, one reduction per step, illustrates Python's order of evaluation. In the following example, each line makes one reduction step to get the next line. **Note!** the (2), (3), (8), (9), and (12) you see to the right on each step refer to numbered priority lines in Figure 7.1.

```
9>1e-4 and {0:"Cavern", 5:'Tunnel'}[0].upper() in 'cave'   →   (8)
     True and {0:"Cavern", 5:'Tunnel'}[0].upper() in 'cave'   →   (2)
                True and "Cavern".upper() in 'cave'   →   (3)
                       True and "CAVERN" in 'cave'   →   (9)
                                True and False   →   (11)
                                        False
```

(1)	$f(\cdots)$	function application
(2)	$\mathcal{E}_1[\mathcal{E}_2]$	index (lookup)
(3)	$\mathcal{E}.f(\cdots)$	method call
(4)	`**`	exponentiation
(5)	$-\mathcal{E}$	change sign
(6)	`*, /, //, %`	multiplication, division, remainder
(7)	`+, -`	addition, subtraction
(8)	`<, <=, >, >=, <>, !=, ==`	comparison operators
(9)	`in, not in`	membership
(10)	`not` $\mathcal{E}$	logical negation
(11)	`and`	logical conjunct
(12)	`or`	logical disjunct

Figure 7.1: Python operator priorities.

The next section of the chapter has a more detailed explanation of how Python evaluates and reduces expressions, but the example above hints at how things occur: there is a series of steps, each step simplifying the expression, and each step consults the table of Figure 7.1. Extra parentheses can override Python's operator priority; the same holds for brackets (used to define lists or indexing) and for curly braces (used to define dictionaries). Consider

```
{3+4:True, 50/2:"quarter"}[12-5]
```

According to the operator priorities, (2) dictionary lookup has highest priority for evaluation. But, the dictionary items have expressions for keys, and these are within the `{ }` symbols; similarly, there is an expression within the `[ ]` for the lookup value, and that also has higher priority to reduce first. The actual order of evaluation would therefore be

$$\begin{array}{lll}
\texttt{\{3+4:True, 50/2:"quarter"\}[12-5]} & \rightarrow & \textit{left-to-right} \\
\texttt{\{7:True, 50/2:"quarter"\}[12-5]} & \rightarrow & \textit{left-to-right} \\
\texttt{\{7:True, 25:"quarter"\}[12-5]} & \rightarrow & \textit{left-to-right} \\
\texttt{\{7:True, 25:"quarter"\}[7]} & \rightarrow & (2) \\
\texttt{True} & &
\end{array}$$

You might notice above that the first three steps, done left-to-right, could instead be done in any order, because they are "independent" expressions. Mentally, this is the simplest way to think about parentheses (or braces and brackets): they surround expressions that have to be evaluated before the operators outside of the parentheses (braces or brackets).

Typical of Python usage is a comparison expression with function application, arithmetic, or string operations in it:

```
len('t'+" E")>2 and not "x" in "axis"   →   parentheses
len("t E")>2 and not "x" in "axis"      →   (1)
3>2 and not "x" in "axis"               →   (8)
True and not "x" in "axis"              →   (9)
True and not True                       →   (10)
True and False                          →
False
```

Many software professionals are not fully cognizant of operator priorities. Having to work with numerous programming languages, system tools, database packages, and a variety of mobile computing devices (plus keeping up with all the latest trends in computing), even professionals cannot be expected to recall obscure details of a particular programming language. Thus, some programmers might rewrite the example above as

```
(len('t'+" E")>2) and (not ("x" in "axis"))
```

Using the added parentheses, it is obvious what is evaluated first, second, and so on. The **and** is clearly the last operation to be evaluated. If you are uncertain or perhaps just want to make expressions more readable, consider adding extra parentheses. Whether you use them or not is up to you: in all areas of life, expression can be a matter of personal style.

Rules of Evaluation

Given the operator priorities, parentheses, and well-formed expression rules, how does Python evaluate an expression? There are different ways to explain this, and we use a simplified explanation here. This section of the chapter is somewhat lengthy, but understanding how Python does the evaluation can be quite important: if you want an expression to give the right answer, you had better understand the way Python will interpret your expression.

Repeating from earlier, the general rule is left-to-right reduction of an expression to a final value. However, as Python evaluates from left to right, it "looks ahead" before it reduces an operator. Consider the expression

```
2-3-4*2**5+1
```

General Rules: Left-to-right evaluation, but look-ahead first, checking if a higher priority operation comes next; parentheses force evaluation order; evaluation work can be "queued up" due to operator priority.

Going left-to-right, the first operator is subtraction: does Python therefore immediately reduce 2-3 to -1? No! First, Python observes that the operator *following* 3 is another minus operator; now, since the operator on the left of 3 and on the right of 3 have the same priority, Python can safely reduce 2-3 to -1 and get

```
-1-4*2**5+1
```

as a partially reduced expression. The next operation to consider is reducing -1-4 to -5: can this be done? No! First, Python observes that the operator to the right of 4 is *. Comparing multiplication to minus in the priority table of Figure 7.1, we see that multiplication has higher priority. Hence, Python should reduce 4*2 before reducing the minus sign to the left of 4. So is that what Python does next? No! Before reducing 4*2, Python looks to the right

of 2 and finds the operator **. Again, we consult the table of Figure 7.1. It turns out that
** has higher priority than *, so Python should first reduce 2**5 before working on the
multiplication. Is that what Python does next? No! Python looks to the right of 5 to see if
there is another operator (if there were no more operators, we would finally be at the end of
the story). To the right of 5 is the plus operator. The plus operator has lower priority than
** in the table. Therefore, finally, Python can get to work actually reducing an operation
to a value. To summarize where things stand at this point in the evaluation, Python has a
"backlog" of two jobs to do,

1. reduce 2**5, getting 32

2. then reduce 4*32, getting 128

The partially reduced expression thus becomes

$$-1-128+1$$

Once again, Python can consider reducing the minus operator to the right of the first 1 in
this expression. Is that what Python does? No! First, look ahead to compare this minus
operator to the operator on the right of 128. It is a plus operator. In the table of Figure
7.1, the minus and plus have the same priority. What is Python to do in this event of equal
priority operators? The answer is simple, just use left-to-right evaluation. Python therefore
reduces -1-128 to -129. The partially reduced expression becomes

$$-129+1$$

One more step gets the final value, -128.

☆   ☆   ☆

A curious illustration of Python's left-to-right order of evaluation occurs with boolean operators or, and. Python *optimizes* the way that these operators are evaluated by skipping
reduction when it will not matter. Suppose Python is asked to evaluate

True or ☺

where "☺" is some expression. It turns out that whether ☺ is True or it is False does
not matter: the final result will be True, just based on the simple definition of "or" in
Python. Therefore, Python skips even trying to evaluate "☺" (so long as it is a well-formed
expression). Here is some evidence of this fact, using interactive Python:

```
>>> (3>2) or (3>(2/0))
True
>>> (3>(2/0)) or (3>2)
ZeroDivisionError: integer division or modulo by zero
```

Evaluating left-to-right, Python gets the partially reduced expression

True or (3>(2/0))

Python can immediately reduce this to True, since it does not matter what value would
be on the right side of the or operator. But, when we switch around the two sides, the
left-to-right rule asks Python to evaluate (3>(2/0)) first, and this is an error.

A similar example would be an expression

`7>1 and "t" in "it" and 4>2+2 and 7>3/0`

According to the priority table in Figure 7.1, all operators (`>`, `in`, `+`, `/`) are higher priority than **and**. However, going left-to-right, whenever Python might encounter something of the form

`False and ☺`

then Python can immediately conclude the reduction to **False** is correct, regardless of the value of "☺," by the definition of **and**. Partial evaluations for the expression above are

```
    7>1 and "t" in "it" and 4>2+2 and 7>3/0    →
   True and "t" in "it" and 4>2+2 and 7>3/0    →
        True and True and 4>2+2 and 7>3/0      →
             True and 4>2+2 and 7>3/0          →
                True and 4>4 and 7>3/0         →
               True and False and 7>3/0        →
                    False and 7>3/0            →
                         False
```

Natural languages, like English, are known to have inconsistencies. In principle, programming language should be free from inconsistencies, but sometimes they do arise. An example of this is the Python expression

`0 in [0] == True`

which Python evaluates to be **False**. Instead, for the expression

`(0 in [0]) == True`

Python's evaluation is **True**. This is logical, since according to the priority table in Figure 7.1, the `==` operator has higher priority; yet, if we try

`0 in ([0] == True)`

Python reports a **TypeError**, because the **in** operator only works with sequences! Here we see an example of an inconsistency in Python's grammar (a bug, which may be corrected in future revisions to the language). Fortunately, such inconsistencies are quite rare and should not be a concern for practical purposes.

Names for Values

Most commonly, programs do not directly have numbers, lists, strings, and so on, in the expressions. Rather, symbolic names for things are used. Conventionally, textbooks introduce *variables* to refer to data. In Python, variables are more complex than in other languages, so we postpone the study of variables (and assignment statements) to Chapter 15. The examples that follow are simple, yet show how expressions can work with names referring to data.

```
            x = len("gravity")      ➡      x = 7
                   y = 81 % 17       ➡      y = 13
          z = [ x, y, x<y and y>0 ]  ➡
        z = [ 7, 13, 7<13 and 13>0 ] ➡
        z = [ 7, 13, True and 13>0 ] ➡
        z = [ 7, 13, True and True ] ➡
              z = [ 7, 13, True]
```

The bottom line for this little example is that x stands for 7, y stands for 13, and z stands for [7,13,True]. When you work interactively with Python, giving names to expressions actually gives names to the *values* of those expressions, after evaluation. Notice that the value for z does not refer to x or y, even though the expression defining z had both x and y in it.

Using names for expressions can dramatically reduce the number of keystrokes needed to express a program. The hard part of learning to use names is that you have to keep track of the type and value of the names. Evaluating an expression requires knowing the values of all the named parts.

```
>>> a = "enter"
>>> b = 4*[a]
>>> c = b[1]+b[3]
>>> "renter" in c
True
```

Python responds silently to defining a name during an interactive session. Python does not respond with "OK," it just accepts what is typed (like "b = 4*[a]") without complaining. This is normal behavior during an interactive session. Python only shows a value if there is something to be evaluated. Above, to understand why Python evaluated the final expression to be **True** requires that you look back to see how c is defined, which in turn means you need to look back further to see where b is given, and so on. As a beginner, when you have trouble with expressions in programs, you should ask Python interactively to show what is the value of a name. For instance, given the above:

```
>>> a, b, c
('enter', ['enter','enter','enter','enter'], 'enterenter')
```

Python shows the value of a name, or a tuple of names.

Terminology Review

Jargon introduced in this chapter includes: expressions, evaluation, order of evaluation, well-formed expressions, runtime errors, syntax errors, left-to-right, operator priorities, reduction, syntax rules.

Exercises

(1) What would be the result of Python evaluating the following?

    1. `"Hello",[21,4)`

    2. `"abcd" + ("mnop")`

    3. `"absolute"[9-5]`

    4. `"amazing" >= "astounding"`

    5. `"and" in "or" or "or" != "and"`

    6. `"california"["f"]`

    7. `"divide"/2`

    8. `"easy" in ("yes we ease"*2)`

    9. `"gb" in (10*"boing")`

  10. `"hand" + "traffic"[2*5-4]`

  11. `"hexadecimal"/2`

  12. `"orange"[(2,9,-2,5)[2]]`

  13. `"w" in "Iowa" and (5!=4*3-7 or "k" not in "Hawk")`

  14. `"xmo/2+57`

  15. `("and" in "or") or ("or" != "and")`

  16. `("hq"*2,("a"<"b")and True)`

  17. `((10<2*5) or (7<7*7)), "a"*2`

  18. `((not ((10-2)==2**3) and (1e5 > 3000))`

  19. `(-1,-2,-3,-4)[-2]`

  20. `(-2**3,"0"+"2")`

  21. `(0*"x") in "Iowa"`

  22. `(1,2)[0]`

  23. `(256**0.5)**0.(256**0.5)**0.5`

  24. `(True,"Sample",False,"Seven")[4]`

  25. `(not True, "to"+"rn", 72/6)[2-4]`

  26. `(type(4*4),type("a"*2),type(3.0*2))`

  27. `-(3**4) <= (-3)**(4)`

  28. `1*2*3*4*5/10`

  29. `not (True and False)`

  30. `1+2*7**2`

  31. `1.-+3**`

  32. `105/2 == 52.5*2.0 (Python2)`

  33. `10>7 or "m">"b" and True`

  34. `15*(3-2*(12+6/(4+8))`

  35. `15//2+1 (Python3)`

  36. `2 in (21,5-1)`

37. `2*((3-1)*"ox")`

38. `2*2+9+2*3-5`

39. `3*(2+(8*(1+(6+7)*2))))`

40. `4*(---2+2)*'stop'`

41. `5-4-3-2`

42. `6/((10*4)+3))` (Python2)

43. `8.1e6-10000 <= (2**3)*(10**6)`

44. `89//2+1e2` (Python3)

45. `True and ((5!=2) or (not False))`

46. `True and (False or not False)`

47. `type( 8>10 )`

48. `8.1e6-10000 <= (2**3)*(10**6)`

(2) What should be in the two blanks so that Python would evaluate the following expression to be 25?

   `((10,11,12),(4,5,25),(7,19,21))[__][__]`

(3) What value should be in the blank so that Python will evaluate this expression to be True?

   `("four","five","six","seven","eight")[__] in "one hundred sixty"`

(4) What value should be in the blank so that Python will evaluate this expression to be 19?

   `(30-19+2,-5+3*8,"19",True)[__]`

(5) What value should be in the blank so that Python will evaluate this expression to be False ?

   `(5>=5,"a"<"m",6==2*3,"f" in "swim",True)[ 2 -  __  ]`

(6) Here is part of an interactive Python session. What line will Python show in response to this?

   ```
   >>> x = [5,6,7,8]
   >>> y = [x,True,x,False]
   >>> z = (y[0]==y[2],y[2])
   >>> z[-1][-1]
   ```

(7) How will Python respond to this interactive session?

   ```
   >>> s = ['taken','surprise','over','come','by']
   >>> (s[0]+s[-1]).upper() + s[-3]+s[3]
   ```

Python's Well-Formed Expressions   The rules that follow are deceptively power-ful. They start with simple statements, but build on each other in perhaps surprising ways. It is best to read them first, then look at examples of expressions, going back to the rules if questions arise. Rules R6 and R7 look more complicated, but the pattern is easy to understand after looking at a few examples.

Rule R1   Every Python value, be it numeric, character, string, tuple, list, dictionary, boolean, and so on, is a well-formed expression.

Rule R2   If $\mathcal{E}$ is a well-formed expression, then $(\mathcal{E})$ is a well-formed expression.

Rule R3   Given any unary operator $\circ$, if $\mathcal{E}$ is a well-formed expression, then $\circ \, \mathcal{E}$ is a well-formed expression.

Rule R4   Given any binary operator $\circ$, and two well-formed expressions $\mathcal{L}$ and $\mathcal{R}$, then $\mathcal{L} \circ \mathcal{R}$ is a well-formed expression.

Rule R5   (Indexing Syntax) If $\mathcal{S}$ is a well-formed expression and $\mathcal{E}$ is a well-formed expression, then $\mathcal{S}[\mathcal{E}]$ is a well-formed expression.

Rule R6   (Function Syntax) If f is a function name, and $\mathcal{E}_1$, $\mathcal{E}_2$, $\mathcal{E}_3$, ..., are all well-formed expressions, then $f()$, $f(\mathcal{E}_1)$, $f(\mathcal{E}_1, \mathcal{E}_2)$, $f(\mathcal{E}_1, \mathcal{E}_2, \mathcal{E}_3)$, ... are also well-formed expressions.

Rule R7   (Method Syntax) If f is a method name, $\mathcal{S}$ is a well-formed expression, and $\mathcal{E}_1$, $\mathcal{E}_2$, $\mathcal{E}_3$, ..., are all well-formed expressions, then $\mathcal{S}.f()$, $\mathcal{S}.f(\mathcal{E}_1)$, $\mathcal{S}.f(\mathcal{E}_1, \mathcal{E}_2)$, $\mathcal{S}.f(\mathcal{E}_1, \mathcal{E}_2, \mathcal{E}_3)$, ... are also well-formed expressions.

This list of rules is incomplete. A more formal, complete list of rules would have provi-sions for lists, tuples, dictionaries, sets, strings, and other features introduced in later chapters. The rules for the types in Chapter 5 can be understood by intuition because of the many examples already presented. The difference here is that expressions can be used in lists. For well-formed expressions $\mathcal{E}_1$, $\mathcal{E}_2$, $\mathcal{E}_3$, the list $[\mathcal{E}_1, \mathcal{E}_2, \mathcal{E}_3]$ is also a well-formed expression; similarly, expressions can be used in tuples, dictionaries, and so on.

Examples. The following examples show that expressions must be well-formed to be valid Python, though there are cases where it is not enough to be well-formed. The first line is not well-formed because only Rules R2, R6, and R7 introduce parentheses, and always in pairs surrounding well-formed expressions: `"xyz" [2` is not a well-formed expression because Rule R5 demands that brackets occur in pairs.

expression	well-formed	valid Python
`len("xyz"[2)]`	✗	✗
`5+"AB"[9]`	✔	✗
`*+3,4`	✗	✗
`"abc"[2]*len("abc")`	✔	✔
`2.5 (3e9 - -4E8)`	✗	✗
`[1+2,True or not False]`	✔	✔

Interlude: Puzzles with Expressions

Here are some puzzles testing knowledge of Python expressions, types, and operators in an indirect way, requiring some imagination, trial, and error. The questions ask you to find Python values (numbers, strings, lists, etc.) for the Greek characters α and β. Some questions are easy, but some are challenging. For some of the questions, it may help to try empty sequences, such as ' ', [], and ().

① Find values for α and β so that the following evaluates to True.

$$\alpha\texttt{<=}\beta \text{ and } \beta\texttt{<=}\alpha$$

② Is there a value for α so that Python evaluates the following to be True?

$$\alpha \texttt{ + 1 == } \alpha$$

(Hint: According to some people, $\infty + 1 = \infty$.)

③ For what values of α being a sequence type (list, string, tuple) will Python evaluate the following to be True?

$$\texttt{2*}\alpha \texttt{ == } \alpha$$

④ Find α and β so that the following evaluates to True.

$$\texttt{type(}\alpha\texttt{)==type(}\beta\texttt{)} \quad \text{and} \quad \alpha\texttt{<}\beta \quad \text{and} \quad \texttt{len(}\beta\texttt{)<len(}\alpha\texttt{)}$$

⑤ Find α so that the following evaluates to True.

$$\texttt{type(}\alpha\texttt{)==type((}\alpha\texttt{,))}$$

⑥ Find α and β so that the following evaluates to True.

$$\alpha\texttt{[}\beta \texttt{ in } \alpha\texttt{]} \texttt{ == } \beta$$

⑦ Does the following evaluate to True for all numbers α of type int?

$$\texttt{1+}\alpha\texttt{\%2} \texttt{ == } \texttt{(}\alpha\texttt{+1)\%2}$$

❶ Find α so that the following evaluates to True.

$$\alpha \text{ in } \alpha \quad \text{and} \quad \alpha + \alpha == \alpha$$

❷ Can you find α and β so that the following evaluates to True?

$$\alpha \quad \text{not in} \quad \beta \quad \text{and} \quad \beta[\alpha] \;==\; \alpha$$

❸ Are there values for α and β so that the following evaluates to True?

$$\alpha \quad \text{in} \quad \beta \quad \text{and} \quad \alpha \;!=\; \beta[\beta.\text{index}(\alpha)]$$

❹ Is it possible to have value α so that False results in the following comparison?

$$\alpha.\text{upper}() \quad == \quad \alpha.\text{upper}().\text{upper}()$$

❺ Find α and β values so that the following evaluates to True.

$$\alpha \text{ in } \alpha \text{ in } \beta$$

❻ Is there an α so that Python evaluates the following to be False?

$$\text{len}(\alpha) >= 0 \text{ or } \alpha[0] == \alpha[-1]$$

❼ Can there be α and β to get True as the result of the following comparison?

$$\beta[\alpha] \quad == \quad \alpha[\beta]$$

Chapter 8:   Printing

A verbal contract isn't worth the paper it's printed on.
— Samuel Goldwyn

Printing is the simplest form of programming. Most people do not even think of printing as a kind of programming, but after some study of what goes on, especially for more complicated cases, writing a correct *print command* can be seen as programming. Even Gutenberg's printing press had, in some sense, to be programmed: the letters had to be arranged the right way so that the desired page got produced.

Basic Print

Chapter 5 describes computer programs as lists of instructions, where an instruction could be some low-level bit operation. For this book, such instructions are classified into two kinds, the computational ones and the commands. Computational instructions do things like addition, exponentiation, counting characters in a string, searching a dictionary, sorting data, and so forth. Commands store data into files, control motors, raise or lower volume on speakers, and the like. Whereas the computational instructions produce the answer to some question, the command instructions do not really answer a question, instead changing something that might even be external to the computer. Printing instructions are traditionally classified as commands, because the historical meaning of "print" is to make an image on paper. The current meaning is broader, so that printing can mean writing on a screen or writing text to a file.

```
> python myscript.py
Hello does
this
work?
>
```

Commands and Scripts. A *command*, sometimes called a *statement*, is a line of text in Python with special syntax. There are many commands in Python, each typically starting with some special word, such as `print` or `del`, followed by text used as an argument to the command. Some commands are a single line of text, but many command arguments have numerous lines of text, with particular conventions about the spacing of the text on each line. Typical commands are print statements, assignment statements, flow control statements, and function definition statements. Within such statements there can be values (of Python types) and expressions. The simplest kind of Python program is a *script*, which is a text file containing Python commands. Using an operating system's command console, running a Python script can be as easy as shown above typing `python` followed by the name of the file in a terminal or command prompt. In the example, three printed lines were displayed, which the script generated.

Important Note: When you work with Python interactively, each line you enter will be followed by Python showing the result of evaluation. For example:

```
>>> "hi" + "now"
'hinow'
>>> print("hi"+"there")
hithere
```

Two things to observe from the example are that (**1**) when Python evaluates `"hi" + "now,"` the result is clearly a string and Python shows quotes surrounding the evaluated result; (**2**) the `print` produced something *without* the quotes. Now, to show a contrasting example, suppose `myscript.py` is a file consisting of *exactly* these two lines:

```
"hi" + "now"
print("hi"+"there")
```

At a command console, the script is run as follows:

```
> python myscript.py
hithere
>
```

What we observe is that the result of evaluating `"hi" + "now"` **is not printed** by running the script. **That is normal:** Python does not print results from evaluating expressions in a script. If we need to have some output, then the script must have an explicit `print` in it.

Print as Function (**Python3**) or Print as Command (**Python2**)

Python3's print command uses the syntax of functions (technically, `print` is a function in Python3, but it is also a command because it outputs to a printer rather than return a value).

```
>>> print(5*7, [True,True and False], "xyz")
35 [True, False] xyz
```

Things to notice from the example are that expressions are evaluated (reduced to a value) before printed and strings are shown without quotes. There can be any number of arguments to the `print` function; however, to prevent source code lines from getting too long, programmers usually separate what needs to be printed into multiple `print` commands.

Python2's Print Statement

Python2's print command consists of the word `print` followed by any number of expressions separated by commas.

```
>>> print 5*7, [True,True and False], "xyz"
35 [True, False] xyz
```

Except for this not being a function application, the syntax is about the same as for Python3. What would happen if we tried the Python3 syntax in a Python2 environment?

```
>>> print(5*7, [True,True and False], "xyz")
(35,[True, False],'xyz')
```

The output shows that Python2 evaluated the statement as a command to print a tuple; in fact, the command could be equivalently written as

```
>>> print (5*7, [True,True and False], "xyz")
```

This rewriting of the command makes it clear that Python2's `print` can print a tuple, and the syntax is not the same as function application. One more example is a script in a file. Suppose `myscript.py` contains these lines of text:

```
print "Hello does"
print "this"
print "work?"
```

The three print commands will, when the script runs, have the output shown earlier in this chapter.

String Interpretation

What explains the different behavior of printing strings, here illustrated with Python2 syntax?

```
>>> print "test\t this"
test      this
>>> print ["test\t this"]
['test\t this']
```

In the first case, Python *formats* the string onto the page (or screen). The tab character ('\t') has been used to guide the formatting. The quotes are gone because they are not part of the string content, they are just there for us to know where the string begins and where it ends, which could otherwise be ambiguous (for strings containing spaces).

In the second case, Python displays a list containing a string value. Python's display of this list has been produced for human readability, though there could be some machine-oriented, bit, or numeric way that the list is encoded in memory: we do not care how the machine does it, we only want to see a readable version of the list. The formatting of a string does not occur until it is printed as a string.

```
>>> print '*'+2*'\t*'+'\nS\nT'
*       *       *
S
T
```

The `print` command can generate many lines of output, shown above. In effect, the special characters '\t' and '\n' are *instructions* to the printer. This is why we may think of printing as a primitive form of programming: the printer is "programmed" by following the instructions embedded into the text. Similarly, if you have seen HTML used in Web page design, it is a programming language for Web browsers, instructing them how to format the content of a Web page.

⮕ web

Print **Is Tricky!**

Though it looks so simple, `print`'s behavior is complicated. A command `print (m)` behaves differently depending on `type(m)`. If m is a string, then its characters (and meta-characters) will be interpreted as instructions to the printer, as shown above. However, if m is not a string, then m will first be converted to a string representation, using something like Python's built-in `str()` conversion function, so that it can be shown using ASCII characters. Thus, in a Python2 statement such as

```
print 1.0+0.5, "$\nX", False, "False"
```

the number 1.5 and the value `False` must be converted to strings, whereas the two strings will be interpreted for printing. The output from this is

```
1.5 $
X False False
```

Remember, `False` is not a string; `"False"` is a string, which may seem confusing because both have the same printed output.

String Trivia

This section has some obscure notation and tricks that can be used with strings. Except for the topic of long strings, the extra notation is not really helpful to a beginner learning Python (but it does not seem to fit elsewhere in the book, so it is here for reference).

Long Strings. Python does not put a limit on how long strings may be. With an interactive Python session, try this:

```
>>> print 1000*"this is a test"
```

and you will see that Python displays a long string (too large to fit onto one screenful of output). Python provides a way to type in a long or multiline string, using a convention of three quotes to start and three quotes to end the string. The syntax works with either single (') or double (") quotes. Example:

```
>>> '''There are so many laws and federal statutes
... that a bookshelf holding them all is over
... nine feet thick.'''
'There are so many laws and federal statutes\nthat
a bookshelf holding them all is over \nnine feet thick.'
>>>
```

The "..." is inserted by Python when, during interaction, it expects more input to be typed that continues what was started on previous lines. The triple quote (''') tells Python that a string definition begins, which can go on for many lines, until finally another (''') ends the definition. Notice how Python automatically created the newline characters ('\n') for the end of each line being part of the string.

Raw Strings and Bytes.

Python supports *internationalization*, meaning that characters from many languages can be represented, including those outside of the ASCII alphabet. Internationalization is an advanced topic outside of this introductory text, but it is worth mentioning that Python supports other kinds of strings or string-like sequences. The `bytes` and `bytearray` types are useful to handle unusual characters. The notation for a sequence of the `bytes` type, given in terms of characters, is to start a string with "b'" instead of a single quote, as in:

```
>>> x = b'some bytes could be here'
```

One motivation for the `bytes` type has to do with internationalization and other representation issues (along with some efficiency concerns). We mention it here only because some software libraries refer to the `bytes` type or a `bytearray` sequence. Recent versions of Python2 allow the use of `bytes`, but do not support this language feature fully in the way Python3 does.

What one has not experienced one will never understand in print.
— Isadora Duncan

Raw Strings.   Both Python2 and Python3 allow strings in *raw string* syntax, which consists of beginning a string with "r'" instead of a single quote. Using raw string syntax bypasses the backslash escape convention that Python normally uses for strings. In a normal string, wherever there are \n, \t, or \\ (the meta-characters introduced in Chapter 5), Python will internally use a single character in the string. But with a raw string, backslashes are not treated in any special way:

```
>>> r'Showing off how \t and \ are treated'
'Showing off how \\t and \\ are treated'
```

Observe that Python converted the backslash symbol within the raw string into the '\\' character. When printed, only the single backslash would be shown in each instance.

Implicit Concatenation.   Another obscure feature in Python, and not guaranteed to work in all cases, is string concatenation without an operator. It works by putting strings side-by-side:

```
>>> "Hello"    "World"
'HelloWorld'
>>> 'Way''Off'
'WayOff'
```

The only reason to mention this obscure feature is that students sometimes encounter this by accident, working on an interactive Python session. It is not good practice to use this feature in programming. The general rule of good style in computing is to make things clear and explicit, rather than use little-known tricks.

⇨ web

Backspace   Long ago, hardware printers were mechanical devices that required low-level instructions, including "form-feed" (to get a new sheet of paper) and distinct commands to move the typing back to the start of a line and to roll the paper forward by one line. These low-level instructions enabled some tricks we do not have today: one could make a program that printed the same character on the same paper until it actually put a hole through the paper! There are still vestiges of the old days. One is the backspace character (\b). Consider this:

```
print ("Please be careless\b\b\bful")
Please be carelful
```

Can you explain the output?

Automatic Newline. Normally, any `print` command automatically adds a newline (`'\n'`) character at the end of what is printed. For instance, suppose a script `myscript.py` contains these Python statements (using Python3 syntax):

```
print("one",1)
print("two",2)
print("three",3)
```

Now, the script is run using a system console (command shell):

```
> python myscript.py
one 1
two 2
three 3
```

What if you would rather not have this behavior? A special syntax for this in Python3 is the following:

```
print("one",1,end='')
print("two",2,end='')
print("three",3)
```

When the script is run, the first two `print` commands will substitute an empty string for the newline character, with the result:

```
> python myscript.py
one 1two 2three 3
```

Python2 has a different syntax to do this. The script would be

```
print "one",1,
print "two",2,
print "three",3
```

The extra comma on the first two `print` commands means, to Python2, that it should skip inserting a newline character.

web

Terminology Review

Jargon used in this chapter (some of it actually defined in earlier chapters) includes: command, statement, script, format, printer instructions, unicode, raw strings, automatic newline.

Exercises

(1) Write a Python script named `ball.py`. Running the script should have this output:

```
     xxx
   xxxxxxxxx
  xxxxxxxxxxxxx
 xxxxxxxxxxxxxxx
xxxxxxxxxxxxxxxxx
xxxxxxxxxxxxxxxxx
 xxxxxxxxxxxxxxx
  xxxxxxxxxxxxx
   xxxxxxxxx
     xxx
```

There are many ways that `ball.py` could be written, but your answer should have these properties:

- The script consists of eight `print` commands.
- In any `print` command, the letter "x" only appears once or twice (to get around this limit, just use expressions like `6*'x'`).

(2) Each of the following `print` examples will generate some output when they run. Can you predict what they will print? To make things clear, all the examples say whether Python2 or Python3 is used.

- Python2 example:
  ```
  print(12,"1"),
  print("2 ")
  ```
- Python3 example:
  ```
  K = '''* "* \'>'''
  M = "(\t)"
  print(K+M+K)
  ```
- Python2 example:
  ```
  s = "abcde\nfghijk"'
  print(3*s[2]+2*s[9]+s[3]+s[5]+2*s[-1])
  ```

(3) Try the following Python `print` command, here shown in Python2.

```
print 1000*(2*' '+'X')
```

Now try replacing the value 2 in this `print` command by 3, 4, 5, 6, 7, 8, and 9. For which values do the X letter line up in columns and for which values do the X letters make diagonal lines on the window?

☆(4) Suppose the Python2 command `print c[0]+c[1]+c[2]+c[3]+c[4]` produces the following output:

```
TTTTTTTT
   TT
   TT
   TT
   TT
```

What could `c` be in order to get such a result?

(5) (Just for fun.) Use a search engine to research the topic "ASCII Art." You will likely find translations from photographs to printer-approximated images from those photographs. While most of these do not use tricks like the `'\t'` (tab) character for formatting and spacing, it is interesting to note that some advanced controls (well beyond what is in this chapter) can even do things like backspace and print over the same character twice—which only has meaning on a real paper printer. There is even animated ASCII art!

Pretty Printing

Python's `print` is not very fancy: you can see data, but there is not much detailed control over how numbers and sequences appear when printed. Chapter 25 introduces some techniques for data formatting. Beyond this book, there are many specialized techniques (even a data formatting "mini-language" in Python) to automate and control the way data is rendered when printed, including how many decimal places are used when showing decimal amounts. The following example shows a "pretty printing" facility that Python offers, which is mainly useful for lists and dictionaries.

Suppose we need to print something in a complicated list, for instance a list that contains tuples, strings, and a dictionary. A typical interactive session might be:

```
>>> a = ("R",False,78)
>>> b = { "white":(255,255,255), "black":(0,0,0) }
>>> c = [ a, b, "+++", b ]
>>> print(c)
[('R',False,78), {'white':(255,255,255), 'black':(0,0,0)},
'+++', {'white':(255,255,255), 'black':(0,0,0)}]
```

What you see is that printing crams all the information together on just one line if it will fit, otherwise breaking it into more than one line of output. Now we continue the interactive session with a technique that is described in Chapter 18 (that chapter explains how to take advantage of a rich library of software that accompanies Python).

```
>>> from pprint import *
>>> pprint(c)
[('R', False, 78),
 {'black': (0, 0, 0), 'white': (255, 255, 255)},
 '+++',
 {'black': (0, 0, 0), 'white': (255, 255, 255)}]
```

The `pprint` is a "pretty print" function, not part of the Python language, which is available in the `pprint` module. The "`from pprint import *`" line tells Python to bring in the `pprint` function from the library of modules. This pretty-printing function makes a nicer display of complicated lists by attempting to present them in more tabular display, spread out over several lines.

Chapter 9:   Functions I

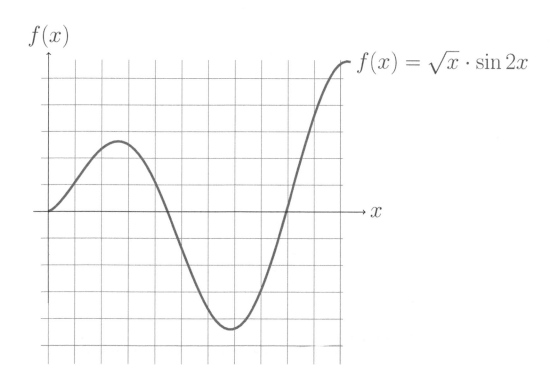

$$f(x) = \sqrt{x} \cdot \sin 2x$$

f = lambda x: x**0.5 * sin(2*x)

def f(x):
    return x**0.5 * sin(2*x)

> *In the old days when people invented a new function*
> *they had something useful in mind.*
> — Henri Poincare

Programming languages are connected to an area of computing called *software engineering*, which asks a simple question: why is the production of software different from designing bridges, manufacturing aircraft, developing pharmaceuticals, or building houses? Architects and construction firms are able to pretty well predict how long it will take to build a house and how much it will cost, but the same cannot be done with software. Also, when it comes to building a house, there is an established marketplace of parts, concrete, structural beams, and so on; there are tools for all aspects of construction. The dream of software engineering is to find the right kinds of tools and "parts" so that creating programs and computing applications can become predictable, reliable, and have acceptably low cost. This dream has influenced the evolution of programming languages and industrial conventions for organizing software systems.

One important discovery of software engineering is the *DRY principle* ("Don't Repeat Yourself"). The basic idea is simple: humans should not need to write software that is repetitive. Instead, we should have tools so that a particular algorithm or symbolic manipulation is done once, and then *reused*, instead of rewriting the same thing over and over. A key technical device for this purpose is the invention of the *subroutine*. A subroutine is a portion of a program that can be reused, possibly for multiple reasons; the goal of a subroutine is typically some limited computation that *returns* a value based on information given to the subroutine. Suppose a subroutine exists for calculating $\sqrt{x}$, call it `sqrt(x)`. Within a program, there can be expressions like `sqrt(801.25)`, `sqrt(4.1129e12)`, or `sqrt(169)`. The method for calculating a square root is a highly researched and optimized numerical procedure, and instead of doing the work of figuring out how to do this ourselves and repeating the effort, it is handy to have an "off-the-shelf" subroutine available.

Function Syntax

Python uses the term *function* rather than subroutine, which can be misleading considering all the different meanings of "function" outside of computing. Within the computing community, *functional programming languages* are a well-known branch of the family tree of languages. These languages consider functions to be types, similar to data types like integers, strings, and lists; Chapter 10 has a section on *function composition* discussing this programming style further.

Python offers two ways to define functions, one for simple, one-line expressions, and another for longer computations or lists of commands. We look first at the one-line style of function definition because of its connection to the history of computing research.

One-Line Functions: Lambdas

Suppose you are asked to solve the following equation:

$$a \cdot x^2 + b \cdot x + c \quad = \quad 0$$

This is the famous quadratic equation, and many students would write down $x = (-b \pm \sqrt{b^2 - 4ac})/2a$ immediately from memory, but there is a curious interpretation of the equation where that answer would be wrong: the person asking tells you that you are supposed to solve for c, not x. Then the answer would be just $-ax^2 - bx$. The point is, to be very precise, you need to be told what are the variables, and what are the given constants in the equation. This is how Python can define a function that computes $-ax^2 - bx$:

```
f = lambda a,x,b:  -a*x**2 - b*x
```

> Lambda is the name of the Greek character λ, which is used in a language of function definition called λ-calculus. Alonzo Church introduced λ-calculus in the 1930s, well before digital computers existed. In the 1950s, when the modern form of digital computing was invented, most intended applications of computing were mathematical functions—and investigation of λ-calculus became important. Can everything computable be expressed using λ-calculus? This kind of research question continues to the present.

The word "`lambda`" is a Python *reserved word* (a special word that is built-in to Python's syntax). The box explains the historical reference for `lambda`. The statement above defines a function `f`, and the "a,x,b:" indicate that this function has three parameters named `a`, `x`, and `b`. The remainder of the line is an expression to say what value the function returns when it is used. The following is a full, interactive example that defines `f` and then uses it twice:

```
>>> f = lambda a,x,b:  -a*x**2 - b*x
>>> f(1,5,7)
-60
>>> f(10,2,100)
-240
```

In fact, a function defined with a `lambda` can be used even without giving it a name:

```
>>> (lambda x,y:  x**2 - y**2)(16,12)
112
```

The first set of parentheses, surrounding the `lambda` expression, are needed so that Python knows where the `lambda`'s definition ends; the second pair of parentheses tell Python what are the values for `x` and `y`. This way of defining a function without a name, using it only once, does not make much sense. However, there are software packages in libraries that may require that a one-line function definition be provided, and for these packages `lambda` expressions could be useful.

```
>>> R = lambda x: "positive" if x>0 else "negative"
>>> R(5)
'positive'
>>> R(-2e10)
'negative'
>>> R(0)
'negative'
```

Lambda definitions can even have conditional definitions, using reserved words **if** and **else**. This syntax is somewhat obscure, and most programmers find better ways to define functions than this style of programming. In case you ever come across this syntax, here is an example to the left. Some might consider function R to have a bug, because it reports zero to be **negative**. However, Python is correctly following the definition of R. Later, in Chapter 10, we see a more flexible way of putting conditions into functions, which would easily allow for making R return something different for zero.

Multiline Functions: The Def Command

In nearly all situations, the **lambda** style of defining a function is impractical. The syntax is hard to remember, it is unlike the rest of Python, and being confined to a single line expression is not enough to do interesting work. The usual way to define a function in Python is to use the reserved word **def**. To the right is a short example. The syntax starts with **def**, then a name for the function, a *parameter list*, and a colon. Thereafter follow one or more lines, one of which is

```
>>> def sqrt(x):
... return x**0.5
...
>>> sqrt(16)
4.0
>>> sqrt(900)
30.0
>>> sqrt(2)
1.4142135623730951
```

a **return** statement. The return statement provides an expression that Python evaluates, reducing it to a value that will be substituted when the function is used. The syntax of *function application* consists of the function name followed by parentheses surrounding arguments (if any) to the function. For instance, the function application **sqrt(16)** first *binds* the value 16 to the symbolic name x, then evaluates the expression 16**0.5, which turns into 4.0 by reducing the expression. The "binding" of 16 to the symbolic name x is temporary, done only for the duration of Python's evaluation of function application; later, values 900 and 2 will be bound to the symbolic name x when they are used in **sqrt** application.

Notice the ... shown by Python during the definition of the function **sqrt**; this was done by Python because it is aware that a function is being defined, and expects one or more lines of code to be part of the function. ***It is crucial that these lines be indented***: you will see many examples illustrating this point. Python uses the notational convention of *indenting* lines of text to tell where a definition starts and where it ends. In the interactive session, a blank line ends the definition.

Rather than define functions interactively, we usually put the function definitions in a script. Suppose **myscript.py** is a file containing these lines (using Python3 syntax for the print statements).

```
def firstlast(s):
   return s[0]+s[-1]
print( firstlast("hold") )
print(firstlast('taxes'))
print(firstlast("Garden Ornament"))
```

Running the script has this output:

```
> python myscript.py
```

```
hd
ts
Gt
```

The function `firstlast` returns a string consisting of the concatenation of the first and last character of the function argument. One way to interpret the function definition, which appears first in the script file, is that it is a command: the command is to define a function. Once the function is defined, it can be freely used in expressions later in the script. A script can contain many function definitions, each following the syntax of function definition, as shown below.

```
def firstlast(s):
    return s[0]+s[-1]
def lastfirst(s):
    return s[-1]+s[0]
print(firstlast("hold"))
print(lastfirst("hold"))
```

Methods. For the sake of completeness, it is worth mentioning that Python has one more way to define functions. Chapter 27, which appears much later in this book, explains how *methods* can be defined. For now, it is not important to know the details, but as a point of curiosity we can see "under the hood"—how Python evaluates expressions using function calls. A *method* is a special kind of function. One example of a method introduced in Chapter 6 is the `upper` method. Recall that an expression like `"Hello".upper()` was explained in Chapter 6 to be effectively a secret function UPPER, as though it were UPPER("Hello") instead of `"Hello".upper()`. Similarly, Python has secret functions for nearly all operators, which are methods. Corresponding to the addition operator +, for example, there is the "__add__" method, demonstrated here:

```
>>> x = 100
>>> x.__add__(1)
101
```

The example shows that `x+1` is the same as `x.__add__(1)`, which is essentially a function call.

Head, Body, Parameters, and Arguments

Looking further into the syntax of function definition, function application, and related conventions, it is helpful to develop some terminology. Much of this terminology is used in other programming languages as well, and is generally "common knowledge" among programmers.

Head and Body. Some jargon for function definition is *head* and *body* of the function. The "head," or *header*, is just the first line, starting with **def** and ending with a colon. The remaining lines of the function definition are the *body* of the function, which have to be indented so that Python knows which lines belong to the function body. For `lambda`-style definitions, the body is the part that follows the colon.

Parameters versus Arguments. Perhaps you have noticed: sometimes functions are described as having parameters, and at other times they are arguments. Are these terms just synonyms? To many students, there seems no difference. Technically there is a clear difference in usage.

On the defining line of a function (beginning with the keyword def and ending with the colon), the symbolic names in the function head are called *parameters*. Subsequently, for each time that function is used in application, what gets evaluated and substituted for the parameter is called an *argument* to the function. A program has one line for defining parameters, but these parameters can be used as arguments many times: a Python program can have many applications of the same function, but with different values in the arguments at different places in a program.

```
def sqrt(x):      x is a parameter
     ...
print sqrt(100)   100 is an argument
print sqrt(225)   225 is an argument
```

Binding. When a Python program evaluates a function application, function arguments get *bound to* the parameters defined for that function. Later in the chapter we will see several ways of binding arguments to parameters. One important observation about binding is that if an expression is used as an argument, Python must first evaluate that expression, reducing it to a value; only then does the symbolic name used as the function parameter have a definite meaning inside the function's body.

Binding Multiple Parameters. The names of a function's parameters appear in the head; in Python, a function's head must provide exactly the number of names that any use of the function will have. Below are some acceptable and invalid cases for function headers.

```
def f(x,y,z):   ✔
def f(x,x):     ✘
def f():        ✔
def f(a,b-1)    ✘
```

The second line is invalid because the head attempts to name two parameters with the same name; the third line is acceptable because Python allows functions with no parameters (the number of parameters is zero); the fourth line is invalid because Python expects *only* names, not expressions. However, for arguments to functions, it is natural to have expressions. The table below shows columns for a function header, a typical usage of that function, and the binding that results.

head	usage	resulting binding
def f(a,b):	f(2,2*3)	a equals 2, b equals 6
def f(a,b):	f(True or False, not False)	a equals True, b equals True
def g(m,n):	g("AK"[1],(2,)+(9,))	m equals 'K', n equals (2,9)

Notice how the third column, the binding of the names (a, b, m, n), resembles how Python allows naming of the values that result from expression evaluation. For example, in the last row of the table, the binding result is m = "AK"[1], and this evaluation of expressions to names is done before Python proceeds to evaluate the body of the function.

Functions as Commands

Functions can return values based on expressions of their arguments, but Python does not require all functions to return values. Some functions are like Python3's print syntax, essentially using the function syntax to accomplish some external effect: drawing on a window, playing a sound, and so on. A simple example using Python3 syntax is this script:

```
def twiceprint(sometext):
  print(sometext)
  print(sometext)
twiceprint("Hello")
twiceprint("there")
```

The function `twiceprint` has no return statement since the point is to print the argument twice, but there is nothing to calculate. Similarly, each function evaluation is simply a line with `twiceprint` and an argument, and nothing is expected to be computed. When run, the output of this script is:

```
Hello
Hello
there
there
```

The same script written using Python2 syntax is:

```
def twiceprint(sometext):
  print sometext
  print sometext
twiceprint("Hello")
twiceprint("there")
```

Function application is the same for Python2 and Python3; the only difference is the **print** statement. Typical command functions may not use any parameter at all: in such cases the parameter list is empty:

```
def shoutout():
  print "one"
  print "more"
  print "time"
shoutout()
shoutout()
shoutout()
```

Notice how the indentation of all the lines in the body is the same. Python does not have a precise requirement of how far lines need to be indented, but they *must* all be indented by the same amount: all the lines in the body should line up along some imaginary vertical line.

Tracing. The ability to insert **print** commands into a function body can help us see how Python works, or perhaps that a function has been incorrectly coded. Consider this definition of a function `calc` and two function applications, in a script:

```
def calc(y):
  print "argument is", y
  return y**(1.0/3.0)/(1.0/y)
print "A:", calc(2**3)
print "B:", calc(2**5)
```

When this runs, the output is:

```
 A: argument is 8
 16.0
 B: argument is 32
 101.593667326
```

The surprising thing about this is that the two `print` commands mingle their output. The first `print` statement outputs `A:`, but then must wait for the function application `calc(2**3)` to be evaluated and reduced to a value before it outputs the rest. However, *inside* of the function application `calc(2**3)` there is a `print` statement (by the way, this adds a newline, as `print` commands normally do). Finally, the value 16.0 is returned, and then output.

Terminology Review

Jargon introduced in this chapter includes: the DRY principle, subroutine, parameter, argument, indented lines, head, body, binding, bound to.

Exercises

There can be many answers to some of the exercises: writing functions calls for some creativity and problem solving. The following exercises can all be solved by returning expressions, drawing from the material covered in this and preceding chapters. Feel free to use built-in functions that Python has (e.g., `len`) or built-in methods, such as the **upper** method on strings or the **index** method for sequences.

(1) Write a function named `MultiCalc` that returns a list of the sum, the product, and the remainder of a pair of numbers. Here would be some interactive calls to `MultiCalc`:

```
>>> p = (85,23)
>>> MultiCalc(p)
[108, 1955, 16]
>>> r = (1,1)
[2, 1, 0]
```

(2) Write a function named `allz` that takes a sequence argument, and returns a string of z characters of the same length as the argument. Here are a few examples of how it should behave:

$$
\begin{aligned}
\texttt{allz([1,2,3,4,5])} &\rightarrow \texttt{'zzzzz'} \\
\texttt{allz("happen")} &\rightarrow \texttt{'zzzzzz'} \\
\texttt{allz([])} &\rightarrow \texttt{' '}
\end{aligned}
$$

(3) Write a function named `lastearly` which returns either `True` or `False`, depending on whether a string's last character also occurs earlier in the same string. Here is what we expect from `lastearly`:

$$
\begin{aligned}
\texttt{lastearly("overland")} &\rightarrow \texttt{False} \\
\texttt{lastearly("wow")} &\rightarrow \texttt{True} \\
\texttt{lastearly("X")} &\rightarrow \texttt{False} \\
\texttt{lastearly("wish for years")} &\rightarrow \texttt{True}
\end{aligned}
$$

The answer is to define `lastearly(value)` so that it returns the "!=" comparison last character's index with the number `value.index(value[-1])`: if they are different then the last character occurs earlier in the string. (Recall that `len(value)-1` is the index for the final character.) See if you can make a working definition of `lastearly` based on these ideas.

☆(4) Every student in an algebra class learns the basic formula for the roots of a quadratic,

$$
\frac{-b \pm \sqrt{b^2 - 4ac}}{2a}
$$

which finds values of x such that $ax^2 + bx + c = 0$. Write a function `quadroot(a,b,c)` that returns the roots, as a pair, for the given parameters.

☆(5) Write a function `foo(s)` that returns a boolean, given a string s: the result is `True` if the first character of s concatenated with the last character of s also occurs as a string within s. Here are some examples:

$$
\begin{aligned}
\texttt{foo("wanted")} &\rightarrow \texttt{False} \\
\texttt{foo("drainer")} &\rightarrow \texttt{True} \\
\texttt{foo("scissors")} &\rightarrow \texttt{True}
\end{aligned}
$$

(6) The `lambda`-style definition allows a parameter to be a tuple. Consider these two definitions of `f`, followed by two calls to `f`:

  (a) `f = lambda x,y:  x+y / x*y`

  (b) `f - lambda (x,y):  x+y / x*y`

  (*i*) `f(2,4)`

  (*ii*) `f((2,4))`

  Which of (*i*) and (*ii*) works with **(a)**? Which works with **(b)**? How many arguments does `f` expect for **(a)** and how many with **(b)** as the definition? (Chapter 10 has more coverage of functions with multiple parameters.)

Return versus `Print`

Some beginners confuse the concepts of `return` and `print`—it can be confusing, as the following example shows. What is the difference between the two versions of the `sqrt` function below?

```
def sqrt(x):                      def sqrt(x):
    return x**0.5                     print x**0.5
```

In fact, the response to *either* looks the same:

```
>>> sqrt(25)
5.0
```

To explain how they differ, it is helpful to make a mental model of what `print` means. Suppose the Python `sqrt` functions are running on a smartphone which has a display and also a wireless link to a printer. The environment has been set up so that the `print` command outputs to the printer, whereas some other function, perhaps `display(s)`, outputs to the phone's screen area. In this situation, we see that `print` outputs on paper, whereas `return` is intended as calculating the square root of parameter x. The original meaning of `print`, dating back to the origin of computing, was to output on paper; only later was printing reinterpreted as output to a console. Such "virtualization" of the physical world is typical in the history of information technology, where we rely on metaphors to explain things (folders, the desktop, etc.). In our smartphone scenario, casual use of `print` will not be helpful if we need to have the result of `sqrt` instead be displayed the screen. Worse, if the result of `sqrt` is to be used in further calculations, `print` is not at all what is needed. To see this, just using Python2 in a typical (non-smartphone) environment, compare what happens when the two versions of `sqrt` are used in expressions:

```
>>> 1 + sqrt(9)                   >>> 1 + sqrt(9)
4.0                               TypeError: unsupported types for +
```

The version with the `print` statement got an error because it failed to return a value (secretly, it does return a value `None`, explained in Chapter 13, but this causes an error).

functions which calculate a result should use return

Chapter 10: Functions II

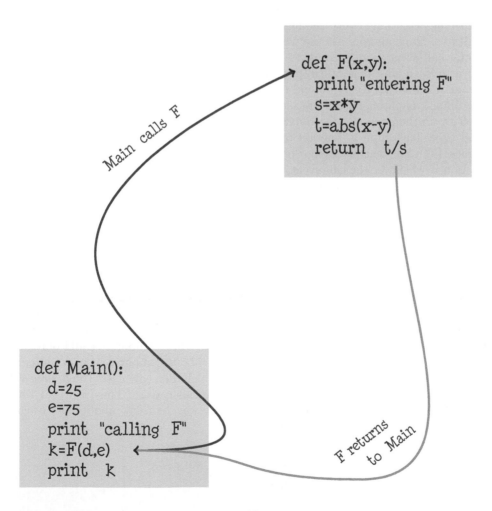

```
def F(x,y):
   print "entering F"
   s=x*y
   t=abs(x-y)
   return  t/s
```

Main calls F

```
def Main():
   d=25
   e=75
   print "calling F"
   k=F(d,e)
   print  k
```

F returns to Main

It is the function of vice to keep virtue within reasonable bounds.
— Samuel Butler

The *functional style* of programming is one that leverages the ability to create functions in nearly extreme ways. In addition to making functions that compute numeric, string, and list values, a function can test what kind of arguments it is given and change what it returns accordingly. This chapter shows how Python functions can work with multiple arguments and even substitute for missing arguments. The functional style encourages programmers to write functions from other functions: some functions are built in to Python, and these can be used to write other functions. There are even functions that have, as inputs, other functions! This abstract way of thinking moves the programmer up to higher layers, so to speak, on the pyramid of software automation. Whereas low-level data processing works with numbers, higher-level computing approaches symbolic reasoning, where operations seem to transform ideas. Fortunately, the material in this chapter is not so abstract: the techniques are mainstream Python language concepts and turn out to be quite practical.

Programmers use a certain vocabulary when talking about the way functions are used and how they behave. In nearly all cases, a program has a "main" function—this is really just jargon for the program itself. The `main` function will usually have statements with expressions, and some of these expressions will refer to other functions. For instance, if the `main` function (sometimes called the *main program*) uses an expression using Python's built-in `len` function, then we say `main` *calls* `len`, and `len` *returns* to `main`. The terms "calling" and "returning" colorfully evoke the musical pattern of call and response, which occurs in many cultures. Some authors use the word *invoke* instead of "call," which lets one refer to a particular call event as an *invocation*. In the example of `main` calling `len`, not only does `len` return to `main` after it is called, it returns a value—the length of a sequence that was its argument for the call. Keep in mind that programming is essentially a way of describing and controlling computing events. In this sense, the events of "calling" and "returning" are controlled by Python commands: `len(S)` calls `len` with argument `S`, and `return n` is a command to go back from a function back to the caller. Since a function could be called many times, from different places in a program, Python has to keep track of who the caller of a function is whenever the call event takes place.

Not all functions have parameters. There could be a function named `monitor` that has no parameters, so a `main` program calling it would have "`monitor()`" in some expression. Perhaps `monitor` returns a list, but the point is that no arguments are needed, so there is nothing between the parentheses, which looks strange at first. What if a function has nothing to return? Python actually insists that every function return some value, however, if a programmer forgets to do this, a substitute value is automatically provided: a later section in this chapter introduces Python's `None`, the special substitute value. There is another sense in which functions "return" to the caller. Whenever Python evaluates an expression using a function, that expression is temporarily put on hold, because function evaluation has high priority. When and where `main` calls `monitor`, we say *control passes to* `monitor`. This terminology originated from the days when computers could only do one step at a time (and most people still reason this way about computing). In a sense, `main` gives control of the computer's facilities to `monitor`, which then calculates the desired value. After `monitor` is finished, it passes control back to the caller, `main`. Thus, `monitor` returns control of the computer back to `main`. The simplest way to think about how programs operate is that they do one step at a time.

Parameters: Binding by Position

To this point, the functions introduced mainly used a single parameter or had an empty parameter list. Technically this is already enough for all programming needs, because a single parameter could be a tuple, dictionary, or list type–each of which can bundle up any collection of data. However, it is usually more convenient to use a parameter list with several symbolic names, one for each parameter.

Positional Parameters. We start with a simple example.

```
def subtract(a,b):
   return a-b
```

Evaluation of `subtract(8,2)` returns 6, whereas `subtract(2,8)` returns -6. Thus, the first argument binds to `a` and the second argument binds to `b`. This style of matching up arguments, first argument to first parameter, and so on, is called the *positional parameter* style. Here is a three-parameter example:

```
def subthenadd(a,b,c):
   return a-b+c
```

When the head of the function contains, say three parameters, any function application needs to have three parameters. So, Python will output an error when the wrong number of arguments is tried for function application:

```
>>> subthenadd(9,2)
TypeError: subthenadd() takes exactly 3 arguments (2 given)
```

Python has some advanced notation to allow the definition of functions with a variable number of parameters (for instance, like Python3's `print` function, which can have any number of arguments).

Function Type. The error in the previous example was reported by Python as a `TypeError`. This error suggests that functions have types. You can see this by asking Python with the `type()` query:

```
>>> type(subthenadd)
<type 'function'>
```

Python is thus aware of the function name much like a data type, such as string, list, or numeric types. Further, the number of parameters is considered to be a characteristic of the type of function, as are some other features described below.

Arguments by Keywords

Python differs from traditional languages, which use the positional style only for functions and subroutines, by offering a variety of styles for application and definition of parameters. First, we show how even functions defined with positional parameters can be called with keyword style arguments. This style uses the "=" symbol to say which argument should be bound with a parameter. The first example refers to the `subtract` function defined previously.

The Web was originally based on pages and links between pages, where each page was named by a **URI** (Uniform Resource Identifier). When search engines and similar content servers came on the scene, **URL**s added programming features to page names, including keywords. You may see some addresses on a Web browser with extra keywords and values, like "`?ref=1&q=cross+file`".

```
>>> subtract(a=9,b=2)
7
>>> subtract(b=1,a=3)
2
>>> subtract(b=100)
TypeError: subtract() takes
  exactly 2 non-keyword arguments
  (1 given)
>>> subtract(16,b=8)
8
>>> subtract(10,a=5,b=0)
TypeError: subtract() got multiple
  values for keyword argument 'a'
```

The Web browser sends a customized request, using these keywords, to a Web server. Python allows a similar style for function parameters and arguments. Advantages of this style are a more programmer-friendly interface and having "default values" when the keywords are missing.

The examples show several features of calling a function with the keyword argument style: (*i*) The arguments bind by the *parameter name*, a and b in the example. It does not matter which is the order of the keyword arguments given. (*ii*) All parameters defined in the function header need to be bound by the function application. (*iii*) An argument for a parameter can only be specified once in the function application. (*iv*) Positional and keyword argument styles can be mixed. The rule here is that positional arguments come first, then any remaining parameters can be specified by keyword. The keyword style of argument specification is not so useful for invoking functions defined with positional parameters; the real purpose of this style is motivated by the next topic, keyword parameters.

Default Parameters by Keyword

Parameters can also be specified as keywords by using "=" and a value to bind to the parameter. During function application, a keyword argument then *overrides* the parameter.

```
def nand(left=True,right=True):
  return not (left and right)
  ...
>>> nand(left=False,right=True):
True
>>> nand(left=5>3, right='a' in "lost")
True
```

The parameter for **nand**'s definition says that the symbolic name `left` has the value `True`; however, the first function application contradicts this, instead specifying that `False` should be bound to `left`. When Python evaluates the function application, what is given in the argument takes over. Though keyword style parameters can be used with the argument style of function application, seen above, the positional style can still be used:

```
>>> nand(False,True)
True
>>> nand(True,True)
False
```

The value given for a parameter in the function header is called the *default value*. There are two motivations for the keyword style: first, people may forget the exact order of what are the parameters to a function, but remember the symbolic names of the parameters. The second motivation is that there may be a parameter which, in 99% of all function applications, tends to get the same value. To streamline programming notation, in the spirit of Don't Repeat Yourself (DRY), Python allows parameters that have default values to be omitted from function application. When omitted from the arguments, the value used in function evaluation will be the default value.

```
>>> nand(right=(16==4*4))
False
>>> nand(left=False)
True
>>> nand()
False
```

The last line above shows that all arguments can be omitted, because the header for `nand` gives default values for all parameters.

Beginning Python programmers tend to avoid using keyword parameters, except where necessary: when using some of Python's library of functions, the use of keywords is practically the only way to take advantage of some functions.

Manual Binding

Instead of writing a function header with parameters (`foo(x,y)`, etc.), Python has syntax to treat positional arguments to a function as a tuple. This is done by naming just one parameter and preceding it with "`*`," as shown below to the left, with an example usage on the right.

```
def numpars(*p):            >>> numpars("one",2,True,"blue")
    return len(p)           4
```

To refer to the kth argument given to `foo` with head `foo(*p)`, a statement in the body would use `p[k]`. Keyword arguments can be accessed by similar syntax. The notation `foo(**p)` in the header allows the body to refer to arguments in a dictionary. For instance, `p["time"]` would equal 5 in a call `foo(time=5)`. If both positional and keyword arguments are used in a function call, the definition's head would be `foo(*p,**k)`, which makes `p` a tuple of positional arguments and `k` a dictionary of keyword arguments.

Return and None

Functions that produce a result based on arguments or default values of parameters have `return` statements to say what is the result value. We have seen that command functions (like ones that only print) do not have `return` statements. You should know, however, that Python actually does have a return value even for functions without `return` statements: it is a special value called `None`. There is even a special type in Python for this:

```
>>> type(None)
<type 'NoneType'>
>>> None
>>>
```

Unlike other values, you see above that Python's display of `None` in an interactive session shows nothing. But, you can see it as part of a tuple or list:

```
>>> [None,False]
[None, False]
```

Here is a demonstration of how `None` gets produced for a function which does not have a `return` statement:

```
def noret(x):
  x + 1
...
>>> [noret(5)]
[None]
```

If you were expecting to see 6 as the result of `noret(5)`, then you have missed an important point about Python functions: they return `None` *unless* you have a `return` statement. Of course, if you really wanted to, you could have a "`return None`" in your function, but why would anyone do that? In fact, there is a reasonable answer to this question, coming up in Chapter 11. Using "conditional logic" it is possible to program a function that returns quickly, without computing all the statements in the body of the function, if the arguments have particular values. Then, either "`return None`" or simply the statement "`return`" is sensible. In Python, the statement `return` (with no value given) is equivalent to `return None`, illustrated by this example:

```
def nothing():
   return
>>> [nothing()]
[None]
```

Using Function Calls and Names

So far, the chapter has not addressed the concern of how functions and parameters are *named*. Previously, function names `sqrt`, `firstlast`, `lastfirst`, `twiceprint`, `shoutout`, `calc`, `subtract`, `subthenadd`, `nand`, and `noret` have been defined as examples. These all happen to be lowercase function names, but uppercase names and mixed names are also permitted, for instance

```
MUL, Fraction, CaLiFoRnIa, EasyThereGuy
```

are valid Python function names. Generally, any combination of alphabetic characters (without any blanks) is an acceptable name. Python discriminates between upper and lowercase names, so `Sqrt` and `sqrt` are considered to be different names. The only restriction is that certain *reserved names*, also called *reserved words* and *reserved identifiers*, should not be chosen as function names. Examples of this are: `and`, `or`, `not`, `False`, `True`, `in`, `def`, `type`, `len`, `print`, `None`, and any other part of the Python language that occurs in statements, types, operators, and such—it can be confusing to define functions with names that conflict with the language.

Similarly, parameter names which symbolically refer to arguments can be any name that does not conflict with the Python language; above examples use parameter names `x`, `y`, `a`, `b`, `left`, `right`, but as with function names, you can use upper- and lowercase or a mixture of cases. As a matter of style, some people prefer to use names that reflect the "meaning" of a parameter and so names like `dividend` or `InvoiceNumber` could be used. Other people like terse names like `x`, `y`, `J`, and so on. Avoid tricky and confusing names like `ILIILI`, `LLILIIL`, and so on, which make reading code very difficult.

Numeric digits can also be used in names, though not as the first character. Thus, names such as `y30`, `alpha1`, `Key003` are admissible in Python.

Building on Functions

It should come as no surprise that you can use function application in expressions, even those that are arguments to functions:

```
>>> nand( subtract(7,3)>0, subtract(2,9)>0 )
True
```

To bind arguments of `nand` to its parameters, Python first has to evaluate the expressions for each argument, which are function applications. Sometimes this is called *nested evaluation*, where in order to evaluate one thing, something inside (here, it is inside the argument list) has to be evaluated. This use of "nest" is an analogy to nesting dolls, a Russian folk toy.[1] As well as putting function application inside of argument expressions, it is quite common to organize function definitions that use function application in their bodies. For example, the formula for distance between two points in two dimensional space, called the Euclidean distance, is

$$\sqrt{(x_2 - x_1)^2 + (y_2 - y_1)^2}$$

Using Python definitions, this formula could be written with several functions:

```
def dimdiff(a,b,ind):
  return a[ind]-b[ind]
def xdiff(v,w):
  return dimdiff(v,w,0)
def ydiff(v,w):
  return dimdiff(v,w,1)
def sqrt(x):
  return x**0.5
def distance(p,q):
  return sqrt(xdiff(p,q)**2, ydiff(p,q)**2)
```

This example probably went too far in using functions, but it makes the point that you can write one function in terms of expressions that rely on other functions. Whether this is a good idea or not depends on the situation.

---

[1]Look up *matryoshka* if you are curious.

Python's Built-In Functions

Python has some functions that are automatically available without needing the programmer to define them. These are called *built-in functions*. Here is a partial list of Python's built-in functions:

abs(x)	returns absolute value
min(x,y)	returns smaller argument
max(x,y)	returns larger argument
type(x)	type query
len(x)	length of sequence

Chapter 18 describes how thousands more functions can be brought into Python, thanks to libraries that are freely available with Python or found via the Web.

Type Conversion

Another set of built-in functions are ones that can convert data from one type to another. The function names are the same as the type names, and all take a single argument. Also, all of these have a default value when no argument is given. The following shows the default values:

int()	0
float()	0.0
bool()	False
str()	''
tuple()	()
list()	[]
dict()	{}
set()	set([])

Common examples of type conversion are string to numeric, float to integer, and anything to a string. Here are some examples:

```
>>> int(1.95)
1
>>> float(999)
999.0
>>> int(False)
0
>>> tuple( [False,-9,"abc"] )
(False, -9, 'abc')
>>> list( "state" )
['s', 't', 'a', 't', 'e']
>>> str( [1,2,3] )
'[1, 2, 3]'
```

Conversion to a string again requires that you comprehend the difference between typed data and the characters that represent that data. This often trips up beginners. Consider these cases:

```
>>> [8,2,5,1][2]
5
>>> str([8,2,5,1])[2]
```

```
','
>>> "home" + 9
TypeError: cannot concatenate 'str' and 'int' objects
>>> "home" + str(9)
'home9'
>>> int("seven")
ValueError: invalid literal for int() with base 10: 'seven'
>>> int("7")
7
```

The examples are not a complete set of rules for how Python does (and does not) convert between types, but show the more common cases. The `print` function in Python3 uses the equivalent of `str()` for each argument before output; the `print` statement in Python2 similarly handles each expression given on the statement.

Namespace Queries

During a Python interactive session, or during the run of a script, Python builds an internal dictionary of the names of defined functions and other things needed to evaluate expressions and to execute programs. There is a built-in function `dir` that returns a list of what are the currently defined names. Here is the output of `dir()` when Python first starts an interactive session:

```
>>> dir()
['__builtins__', '__doc__', '__name__', '__package__']
```

All the special names used by Python start with underscore characters—these have special significance for the Python environment. Now suppose the session continues with:

```
>>> def sqrt(x):
...     return x**0.5
...
>>> def double(x):
...     return 2*x
...
>>> dir()
['__builtins__', '__doc__', '__name__', '__package__', 'sqrt', 'double']
```

This example hints at how Python does its job: it uses concepts from Python itself in order to interact with users, evaluate what they type, define functions, and so forth. It uses integers, strings, lists, dictionaries, and other data types, with extensive use of functions to do all the work.

> *The smaller the function, the greater the management.*
> — C. Northcote Parkinson

Function Composition

Building new functions in terms of old ones is a standard way to write software. A term for this is *function composition*, which means putting functions together in some combination to get new functions. For some examples, recall that Chapter 6 explained how the operators == and < work for sequences, but did not define other comparisons between sequences. Using function composition it is easy to explain how the operators work. Below, let leq be a function for the <= operator, neq for != (and its synonym <>), gt for >, and geq for >=.

```
def geq(x,y):
    return not (x < y)
def neq(x,y):
    return not (x == y)
def gt(x,y):
    return geq(x,y) and neq(x,y)
def leq(x,y):
    return not gt(x,y)
```

Function composition has another meaning for a style of programming called *functional programming*. The idea of functional programming is that parameters of functions, and more broadly inputs to algorithms, can be **functions** as well as ordinary data values. It is difficult to appreciate this without looking at an example.

```
def addOne(x):
   return x+1
def addTwo(x):
   return x+2
def appFtoVal(f,v):
   return f(v)
def appFFtoVal(f,v):
   return f(f(v))
...
>>> appFtoVal(addOne,100)
101
>>> appFFtoVal(addOne,100)
102
>>> appFtoVal(addTwo,100)
102
>>> appFFtoVal(addTwo,100)
104
```

The interesting thing here is that you cannot see, by looking at the body of appFtoVal, just what exactly the function f does. Indeed, Python gives the freedom of selecting what function f will be up to the caller of appFtoVal, as the example shows.

Local Functions

Sometimes it is handy to write a function only to make it easier to write another function. Suppose three (x, y) points are given and we need to know whether all these points lie on a common line or they are corners of a triangle. A test for this (not foolproof because float is imperfect) is to check whether two of the interpoint distances add up to the third distance. The following example uses syntax explained in later chapters: Python's if is explained in

Chapter 11, but can be understood intuitively here; the simultaneous definition of d1, d2, d3, to the respective values of `distance`, is syntax explained in Chapter 15.

```
def colinear(a,b,c):
  def distance(p1,p2):
    x1,y1 = p1
    x2,y2 = p2
    return ((x2-x1)**2 + (y2-y1)**2)**0.5
  if a==b or b==c or a==c:
    return True
  d1,d2,d3 = distance(a,b), distance(b,c), distance(a,c)
  if d1+d2==d3 or d2+d3=d1 or d1+d3=d2:
    return True
  return False
```

The point of the example is that the "interior" function `distance(p1,p2)` has no use outside of the `colinear` function, so it is defined inside of `colinear`. The body of `colinear` first defines `distance` and later uses it. The parameters a,b,c are each (x, y) pairs, which is why the statement `x1,y1 = p1` is sensible: p1 is a pair of values. An important point of this example is that `distance` is *local* to `colinear`. Had this code been part of a larger program, other places in the program would not be able to call `distance`, because it is local to `colinear` and Python wo not allow code outside of `colinear` to use it. (Though there is an exception to this rule: see the box "Currying and Made-to-Order Functions" later in this chapter.)

Terminology Review

Jargon introduced in this chapter includes: positional parameters, keyword parameters, default values, keyword arguments, the `None` type, type conversion functions, namespace, function composition, and functional programming.

Exercises

(1) Write a function `IsDiff(a,b,c)` that returns `True` if a-b equals c, and otherwise returns `False`.

☆(2) Write a function `IsUpper(r,s)` that returns `True` if s is the uppercase version of r. An interactive test of `IsUpper` would be the following:

```
>>> IsUpper("Tent",'TENT')
True
>>> IsUpper("ground","EARTH")
False
```

(3) This is almost the same question as (2). Write a function `TestUpper(c)` that returns `True` if c is an all uppercase string. Here are test cases:

```
>>> TestUpper('BIG')
True
>>> TestUpper("Sun")
False
```

(4) Write a function named `sandwich(a,b,c)` that returns `True` if b is equal to the concatenation of a and b. Some test cases for `sandwich` are:

```
>>> sandwich("the","theplay","play")
True
>>> sandwich([False],[False,True],[True])
True
>>> sandwich((),(1,2),(1,2))
True
>>> sandwich("X","J","Y")
False
```

(5) In mathematics, a function is *idempotent* if multiple applications get the same result as a single application of the function. Python has a built-in function `abs` with this property: `abs(-7)` returns 7, the absolute value of the argument. Clearly, `abs(abs(x))` returns the same number as `abs(x)` for any number x. This exercise is to write a function named `idem` that returns `True` in case `f(f(x))` is equal to `f(x)` for given arguments f and x. Here would be some interactive test cases for a correctly designed `idem`:

```
>>> idem(abs,-3)
True
>>> x = type(True)
>>> y = type(x)
>>> idem(type,y)
True
>>> def subtractOne(x):
...     return x-1
...
>>> idem(subtractOne,50)
False
```

(The test case using Python's `type` query is a bit tricky, but may make sense if you experiment with `type(type(True))`.)

☆(6) The following function definition has several errors. There are two syntax mistakes, a possible runtime error (which might or might not occur when trying to use the function), and what is probably a design flaw, namely a suspicious way the function is coded. Can you find the errors?

```
def multicat(prefix=(1,2),value,suffix=(9))
    a = prefix + value
     b = a + suffix
    return
```

(7) What will this script print when it runs?

```
def switch((left,right)):
  return (right,left)
def insert(a,(b,c)):
  return (b,a,c)
print insert(True,switch((True,False)))
```

Currying and Made-to-Order Functions

Currying is a technique that reframes the computing of functions with multiple parameters into computing that only uses single-parameter functions. This technique is named after logician Haskell Curry (functional programming language Haskell is named after him). It is simple in Python to illustrate this technique, and also emphasizes some novel programming ideas. Suppose we need a function `increase(x)` that returns x+k for some desired value k. One way to do this would be to define `increase(k,x)` so that the value of k is a parameter. A disadvantage of this definition is that a program needs to have the value for k known and remembered so that it is available when using `increase`. Instead, is there some way to define `increase(x)` so that the value of k is "built in" to the definition, yet this value is not a fixed number (like 1, 2, or 99) in the definition?

```
def makeIncrease(k,x=0):
    def bump(x):
        return k+x
    return bump
```

```
>>> increaseFive = makeIncrease(5)
>>> increaseTen  = makeIncrease(10)
>>> increaseFive(1)
6
>>> increaseTen(2)
12
>>> bump(3)
NameError: name 'bump' is not defined.
```

The body of `makeIncrease` is peculiar: it defines a *local function* named `bump`. This local function is returned to the caller of `makeIncrease`. The last line in the interactive session (`bump(3)`) demonstrates that `bump` is not known outside of the `makeIncrease` function. Yet, `increaseFive` is a function: it is equivalent to `bump`, where k equals 5. The net effect is that `makeIncrease` *creates* a specialized function, which can be used later. Two examples of this are `increaseFive`, a one-parameter function which adds 5 to its argument, and `increaseTen`, which adds 10 to its argument.

This technique of writing a function that returns a new function is typical of the style of advanced functional programming. It can be used to "Curry" functions and to reduce the number of parameters in some situations. As a beginner, you should not be expected to use or master such an advanced technique. Nonetheless, there are some useful takeaways from the example above:

- In Python, a function is a type, much as sequences, booleans, and numbers are types.

- It is possible to return a function as the result of some calculation.

- Conversely (not shown above, but made useful in Chapter 13), it is possible to have a function as an argument. For example:

    ```
    app = lambda f,g,x:  f(g(x))
    ```

    defines `app(f,g,x)` to be `f(g(x))`.

Interlude: Table Lookup Functions

Recall the inventory problem of Acme Perfume, the essence of which was the representation of tables using Python types. What good are tables without being able to use them? Once there are Python *data structures* to represent the tables, such as lists, tuples, and dictionaries, the practical *use cases*[2] motivate the invention of functions to access the tables.

How does one decide whether or not new functions should be written, what parameters they should have, and what they should compute? Two schools of thought are *top-down design* and *bottom-up design*. The top-down approach proceeds from thinking about how software will be used, what the goals are, and then breaking down action by users into small enough sub-actions that they look like desirable functions. For example, suppose Acme's employees need to frequently make a list of Web sites for an ingredient. A desirable function thus might be `lookup(T,ingred)`, where parameter T refers to Acme's tables and parameter `ingred` names an ingredient. Function `lookup`'s action would be to make a list of Web sites and return that. The bottom-up method is more difficult to motivate, coming mostly from the experience of having previously designed many systems and then anticipating what will be useful even before users ask for it! A typical bottom-up tactic is to write functions that search, update, and delete rows of a table. Such functions can be designed, written, and debugged even without knowing whether or not the application will need them. One advantage to the bottom-up method is that users, perhaps the employees and managers at Acme, are not certain about what they want. It could be useful to have a family of potentially useful functions ready when Acme's management finally nails down all the requirements for the software.

Recall the two tables mentioned earlier, one for ingredients and the other for suppliers. Here we show two rows of each, but the columns are designated A, B, C, and so on, and values under the columns are numbers.

ingredient	A	B	$\cdots$
oakmoss28	100	101	$\cdots$
lavender4	200	201	$\cdots$

supplier	M	N	$\cdots$
Botanisco	300	301	$\cdots$
Olfaktikov	400	402	$\cdots$

Let `ingredients` and `suppliers` be Python representations of these two tables. We assume that each row in the ingredient table names a different ingredient than all the other rows (we can arrange for this to be true by design for Acme's database). Similarly, we suppose each row in the supplier table differs from the other rows. These assumptions motivate using dictionaries: `ingredients["oakmoss28"]` could be a list of the values for columns A, B, and so on, and `suppliers["Botanisco"]` could be a list of the values for columns M, N, and so on. Alternatively—and this will be our choice—each row of the ingredients table can be a dictionary. Thus,

```
ingredients["oakmosss28"]["B"]    ➔    101
```

One column of the ingredient table, say D in the ingredient table, is a list of all the suppliers for an ingredient. The Acme management would like a simple query that, given an ingredient, responds with the Web site of a supplier for that ingredient (the query just returns the site of the first supplier in the list). The following `oneWeb(ingred)` functions implements this query.

---

[2]In software engineering, the term *use case* refers to analysis of how people will likely use a system. Use case analysis is a first step in figuring out what functions would be useful to the users of a proposed system. If you query a search engine on "use case analysis" you are likely to find diagrams which illustrate how users of a system interact with its parts.

```
def oneWeb(ingred,T1=ingredients,T2=suppliers):
   ingredRow = T1[ingred]
   suppList  = ingredRow["D"]
   oneVendor = suppList[0]
   suppRow   = T2[oneVendor]
   webSite   = suppRow["P"]
   return webSite
```

The `oneWeb` is a textbook example of a table lookup. Each line of the function is either a table lookup (we see lookups in `T1`, `T2`, and for rows `D` and `P`) or an index operation: the `suppList[0]` effectively "looks up" the first item of a list.

Example: Suppose the above `oneWeb` function is called with `oneWeb("lavender4")`; defaults on the `T1` and `T2` keywords will be the `ingredients` and `suppliers` tables, represented below as dictionaries. Here is a picture of how Python will relate the names given to values when it evaluates `oneWeb("lavender4")`:

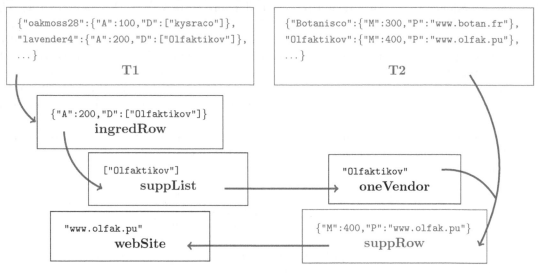

Each arrow above stands for a name definition in the script. The arrow from `T1` to the `ingredRow` box just below represents "`ingredRow = T1[ingred]`," since we know `ingred` is `"lavender4"` for this example. The rightmost arrow from `T2` to the `suppRow` box joins up with a line from `oneVendor`—that is because this arrow represents the "`suppRow = T2[oneVendor]`" definition in the script.

Table lookup is a core problem-solving technique in computing. Lookup is so simple that it is often overlooked. In order for table lookup to be practical, we also need ways to create dictionaries, update dictionaries, and load tables into dictionaries from files. Ways to update dictionaries are presented in Chapters 15–17. Reading from files is a topic of Chapter 25.

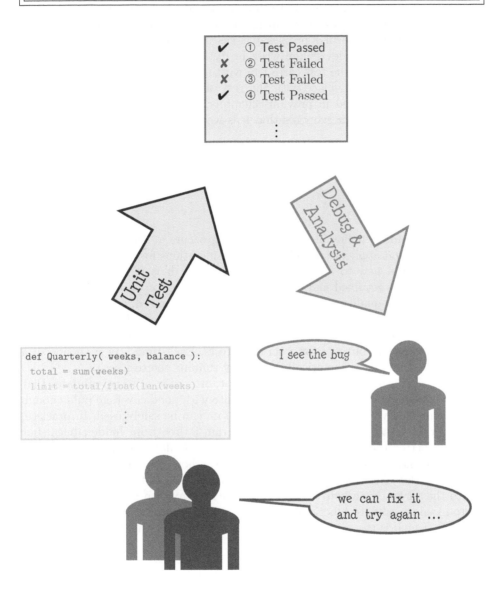

How can one become proficient in writing functions? Printed exercises only go so far: they encourage the reader to think about a problem, but fall short of an interactive experience. The following few pages in the book explain a Python framework for testing programs. With a testing facility, a suite of training exercises opens up, provided online as a companion to this text. These exercises take the form of puzzles: test cases for a function (which is missing) are provided, and the puzzle is to devise and write in Python a satisfactory function. You know you have the solution when the test cases run with no errors.

The unit-testing topic is out of place with the rest of the text: it uses some Python syntax that has not been discussed in previous chapters. Later chapters do explain the syntax, but the topic is so useful for exercises that it is worth seeing here.

Test Suites

Trust, but verify.
— Russian saying

Testing software is a standard policy in industry. Testing occurs at multiple times during development of systems and applications. The main considerations for testing are deciding what should be tested and how to automate testing, because it is tedious and likely to be done repeatedly as bugs get fixed and software evolves. Large software companies have separate testing divisions for quality control. Some testing is randomized, but randomization may not be a guarantee that certain important cases are tried, which can be vital for software used in safety-critical missions. Most often, automated testing relies on scripts that give inputs and expected outputs for a series of tests. Each time a new version of a program is developed, it can be automatically tested by running the test script.

Testing *coverage* refers to how extensive a test script, or a *suite* of tests, validates that software correctly implements a specification. A test suite with good coverage puts enough "stress" on a program to give confidence that the program can be safely used. In practice, even the best coverage is no guarantee that the program is free from hidden bugs, but running tests is far better than doing nothing. Testing can be done at different levels of detail. For interactive games, testing might need to cover how the game performs with simulated user input; for Web servers, testing would cover different browsers and their interactions with the server. Even individual parts of the software can be tested by making test suites customized to validate functions or methods making up a software application. This last technique, which is the unit testing of individual functions, is described next for Python.

Formal Methods

The design of software is driven by imagination. In the case of an individual software designer, the imagined application or system may be based on a coherent vision, free from internal conflicts or bugs. More often, software is the result of team efforts combining design ideas from many people, from customer suggestions, or brainstorming under the influence of late night pizza consumption and crazy music. Little surprise that much software really is vaguely imagined, so the vision probably would have some unforeseen problems when it is actually built.

Software engineering researchers are well aware of the problems going from vision to reality. Various design disciplines and tools can be used, which try to coerce people doing design into using techniques that double-check the designs, motivated in part by the success of double-ledger bookkeeping in finding accounting mistakes. One research contribution is the area of *formal methods*. Within formal methods, the starting point is to have a *specification* of software. By "specification" we mean that the details of imagined software are pinned down precisely so that there is no confusion about what a design means and does not mean. Creating a truly unambiguous specification is quite difficult. Consider students taking courses, particularly courses where homeworks are programming assignments. Invariably, students find the assignments confusing, because questions come up about how a program should behave. Even for extremely simple assignments like "write a function to compute square root" a student might ask, what if the input is a negative number, what if the input is a character string, and so forth. We do not want to write a book, the equivalent of an income tax regulation, dealing with every question that could conceivably be asked. In practice, specifications will make some compromises to avoid overly long and complicated descriptions.

Practical specifications of software fall short of the ideal, leaving some details unmentioned. This could be a problem during software development and show up during program testing, but it is better than not having any kind of specification. Complete discussion of specifications is beyond what this book covers. One limited kind of specification, which is very practical for beginners, is *unit testing*. The idea of unit testing is to make a series of software tests. Each test consists of an input for what is being tested and the expected output. In principle, specification of software might be achieved by unit testing; in practice, the number of tests that would be needed to represent a full specification is too large to describe. Even for something as simple as a square root function, a full suite of test cases could number 10^{40} or more. Researchers have devised clever ways of reducing the number of tests to a small number so that the probability is good for finding defects in software. In this discussion, things are less formal. We limit unit testing to functions, and the test cases are typically only a few.

Python Doctest

```
'''
>>> sqrt(16)
4.0
>>> sqrt(3)
1.7320508075688772
>>> sqrt(-1)
Traceback (most recent call last):
    ...
ValueError: negative number cannot
    be raised to a fractional power
'''
def sqrt(x):
    return x**0.5
if __name__ == "__main__":
    import doctest
    doctest.testmod()
```

Here, using the `sqrt` function, we show basic unit testing with Python. The syntax is shown to the left, which is a testing script for `sqrt`. The file begins with a long string (Chapter 8 explains the notation for a multiline string). This string contains something that should look familiar: it is a transcript of an interactive Python session, which exercises some `sqrt` calls. This transcript has been edited slightly; the "..." line in a real Python session would be several lines of diagnostic information. At the end of the script, there are some mysterious lines with underscores and the name `doctest` in a couple places. The "doctest" is Python's *test harness*, meaning that it is a part of Python that drives the testing procedure. What `doctest` does is to read the long string at the beginning of the script, and use that to formulate tests. The transcript in the long string says what is to be tested and what values to use and expect.

Without Bugs

Running the unit test is easy from a command prompt. Suppose the script shown above is in a file `sqrt.py`. Just running the script does the testing:

```
> python sqrt.py
>
```

The script has no output if the function `sqrt` passed all of the tests. Should some kind of report be desired, there is a slightly different way to run the script, shown to the right (notice the "-v" on the `python` command, which requests verbose output). There are three test cases in the script `sqrt.py`. The output, presented to the right, shows "ok" for each test case. The perhaps confusing part is that the test verifies that `sqrt` *should have an error* when the argument is -1. The designer of the test cases *wanted* the square root function to fail for negative numbers. If instead, the `sqrt` function returned some value instead of getting the `ValueError`, that would be wrong in the opinion of whoever wrote the test cases. In normal life, we see tests with only positive results to mean satisfactory performance; but in software, a thorough specification can also say just when a function should get an error.

```
> python sqrt.py -v
Trying:
    sqrt(16)
Expecting:
    4.0
ok
Trying:
    sqrt(3)
Expecting:
    1.7320508075688772
ok
Trying:
    sqrt(-1)
Expecting:
    Traceback (most recent call last):
        ...
    ValueError: negative number cannot be
    raised to a fractional power
ok
3 tests in 2 items.
3 passed and 0 failed.
Test passed.
>
```

With Bug

Let's suppose the example is changed to introduce a **bug** by defining `sqrt` incorrectly (raising x to the power 0.25 instead of 0.5). Below, the incorrect definition is on the left, and part of the unit test run is shown on the right.

```
def sqrt(x):
    return x**0.25
```

```
> python sqrt.py
***********************
Failed example:
    sqrt(16)
Expected:
    4.0
Got:
    2.0
***********************
```

The output shows only tests that fail, with input and expected output. Seeing the difference between "expected" and "got" is valuable when debugging the function.

Syntax Explained

While the general picture of unit testing should be clear from these examples, the syntax is mysterious. Some parts of the `sqrt.py` script use Python features explained in later chapters. Figure 10.1 shows a simplified look at the script. The key points to observe are:

- The script starts with triple quotes—a long string (explained in Chapter 8)—which continues down to the triple quotes some lines below. Recall that scripts, unlike interactive Python, do not print expressions. So, starting a script with a string will not harm anything.

- Beginning a script with a long string is a sneaky way for a programmer to write a message, usually an explanation, to anyone (human) reading the program. This is a *commenting convention*, described later in Chapter 20. For the present, simply accept this as some strange kind of remark that starts the script.

- **Do not be confused that the long string contains Python code.** Yes, it happens to look like some Python test cases, but technically it is just a string, used as a commenting convention.

- The definition of `sqrt` is the normal way of defining functions, explained in Chapter 9.

- The line starting with "`if`" is the first point in the script where computing occurs. Earlier lines of the script are either documentation (the long string) or function definition (for `sqrt`). The meaning of `if` is made clear in Chapter 11; for now, just think of this as a way to turn on unit testing under certain conditions. The "`__main__`" refers to the concept of the main function, talked about informally in Chapter 10. The "`import doctest`" tells Python to use a *module* from the standard Python library; Chapter 18 explains the syntax of importing. Finally, the `doctest.testmod()` is a function call, which kicks off the unit testing.

- Once the actual unit testing takes control, it uses a devious trick. The unit testing function `doctest.testmod` *reads* the comment at the beginning of the script. It extracts from the long string a specification of test cases. These test cases, which were painstakingly copied from an interactive Python session (which had a working version of `sqrt`) show exactly how `sqrt` should behave for certain arguments (16, 3, and –1).

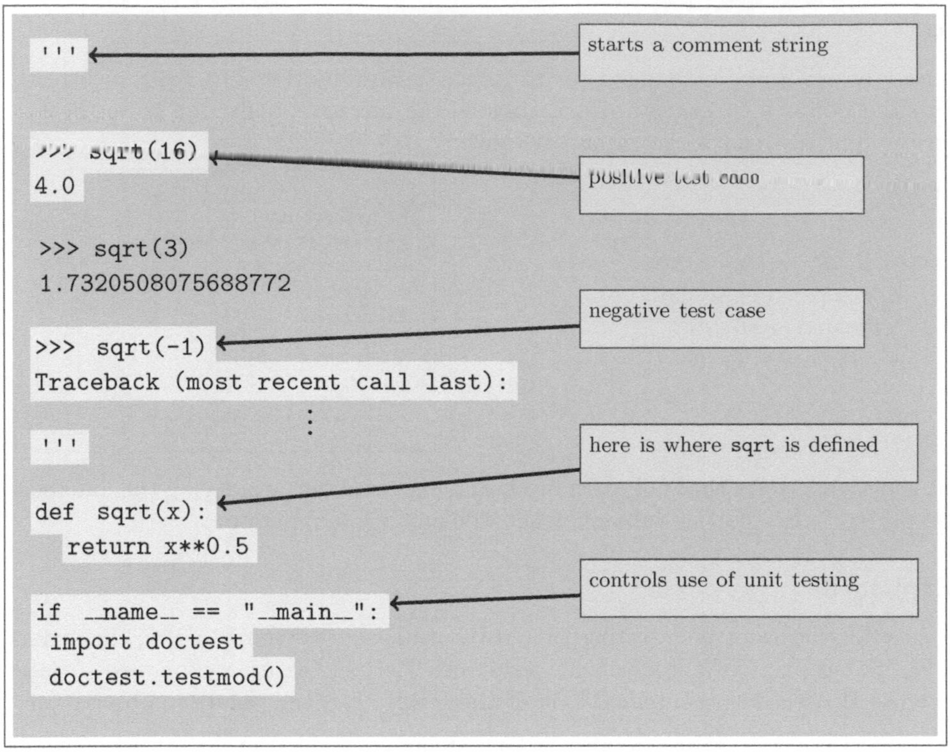

Figure 10.1: Simplified view of test script.

Separating Test from Function

Another way to test a function is to define it in one file and put the testing script in another file. An example testing script is shown in Figure 10.2. Notice that it does not contain a definition of `sqrt`, but has an `import` line in its place; Chapter 18 explains the syntax of this line. Suppose the file `testsqrt.py` contains that which is in Figure 10.2. To run the script, first there needs to be a file `sqrt.py` containing the definition:

```
def sqrt(x):
    return x**0.5
```

Testing occurs by entering the command

```
> python testsqrt.py
>
```

Going Further

In addition to the `doctest` feature, Python has a `unittest` and other facilities to support testing, most of which are more advanced than needed for beginners. One thing worth pointing out is that it is possible to test many functions in one script. The long string with test cases can use a number of test cases and test multiple functions. These functions might use built-in functions, refer to each other in expressions, and use other Python syntax defined in later chapters.

```
'''
>>> sqrt(16)
4.0
>>> sqrt(3)
1.7320508075688772
>>> sqrt(-1)
Traceback (most recent call last):
    ...
ValueError: negative number cannot be raised to a fractional power
'''

from sqrt import *

if __name__ == "__main__":
    import doctest
    doctest.testmod()
```

Figure 10.2: Unit test script.

Exercises

The Web site support of this textbook has many unit tests. Each of the unit tests is a script with missing function definitions. Your task is to write the missing functions so that running the scripts completes testing with no errors. A typical exercise is shown on the right. The two lines staring with `#--------` are comments (see Chapter 20 for the syntax of a Python comment). The exercise is to define a function named `allz` that has the behavior shown in the three test cases. As explained in this chapter, these test cases are copied from an interactive Python session using a working `allz` function. Your definition of `allz` should be put between the two `#--------` lines. Once you have put a definition of `allz` between these two lines, run the example, using an Integrated Development Environment (IDE) such as IDLE, or from a system console. For instance, if the file is `allz.py`,

```
'''
The allz function returns a string
in which every letter is 'z';  the
length of the returned string is the
same as the length of the argument
given to allz:

>>> allz( [1,2,3,4,5] )
'zzzzz'
>>> allz( "happen" )
'zzzzzz'
>>> allz( [] )
''
'''
#-------------------------------
#-------------------------------
if __name__ == "__main__":
    import doctest
    doctest.testmod()
```

and you have edited it to have `allz` defined, then a command from the console

```
> python allz.py
```

tests your program.

In general, with running Python programs (not just with unit testing), Python will report errors. The way that Python indicates the source of an error, whether it is a syntax error or runtime error such as division by zero, is supposed to inform the user about the type of the error and the line number in the program. Unfortunately, the terminology that Python uses often contains too much detail, some advanced concepts, and other information not so helpful to debugging. Sometimes IDEs do a better job of indicating the error, perhaps highlighting the line in a different color to emphasize the location. Chapter 21 offers some advice on debugging, but for unit testing there is a different strategy. If the unit test fails because your function definition has a bug, the best debugging method is to first *isolate* the bug: make a copy of the python program, and in your copy take out the unit testing. As an example, you could make a file `copy-allz.py` that contains *only* your definition of `allz`, followed by one print statement, say `print(allz([2,3]))`. When you run `copy-allz.py`, the only thing the program does is to try evaluating `allz([2,3])` and print the result. This makes debugging simpler because the program has fewer actions.

```
def allz(S):
  if len(S)==5:
    return 5*'z'
  elif len(S)==6:
    return 6*'z'
  else return ''
```

The English description of `allz` at the beginning of the exercise conveys a general meaning, but the test cases are far more precise. Obviously, each exercise has only some test cases. Defining a function to satisfy these cases exclusively, and not the more general description, is not really solving the problem. The proposed definition of `allz` on the left (which uses Python condition syntax from Chapter 11) will pass the three unit tests: it is correct for sequences of length 0, 5, and 6. Yet the intent of the problem was to provide a correct result for *any* length sequence, not just the three instances shown. To overcome this situation, some systems inject random tests, using random values for test arguments. For beginners, it is better to use known unit tests without randomness, since this makes problems more concrete and is less confusing during debugging.

The Web site unit test supplement to this book arranges the unit tests into topics that roughly correspond to the progression of chapters. There is a section **Basic** that can be solved using techniques of previous chapters; a section `Condition` needs material from Chapter 11, and `Slice` exercises ideas of Chapter 12. Other sections depend on later chapters. Solving a few of these unit tests really helps one get the hang of functions, problem solving, and the simple tasks of typing in Python, testing it, and debugging.

The way to understand a system is
to learn how it breaks.

Chapter 11:   Conditional Logic

12 coins and a balance

one coin is counterfeit—it is either
heavier or lighter than other coins

find the counterfeit coin in three
weighings

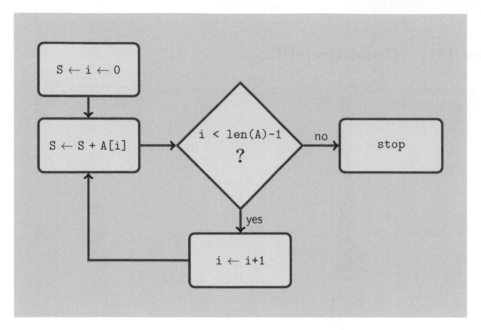

Figure 11.1: Small flowchart example.

Over a century ago, railroads were hot technology, pushing innovation and driving the economy. The buildup of rail infrastructure put tracks between cities, essentially creating a road network for trains. Unlike natural paths or roads for people, horses, and livestock, trains cannot turn by themselves from one track to another. It took the invention of the rail switch to get trains from one track to another. Eventually a network of tracks and switching junctions emerged.

Early train locomotives were fueled by wood or coal and railway engineers managed the switches. Major junctions in most cities, the railway switchyards, concentrated the switching jobs. The junctions also had repair facilities, shunting engines, stocks of water (needed for steam engines), and supplies. Imagine a train heading from Chicago to Kansas City. Rather than have a single track dedicated to this route, the train goes along many track segments, guided by switches. First might be a track from Chicago to Rockford; then a track from Rockford to Dubuque. At each junction, an engineer had to set the switch for the train changing track segments. Every switch setting was a decision by an engineer, hopefully getting the train closer to Kansas City. Looking at this situation more generally, the picture we see is many trains moving simultaneously to lots of destinations. We see that the train network is essentially programmed by engineers to keep train traffic flowing smoothly. Most rail switches are binary: either the switch is set one way or the other. Consequently, the logic of switching resembles a primitive form of computing.

Some decades later, another new technology arrived, again using manual switching and junction stations: the telephone network. A telephone call in the early days made an electrical circuit between two telephones. Telephone operators made this possible by patching wires between contacts of other wire segments. Each patch wire can be regarded as a switch, and the operation of the overall network facilitated calls flowing through the system.

Similar to the telephone network, the earliest computing devices required manual setup of the machinery. What was computing's analog to train traffic or a network of telephone calls? Data is what flows through a computing process: input flows to output. The nature of the input data dictates how data gets "switched" through a network of logic, just as a train's destination guides how switches have to be set for proper flow. Concentrating our attention on the switching, we see the *control flow* of the network. Each junction or decision point controls where things flow. Chapter 10 also refers to control flow in the motivation for the `return` statement of a function.

Even before programming languages came on the scene, people devised notation for the logic of control flow—we use the term *logic* because the fundamental units for switching are often binary, hence there is a kind of boolean status for a switch, setting it one way or another. A graphical view of control flow (along with other processing descriptions) is the *flowchart*. The idea of a flowchart is to show how inputs drive the sequence of steps through a procedure. Figure 11.1 shows a fragment of such a flowchart. Diamond shapes represent decisions, with a question in the diamond and arrows leading away according to the answer.

Programming languages all need some kind of way to let switching be represented, since control flow is a central issue in software design. The typical feature in programming languages is an if syntax to control which parts of the code handle data depending on the circumstance. Associated with if is a *condition* and some kind of action clause. The condition is an expression that evaluates to a boolean value; when the condition is *true*, the action clause takes over processing of data. When the condition is *false*, the action clause is skipped. The overall structure of a program may string together many such if statements, just as a flowchart may have many decision points within it. This way of describing decisions in programs is sometimes called *conditional logic*, because the logic of decisions is guided by the if conditions.

Control Flow Using If

Before examination of Python's if statement, let us take a look at how equivalent concepts might be expressed in other areas of science. The state of water (H_2O) is either liquid, solid (frozen), or gaseous (vapor). The particular state of water depends on the temperature. Notation for this fact could be:

$$H_2O \quad \text{is} \quad \begin{cases} \text{solid} & \text{if} \quad \text{temperature} \leq 0 \\ \text{liquid} & \text{if} \quad 0 < \text{temperature} \leq 100 \\ \text{gas} & \text{if} \quad \text{temperature} > 100 \end{cases}$$

The same notation is used in mathematics. Here is an example taken from a math textbook, defining some term $\delta_{i,j}$:

$$\delta_{i,j} \quad = \quad \begin{cases} -1 & \text{if} \quad i < j \\ 0 & \text{if} \quad i = j \\ 1 & \text{if} \quad i > j \end{cases}$$

By this definition, $\delta_{5,5} = 0$, $\delta_{3,1} = 1$, and $\delta_{2,7} = -1$.

Python. To the right, the box shows how the definition of $\delta_{i,j}$ could be expressed as a Python function. The body of `delta` consists of three `if` statements. The syntax for `if` resembles the syntax for `def`: first the word `if`, then some expression which evaluates to a boolean value, then a colon. Each `if` statement has an associated "body" which is indented. A function application of `delta` goes through the `if` statements sequentially; if the expression `i<j` evaluates to `True`, then the function application immediately returns `-1`, and the other two `if` statements are ignored. Only if the expression `i<j` evaluates to `False` will Python go on to look at the second `if` statement.

```
def delta(i,j):
  if i<j:
    return -1
  if i==j:
    return 0
  if i>j:
    return 1
```

The function `delta` can be rewritten using only two `if` statements and get exactly the same results, shown in the left box. When evaluating `delta(8,2)` with this definition, Python first binds `i` to 8 and `j` to 2. The first `if` condition evaluates `8<2` → `False`, so Python evaluates the second `if`, which also evaluates to a `False` condition. Finally, the only remaining statement in the body executes, so `delta(8,2)` returns 1. Contrast this definition with the *incorrect* definition, shown next.

```
def delta(i,j):
  if i<j:
    return -1
  if i==j:
    return 0
  return 1
```

The mistake here is the indentation of the last `return` so that it belongs to the body of the second `if`, rather than being the final statement of `delta`'s body. Since this mistake is valid by the syntactic rules of the Python language, there would be no error message from Python. The program would simply give an incorrect result: for this buggy version, `delta(8,2)` returns `None`, because no `return` statement gets executed. This is a particularly insidious kind of error, one that some programmers blame on the syntax of Python. Java and C use curly braces ({ }) to explicitly say where the body of an `if` starts and where it ends, so they do not typically encounter this problem.

```
def delta(i,j):
  if i<j:
    return -1
  if i==j:
    return 0
    return 1
```

Tracing. By adding some `print` statements, the flow control is illuminated by looking at the program's output. Tracing shows a "history" of what happens when the program proceeds from one line to the next. Below, the definition of `demo` is changed to include `print` statements which uniquely identify different points in the program. When the program runs, it will be clear exactly which `print` statement caused something to be output. An interactive experiment with `demo` is shown on the right.

```
def demo(flag):
    print 1
    print 2
    if flag:
        print "XX"
    print 3
    print 4
```

```
>>> demo(False)
1
2
3
4
>>> demo(True)
1
2
XX
3
4
```

Nested If

Using the `if` statement added a second level of indentation to the body of a function. You can take the syntax even further, putting `if` statements inside the body of an `if`.

```
def nestif(x,y,z,a,b,c):
    if x:
        if y:
            print a
        print b
    if z:
        print c
```

Sometimes it helps to visualize the indentation with vertical lines showing the levels of indenting. Below, on the left, the nested `if` example is enhanced to show lines at the same level of indentation. It is clear from looking at the vertical lines there are three levels of indentation. You can see that "`if x:`" and "`if z:`" align on the left at the same level. Some text editing programs are aware of Python syntax, even showing the vertical lines when you edit a script. Further, they can allow you to *collapse* the body of an `if` statement or even the body of a function. For instance, on the right, there appears a view which one such editor has "collapsed" the body of one `if` statement.

```
def nestif(x,y,z,a,b,c):
    if x:
        if y:
            | print a
        print b
    if z:
        | print c
```
```
⊟   def nestif(x,y,z,a,b,c):
⊟   if x:
⊞       if y:
            print b
⊟   if z:
        | print c
```

The ⊟ symbol on the left indicates that a body can be collapsed by clicking on the symbol. The ⊞ and the horizontal line show that the body has been collapsed. If you want to see the body again, click on the symbol and it will un-collapse. Not all "smart editors" work this way, and there might be other conventions for collapsing and expanding nested statements. Also, there are other helpful features in Python-aware text editors, such as coloring the special words (`def`, `if`, etc.) or using different fonts for different parts of the Python language. Such editors can help you navigate through different levels of nesting. Of course, it does not hurt to have Python evaluate the function a couple of times to verify that it works as expected:

```
>>> nestif(True,True,True,1,2,3)
1
2
3
>>> nestif(False,True,True,1,2,3)
3
>>> nestif(True,False,True,1,2,3)
2
3
>>> nestif(False,False,False,1,2,3)
>>>
```

The x, y, z parameters act as switches for the control flow, determining which of a, b, c will be printed. The example shows nesting (that is, putting an if statement inside of the body of an if) with just one more level of indenting. In principle, you can use if inside if inside if ...to as many levels as you need, but doing so tends to make programs less readable. Another way to write the same nestif function above would be

```python
def nestif(x,y,z,a,b,c):
    if x and y:
        print a
    if x:
        print b
    if z:
        print c
```

Levels and Statement Blocks

When describing Python code in a script or in the body of a function, two if statements are said to be *at the same level* if they are indented by the same amount and no other statement between them is indented by a smaller amount. Figure 11.2 shows an example with nested if statements that are shaded in gray (or colored, if you happen to be seeing a colored version of the text): all the ifs at the same level have the same shading.

Notice that it is *not* the case that all ifs with the same amount of indentation are at the same level in function R(a,b,c). The if's associated with printing 4 and 5 are indented the same as those for printing 9 and 10, yet they have different colors. The reason is that the statements printing 7 and the if testing a==c have lesser indentation; this "breaks up" the structure of the levels.

```
def R(a,b,c):
    print(1)
    if a>b:
        print(2)
    if a==b:
        print(3)
        if b>c:
            print(4)
        if b==c:
            print(5)
    print(6)
    if a>c:
        print(7)
    if a==c:
        print(8)
        if b>c:
            print(9)
        if b==c:
            print(10)
```

an outline

1. topic

    a. subtopic

    b. subtopic

2. topic

    a. subtopic

    b. subtopic

Figure 11.2: Levels of `if` and outline structure.

Now consider the outline shown in the figure. Here we see that numbering for subtopic is reused: even though the subtopics for topic 2 are at the same level as those for topic 1, they do not need to be numbered as "c" and "d," which would carry on from the "a" and "b." It is natural to consider each new subtopic list as something new, and number it by starting over. Similarly, the levels of `if` statements are only considered the same when they belong to the same **block** of statements. A *block* of statements is a group that is indented by the same amount or more.

In the figure, all the statements below `def R(a,b,c)` are a block: they are all indented more than the `def` statement. Likewise, following `if a==b` there is a block of five statements, all indented more than this `if` statement.

Else and Elif

Python's `if` statement is adequate for the conditional logic in any function definition imaginable. Yet, the language can do better than just having `if` alone, because certain patterns of conditional logic occur frequently in programs. A recurring theme in the evolution of programming languages is to watch how people use the language, then ask if some change in the language, perhaps a new feature added to the language, will simplify things. The `else` statement is a good example of this theme.

First, consider a function `questin(s)` returning `True` if string s contains a question mark.

```
def questin(s):
    return '?' in s
```

This function does not even need conditional logic! But, just to make a point, we rewrite it using `if` and add some `print` statements.

```
def questin(s):
    if '?' in s:
      print("positive")
      return True
    if not ('?' in s):
      print("negative")
      return False
```

The pattern here, occurring quite often, recalls the flowchart diamond shapes, where a decision has two outcomes. The decision is a condition (boolean). Above, the pattern is expressed with `if`s, one for the case *true*, the other for the case *not true* (*false*). A drawback to this style is that the condition (`'?' in s`) had to be typed in twice. An `else` statement overcomes this drawback. The same function is rewritten by:

```
def questin(s):
    if '?' in s:
      print("positive")
      return True
    else:
      print("negative")
      return False
```

Notice that the `else` statement aligns (same indentation) as the `if` statement—*this is crucial* in Python. The only way that Python can know what condition `else` refers to is by the indentation. Computing jargon for this pattern is that `if/else` has two *branches*, one handling the *true* condition, the other handling the *false* condition.

Else Association. Python's rule for evaluating `else` is that the block of statements following `else` runs only when the condition of the preceding `if` *at the same level* evaluates to `False`. To see why this rule is needed, consider an example.

```
def K(m,n):
    if len(m)>len(n):
      print(m)
      if n in m:
        print(n)
    else:
      print(n+m)
```

The `else` is *not* associated with the immediately preceding `if` statement (which has condition "n in m"), because of the different levels. The preceding `if` at the same level as `else` is the first `if` in the example.

Elif

The same theme that motivated `else`, namely that programming languages cater to common patterns used in practice, can be extended much further. Python does not go very far in this regard, unlike some other languages. There is a trade-off between adding language features for convenience and burdening people who are learning the language with too much syntax. The only other statement Python has is the `elif` statement. An example shows how `elif` helps.

```
def whichstate(s):
    if "Iowa" in s:
        return 0
    else:
        if "Illinois" is s:
            return 1
        else:
            if "Wisconsin" is s:
                return 2
            else:
                return -1
```

Examination of this function and careful counting shows that it uses four levels of indentation. This seems unfortunate, since what is really happening here is a three-way decision, either return 0, 1, or 2. The `elif` statement abbreviates `else` followed by an indented `if`, and this reduces the nesting and indentation, making things more readable. Further, you can have any number of `elif` statements associated with an `if` statement, all aligned at the same indentation as the `if`.

```
def whichstate(s):
    if "Iowa" in s:
        return 0
    elif: "Illinois" is s:
        return 1
    elif "Wisconsin" is s:
        return 2
    else:
        return -1
```

Notice the final `else` statement: it takes over when none of the previous `if`/`elif` conditions evaluate to `True`. It would be easy (but quite boring) to expand this function with 47 more `elif` statements dealing with the remaining state names. Later, we learn there are much nicer ways of getting the same result using dictionary methods and other Python statements.

Example: Reacting to Type Comparison

Most functions expect a parameter to be a particular type. The function might use an operator or a method that is only valid if the parameter is known to be a string, for example. Many languages that use typed data permit the design of functions that behave differently depending on the type of the argument the caller supplies. The `if` statement can control which way a function behaves by comparing the argument's type to what is expected. To illustrate this, we first look at Python type names.

`type(x) == list`	➡	True if x is a list
`type(x) == dict`	➡	True if x is a dictionary
`type(x) == str`	➡	True if x is a string
`type(x) == tuple`	➡	True if x is a tuple
`type(x) == int`	➡	True if x is an integer
`type(x) == float`	➡	True for floating point x
`type(x) == bool`	➡	True if x is boolean

As a demonstration of testing types, the function `first` defined below prints an error message if the argument is not a sequence:

```
def first(S):
    if type(S) not in [list,str,tuple]:
        print "first expects sequence argument"
    elif len(S) == 0:
        print "first expects nonempty sequence"
    else:
        return S[0]
```

Notice that `first` only has a `return` in the case of a nonempty sequence argument. For other kinds of arguments, `first` would return `None` by default.

Terminology Review

Jargon introduced in this chapter includes: flowchart, condition, conditional logic, block of statements, nested if, type comparison.

Exercises

(1) Write a function `even(x)` that returns `True` or `False` depending on whether integer parameter `x` is an even or an odd number. The `even(x)` could be written in a single line, as

```
even = lambda x:   x%2==0
```

But for this chapter, the exercise is to write function `even` using `def` and the `if` statement.

(2) Write a function `hasVowel(S)` that returns `True` or `False` depending on whether a string `S` contains a vowel (where a vowel is one of the letters a, e, i, o, u). Again, the function can be written in a single line using `lambda`, but the question is to write it using `def` and `if`.

(3) Write a function `tpr(G)` that prints a string `G` twice if the length of the string is even, and prints it three times if the length of the string is odd. *Hint: Use the `even(x)` function from problem (1).*

(4) Look up the *signum* function on Wikipedia; then write a Python definition for this function.

(5) What does the following script print?

```
def score(weight,velocity,color):
  print("testing permit validity")
  if weight>10 and velocity>5:
     print("weight is too much for speed")
  if weight<10 or color=="black":
     print("light enough or")
     print("unmarked for permit")
  if weight>=10:
     if color!="black":
        print("needing further test")
  print("done testing")
print("first: 11, 10, white")
score(11,10,"white")
print("second: 12, 3, black")
score(12,3,"black")
print("third: 6, 8, black")
score(6,8,"black")
```

☆(6) Using Python, find out what this script prints. Can you explain its output?

```
def selpow(value):
  print("value =",value)
  if 0<=value<1.0:
     return value**2
  if 1.0<=value<2.0:
     return value**1.5
  if value>=2.0:
     return value**0.5
  print("done")
```

```
print("Testing")
print( selpow( selpow( selpow(3.0) ) ) )
print(selpow(-1.0))
```

☆(7) Here are two definitions of a function `aei` to determine whether or not a string contains the letter "a," "e," or "i."

```
def aei(String):                                def aei(String):
    if 'a' not in String:                           u = 'a' in String
        if 'e' not in String:                       v = 'e' in String
            return ('i' in String)                  w = 'i' in String
        else:                                       return (u or v or w)
            return ('i' not in String)
    elif 'e' not in String:
        return ('i' not in String)
    else:
        return False
```

What is the result of evaluating `aei("invalidate")`? One version above returns `True`, but the other returns `False`. What if we change the problem to ask whether a string has *only one* of "a," "e," or "i?" What we would like, for instance, is that `aei("tame")` returns `False`, because "tame" has both "a" and "e"; however, `aei("finish")` should return `True` because "finish" has only "i" and does not have "a" or "e."

- Which of the two definitions of `aei` correctly determines whether the string has just one of "a," "e," or "i?"

- Can you rewrite the definition of the `aei` on the left (the one using nested `if`) so that it does not use nesting, and is thereby easier to understand?

(8) Write a body for function `multival()` so that it has at most one `if` statement and has no `else` or `elif` statement. Your definition of `multival()` should return the same values that the one shown below does, for any argument.

```
def multival(Xlist):
    if 7 in Xlist:
        if len(Xlist)==3:
            return "K"
        else:
            return "M"
    else:
        if len(Xlist)==2:
            return "K"
    return "M"
```

Syntactic Sugar.   Purists of computing might argue that Python's "if" statement is *syntactic sugar*, meaning that while it makes the language sweeter for programming, no new capabilities are added to the language. To appreciate their point of view, consider a function which appears to need if, but actually does not. Suppose we need to write a function $f(x)$ that behaves like x^2 when $x \leq 5$, but is the constant 5 if $x > 5$. A mathematician would define f like this:

$$f(x) \quad = \quad \begin{cases} x^2 & \text{if } x \leq 5 \\ 5 & \text{otherwise} \end{cases}$$

Surprisingly, function f can be written in Python without using if:

```
def f(x):
    D = { True:5, False:x**2 }
    return D[x>5]
```

It is not hard to see that f(3) returns 9, because 3>5 is False, so D[False] evaluates to 3**2. But what about more complicated situations, where a function might need to print and do more than will fit in a dictionary? We can take the same idea used above and make it more general:

```
def g(x):
    return 5
def h(x):
    return x**2
def f(x):
    D = { True:g, False:h }
    K = D[x>5]
    return K(x)
```

The remarkable thing about the dictionary in this second version is that the items are names of functions rather than ordinary data items like numbers, strings, lists, and so on. Python allows functions to be treated like data; hence functions can be in lists, tuples, and dictionaries. After Python evaluates K = D[x>5], the name K refers to the appropriate function, g or h. Once we have a function being called in the **return** statement evaluating K(x), that function could be some arbitrary script of statements, including printing, other function calls, expressions, and so on. In principle, the logic of elif, or nested if could be done in a similar way. However, even purists would admit that using if, elif, and else improve the readability of programs. Because we live in a world where software is shared, modified, and reused, it makes sense to emphasize techniques that make programs simpler to understand.

Chapter 12:   Slice, Split, Join

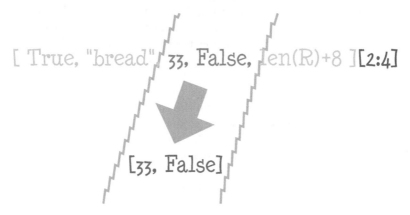

[True, "bread", 33, False, len(R)+8][2:4]

[33, False]

Slicing, Splitting, and Joining

T = "word play in python".split()

T = ["word",   "play",   "in",   "python"   ]

"/".join(T)

"word/play/in/python"

It slices, it dices, it even purées!
— Never actually said by Ron Popiel

Indexing is a standard feature of most programming languages. Java, C#, C++, and C all have syntax like E[i] whereby an item with index i can be referenced in E (which might be a character string, an array of numbers, etc.). Python goes further: it is possible to refer to "chunks" of a sequence instead of indexing items one at a time. This feature is called *slicing* a sequence. Other techniques, like *split* and *join*, make it easy to take apart strings and assemble lists of strings into new strings.

In the same way that hand tools allow people to cut, shape, and put together wood into furniture, slicing, split, and join operations form the "carpentry" of Python's text processing tasks. Even more powerful methods, notably *regular expressions*, could be likened to the "power tools" of text and string processing. This chapter only covers the basic techniques, leaving regular expressions and other more advanced libraries of software as later topics to explore.

Working with slices, particularly Python's syntax for slices, takes some getting used to. With practice, it becomes easy to write expressions that take apart sequences in creative ways and use operators to assemble slices into new sequences. For strings, slicing is only the beginning. String methods provide ways to search, replace, and form new strings from sequences of strings.

Slices of Sequences, Slices Are Sequences

A portion of a sequence is called a *slice* in Python. It is helpful to visualize a slice in a sequence and name some qualities of the slice.

$$[9, 8, \boxed{7, 9, 2,} 3, 8, 6, 6]$$
$$\qquad\quad \uparrow \qquad\quad \uparrow$$
$$\qquad\quad \text{start} \qquad \text{end}$$

Above, the shaded box marks a slice of the sequence and arrows label the places where the slice starts and ends. The Python notation for this slice is

$$[9,8,7,9,2,3,8,6,5][2:5]$$

This expression looks a bit confusing due to the square brackets. It is easier on the eyes to see a similar string slice, seen to the right. The notation for slicing is like indexing, but uses a colon to separate the start and end of the slice: [start:end] specifies the slice to Python. The start index comes before the colon; the end, however, is

```
>>> "wonderful"[2:5]
'nde'
>>> "wonderful"[2:2+3]
'nde'
```

not the index of the ending item—instead end is just beyond the index of the last item of the slice. Initially, this might seem like bad language design. Why not be consistent, why not use an index value for both start and end positions of the slice? To answer this (and also give students an easy way to remember how slicing works) consider the rewriting of the endpoint using 2+3 instead of 5. Of course, these are equivalent, but the point is that we look at 2+3 here as being the start index (2) plus the length of the slice (3 characters). Seen this way, the notation makes sense. The length of the slice is end−start (subtracting start from end).

Slices Are Sequences.   One deceptive behavior of slicing is *a slice of length one*, shown next. A function `slicomp` is defined to show a slice of length one, then an element of the same sequence using indexing, and then the result of comparing the two to see whether they are equal or not. Turns out, they are equal for strings, but not for other sequence types.

$$\boxed{\text{caution - subtle example follows}}$$

```
def slicomp(seq,start,end):
  print ( seq[start:end], seq[start] )
  print ( type( seq[start:end] ), type( seq[start] ) )
  return seq[start:end] == seq[start]
...
>>> slicomp('tambor',3,4)
b b
<class 'str'> <class 'str'>
True
>>> slicomp( [True,7,False,9,True,5], 3,4)
[9] 9
<class 'list'> <class 'int'>
False
```

What this example reveals is that indexing works slightly differently for strings than it does for lists or tuples. On strings, indexing returns a string, whereas on the other types, indexing returns an element of the list or tuple. Notice that Python finds `[9]` and `9` have different types and therefore are not equal (they are not the same thing). This fact is obvious for slices of length 2 or more, but it is easy to forget this with a slice of length 1. The simple rule to remember is that a slice is *always* a sequence, even if its length is 1.

Maximum Slices.   Another special case for a slice is taking the entire sequence as a slice. The example here shows what happens when a slice starts with 0, the index of the first item in the sequence, and ends just after the index of the last item, that is, `len(seq)`. The value of `len(seq)` is not a valid index value—it lies outside of the sequence; however, it is meaningful for slicing. One can get away with writing an ending index value that would be out of bounds for ordinary indexing of a sequence, and a maximum slice will be returned.

```
def reprod(seq):
  print seq, seq[0:len(seq)]
...
>>> reprod("deals")
deals deals
>>> reprod([9,8,7])
[9, 8, 7] [9, 8, 7]
>>> reprod( (False,True) )
(False, True) (False, True)
```

```
>>> "abc"[0:999]
'abc'
>>> "abc"[1:1+99]
'bc'
```

Thus, slicing notation is more forgiving than indexing: any value beyond the index of the sequence's last item works to get a slice including the rightmost item of the sequence. Of course, if a large value is used for the end, that will violate the earlier "+" observation for the length of a slice. For `1+99`, Python cannot give back a slice of length 99 when the original sequence, starting at index 1, only has two items. Thus, Python returns the longest slice possible with the specified starting index value.

Empty Slices. Many expressions for slicing result in empty sequences: `'hello'[0:0]`, `'hello'[1:1]`, `'hello'[2:2]`, `'hello'[3:3]`, and `'hello'[4:4]` are all empty slices. Visually, these examples correspond to putting the end so close to the start that there is no room for any item shown here for start/end `[2:2]`

$$[\ 9,\ 8,\ 7,\ 9,\ 2,\ 3,\ 8,\ 6,\ 5\ ]$$

start   end

Again, Python is rather tolerant about what can be put as start and end of a slice that is empty; even `'hello'[999:999]` will produce an empty slice. Also, if the end is smaller than the start value, say `'hello'[3:0]`, that is an empty slice. A takeaway from this is that sequences contain lots of empty slices, so to speak.

Negative Index Values. Just as some negative numbers work as index values (`-1` for the end of a sequence), you may use negative numbers to specify both start and end of a slice. For instance, here is an expression to get a slice starting with the second character and ending just before the end of a string.

```
>>> "imagine"[1:-1]
'magin'
```

```
>>> "tertiary junction"[10:]
'unction'
>>> "anthropology"[:8]
'anthropo'
>>> 'anthropology'[:-8]
'anth'
>>> "empire"[:]
'empire'
```

Default Values. The syntax for slicing has some handy ways to say that a sequence starts with index 0 or that it includes everything up to the last item. If you omit the start value, the default is 0; if you omit the end value, the default is to include the rest of the sequence. The last idiom shown, namely `S[:]` to make a copy of a sequence, turns out to be quite useful and is worth remembering.

Splitting Strings

The `split` method works for strings only, not for other species of sequence. The idea is to split up an input string into multiple strings, where the splitting points are determined by a pattern. Date formats typically have slash characters separating the date fields. Using `split` the fields of a date are extracted.

```
'10/25/2006'.split('/')
['10','25','2006']
```

Notice that the pattern, the `'/'` character in this case, is not present in the output: the splitting pattern is removed. Also, the output is not a string, but a list of strings. There are several natural questions one might have about the `split` method:

- What happens if the pattern is not found in the input?

- What happens if the input is nothing but the pattern?

- Can the pattern be anything? What about a pattern with more than a single character? How about an empty string?

- Is there some way to have more than one pattern?

These questions are answered later by showing examples. The point of listing the questions is that a single example is rarely enough to fully understand an operator, function, or method. How a method or function or operator behaves with exceptional inputs, like corner cases, needs to be investigated for full understanding. Good reference manuals for programming languages (*not* textbooks) should explain all the details of functions and methods, answering all questions about what happens with unusual inputs. One problem in practice is that even when reference manuals do explain details, the explanations could be mathematical or use "legalese," that is, English found in laws, regulations, or bureaucratic text that is hard to fathom. Fortunately, you can always try examples with Python and discover for yourself the answers.

More generally, the problem of clearly describing how software works or should behave is a profound, core challenge in computing. Misunderstandings by users, by programmers, and by software vendors can have serious consequences. In this introductory text on computing we will not see much that helps to resolve such problems; this is a more advanced topic. Some years ago, IBM developed a new computer and new programming language and wanted to test the new system. The company chose a novel strategy. They loaned some early models of the new system to local schools, where kids could play with them. What IBM found is that the system quickly broke, both hardware and software, and it broke in many different ways. It seems that kids tried doing things that the programmers and engineers had never imagined. Probably, had the system only been sold to other companies with business applications, the bugs associated with unanticipated inputs and surprising usage patterns might have taken years to be exposed, if ever. For high quality software, the old saying "expect the unexpected" is good advice to software designers. On a small scale, this is another reason to explore the corner cases of inputs to methods and functions.

```
>>> 'testing 123'.split('/')
['testing 123']
```

This shows what happens when the splitting pattern is absent from the input string: the result is a list, but it only contains the original input string.

```
>>> "on knowing the price of dice".split('e ')
['on knowing th', 'pric', 'of dice']
```

Yes, you can use a pattern that is a string longer than a single character. But, it can be confusing:

```
>>> "oooo ooooo oooooo".split('oo')
['', '', ' ', '', 'o ', '', '', '']
```

To make sense of the result, it may help to put lines under and over the places where the pattern occurs (we use both under and over to make it easy to see).

$$\overline{\underline{oo}}\,\overline{\underline{oo}}\,o\ \ \overline{\underline{oo}}\,\overline{\underline{oo}}\,o\ \ \overline{\underline{oo}}\,\overline{\underline{oo}}\,\overline{\underline{oo}}$$

Between $\overline{oo}$ and $\underline{oo}$ in $\overline{oo}\underline{oo}$, there is an empty string (see it?). This is the rationale for some of the empty strings in the output. All the overlined and underlined portions, which match the pattern, are removed. The resulting list only contains strings that are between the removed patterns, or between a removed pattern and the start or the end of the original string.

When an example is confusing, like the previous one, it can help to try a simpler one. Here is a simpler split using `"oo"` (for both string and pattern). A way to understand the result is to observe that

```
>>> "oo".split('oo')
['', '']
```

`"oo"` is obtained by evaluating (`'' + "oo" + ''`)

and removing the pattern `'oo'` leaves an empty string representing the start and another representing the end of the original string. By rewriting a string containing the pattern as a concatenation expression (`+`), the output result makes sense.

The `split` method does not work for just any pattern: the pattern cannot be empty, or Python will output an error message.

```
>>> "abc".split('')
ValueError: empty separator
```

Strings to Words

One other special case for a pattern is for splitting by *whitespace*. Whitespace refers not to a single string, but any combination of characters that are invisible when printed, such as blanks, tabs, newlines, and such. The aim of whitespace splitting is to derive a list of the words in an input string without having any empty strings, blank strings, or similar, in the list. The whitespace split is signaled to Python by having *no argument* for the pattern. Thus,

```
>>> "One\n\tTwo Three Four\n\nFive\n".split()
['One','Two','Tree','Four','Five']
```

The whitespace split is especially useful for functions that might get input text lines in either Unix/Linux format or in Windows format: the usual way lines end in Windows is with the string `'\r\n'`, whereas in other systems lines end with just `'\n'`. The whitespace split produces the same result with either convention for ending a line of text.

Joining List of Words

The `join` method does the opposite of `split`, roughly speaking. The `join` method thus takes a *separator string* and uses that as the "glue" when joining up (actually, concatenating) a list of strings. Suppose there is a list of strings to be concatenated all together;

```
>>> " ".join( ['how','big','is','the','storm'])
'how big is the storm'
>>> "/".join( ['12','31','15'] )
'12/31/15'
>>> "--".join( ["a","b","c","d"] )
'a--b--c--d'
```

then use the empty string for the separator, and `join` does the work:

```
>>> ''.join( ['how','big','is','the','storm'])
'howbigisthestorm'
```

Other Handy String Methods

Many other string methods are built-in to Python and yet more are available in the Python libraries of functions and methods. A few are shown here with examples.

```
>>> 'round Table'.upper()
'ROUND TABLE'
>>> 'round Table'.lower()
'round table'
>>> 'Inventory'.center(30)
'          Inventory          '
>>> "mississippi".replace('i','x')
'mxssxssxppx'
>>> "mississippi".replace('ss',' ss ')
'mi ss i ss ippi'
>>> "mississippi".replace('ss','')
'miiippi'
```

```
>>> "oooooo".replace('oo','')
''
>>> "ooooooo".replace('oo','')
'o'
>>> "whole".strip()
'whole'
>>> " tacit approval given \n".strip()
'tacit approval given'
>>> "eventually exit".count('e')
3
>>> 'ooooooooo'.count("oo")
4
```

The `center` method produces an output string of the specified length, roughly centering the input string into the output. The `strip` method removes whitespace to the left and to the right of any nonwhitespace text in the input. There are also `lstrip` and `rstrip` methods that, respectively, remove only from the left or right. The `count` method reports how many times the method's argument occurs in the string. The `count` method is notable in that it also works for lists:

```
>>> [6>5, 5>4, 1>2, 'e'>'g'].count(True)
2
```

Method on Method

Though Chapter 7 explains how an expression can use multiple function applications and method calls, there are some tricks of the trade you might not think of initially using Python. It is helpful to see some examples.

```
>>> ''.join("1/2/3".split('/')) == "123"
True
```

The first example shows that expressions with methods can be arguments to other methods. The next example deals with an unanswered question posed earlier in the chapter. How can we split on multiple patterns, that is, do something like the whitespace split, but for some custom patterns? Below is Python code to split either using a colon or a semicolon.

```
>>> 'e;f or g:t m;d'.replace(':',';').split(';')
['e', 'f or g', 't m', 'd']
```

The example exploits the way that Python evaluates expressions left to right, with expectations for operator priorities. The `replace` method is the first to be evaluated, and it creates a string with colons changed to semicolons; then the `split` method divides that string into a list of strings according to where semicolons were found.

```
def anycompare(S,T):
  return S.upper() == T.upper()
...
>>> anycompare("Fast",'FAst')
True
>>> anycompare("slow",'sloWW')
False
```

The previous examples used the **replace** method to *transform* (get a new string) data into a form easier to work with. The same idea is used here to compare an input string without caring about the difference between upper- or lowercase. This technique is a case that disagrees with human intuition. For a human, it would be more work to first convert a string to uppercase than to compare without caring about the upper/lowercase distinction. In computing, however, transforming data to a "normal form" is often a key principle in problem solving.

Terminology Review

Terminology introduced in this chapter includes: slicing, whitespace, separator string, and empty slice. Important methods introduced are **split, join, upper, lower, center, replace, strip,** and **count**.

Exercises

(1) What does Python evaluate the following expressions to be?

1. `"agility"[2:5] + "taxonomy"[3:6]`
2. `[115,202,192,334,257][:4]`
3. `len("crazy"[3:3+4])`
4. `[9,8,7,6,5,4,3,2,1][-3:]`
5. `type([False,True,False,True][2:3])`
6. `"---".join( "this is important".split() )`
7. `int( ''.join( "7/7/07".split('/') ) )`
8. `"too soon to tell".replace('o','*').replace('* ','')`

(2) What does the following script print?

```
def midcap(f):
    return f[:f.index("t")].split()[2]
print f("going far in a boat over a river")
```

☆(3) Write a function `trisect(String)` that splits `String` into a tuple (`left`,`middle`,`right`).
Examples using `trisect` in an interactive session:

```
>>> trisect("abcdefghi")
('abc', 'def', 'ghi')
>>> trisect("567")
('5', '6', '7')
```

For simplicity, you may assume that any argument of `trisect` is a string of length $3n$,
for some number n. If you are careful in how you use splitting, your `trisect` function
should even give a sensible result for `trisect("")`.

(4) Create a function `first`, using slicing, that returns `True` if the item at the specified
index is the first occurrence. Here is a definition of `first` without slicing:

```
def first(Seq,i):
    a = Seq.index(Seq[i])
    return (a == i)
```

Examples using `first` are `first([1,2,3,4],2)` → `True`; and `first([2,2,2,2],2)`
→ `False`. Your definition should use the slice `Seq[:i]` and return `True` if `Seq[i]` is
not in this slice.

☆(5) Suppose there is a string containing one period and all alphabetic characters are
lowercase. Write a function `fsub` that returns a new copy of the string in which all
"o" characters before the period are removed, and all "y" characters after the period
are changed into "ia." For example,

```
fsub("you fool ophelia. oh my say") → "yu fl phelia. oh mia saia"
```

(6) Write a function `halfmerge(V,W)` that returns a sequence composed of the first half
of V followed by the last half of W. Some interactive examples:

```
>>> inmerge([1,2,3,4],[5,6,7,8])
[1,2,7,8]
>>> inmerge(['a','b','c','d'],[True,False])
['a','b',False]
```

You might wonder what `halfmerge` is supposed to do if V or W do not have an even number of items (it is unclear how to cut a sequence of three items in half). The answer is that the specification is not clear on this point; the only examples above are even-length sequences. Your answer need only be valid for the cases where sequences can be halved, and for odd-length sequences, your `halfmerge` can return anything or even generate an error.

(7) Write a function `Paf(S)` that returns a string that is like S except that letters after the first x (if there are any x characters) are all uppercase. Here are interactive examples with the `Paf` function.

```
>>> Paf("Normal input")
'Normal input'
>>> Paf("Mixing words")
'MixING WORDS'
>>> Paf("xray")
'xRAY'
```

Hints: Use `if` to return if the argument S contains no x; use the `index` method to find the location of the first x; use a slice expression to represent the substring of S that occurs *before* x, and another slice expression to represent the substring after the x. Note that slices can be empty (hence the substring before x in the `xray` example is empty).

(8) Here is a function with a bug:

```
def rotate(seq,amount):
    if amount<0:
        return seq
    return seq[amount:]+seq[amount]
```

The desired behavior of the function was to "left rotate" a sequence by a number of places in the `amount` parameter. Here would be examples of a working function:

```
>>> rotate([1,2,3,4,5],1)
[2,3,4,5,1]
>>> rotate([1,2,3,4,5],3)
[4,5,1,2,3]
```

Can you find the bug and fix the definition of `rotate`?

(9) Use a search engine to look up the Python `endswith` method and the Python `rstrip` method. Then write a function `ing(w)` that returns `True` if w is a string that ends with "ing," but ignoring any whitespace.

```
>>> ing("barely")
False
>>> ing("run or walking   ")
True
>>> ing("Douglas and Boeing")
True
```

```
def primes(x,y):

    return [i for i in range(x,y) if

    all([i%j != 0 for j in range(2,i) if

    i%j == 0]) ]
```

Comprehensions and Generators

```
>>> primes(200,300)

[211, 223, 227, 229]
```

Map, Reduce, Filter

```
>>> Words = "Three functional paradigms"

>>> map( len, Words.split() )

[5, 10, 9]

>>> f = lambda x: "r" not in x

>>> filter( f, Words.split() )

["functional"]
```

Most people find the concept of programming obvious,
but the doing impossible.
— Alan Perlis

It is remarkable how often we list or enumerate information. Lists help shoppers remember what to buy; checklists are essential for pilots going through complicated procedures on takeoff and landing; businesses continuously scan lists of sales and production figures; scientists analyze lists of experimental data looking for patterns. Python has the `list` data type, but that is only the starting point toward automating the many things people routinely do with lists. Learning how to manipulate data in lists is the gateway to mastering more sophisticated structures of information: databases built of tables, scientific matrix operations, and search engine statistics. This chapter reviews useful methods and functions for working with lists. Python has a special syntax for generating new lists from existing lists, which is quite powerful and interesting.

List Functions: max, min, sum, all, any, zip

Earlier chapters introduced the basic list operators for indexing and slicing. The `len` function tells you the number of items in a list. Here are some other useful built-in functions for lists.

```
>>> max( [12,16,5,-8,20,7,14] )
20
>>> max( "four five six
seven".split() )
'six'
```

max. The `max()` function is typically used on numbers (`max(9,3)` returns 3). However, `max()` can also be used with a list argument. A restriction on the list is that all the items be comparable, that is, they should have the same type for comparison purposes: all items can be numeric, all items can be strings, and so on. The string example above returns `'six'` because it is the largest string (alphabetically). Python prints an error message if the input list is empty.

min. The `min()` function returns the smallest item of a list.

sum. Use the `sum()` function for numeric lists only: it adds up the numbers of a list. For an empty list, the `sum()` result is zero.

```
>>> sum( [1.5,30,21.25,12.4] )
65.1500000000000006
```

all and any. Use `all()` to test for the presence of `False` in a list of booleans. Intuitively, `all(x)` returns `True` if all the items of list x are `True`; or `True` if x is empty. Contrasting with `all()`, the function `any()` changes the logic of the test: `any(x)` tests for the

```
>>> all( [] )
True
>>> all( [True,True,False] )
False
>>> all( [ 10>9, 'x' in "max", 0 == 5*0 ] )
True
```

presence of *at least one* `True` value in list x. If there is not any `True` found, the function `any([])` returns `False`.

zip. The name `zip()` is inspired by an article of clothing: the zipper. The teeth of the two parts of a zipper are merged by connecting one tooth from each part as the zipper slides. The `zip` function takes two lists and puts them into a single list of pairs, where each pair has one item from both lists. It is best to start with an example:

```
>>> zip( [1,2,3], ['a','b','c'] )
[(1,'a'), (2,'b'), (3,'c')]
```

It is typically expected that both arguments to `zip()` will be sequences of the same length; if not, then `zip()` will stop building output with the length of the shorter list. Also, `zip()` permits strings to be used as arguments, as shown to the right. Why would the `zip()` function be useful? One answer is the building of dictionaries from lists. It turns out that the type conversion function `dict` takes an argument of the form of `zip`'s output:

```
>>> zip( [0,9,5], "talk" )
[(0,'t'), (9,'a'), (5,'l')]
>>> zip( "talk", [0,9,5] )
[('t',0), ('a',9), ('l',5)]
```

```
>>> dict( [(0,False), (-1,"hi"), (7,2) ] )
{ 0:False, -1:'hi', 7:2 }
>>> dict( zip([4,5,6],"xyz") )
{ 4:'x', 5:'y', 6:'z' }
```

```
>>> zip(*zip([2,2,5],"efg"))
[(2,2,5), ('e','f','g')]
```

The `zip()` function can even "unzip" with different syntax, which we do not explain in this chapter (because it is seldom used). As a teaser, here is an example using `zip()` to both zip and unzip, using the *unpacking* operator (this is trivia you need not know for learning Python). We mention it here mainly so you can look up "unpacking arguments" in a reference manual, should you be curious.

List Functions: filter, map, reduce

filter. With `filter()` we encounter an example of true *functional style* of programming languages: it is a function that expects a function argument (an initially confusing concept). To use `filter()`, you need to define your own function that returns a boolean. The code shown here illustrates two usages of `filter`. Can you see what `filter()` does? Functions `big()` and `small()` are defined to report `True` for some numbers, but `False` for others. The output of `filter()` uses a function like `big()` or `small()` to screen the items given in the second argument, a list.

```
def big(x):
    return x>10
def small(x):
    return not big(x)
...
>>> filter(big,[6,8,14,2,19,6,10])
[14,19]
>>> filter(small,[6,8,14,2,19,6,10])
[6,8,2,6,10]
```

Note for Python3: *The* `filter` *function returns a "filter object" rather than a list. Later in this chapter, the concept of generator/iterator is introduced;* Python3 *returns generators or generator-like things, such as the filter object, where* Python2 *would return a list. Fortunately, for many purposes, a generator behaves like a list.*

```
def square(x):
  return x*x
def double(x):
  return x+x
...
>>> map(square,[3,6,9])
[9,36,81]
>>> map(double,"fine")
['ff','ii','nn','ee']
```

map. Another functional-style tool is the `map()` function. Like `filter()`, the `map()` function needs a list and a function. The output list has the same number of items as the input list; all that happens is to apply the given function to each item of the input. You might notice to the left that `map()` can take a string as input as well as list (any sequence type is accepted).

Note for Python3: *The result of using* `map` *is a generator-like thing called a map object.*

reduce. The idea of `reduce()` is to let programmers define their own versions of `sum()`, replacing addition with a function of their own design. As with `filter()` and `map()`, a function needs to be defined first. The first example with `multiply` is easy to comprehend, but the second example may require some thought to figure out.

```
def multiply(x,y):
  return x*y
def fun(a,b):
  if len(b)>3:
    return b
  return a
...
>>> reduce(multiply,[8,9,0.5,2])
72.0
>>> reduce(fun,"one and two and three".split())
'three'
>>> reduce(fun,"one and two and end".split())
'one'
```

Note for Python3: *To use* `reduce` *in* Python3, *you need to have this statement earlier in your script or interactive session:*

```
from functools import reduce
```

The syntax of importing modules is introduced in Chapter 18.

➡ An exercise at the end of this chapter suggests that you explore two other handy built-in functions, `sorted` and `reversed`. It is worth knowing about these.

⟩ web

Functions `map`, `filter`, and `reduce` predate the Python language, and were in common use by functional programming experts in the 1960s. These functions are *paradigms*, or patterns, of frequently used ideas in problem solving—they automate some of the steps of programming. More recently, Google built much of their Web indexing on a pattern called MapReduce, which does something like a combination of `map` and `reduce` (but in a way that can scale to using thousands of computers working together). All the abstract thinking behind these functional paradigms, which may initially seem artificial, does turn out to be useful in practice!

Streams, Generators, and Iterators

Imagine a graphical game where players can explore a fantastic, fictional landscape with rivers, mountains, lakes, forests, trails, villages, and more. Without knowing how such a game might work, we might conjecture ways the software makes it possible to view the landscape in some detail. One way would be to have a massive dataset of images—needing lots of storage area to hold the dataset. Another idea would be to *generate* the landscape on demand, using algorithms. Computer scientists have researched the natural characteristics of landscapes, weather, and lighting at different times of day and night, and published algorithms that create realistic landscapes (such research is ongoing). The great advantage of such algorithmic generation is that relatively little storage is needed, because instead of storing an image, it can be created on demand by an algorithm.

Returning to Python and lists, suppose we would like to have a list of all the integers between one and ten thousand. Let's say what we want is:

$$A = [1,2,3,\cdots 10000]$$

Of course "$\cdots$" is not a symbol one can type, and it is not in the Python language. But why do we need such a list? Instead of having such a long list of ten thousand numbers, Python can *algorithmically generate* the list on demand.

Python has provisions for two kinds of generated lists (or generated tuples). These two kinds were added to the Python language based on observing how programmers typically use long sequences of data. The two patterns commonly seen in practice are *random access* and *sequential access*. In the pattern of *random access*, programs may select different items in lists at seemingly "random" places (well, it looks random to Python, because the pattern is unpredictable). For random access, indexing is used: a program might have an expression using A[237], and immediately after another expression could use A[608]. Thus, the program "jumps" from one place to another in the list named A. The second typical pattern is *sequential access*. Programs that use sequential access are predictable: the first reference to list A would be A[0], then A[1], and so on, proceeding up to the end of A (unless the program decides to finish looking at A prematurely).

It is the pattern of sequential access where algorithmic generation excels. Indeed, Python has notation to define a *generator* of lists or sequences. More broadly speaking, Python language experts use the term *iterator*, and sometimes the term *iterable* appears in documentation and error messages. For the present, it is enough to think of both terms, iterator and generator, as having the same meaning.

The concept of sequential access is not limited to lists and the Python language. Most programs that read files, write files, and communicate through networking software depend on sequential access to data. Humans read text sequentially (except when skipping over the boring parts). Usual jargon for software that processes data, whether from a file, a list, or some other memory device, is *data streaming*. When a file is "viewed" as a data stream, the data in the file flows out from the file to the software, in sequential order, from first byte to last byte. Similarly, a program's output (like Python's `print`) is a data stream flowing from the program to some storage area or possibly to a text area in a window.

Range/Function Generator

Range

The `range()` function generates a list of integers, controlled by a few parameters. As the Python language evolved, the `range()` function became more important and frequently used in expressions, which caused some practical problems. The situation culminated with a change in the meaning of `range()` between Python2 and Python3. Below, we first look at Python2's `range()`, and then explain how the Python3 version of `range()` differs. Fortunately, for nearly all programming concerns, the two versions get the same results.

Range in **Python2**

When Python2 evaluates `range(k)`, for some integer k (not a negative integer), a list of k items is returned. Before a technical explanation is given, a few examples for `range()` are shown.

$$
\begin{array}{rcl}
\texttt{range(0)} & \to & \texttt{[]} \\
\texttt{range(5)} & \to & \texttt{[0,1,2,3,4]} \\
\texttt{range(0,5)} & \to & \texttt{[0,1,2,3,4]} \\
\texttt{range(4,10)} & \to & \texttt{[4,5,6,7,8,9]} \\
\texttt{range(4,10,1)} & \to & \texttt{[4,5,6,7,8,9]} \\
\texttt{range(4,10,2)} & \to & \texttt{[4,6,8]} \\
\texttt{range(10,4,-2)} & \to & \texttt{[10,8,6]}
\end{array}
$$

There are three forms using `range()`, either one, two or three arguments can be given. The main form is the two-argument case, which is `range(`*start,limit*`)`. Here, *start* is the first item for the result list; *limit* is a value beyond which the list does not go. An optional third argument, *step*, is the value added going from one item to the next. When `range()` has only one argument, then *start* is zero and the argument is the `limit` value. All arguments should be integers.

```
>>> sum( range(1000) )
499500
>>> range(8)
[0,1,2,3,4,5,6,7]
>>> type( range(8) )
<type 'list'>
```

Range in **Python3**

An example given for Python2 contains the function application `range(1000)`. When Python2 evaluates this function application, it builds a list with a thousand integers, which occupy some space in memory. While memory is not so expensive, some programmers did use `range()` with some very large arguments, which caused some performance problems with evaluating expressions (slow running times for programs).

To counter the performance problems with `range()`, the language designers decided to make `range` algorithmically generated rather than build a list. In Python3, `range(100)` is a "range object" rather than a list. However, it behaves exactly like a list in nearly all respects. For instance, `range(5,15)[-2]` is 13, just as one might expect for a list. Repeating an example used earlier, the `sum()` is the same as

```
>>> sum( range(1000) )
499500
>>> range(8)
range(0,8)
>>> type( range(8) )
<class 'range'>
```

for Python2; what you cannot see is that Python3 created the list starting with 0, then 1, then 2, and so on, only when `sum()` asked for the next item of its argument. That way, sum added up the numbers in the list sequentially, but the entire list was not needed in memory.

Only after a list item was given to `sum()` and added to a total, then did `range()` supply the next item.

One can generally observe that as the Python language has evolved, from Python2 to Python3, the evaluation has become "smarter" in the way it treats sequences. The approach of Python3 for `range`, `map`, and `filter` (among others) is called *lazy evaluation*. The idea of lazy evaluation is that the Python interpreter delays actually evaluating expressions until it is certain they will be needed. This clever idea does save the amount of memory needed for computation, but the situation for Python3 is not easy to explain to beginners.

Bottom Line.   Use `range()` in Python3 just as you would in Python2: for all computing purposes they have the same behavior. `Note:` in Python2, if the advantages of an algorithmically generated version of `range` is needed, it is available as "`xrange`." If you wish to see a list for some `range` object in Python3, simply write `list(range(4,100))` to see the list (which does nothing more than convert the `range` object to a list).

List Comprehensions

To this point, a limited number of operators and functions have been introduced that *create* lists: `range()` can generate a list; slicing extracts a portion of a list; list concatenation (using the `+` operator) creates a new list from two input lists; functions `filter()` and `map()` each take one input list and produce one output list. This section explains a special syntax to create new lists from existing lists. The formal name for this syntax is *list comprehension*; informally, a simpler name for the syntax is custom list.

Illustration.   To motivate the syntax, think about the following somewhat artificial problem. Suppose a list is needed containing numbers of the form $x^2 + 2$, where x is some integer in the range 20–25. Such a "custom list" is expressed by the Python syntax:

```
>>> [ x*x+2 for x in range(20,26) ]
[402, 443, 486, 531, 578]
```

The general form of this syntax uses an implicit parameter, `x` in the example above. To explain the general form, let "*expr*(`x`)" stand for some Python expression which uses parameter `x` in it. This expression can use operators, functions, and methods, and `x` can appear numerous times in the expression. In fact, the expression might not even contain `x` (we will see examples where that makes sense). Also, let *elist* stand for some expression that evaluates to a sequence (list, tuple, or string). Basically, *elist* can be anything handled by the `in` operator—even a dictionary will be acceptable. Another term for the list represented by *elist* is the *source list*. Items are taken from the source list, fed to the expression as parameter `x`, which produces the output items. The general form for a custom list (*list comprehension*) is:

$$[\; expr(\text{x}) \; \texttt{for} \; \text{x} \; \texttt{in} \; elist \;]$$

Of course, rather than always naming the parameter "`x`," any other name could be chosen.

Examples

```
>>> [ word+'!' for word in "have a good day".split() ]
['have!', 'a!', 'good!', 'day!']
>>> [ T>5 for T in range(4,9) ]
[False,False,True,True,True]
>>> [ 8 for m in range(4) ]
[8,8,8,8]
>>> [ min(i,10) for i in range(8,16) ]
[8,9,10,10,10,10,10,10]
```

The last example builds a list using `min()` for the expression of items. Though this makes the point that functions can be used, a more dramatic example is to use tracing in the function evaluation. The next example only works for Python3, though the same idea can be carried out for Python2.

This result looks surprising at first. You can see that the `print()` function is applied four times, once for each item in `range(6,10)`, and each time the `print()` function adds a newline character, which is why you see four lines of output. But then there is a list of four `None` values. Why is this? The answer is that the custom list

```
>>> [ print(i) for i in range(6,10) ]
6
7
8
9
[None,None,None,None]
```

notation does build a list, and the value returned by `print` is `None` (because `print()` returns `None` in Python3).

```
def show(i):
  print i

>>> [ show(i) for i in range(6,10) ]
6
7
8
9
[None,None,None,None]
```

The same example can be shown in Python2, but using an additional function definition. Because `print` is a command rather than a function in Python2, we make up a function `show()` here, which does nothing more than print its argument. Recall that functions return `None` by default, so each call `show(i)` returns `None`. Thus, the custom list has only `None` items because the `show` function has no `return` statement.

Adding a Condition.   *But wait, there is more!* Yes, the general form of list comprehension has further syntax, optionally adding a condition on what items are used from the source list. The form is:

$$[\ expr(\mathtt{x}) \ \mathtt{for} \ \mathtt{x} \ \mathtt{in} \ elist \ \mathtt{if} \ condition \ ]$$

Of course, rather than always naming the parameter "x," any other name could be chosen. The *condition* is a Python expression that evaluates to a boolean, and may have parameter x in it.

Examples

```
>>> [ i-1 for i in range(12,20) if i%5 in [2,4] ]
[11, 13, 16, 18]
>>> [ c for c in "king kong" if c>'m']
['n', 'o', 'n']
>>> ''.join( [ c for c in "king kong" if c>'m'] )
'non'
```

These examples just show the notation, they do not really indicate how useful custom lists could be for real programming. The next example is the first to suggest some potential for more ambitious problem solving.

Problem Example. A typical puzzle asks a question that is simple to read and understand, but does not have an obvious or trivial answer. Here is a puzzle question: How many numbers between zero and one thousand contain the digit 7 somewhere?

Someone with a math background will jump to thinking about arithmetic operations to do the job. For instance, you can tell if a number n ends with the digit 7 by the expression $n\%10 == 7$; to detect whether 7 occurs elsewhere in the number, more arithmetic is needed. However, a person with a computing background will try a simpler idea. If we first convert the integer from numeric type to a string, then all that is needed is to look for the character '7' in the string. So, the strategy to solve this problem is to first generate integers in the range 0–1000 (the **range** function can do this), and then filter out those numbers with a digit 7. As a final step, the **len** function reports how many items there are in the filtered list.

str(n)	convert n to a string
'7' in str(n)	test for digit 7
[n for n in range(1000)]	source list

Given this progression of the elements of our solution, the following should be understandable.

```
>>> len([n for n in range(1000) if '7' in str(n)])
271
```

Notice that we did not really write the solution all in one go: it is best, even for experienced programmers, to first write the elements of an expression, make sure the syntax is right, and perhaps even test corner cases of these elements using Python interactively. After such preparation, putting together the solution is easier and more reliably done.

Two Source Lists. It is conceivable that a custom list is needed from the combination of items from two source lists. In principle, any number of source lists could be combined, but the main idea is best seen with two source lists. The custom list syntax enables expression of this idea, though it is not very useful in practice. The reason for showing it here is a hint about how database queries are done. Queries of databases are usually questions about the content of tables. There might be a table for inventory and another table for part number. The table for inventory has part numbers and quantity in stock. The table for part number has the numbers and a text description of that part. Perhaps a question is "What are the part descriptions for items not in stock?" In order to answer this question, the two tables somehow need to be combined. As a warmup to this kind of question, we show first a custom list based on combining characters from two strings.

```
>>> [ a+b for a in "12" for b in "xy" ]
['1x', '1y', '2x', '2y']
```

The example shows that every combination of items from the two source lists "12" and "xy" appear in the output.

Database Example. The combination of two source lists to produce one output list illustrates the kind of processing typical of database queries. To show this using Python (real databases use specialized languages like SQL), suppose that inventory is a list of pairs of the form (p, q) where p is a part number and q is the quantity of that part in current stock. The other list, the part description list, has the form (p, d) where p is a part number and d is a text description of that part. The part description list is probably derived from catalogs supplied by part vendors, and it usually has more parts than are offered as inventory. Thus, the part numbers that occur in the inventory list are just a subset of the parts in the description list. The problem now is to write a function reorder() that produces descriptions of the parts that need to be reordered, because they are not in stock, but should be. Here is the function's header:

```
def reorder(Desc,Inv):
```

Parameter Desc is the description list; parameter Inv is the inventory list. Suppose d is an item of Desc and let k be an item of Inv. Here are a few expressions that will be useful for writing the function body:

d[0]	part number from Desc item
k[0]	part number from Inv item
d[0]==k[0]	True when d, k
	refer to the same part
d[1]	text description of item
k[1]	quantity in stock for an item
k[1]==0	True if item out of stock

The expressions above may seem obvious, but it is still a good idea to see that we have all the ammunition needed to attack the problem. The final step is to combine both lists, but filter the combination so that we only get those part descriptions where the quantity in stock is zero.

```
def reorder(Desc,Inv):
    return [d[1] for d in Desc for k in Inv if d[0]==k[0] and k[1]==0]
```

Let's try this with some simple inputs:

```
>>> reorder( [(1,"abc"),(2,"def")], [(1,5),(2,0)] )
['def']
```

Though just one test does not prove the expression is correct, the output is what we expect to see.

Python Generators

Creating a generator in Python is as simple as using the comprehension notation, but with parentheses instead of square brackets. An interactive example:

```
>>> M = (i**2 for i in range(4,35))
>>> type(M)
<type 'generator'>
>>> M[12]
TypeError: 'generator' object is not suscriptable
```

Unlike a real tuple or a list, the generator M does not support the random access pattern. No indexing is allowed. Also, some typical list or tuple functions do not work with generators. Even when they work, there is a surprise: **generators get "used up"** as

```
>>> M = (i**2 for i in range(4,35))
>>> max(M)
1156
>>> max(M)
ValueError: max() arg is an empty sequence
```

the example to the right illustrates. What is going on here? The first response to `max(M)` is correct, it is `34**2`, is equal to `1156`. But the second try of evaluating `max(M)` got an error. The explanation is that a generator can only be "used" (going through all the items it generates) once. This may seem quite surprising, but it is a typical way to do things in software. New generators can easily be created, so there really is not any limitation if one of them "expires" after using it. After seeing how generators are defined and how they work, it should be clear that Python3's `range` object (and Python2's `xrange`) are more flexible than generators, because they do not get used up and because they support random access by indexing.

```
>>> Y = enumerate("Precipitation")
>>> [ x for x in Y ]
[(0,'P'), (1,'r'), (2,'e'), (3,'c'), (4,'i'),
 (5,'p'), (6,'i'), (7,'t'), (8,'a'), (9,'t'),
 (10,'i'), (11,'o'), (12,'n')]
>>> [ x for x in Y ]
[]
```

Much of the software in Python libraries uses generators or iterators. There are also built-in functions that return generators, and advanced techniques where functions can become generators (so that they algorithmically "stream" what they return to callers). One example is the `enumerate` function. The `enumerate` function returns a generator for a sequence; the generator creates pairs of index values (numbers) and the corresponding item in the sequence. Why this should be useful is a subject for later chapters. The point to observe above is that the generator returned by `enumerate` is "used up"—it appears to be empty when the interaction above tries to use it again.

Dictionary Comprehensions

Comprehension notation also works for building dictionaries.

```
>>> WordList = "a wakeup call from the team".split()
>>> N = enumerate(WordList)
>>> D = { t[0]:t[1] for t in N }
>>> D
{0:'a', 1:'wakeup', 2:'call', 3:'from', 4:'the', 5:'team'}
```

Recall how *binding patterns* enable functions to name the parts of sequences in their parameters. A similar idea is also allowed in comprehensions or generators. If it is known that items from a sequence (or a generator) will be tuples, we can use patterns to name the parts of the tuple. Hence, the example above could have been written this way:

```
>>> WordList = "a wakeup call from the team".split()
>>> N = enumerate(WordList)
>>> D = { a:b for (a,b) in N }
>>> D
{0:'a', 1:'wakeup', 2:'call', 3:'from', 4:'the', 5:'team'}
```

Other Comprehensions

Strings are sequences, which can be indexed, sliced, and concatenated. So can we also use comprehensions to make new strings from existing sequences? Sorry, current Python does not offer string comprehensions. Nor does Python have tuple comprehensions. The way to get the equivalent of string or tuple comprehensions is to use a type conversion function. Problem (7) at the end of the chapter asks you to write the equivalent of tuple comprehension. Here, we show two examples of getting string results from comprehensions.

```
>>> P = "surveys show about one third of people"
>>> U = [c for c in P if c not in "aeiou "}
>>> ''.join(U)
'srvysshwbtnthrdfppl'
>>> M = [ord(l) for l in "antiques"]
>>> M
[97, 110, 116, 105, 113, 117, 101, 115]
>>> ''.join( [chr(x+1) for x in M] )
'boujrvft'
```

Both examples use the string `join` method to create a new string from a list of strings. The first examples shows some filtering (removing vowels). The second shows what happens by incrementing the numeric code for each letter: the a becomes b, the n becomes o, and so on in the result.

Multiline Expressions

As more syntax features of Python are exposed in this chapter, the examples get longer and it becomes more difficult to demonstrate Python features with single-line statements. There are several ways to make a Python statement that is longer than a single line of text. One of these has already been mentioned in Chapter 8, the triple quote (''' or """) convention. Python evaluates the following as if it were, logically speaking, a single long line:

```
len( '''This anecdote produced an extraordinary effect, not only
upon Mr.  Slithers, but upon the housekeeper also, who evinced
so much anxiety to please and be pleased, that Mr. Weller, with
a manner betokening some alarm, conveyed a whispered inquiry to
his son whether he had gone 'too [far].'''')
```

Besides the triple quote convention, Python permits a statement to span multiple lines if a parenthesized expression has been started, but not completed. Hence,

```
5.32E12 * ( 3.692 -
   4.105 )
```

is valid syntax for an expression spanning two lines. Similarly, a left parenthesis (used to start a tuple, used to enclose arguments for function application, used to enclose parameters in a function header, and so on, can all span any number of lines, up to where the closing right parenthesis) is found. The same idea works for a left bracket [or a left brace {, since Python can detect that more lines are needed in order to find the matching right symbol for the statement to end. Thus, an earlier example could be rewritten as:

```
def reorder(Desc,Inv):
   return [ d[1]
            for d in Desc
            for k in Inv
               if d[0]==k[0] and k[1]==0
         ]
```

When single statements span lines, the rules about indentation (all statement text aligning on the left) are suspended, at least for the continuation of the statement spanning lines. After the statement's final line, the rules about indentation go back into effect. Sometimes using more lines can make statements more readable.

One other technique to make a Python statement span multiple lines is to use a *continuation marker*, represented by a single "\" character. For example,

```
def myfunction(r,s):
   return r + \
          s * 2 + \
          200
```

Each backslash ending a line tells Python that the next line below is a continuation of the previous line. The continuation lines do not need to have the same indentation, but it can look nicer to use some amount of indenting. One tricky point about using "\" to continue lines: **there should be no characters (not even a blank) after the "\" character.** This is tricky because a blank is not visible, and Python does *not* consider "\ " to be a line continuation marker.

Terminology Review

A few *list functions* are introduced in this chapter: `max`, `min`, `sum`, `all`, `any`, and `zip`. Three important *functional* list functions are `filter`, `map`, and `reduce`. The `range` function produces a list of integers (or in Python3, a function "object" that later will behave like a list). Powerful syntax for *list comprehensions* enables concise specification of new lists from existing ones. Python *generators* and *iterators* provide a way to algorithmically generate sequences. Other syntax shows how multiline expressions work in Python.

Exercises

(1) What does Python evaluate the following expressions to be? These are best answered using an interactive Python session, possibly trying different parts of the expression to understand how they fit together for the result.

   1. `min(range(20))`

   2. `len( range(10,20) )`

   3. `range(20)[11:17]`

   4. `[ -x for x in range(5) ]`

   5. `sum(range(6))`

   6. `any( [c=="X" for c in "ejkXrq"] )`

   7. `map( len, "the overall picture is good".split() )`

   8. `range(5) + ['+'] + range(5)`

   9. `504 in range(85,12,900)`

  10. `sum( range(-5,5) )`

  11. `''.join( [ "-"+c for c in 'python' ] )`

(2) A function `foo(C)` is needed that returns the "backwards" version of a character string:

```
>>> foo("hawk")
'kwah'
>>> foo("amazing")
'gnizama'
```

Write function `foo(C)` in Python. Here is a strategy for writing `foo`. First, see if you can write a **range** term that steps from the rightmost index down to the first index of a string. For instance, if the string is `"thousand"` then the **range** expression should return `[7,6,5,4,3,2,1,0]`. Once you have this range expression, use it to make a custom list, something along the lines of

```
[ C[i] for i in range( ... ) ]
```

It can help to just make a simpler version of `foo(C)` that returns this custom list and test it with a few examples. Once you have this working, the remaining task would be to convert the list of characters into a string. Use the `join` method to do this. Recall this:

```
>>> ''.join( ['r','i','s','k'] )
'risk'
```

You can use this kind of `join`, but with your custom list as its argument.

☆(3) Write a function `allvowels(P)` that returns `True` if the argument is a string consisting only of vowels.

☆(4) How many positive integers smaller than 100,000 are divisible by both 11 and 13? Write a Python expression or function to answer this question.

(5) Write a function `issorted(X)` that returns `True` if the argument is a sequence in which each item is less than or equal to the next item in the sequence. Examples:

```
>>> issorted([3,9,10,5])
False
>>> issorted(range(8))
True
>>> issorted([2,4,6])
True
```

The recommended way to write `issorted(X)` is to first create a custom list of booleans in which each item corresponds to a "<=" comparison between consecutive items of X. For instance, such a custom list for input `[3,9,10,5]` should be `[True,True,False]` (notice that the custom list is shorter by one than the input list). The way to get an item of the custom list is to use a comparison like `X[k]<=X[k+1]`. Once you have the custom list working, you can use the `all` function to get the final definition for `issorted`.

☆(6) Scientific and engineering applications make extensive use of matrices, often shown as tables of numbers:

$$
\begin{array}{cccc}
805 & 201 & 327 & 588 \\
612 & 119 & 351 & 292 \\
982 & 779 & 238 & 153 \\
201 & 202 & 496 & 644 \\
484 & 670 & 295 & 517 \\
683 & 109 & 256 & 164
\end{array}
$$

In Python, such a matrix would be represented by a list, where each item of the list is a row of the matrix:

```
[ [805,201,327,588], [612,119,351,292], \
  [982,779,238,153], [201,202,496,644], \
  [484,670,295,517], [683,109,256,164] ]
```

Write a Python function `column(p,M)` which returns a list of the items in column p of matrix M. Example:

```
>>> column(0,[[1,2],[3,4],[5,6]])
[1,3,5]
>>> column(1,[[1,2],[3,4],[5,6]])
[2,4,6]
>>> column(2,["over","take","road"])
['e','k','a']
```

(7) Python list comprehension is used to create a custom list; dictionary comprehension creates a dictionary. What if we need to create a tuple? The generator syntax uses parentheses, so there does not seem to be any way to create a custom tuple. Explain why tuple comprehension is not really needed in Python. (*Hint:* Consider that the built-in `tuple` function can convert a list into a tuple.)

(8) Two more handy, built-in list functions are `sorted` and `reversed`. The idea of `sorted` is to return a sorted version of a list, whereas the idea of `reversed` is to make a backward copy of a list. One of these functions does return a list, but the other returns a generator. Which one returns a generator? Experiment with Python, then consider problem (2) above and how a generator might be the answer.

Chapter 14:   Functional Patterns

Let us train our minds to desire what the situation demands.
— Lucius Annaeus Seneca

Programming languages teach you to not want what they cannot provide.
— Paul Graham

This chapter finishes our functional-first introduction to computing; the remainder of the book starts another style of programming commonly found in languages like C, and Java. The many definitions from previous chapters about types, operators, expressions, function arguments and parameters, are enough in theory to do just about any kind of computing. However, something is missing: a certain "wisdom" of experts is not captured by these definitions. This chapter aims to reveal some tricks of functional programming.

Much human reasoning is not based on deduction from facts. People tend to recognize a situation by pattern matching: if a problem you encounter resembles one you've previously seen, you can likely just rely on a solution you remember to solve the task at hand. Over time, we build internal catalogs of situations and ideas of how to deal with them. The entries in such a mental catalog are *patterns*, and the solutions we remember could be "idioms" that we tend to use. This chapter introduces idioms for functional programming. Later, Chapters 22 and 23 explain other patterns and idioms, but for an imperative style of programming.

Much of the wisdom about functional programming in Python can be found using this link: `http://docs.python.org/howto/functional.html`, however, the explanations there assume more knowledge by the reader than you might have. A goal of this chapter is to provide more motivation and give more examples than the official Python documentation.

Tail Recursion
Suppose you are given a problem of "processing" all the items of a sequence (list, tuple, or string). The word "processing" is purposefully vague: it could be that the problem calls for accumulating (like summing, or filtering) values of the items, or it could be that the problem calls for searching for particular values. The more generally one thinks about what "processing" might mean, the better: we would like to have a pattern that works for the widest range of problems imaginable. Next in this chapter, four examples show tail recursion in Python. By working through these examples, the pattern of tail recursion should emerge.

Printing Items of a Sequence. *Tail recursion* is the pattern of processing the items of a sequence one by one, starting from the first item, and continuing until the last item. The example shown here is **prupper**, which uses tail recursion to print words in uppercase. The first time seeing tail recursion can be puzzling. The output example makes it clear that "**print L[0].upper()**" is going through the three words of the argument string L, but exactly how does this work? The answer is seen by substituting

```
def prupper(L):
    if len(L)==0:
        return None
    else:
        print L[0].upper()
        return prupper(L[1:])

>>> prupper("one two three".split())
ONE
TWO
THREE
```

repeatedly for arguments in the body of **prupper**, taking care to think of each substitution separately.

① When **prupper** is first called (by the ">>>" line), the value of L binds to the list of strings ["one", "two", "three"]. Thus L[0] is "one" and L[1:] is ["two", "three"]. Hence, ONE is printed. Now, notice that the body of the function ends with **return prupper(L[1:])**— this needs to be carefully examined *as a separate, new evaluation*.

> Functional language experts use jargon for L[0] and L[1:]: the item L[0] is called the *head* of L, and the remainder of the sequence, L[1:], is called the *tail* of L. This jargon motivates the name *tail recursion*.

② The new task, namely to evaluate **prupper(L[1:])**, should be thought of as **prupper(["two", "three"])**. Do not be confused that L is used in the argument (as L[1:]). Instead of thinking about L, concentrate on the value, which is ["two", "three"]. When you just look at the argument as a value, it becomes clear that L is ["two", "three"] *in the new evaluation* (not the old evaluation). By this way of understanding, it is sensible that L[0] is "two", hence TWO is printed.

③ By the same reasoning, Python will need to evaluate **prupper(L[1:])** by substituting the value of the slice, which is **prupper(["three"])**. Thus, L is ["three"], L[0] is "three", we see THREE printed, and L[1:] is the empty list []. What remains is to examine **prupper(L[1:])** as a new evaluation.

④ Finally, we have **prupper([])** to evaluate. The if statement causes the function to exit early with **return None**.

Figure 14.1: Some steps to evaluate **prupper("one two three".split())**.

Figure 14.1 analyzes how Python evaluates the **prupper** example. To understand the figure, an idea explained in Chapter 16 needs to be briefly given here. Hypothetically, consider a function **hoo(v)** and a function **ray(v)**; suppose in the body of **hoo** there is an expression **T+ray(5*v)**. In order to evaluate, say **hoo(21)**, Python would need to evaluate `ray(5*v)`—in this case it is `ray(5*21)`. To do so, Python would bind 105 (obtained by `5*21`) to v in `ray(v)`. At this point, we might become worried, because technically there are two valuations for v, 21, and 105. Do not be confused! These are *different* parameters, the v that is a parameter of `hoo` and the v that is a parameter of `ray`. When Python evaluates `ray(105)`, all the preparations and remaining work for `hoo` is put in the background, so to speak. Until Python finishes evaluating `ray(105)`, progress on `hoo` is suspended and `hoo`'s v remains equal to 21.

Now consider the code for `prupper(L)`. Unlike the situation with `hoo` and `ray`, the body of `prupper` requires Python to evaluate an expression with `prupper` before it can progress in the program. Again, we are faced with possible confusion: what value does L have, `["one","two","three"]` or `["two","three"]`? For Python, there is no confusion, because each evaluation of a function *is performed in a fresh, new context*. That is, when such a *recursive* use of `prupper` is encountered—meaning that there is an expression needing evaluation of `prupper` in the body of `prupper`—Python will put the current work of evaluation, which is part-way, finished into the background, and concentrate on a new task of evaluating the recursive expression. When this happens, in the new evaluation, L will bind to a value pertinent to that evaluation. Your mental model for this should be like a virtual desktop, where work stacks up, gets finished, and then resumes at the point where the most recent previous work was suspended.

Steps in Figure 14.1 show how, in tail recursion, Python had to evaluate `prupper` four times: once for each item in the original list, and one extra time with an empty list. There is more to the story: we did not look at how the `return None` participates in the evaluations. A different example will show us that.

Summing Items of a Sequence. A nice trick of using tail recursion is to change a function's definition to have an extra parameter. This parameter represents a "continuation" of some calculation, which was not finished in the body of a function, but will be finished later by some new evaluation on the tail of the sequence. The `tailsum` example shows tail recursion calculating the sum of numbers in a sequence.

```
def tailsum(S,L):
    if len(L)==0:
        return S
    else:
        return tailsum(S+L[0],L[1:])

>>> tailsum(0,[1,10,100])
111
```

Again, it can be confusing for beginners how tail recursion calculates the results, but it is sensible by following a detailed tracing of how Python evaluates `tailsum(0,[1,10,100])`, shown in Figure 14.2. The figure indents further for new evaluations, and un-indents at steps that resume suspended evaluations. It may seem strange that steps ⑤–⑦ do not accomplish anything other than resuming evaluations that simply resume other steps. This is just the way tail recursion works. Later in this chapter, we will see a way to exploit this behavior in a different kind of recursion.

```
def vecsum(S,L1,L2):
    if L1==[] or L2==[]:
        return S
    else:
        head1, head2 = L1[0], L2[0]
        tail1, tail2 = L1[1:], L2[1:]
        return vecsum(S+[head1+head2],tail1,tail2)

>>> vecsum([],[1,2,3],[100,200,300])
[101, 202, 303]
```

Summing Items of Two Lists. Using tail recursion to add up items of a list is not really useful, since Python already has the built-in `sum` function. However, the same pattern can be used to add two lists, element-wise. The code for `vecsum` does this by using tail recursion on two lists. In the evaluation of `vecsum([],[1,2,3],[100,200,300])`, Python names `head1` as 1 and `head2`

as 100. Then a new evaluation is needed, for vecsum([]+[1+100],[2,3],[200,300])
→ vecsum([]+[101],[2,3],[200,300]) → vecsum([101],[2,3],[200,300]).
The value of S is a list, empty for the first vecsum evaluation. As new evaluations occur
during the computing of the answer, each new evaluation will get a longer list for S, and
also shorter lists for the L1 and L2 parameters.

```
def tailfind(S,value,L):
    if L[0]==value:
        return S
    else:
        return (S+1,value,L[1:])
def indx(M,v):
    return tailfind(0,v,M)

>>> "property".index('e')
4
>>> indx("property",'e')
4
>>> "property".index('s')
ValueError: substring not found
>>> indx("property",'s')
IndexError: string out of range
```

Searching for an Item in a Sequence. Recall
that Python's index method calculates the smallest
nonnegative index of a value in a sequence:
for example, "jaded".index("d") is 2. We can
use tail recursion to do the same task. The examples
change a few things about the tail recursion
pattern. First, the tail recursion is in the three-
parameter tailfind function, but to make a simpler
interface for using it, a two-parameter indx
function was invented. A second difference is how
the tail recursion here omits the test for an empty
sequence. Arguably, this is poor style, not checking
for an empty sequence; however, you can see that
the behavior of Python's built-in index is similar—
it also generates an error when the value to be
found is not present. A third, less obvious difference is that the tail recursion done by
tailfind differs from previous examples because it may not go through the entire sequence.
For instance, tailfind(0,"absorbing","a") finishes the evaluation with the first
if statement, rather than needing any new evaluation.

---

① Looking at tailsum(0,[1,10,100]), we see that S is 0 and L is [1,10,100]. Here, Python
is forced to evaluate tailsum(0+1,[10,100]) to know what number to return.

   ② Looking at tailsum(1,[10,100]), notice that S is 1 and L is [10,100], so Python
   needs first to evaluate tailsum(1+10,[100]) to obtain the number to return.

      ③ With tailsum(11,[100]), Python will make a separate evaluation of
      tailsum(11+100,[]).

         ④ Evaluation of tailsum(111,[]) is just the "return S" line, where S is 111.

         ⑤ Having finished the evaluation of tailsum(11+100,[]), Python returns the value
         sought in step ③ (it is 111).

      ⑥ Python resumes step ②, where the value of tailsum(1+10,[100]) is needed—as
      provided by step ⑤.

   ⑦ Finally, Python resumes step ①, giving it the awaited value (111).

Figure 14.2: Steps to evaluate tailsum(0,[1,10,100]); the right-pointing arrow indicates
work suspended to perform a new evaluation; the down-pointing arrow indicates the value
returned to resume the previous evaluation.

Pythonic Style

The pattern of tail recursion is quite powerful. Tail recursion could be used to program Python's built-in functions `sum`, `min`, `max`, `all`, `any`, `filter`, `map`, `reduce`, `zip`, and even `len`. It is worth memorizing the pattern of tail recursion and using it yourself a few times to master this style of programming. The inventor of Python, Guido van Rossum, has a different style preference. At one time, he suggested that such built-ins as `map`, `filter`, and `reduce` be removed from Python, arguing that comprehensions can be used for all situations where these built-ins are used. Later in this chapter, we show why tail recursion, or something like it, remains valuable even when comprehensions are used. The next section shows patterns of using comprehensions; interesting patterns using comprehensions epitomize the so-called *pythonic* style of programming.

Comprehension Patterns

The ways that comprehension can be used are so varied that it is not possible to show them all in one concise chapter. By some examples that follow, a few of the main themes are explored. Beyond these examples, some patterns found in Python's standard module library facilitate other patterns.

Word Problems

Many practical applications focus on text processing. Problems of parsing documents make excellent exercises for learning programming techniques. Suppose `story.txt` is a file containing some natural language text. One line of `story.txt` might be a line such as

```
or tells one everything about them except what one wants to know
```

The programming problem to solve is this: write a function to calculate the percentage of words in the file which contain the letter "e." Above, there are 12 words and half of them contain "e," so 50% is the answer for the line shown.

To solve this problem, a bit of Python's file-reading technique is needed; details about input and output are given in Chapter 25. The code for `eCount` uses two techniques: first `F` represents an opened file, which is the way most computer languages make data in files accessible; second, the `F.read()` method returns all the data in the file as a string. The program defines `words` to be the list obtained by splitting the file wherever strings are sepa-

```
def eCount(fname):
    F = open(fname)
    words = F.read().split()
    eWords = [w for w in words if "e" in w]
    p = 100*len(eWords)/float(len(words))
    return int(p)

>>> eCount("story.txt")
31
```

rated by whitespace (tabs, blanks, and newlines). The comprehension does effectively what Python's `filter` does, making a list of only the items from `words` that contain "e." The line defining `p` takes care to calculate the fraction using floating point, avoiding the crude rounding of integer division. The themes of this example are (*i*) comprehension can go through data taken from a file, (*ii*) comprehension can filter (using `if`) selected values, and (*iii*) the result of comprehension can be used in other sequence functions, such as `len`.

Perhaps the `eCount` function is incorrect, because what was really meant was to calculate the percentage of *unique* words. For instance, if "the" occurs thousands of times, maybe the intent of the problem was to count "the" only once. Python offers a simple way to deal with such a requirement. The `uCount` function uses two comprehensions, one that creates a dictionary of all the words from `story.txt`, and the same list comprehension that `eCount` used to filter only the words containing "e." The theme of this example is that dictionary comprehension can be used to boil down input into just the unique items of the input.

```
def uCount(fname):
  F = open(fname)
  words = F.read().split()
  uniqs = {w:0 for w in words}
  eWords = [w for w in uniqs if "e" in w]
  p = 100*len(eWords)/float(len(uniqs))
  return int(p)

>>> uCount("story.txt")
24
```

As one more variation on the theme of counting e's in a file, here is a program to answer the question, what is the most number of e-containing words on a line? To answer this question, the function `mCount` uses two comprehensions, one of them within an internally defined function `f(t)`. The function `f(t)` is indented and defined *within* the body of `mCount` because `f` is only used inside `mCount`, and not meant to be used in the rest of the program. Function `f` makes a generator, which will produce all the e-containing words in a line `t`. The code of `mCount` defines `lm` as another generator, which yields the length of each filtered sequence that `f(t)` gives, for each line `t` in the file. The themes of this example are (*i*) comprehensions can build upon other comprehensions by introducing functions, like `f(t)`, and (*ii*) for many situations, using a generator instead of list comprehension does the same job. Why is point (*ii*) significant? The issue is one of computer resources. The previous example created a dictionary, obtained by first letting `words` contain the entire file. Had this file been many gigabytes of text, the computer would not be able to run the program due to lack of sufficient memory. However, for the case of counting e's line by line, we can use a generator that only consumes memory enough to take care of one line at a time. Python is smart enough in how it manages generator evaluation to reuse memory. If `lm` had been a list comprehension instead of a generator, all the lengths of all the filtered lines would be needed in memory at the same time. Though you cannot get away with using generators for every programming problem, it is a good strategy when faced with large datasets.

```
def mCount(fname):
  def f(t):
    r = (w in t.split() if "e" in w)
    return len(r)
  F = open(fname)
  lm = (len(f(t)) for t in F)
  return max(lm)

>>> mCount("story.txt")
15
```

Creating Structures

$$\begin{pmatrix} 1 & 0 & 0 & 0 \\ 0 & 1 & 0 & 0 \\ 0 & 0 & 1 & 0 \\ 0 & 0 & 0 & 1 \end{pmatrix}$$

An *identity matrix* is a square arrangement of 0s and 1s with 1s on the diagonal and 0s everywhere else. The problem we consider is how to make a function, using comprehensions, to create an identity matrix. The matrix shown on the left is a 4×4 matrix, because it has 4 rows and 4 columns. The general problem is to create an $n \times n$ matrix, where n is a parameter. Python does not have a data type for matrices, so we use lists: a matrix is a list of its rows, each of which is itself a list of numbers. The 4×4 identity matrix is represented by [[1,0,0,0], [0,1,0,0], [0,0,1,0], [0,0,0,1]]. The general shape of this representation suggests how we can use comprehension: the function will use a list comprehension [`row(i) for i in range(n)`], where `row(i)` is a function that creates a row.

The `idMatrix(n)` function builds an identity matrix, where `n` is the number of columns (and rows). The list comprehension creates the matrix as sketched in the previous paragraph. The trick here is finding a way to define `row(i)`. Here, the function `row(i)` was found by some experimentation and observations about the repetitive structure of the identity matrix.

```
def idMatrix(n):
  def row(i):
    prefix = i*[0]
    suffix = (n-i-1)*[0]
    return prefix+[1]+suffix
  I = [row(i) for i in range(n)]
  return I
```

Observe that row j of an identity matrix consists of j 0's, followed by a 1, followed by more 0's. That observation suggests we try an expression like `j*[0]+[1]+t*[0]` where `t` is some number to be determined. Now observe that each row is a list of n numbers: that implies `t` should satisfy: `j+1+t` equals `n`. Hence `t` is `n-j-1`. This kind of thinking leads to the definitions of `prefix` and `suffix` in the code, but we should also check to see that corner cases, that is, when j is 0 or j is $n-1$, also work out properly. Fortunately, these cases work: in Python, `0*[0]` evaluates to `[]`, which is perfect for row 0 of the matrix. The theme of this example is that list comprehension can describe structured data in controlled, periodic structures.

Searching and Filtering

To a mathematician, computers are most useful when they search a large set of candidates to see which of them are acceptable solutions to a problem. The pattern is thus (*i*) creating a set of candidates, and (*ii*) selecting which ones should be kept. This example here is a program to draw a circle. Mathematically, a circle on the plane centered at the point $(0,0)$ is the set of points satisfying $x^2 + y^2 = r^2$ where r is the radius of the circle. Unfortunately, Python cannot search through infinitely many (x, y) pairs to discover which ones are on the circle, though we can approximate this idea.

Suppose we try (x, y) pairs with $x \in [-200, 199]$ and $y \in [-200, 199]$, but filter for a radius of approximately 150 (which is $r^2 = 22500$). The code used in our example filters by allowing any (x, y) that would fit an r^2 in [22400, 22600]. This program uses a technique from Chapter 18, the `import` statement to gain access to drawing software.

```
import teken
C = [(x,y) for x in range(-200,200)
      for y in range(-200,200)
        if 22400 <= x**2 + y**2 <= 22600]
[ teken.label(start=(x+200,y+200),text="/",
  color="green") for (x,y) in C ]
teken.show()
```

Chapter 24 discusses the `teken` module, which can be used to draw simple figures using a Web browser's canvas area. The method `teken.label` puts text at a specified coordinate, here the slash (/) character. Figure 14.3 shows two outputs for this program, one with the slash character, and another run of the same program with an underscore instead of the slash.

Figure 14.3: `Teken` drawings of approximate circles.

Operator, Functools, Itertools

Python has tools in its standard library which epitomize many patterns used in functional programming. A presentation of Python's language features to access libraries comes later, in Chapter 18, but it is worth describing some of the function tools here. Three library modules are relevant to this chapter, `operator`, `functools`, and `itertools`. To access all of these, the following three lines should be put at the start of a Python script:

```
from operator import *
from functools import *
from itertools import *
```

The effect of these lines is to bring in extra function definitions from Python's standard library. Before launching into more patterns of functional programming that the tools provide, we look at an idiom of Python programming, based on the `itemgetter` function from the `operator` module.

Customized Sorting. Many applications print reports from datasets, calculate statistics, or look for particular situations in files. Quite often, data needs to be summarized and sorted. To the right is a transcript of making a list comprehension and sorting it. Because the items of the list are tuples,

```
>>> C = [(x,x**2,2*x) for x in range(-5,4)]
>>> sorted(C)
(-5,25,-10), (-4,16,-8), (-3,9,-6),
(-2,4,-4), (-1,1,-2), (0,0,0),
(1,1,2), (2,2,4), (3,9,5)
```

the tuple-comparison algorithm described in the box "Python's Algorithm for Comparison" (Chapter 6) is used to order the sorted result: it starts by comparing the first element of one tuple to first elements of other tuples. What if this is not what we want? Is there some way to have the sorted order only look at the second element of each tuple? This is where the `itemgetter` idiom is handy.

A revised transcript is shown to the right. An extra keyword argument to `sorted` specifies that the second element should be used for comparison (whereas `itemgetter(0)` would specify the first element, and `itemgetter(2)` would be for the third). The result is in increasing order by the second element of the tuples. This may

```
>>> from operator import *
>>> C = [(x,x**2,2*x) for x in range(-5,4)]
>>> sorted(C,key=itemgetter(1))
(0,0,0), (-1,1,-2), (1,1,2),
(-2,4,-4), (2,4,4), (-3,9,-6),
(3,9,6), (-4,16,-8), (-5,25,-10)
```

seem a rather obscure part of Python, but sorting is an important pattern in solutions to many problems, and the `itemgetter` technique is worth knowing.

Patterns from Functools. The `functools` module defines `reduce`, which Python2 already has, but Python3 does not. The other significant function in `functools` is `partial`, which does the trick of currying discussed in the box "Carrying and Made-to-Order Functions" in Chapter 10.

Patterns from Itertools. The `itertools` module provides a rich variety of patterns useful for functional programming styles. There are too many of them to describe here, so we look at one of the functions, `groupby`, to get a flavor of what `itertools` has. The official Python documentation on `itertools` (see `http://docs.python.org/library/itertools.html`) has a section on recipes, showing more of the tools in action.

The `groupby` function is designed for processing items of a sequence, where items may be duplicated. The list `[1,1,2,3,3,3,4]` is an example of such a sequence. The point of `groupby` is to process the duplicates as groups. For the example list, there are four groups for the values 1, 2, 3, 4. Within a group, the items can also be sequentially processed. We illustrate this with the problem of finding what is the most commonly occurring word in a text file. Figure 14.4 shows the code, with comments written in italics after some statements. In the figure, `ordered` is a sorted list of the words in a file, and most likely there will be duplicates, because common words "a", "and", "the" occur frequently in normal text. The next line of code calculates, for a given `word`, what is the length of the list of values in a group, all of which are the same word: this tabulates the number of duplicates. If a word only appears once in the file, this length will be 1. To get a group, named as `obj` in the code, the `groupby` function is called, which returns a generator. Items from this generator are pairs of the form `(word,obj)`. The outcome of this work is the list `T`, which contains pairs `(word,c)` where `c` is a count of duplicates. To complete the task, `T` is sorted according to the count; this uses `itemgetter` to specify which element of the tuple is the count and also adds the optional keyword argument `reverse=True`, so that the sorting will be in decreasing order by count. That puts the most frequently occurring word at the beginning of list `R`.

```
from itertools import *
from operator import *
def topword(fname):
  F = open(fname)
  words = F.read().split()              makes list of words in the file
  ordered = sorted(words)               now a sorted list with duplicates
  T = [ (word,len([x for x in obj]))    obj is a group of duplicates
      for (word,obj) in groupby(ordered) ]   groupby gives (word,obj) pairs
  R = sorted(T,key=itemgetter(1),       sort by number of duplicates
      reverse=True)
  top = R[0]                            top is highest dup count pair
  return top[0]


print topword("report.txt")
the
```

Figure 14.4: Finding most frequently occurring word in a file.

As a beginner, you should not be expected to master the patterns in `itertools`. Our purpose in looking at `groupby` is to show the pythonic style of programming, which leverages patterns in libraries. You may encounter this style in browsing Python programs found online or in various software packages.

More Recursion

Tail recursion is only one pattern that uses recursion in functional programming. A few more important patterns are shown here with some examples. Later, in Chapter 19 there is a more general explanation of recursion, and how it also fits with an imperative style of programming.

Summation Revisited. A key property of tail recursion is that functions end either by returning a value or returning what is returned by a recursive call. Another option would be to take the value returned by a recursive call, and then use that value for other purposes before returning. An illustration is a different way of summing items in a sequence than was presented in "Summing Items of a Sequence" earlier in this

```
def tailsum(L):
    if len(L)==1:
        return L[0]
    else:
        return L[0]+tailsum(L[1:])

>>> tailsum([1,10,100,1000])
1111
```

chapter, where `tailsum` was defined with two parameters, the "sum so far" parameter, and the "remainder of the sequence" parameter. The version of `tailsum` shown here looks simpler, because `tailsum` has one parameter. In fact, this version forces Python to do a bit more bookkeeping in its evaluation. Only *after* evaluating the result of recursion on the tail does the code in `tailsum` add the head to what is returned. Consequently, the actual order of summation for the example is forced to be `1+(10+(100+1000))`. The first two items to be added are the last two in the list; additions of all previous items in the list are put in the background by Python, as it waits for recursive calls to finish. For a list of a thousand items, that would mean stacking up nearly a thousand suspended function calls waiting for the last two elements to be added.

Trees

Real computer scientists love trees. Not necessarily the woody kind that grow in nature reserves, but rather the kind of organizational tree found in scientific taxonomies. Figure 14.5 shows an example of a classification hierarchy and how a list in Python might represent this information. The figure shows the Python list twice, first to the right of the diagram, in a form that emphasizes the nesting of lists; and the second underneath, in a linear way on two lines, typical of how Python prints a list.

In the figure's diagram, each of the terms (`life`, `plant`, etc.) is a *node* of the tree. The node at the top, for `life`, is call the *root node* of the tree. (Standard computing terminology for trees turns the tree upside-down compared to what one might see in a biology text.) Underneath `life` are three *child nodes*: `plant`, `bacteria`, and `animal`. The `plant` node has, in turn, two children, `cactus` and `grass`. Nodes that do not have children are called *leaf nodes*. Notice that if we concentrate on the `plant` node, we can think of it as a tree with root `plant` and children (leaves) `cactus` and `grass`. In effect, `plant` is a *subtree* of the `life` tree. Thinking of things this way, the general pattern for a tree is that a node in a tree has possibly two kinds of children, leaves or roots of subtrees.

With this terminology, the rule for how Python can represent a tree as shown by lists in Figure 14.5 is this: a tree is a list with the root as the first item (a nonlist) and children as remaining items. If a child is a leaf, it is not a list; if a child is a subtree, it is a list, following the same rule of representation. Other ways of representing trees may use dictionaries or

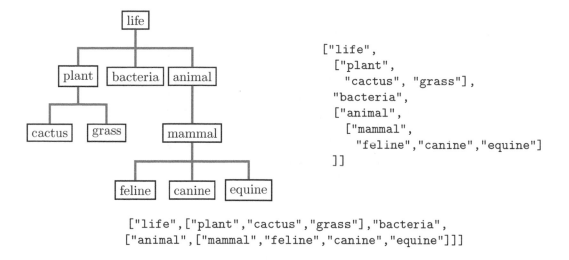

Figure 14.5: Classification tree and Python representation.

even encode all the information in a string. We use this list representation here to motivate a functional programming pattern.

The example problem for trees is a function that counts the number of leaves in a tree. The `return 1` statement produces the count of 1, done for each leaf node. Recursion takes care of trees and subtrees, by calling `leafCount(i)` on each item in the tail of a tree or subtree. Though the function looks simple, it is helpful to check the example's tree argument, `[1,2,[3,4],[5,[6,7]]]`. The root node 1 has three children, but only 2 is a leaf; node 3 has one child, the leaf 4. Node 5 has one child, the subtree 6, which has one leaf 7. The leaves

```
def leafCount(Tree):
    if type(Tree)!=list:
        return 1
    else:
        return sum(leafCount(i)
            for i in Tree[1:])

>>> leafCount([1,2,[3,4],[5,[6,7]]])
3
```

are thus 2, 4, and 7. The example sneaks in another trick of Python syntax: the parentheses used in the notation for a generator are missing in the code; Python allows this when the generator is the argument to a function that has a single parameter (`sum`, in the program).

Suppose that instead of counting leaves, the problem is to count *all* nodes in a tree. A small change to the program gives us the function needed. Instead of `return sum(LeafCount(i) ...`, make it `return 1+sum(LeafCount(i) ...` to include the root of the tree (or subtree) in the count. The same pattern shown by this example can be adapted to many other purposes. If the nodes are numbers, it is not difficult to add up all the values in leaf nodes, using a similar idea.

Nested List Type Similarity. The tree representation has lists that could, in turn, have lists as items. More generally, we can think of lists that are mixtures of numbers, booleans, strings, and lists. The problem we solve here is to say whether two lists A and B are "similar" in the sense that the types at the corresponding places are the same in both lists. The logic of the function is straightforward, with four cases (*i*)–(*iv*). Since each of these cases has a **return** statement, the **elif** or **else** statements are not needed: each of (*i*)–(*iii*) is an **if** statement with a **return**. The four cases are: (*i*) if A and B

```
def similar(A,B):
    if type(A)!=type(B):
        return False
    if type(A)!=list:
        return True
    if len(A)!=len(B):
        return False
    R = (similar(A[i],B[i])
        for i in range(len(A)))
    return all(R)
```

have different types, they are not similar; otherwise, for cases (*ii*)–(*iv*), we know that A and B have the same type, though further checking is needed to determine similarity. Case (*ii*) is when A (and also B) are not lists, in which case they are similar, hence the **return True** statement is appropriate. Notice that for the remaining cases (*iii*)–(*iv*), both A and B are lists. Case (*iii*) returns **False** if the two lists are not the same length, because similar lists must have the same number of items. In the final case, a generator R is created by comprehension, which applies (recursively) the **similar** function to determine whether items at the same index position in A and B are similar. The generator R will therefore behave like a sequence of booleans. The last statement of the function returns **True** only if all the items of the generator are **True**. Examples of similar (✔) and dissimilar lists (✘) follow.

`[True,[3,"x"],False,False]`	`[False,[88,''],False,True]`	✔
`["crack",[[True]],17,["up"]]`	`["Case",[False],9,["down"]]`	✘
`list(range(12))`	`list(range(10))`	✘
`list(range(12))`	`list(range(-4,8))`	✔
`[[["one",3],2:True],0]`	`[[['''J ''',-8],],900]`	✔

⇨ web

Regular Expressions

To programmers who use the Perl scripting language, a facility called *regular expression* is fundamental. Applications that need to scan text for patterns can use regular expressions to define these patterns. For instance, pattern "ab+" stands for text of the form ab, abb, abbb, and so on—an a followed by any number of b's. Regular expression patterns can be extremely complex; there is even a mini-language of regular expressions, which has meta-characters that act like constrained wildcards in matching patterns. These meta-characters, which begin with the backslash character (\), can lead to a "backslash plague" of writing and understanding regular expressions. Chapters and books have been written about regular expressions (Chapter 27 of this book has further information on the topic). The precise details of regular expressions vary from one programming language to another (Perl's differs from Python's). The official Python Web site has a how-to document on the subject (http://docs.python.org/dev/howto/regex.html). Despite the intimidating setup for using and learning regular expressions, the payoff can be worthwhile: careful use of regular expressions can eliminate the need to write functions that look for patterns of text.

This regular expression example searches for a phrase of the form "top yada yada day" where "yada" can be any string of visible text. The line defining `pattern` has the regular expression: you can see `top` and `day` in the expression, with other things such as `\w+` to represent "yada" and `\s+` to stand for white space characters. The string starts with `r'` instead of a single quote to overcome some backslash confusion. The `match.finditer` creates an iterator for all the places that the desired phrase occurs in the text. The function `showplace(d)` is called to print the actual matching text. If you are interested in using regular expressions, it is best to seek tutorials, recipes, and helpful documentation rather than the pages of this book.

```
import re
def showphrase(text):
    def showplace(p):
        start, end = p
        print text[start:end]
    pattern = r'top\s+\w+\s+\w+\s+day\s+'
    match = re.compile(pattern)
    places = ( e.span()
        for e in match.finditer(text) )
    v = [showplace(d) for d in places]

>>> text = '''wish top of the day was
top in each day for me'''
>>> showphrase(text)
top of the day
top in each day
```

Don't Be Too Clever

You may get the impression, reading this chapter, that the aim of functional programming is to find very compact function definitions that are mysterious, because they use lots of tricks of comprehensions and recursion. This is not the case. The patterns that occur repeatedly in programming should be reused, rather than starting from scratch in problem solving. The tools used in Pythonic style take advantage of existing patterns; becoming familiar with these patterns is the equivalent to learning expressions of speech and a larger vocabulary in natural language.

Trying to be too clever defeats one goal of software engineering, which is to make your work easily understandable to other team members (and even to yourself, after a few months). Regular expressions are a technique sometimes abused, resulting in long, inscrutable strings of symbols that somehow match patterns. Functional programming can also be too clever. Here is an example, an expression (written by Ulf Bartelt) that calculates the first 30 numbers of the Fibonacci sequence [1,1,2,3,5,8,13,...] (except for the first two, each number is the sum of the previous two in the sequence):

```
map(lambda x,f=lambda x,f:(x<=1) or (f(x-1,f)+f(x-2,f)): f(x,f),
                        range(30))
```

It takes far too much work to understand why this expression works. There are programmers who enjoy this kind of challenge, but it is generally considered poor style. Chapter 20 has more to say on the topic of style.

Terminology Review

This chapter presented the first usage of recursion, especially tail recursion, in function definition. Along the way, terms like head, tail, and trees (root, nodes, leaves, child) came up in examples. Other examples were used, but did not fully explain such things as files, modules, and regular expression.

Exercises

(1) Show how the expression here, which has two list comprehensions, could be replaced by a single list comprehension.

```
>>> [i for i in range(3)] + [j for j in range(8,11)]
[0, 1, 2, 8, 9, 10]
```

(2) Here is a function definition `foo(f,b,L)` returning a generator.

```
def foo(f,b,L):
    return (f(x) for x in L if b(x))
```

The question is this: Which of the following two expressions would be equivalent to `foo(f,b,L)`?

(a) `map(f,filter(b,L))`

(b) `filter(b,map(f,L))`

(3) A student hears that tail recursion can be used to write the equivalent of what Python's built-in `reversed` function does, namely to produce a reversed-order version of a sequence: `list(reversed([1,2,3]))` ➙ `[3,2,1]`. The student tries the following definition:

```
def myrev(M):
    def brev(S,M):
        if len(M)<2:
            return M+S
        else:
            T = S+[M[0]]
            return brev(T,M[1:])
    G = []
    return brev(G,M)

print myrev([1,2,3,4])
```

When the student ran the program, the output was `[4,1,2,3]`, which is not what a reversing function should do. What is wrong with this program? (*Hint:* It is just a change to one line of the code to make it correct.)

(4) Write a function `mergedict(A,B)` that returns a dictionary equal to the "merge" of dictionaries A and B. An example of testing `mergedict` might be:

```
>>> A = {"E":3, "J":10, "F":12}
>>> B = {"a":1, "t":0, "E":15}
>>> mergedict(A,B)
{"a":1, "J":10, "E":3, "t":0, "F":12}
```

Hints: (*i*) Use dictionary comprehension; (*ii*) use `A.keys()` to get the list of keys that dictionary A contains, and similarly `B.keys()` for B; (*iii*) make a local function that returns the value associated with a key, by looking in A and, if necessary, also in B.

(5) The `diffs(L)` function is supposed to take a list of numbers L and make a corresponding list of the differences between consecutive items in L. An example of `diffs` would be this:

```
>>> diffs([5,2,9,3,0])
[3, -7, 6, 3]
```

The result of `diffs(L)` is thus a sequence with length equal to `len(L)-1`. Write a definition of `diffs` using a comprehension which has the expression `range(len(L)-1)` in it.

(6) Let A and B be lists of the same length. List A can have any kind of item in it, but list B contains only booleans. The problem is to define a function `select(A,B)` that filters A by what the corresponding item of B is: where an item of B is `True`, the corresponding item of A should be in the result. It is easy to understand with an example:

```
>>> A = [3,9,6,12,2,0,10]
>>> B = [True,False,False,True,True,False,True]
>>> select(A,B)
[3, 12, 2, 10]
```

Write a definition of `select` that uses one comprehension, but *does not* use indexing. *Hint: Use the* `zip` *function in your comprehension.*

(7) An inexperienced programmer tried the following function based on tail recursion, to do the equivalent of what Python's built-in `zip` does.

```
def myzip(listA,listB):
    def loczip(S,X,Y):
        if X==[] or Y==[]:
            return S
        newS = S + [(X[0],Y[0])]
        return loczip(newS,X,Y)
    return loczip([],listA,listB)
print myzip([1,2,3],[7,8,9])
```

The programmer was expecting this code, when run as a script, to print `[(1,7),(2,8),(3,9)]`. Instead, Python reported an error, something about "maximum recursion depth exceeded" when it ran. Can you find and correct the bug in this code?

(8) Show that a comprehension expression can give the same result as `zip(A,B)` for lists A and B. *Hint:* The easiest way to do this is by making the term of the comprehension something like `(A[i],B[i])`; but take care to think about corner cases when A and B have different lengths. This problem is, in some sense, the opposite of problem (6).

(9) The `operator` module gives names to most of the Python standard operators described in Chapter 6. For example, after the statement `from operator import *` is in a script (or done interactively), `iadd(5,3)` returns 8,   `mul(5,3)` returns 15, `and_(True,False)` returns `False`, and `or_(True,False)` returns `True`. Using these functions supplied by `operator`, plus the built-in `reduce` function, write expressions equivalent of `sum`, `any`, and `all`.

(10) Use tail recursion to write the equivalent of Python's built-in `reduce` function. The head for your function can be

```
def treduce(func,seq,init=0):
```

where the optional keyword parameter `init` says what is the default value for an empty sequence (it is zero for `sum`). To define `treduce`, it is helpful to first define `tailreduce`, with a head like

`def tailreduce(S,seq):`

which uses `S` for an argument that represents the accumulated value passed on in tail recursion. Once you have written `tailreduce`, the `treduce` function can call `tailreduce` for the tail recursion.

(11) The `map` function creates a list (or generator) from a function `f` and a list `L`: `map(f,L)` returns `[ f(e) for e in L ]`. The goal of this exercise is to turn things around. Write a function `pam(x,F)` where `F` is a list of functions, which returns a list `[`f_1`(x),` f_2`(x), ...]` for the functions $f_1, f_2, \ldots$ in `F`. For example, `pam("test",(len,max,type))` should return `[4, "t", <type 'str'>]`.

(12) Write a function `treemap` that does what `map` does, but for a tree. Here is an example usage of `treemap`:

```
>>> treemap(len,["one","two",["three","four","five"],"six"])
[3, 3, [5, 4, 4], 3]
```

(It is the same tree "shape," but has lengths of the strings instead of the strings in the result.)

Case Study: Tic-Tac-Toe

Software should make life simpler, not more complicated. Mastery of computing includes skills to reduce complexity of programs and algorithms. If there are two ways to write a function, one with four `if/elif` cases and other with just two cases, we generally prefer the latter. The design considerations for a game function is discussed below, stressing ideas to keep things simple and show pythonic style in function definitions.

> **Advice on Design**
>
> The most important advice to beginners about designing programs is this: **don't do it at the keyboard**. As a rule, developers should spend at most 25% of the time actually writing functions, program, and code. About 75% of the time should be spent researching the problem at hand, learning about what techniques are available (including libraries of existing software), asking questions to clarify requirements, experimenting with different representations of the information, and discussing alternatives with other team members. Considerable thought should precede formulation of a plan. Even after you have a plan of attack and thoughts about what functions need to be written and tested, you should think through the consequences of having the functions you imagine writing, and ask yourself if there are corner cases or exceptions.
>
> The case study here shows the finished product of design, skipping over missteps and experiments that were part of the work. The emphasis is on techniques that manage complexity.

Tic-tac-toe is an easy game, made somewhat more interesting if the number of rows and columns is larger than the traditional 3×3 number of cells. Our goal is to write a function which returns `True` if a game position is a win for one play or another, and returns `False` if neither player has won. A first step is to agree on how a particular game position is represented using Python data types. Suppose an $n \times n$ game board is associated to a list of n rows, with each row being a string of n characters: represent an empty cell with `'-'`, and `'X'` and `'O'` for cells that have been marked. An example with this representation appears in Figure 14.6.

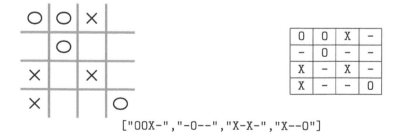

["OOX-","-O--","X-X-","X--O"]

Figure 14.6: Tic-tac-toe game position represented by Python list.

The second part of the design is to look at what is needed to answer the question, is the position a win or not. This amounts to determining whether there are three X's or three O's in a row. However, three in a row means looking in horizontal, vertical, and two diagonal orientations. The obvious way to check this would be to write four functions (or

176

expressions), one for horizontals, one for verticals, one for right-tilted diagonals, and one for left-tilted diagonals. Before we investigate such a design, consider this alternative: if we had a function that rotated a game by 90 degrees, then columns become rows and diagonals flip orientation in the rotation (try it!). So, with a rotation function, we can use just two win-checking functions, one for rows and one for diagonals: the idea is to first check rows, then one diagonal in the game position, then rotate and repeat. We thus have only three functions to write.

How can a function check for three X's or O's being consecutive in a row? Since strings represent the game rows, a slice comes to mind. Some expression like `row[i:i+3]=="XXX"` in an `if` statement checks for three X's being consecutive. To simplify treating both X and O together in one test, the expression could be `row[i:i+3] in ("XXX,"OOO")`.

 What about diagonals? Unlike rows, where the length of each row is n cells in the game, diagonals have differing numbers of cells. The longest diagonal is n cells, while the shortest diagonal we need to examine is 3 cells (we can ignore the two diagonals that have 2 cells and also the diagonals with 1 cell). The diagram shows downward-right oriented diagonals, in two shadings. The darker arrows cover the longest diagonal and extend through the upper right portion of the game board. The lighter arrows are for the lower left part. The dark arrows have in common that they all start on row 0; the lighter arrows have in common that they start on column 0 of the board. The longest diagonal could be given by a list `[ pos[i][i] for i in range(n)]`, where `pos[i]` denotes row number i and `pos[i][i]` is cell number i in row i. What about other diagonals, say for the upper right part of the board? Before conjecturing a pattern, it helps to work out on scratch paper a few of the diagonals, here done for a 5×5 board, starting with the longest diagonal.

```
[pos[0][0], pos[1][1], pos[2][2], pos[3][3], pos[4][4]]
[pos[0][1], pos[1][2], pos[2][3], pos[3][4]]
[pos[0][2], pos[1][3], pos[1][4]]
```

The pattern we conjecture from this example is that the k-th diagonal in the upper-right part would be the list `[pos[0][i] for i in range(k,n-k)]`. The comprehension uses k twice, once to say where the list starts within the position and the other to say where it stops.

Recounting the design to this point, the following functions would be helpful for the solution: **rotate**, to return a 90-degree rotation of a position; **checkrows** to see whether there are three X or O values consecutive in a row; and check-diagonals function to see whether there are three consecutive along the diagonals. Earlier we saw there are two kinds of diagonal, one

```
def check3(seq):
    def grab3(k):
        return seq[k]+seq[k+1]+seq[k+2]
    m = len(seq)
    S = (grab3(i) for i in range(m-3))
    A = (x in ("XXX","OOO") for x in S)
    return any(A)
```

for the upper right part and another for the lower left part of the board. Hence, it would be a reasonable design to have **checkURdiags** and **checkLLdiags** functions. Notice that three of the desired functions need to look for three consecutive X or O values being consecutive, so let's add **check3** as another desirable function to have. Code for **check3** is shown above. The only tricky part of the function is **range(m-3)**, which makes sure Python stops short of looking for three consecutive values too near the end of a sequence. **If in doubt about such things, try an example argument.** Suppose that `seq` has length 10. Starting at `seq[10-2]` (equals `seq[8]`) would cause trouble, because `grab3` would try to access `seq[10]`, and 9 would be the maximum index value allowable.

```
def checkURdiags(pos):
    n = len(pos)
    def diag(k):
        return [pos[0][i]
                for i in range(k,n-k)]
    D = (diag(k) for k in range(n-2))
    A = (check3(e) for e in D)
    return any(A)
```

Function `check3` returns `True` if either player has a win in the argument sequence. Since we have seen a conjectured pattern for upper right diagonals, the `checkURdiags` function is a reasonable next development. The logic of `checkURdiags` direct: `D` is a generator of the diagonals, with each diagonal being a sequence generated by the local `diag` function. Note that `D` stops short of including the two tiny diagonals that have fewer than three items (so that no trouble is caused for `check3`).

```
def checkLLdiags(pos):
    n = len(pos)
    def diag(k):
        return [pos[i][0]
                for i in range(k,n-k)]
    D = (diag(k) for k in range(n-2))
    A = (check3(e) for e in D)
    return any(A)
```

The `checkLLdiags` function, which examines diagonals in the lower-left part of the board, has code nearly identical to `checkURdiags`. The difference is that the diagonals all start on the first column (hence `pos[i][0]` starts the `diag` list comprehension). For the sake of simplicity, the code also checks the longest diagonal: thus the longest diagonal belongs to both the upper right and lower left parts of the board. This redundancy does no harm. For future improvement, the two functions `checkURdiags` and `checkLLdiags` could be combined into a single function `checkdiags`; the combined function would have a parameter to say which of `UR` or `LL` to check.

When a position is turned by 90 degrees, columns become rows. The first row of the rotation, call it `row(0)`, is given by listing the items in the first column (at index 0) of every row of `pos`, namely `[pos[k][0] for k in range(n)]`, where `n` is the number of rows. For the `rotate` function, we are careful to use list comprehension rather than generator notation,

```
def rotate(pos):
    n = len(pos)
    def row(k):
        return [pos[i][k]
                for i in range(n)]
    newpos = [row(j) for j in range(n)]
    return newpos
```

so that indexing can be used on the result. The expression for the second row is similar, but using `pos[k][1]` to get the second column. Extending this pattern of building a row from a column in `pos` gives the code shown to the right.

The final function to write, `winning(pos)`, returns `True` if any of the above `check`-functions returns `True` on either the position or the rotated position. This completes the case study, but we caution the reader: *something important is missing* from this program. What is missing is a document or commentary explaining its logic,

```
def winning(pos):
    rot = rotate(pos)
    R = [ f(pos) or f(rot)
         for f in (checkrows,
             checkURdiags,checkLLdiags)
    return any(R)
```

stating what assumptions are made about the arguments, and discussing restrictions on using these functions. Documentation is quite important, and is the subject of Chapter 20. Each of the functions in this case study deserves documentation and comments about how the functions calculate their results.

Part III

Imperative-Style Python

Chapter 15:   Names for Data

X = 42

X += 5

X = list(range(X))

X[3], X[5] = X[17], X[22]

X[4:12] = []

del X

> *One man's constant is another man's variable.*
> — Alan Perlis

Throughout science, descriptions of quantifiable data use specialized terminology to name measurements. Especially where there are formulas and equations, one finds variables and constants. The famous $e = mc^2$ equation has variables e for energy, m for mass, and the constant c for the speed of light. Economists talk about quantities in markets, sometimes using vocabulary like "exogenous variables" of an economic system. Common to different areas such as physics or economics is the root meaning of the word *variable*, the verb *vary*—the variables of a system are the things that vary over time. A constant, however, is something that does not change.

In the early days of computing, the purpose of having a computer was to support scientific or economic (business) needs, and it was natural to carry over the terminology of variables and constants. Now things are different. Arguably, the most common purposes for computing are entertainment, social networking, and data warehousing. Programming languages have evolved to suit the needs of applications, and the meaning of the word *variable* is no longer closely related to quantities of physical experiments or economic models. New programming languages have corrupted the use of the word *variable*, to some extent. Actually, a better description of what is used in programming would be *symbolic names* for structured data in memory. However, to be consistent with other textbooks and programming jargon, the word *variable* is used in this chapter.

Although the original inspiration for the use of variables is simple and intuitive, Python has many powerful features for manipulating data and dynamically changing the meaning of a variable; languages C, C++, C#, and Java offer comparatively less freedom in working with variables.

Constants

All primitive values in Python can be considered as constants. The value "25" in a Python program represents the same number no matter how often it is used.[1] However, what is usually meant by *constant* in a programming language is a symbolic name for a value, which is defined once, and does not change after being defined. In mathematics, the best known constant is the legendary value $\pi = 3.1415926535897931 \cdots$ the ratio of a circle's circumference to its diameter. A Python definition for π could be the code shown here.

```
>>> pi = 3.1415926535897931
>>> print pi
3.1415926535897931
```

---

[1]In the early days of computing, the FORTRAN language accidentally allowed programmers to change the value of a number, so it could be that "25" might later represent 26 in a program; this was a bug in the programming language.

```
x = 1.121e-2
y = 0.0092
u = 1.05
v = 1.19
w = 2.07
z = 6.502
t = u**(v*w)
((x-y)/t/z + 200.8
```

A constant's name can be any string of characters, subject to the same restrictions explained for function names and their parameters in Chapters 9 and 10. The obvious advantage of having `pi` defined is that we can type "`pi`" into statements rather than a long string of digits. Thereby, Python functions and scripts are easier for us to read. One curious fact, reported in several research papers on education, is that many students are better able to calculate with values than with constants. The studies suggest it is easier to calculate

```
((1.212e-2 - 0.0092)/1.05**(1.19*2.07))/6.502 + 200.8
```

than it is to calculate the value of the final expression shown in the code above, involving `x, y, t,` and `z`.

The two forms are logically equivalent, so why is the first easier for calculation than the second? Apparently, the simple act of substituting actual values for the symbolic names adds to the cognitive load for doing calculations. Nonetheless, programming would be impossible without using symbolic names for values; Python does not have any trouble using symbolic names.

A Python script can have any number of definitions for symbolic names. The definitions are processed sequentially: an expression cannot evaluate a symbolic name before it has been defined. A valid script is the following:

```
kstring = '''Trivial names are those given to a particular
agate by a collector or dealer to honor some special
occasion such as a family event or celebration.'''
words = kstring.split()
print words[0].upper(), words[-4].upper()
```

An example which is *not* correct would be:

```
Tpr = "named specimens were worth more than unnamed ones"
print Words[1:5]
Words = Tpr.split()
```

The bug is that Python is asked to evaluate `Words` before it has been defined. By switching the order of the last two statements, the bug is eliminated. Some other programming languages do not have this restriction: symbolic names can be used before they are defined in the text of a program, because the compiler will search for the definitions throughout the program.

Temporary Constants. Even formal mathematicians reuse symbolic names. Today, in a lecture, x has one meaning, but later in the week x will have a different interpretation. Even though x changes, it can still be understood as a constant, because the scope of a lecture or a journal article is limited. Within the scope of a presentation, it could be that x has only one meaning or one value. Thus, x is a constant if we look at the intended scope for using x and we do not look outside that scope. Likewise, for a Python function `sqrt(v)`, parameter `v` may refer to different arguments at different times: perhaps `sqrt(100)` and `sqrt(225)` are expressions in the same program. If we focus only on the definition of `sqrt`, then `v` is a constant; this is because the *scope* of `v` is just within the body of `sqrt`, where the value of `v` refers just to one value for the duration of computing `sqrt`. It does not change reasoning that different evaluations of `sqrt` get different arguments, because these are independent, do not interfere with each other, and take place at separate times. The examples of x and `sqrt` show that it is reasonable to think of symbolic names as constants, even though there may be some wider context where a name could have different meanings in different places.

Part II of this book (Chapters 5 through 14) does use names for values computed within scripts and functions, but carefully so. Consider the solution to exercise (4) of Chapter 9:

```
def quadroot(a,b,c):
    d = (b**2 - 4*a*c)**0.5
    m = d/(2*a)
    n = -b/(2*a)
    roots = (m+n,m-n)
    return roots
```

There are names `d`, `m`, `n`, and `roots`, for calculated values. However, these *are not variables*, because once a name is equated to a value, it does not change within the body of the function. In effect, they are temporary constants.

Variables

```
x = "types are the cactus needles of programming"
x = x.split()
x = x[3]
x = x[3]
print x
```

The code shown here is a valid Python script. Just looking at this script raises many questions. What does it print? How does one answer the question *what is* x? Is this good programming style or bad style? Before answering these and related questions, it is helpful to step back and make some observations.

One important takeaway comparing the example above and the earlier examples is that the "=" symbol has a different meaning. In good scientific or mathematical presentations, "=" either relates variables in an equation ($e = mc^2$) or means *defined by*, thus giving a definition to a symbolic name, which remains constant for the duration of some intended scope of discussion. For a definition, one should not have one thing and then later a conflicting, different statement. In mathematics, there is no value for x satisfying $x = x + 1$. But the meaning of "=" in the Python example above is *redefine* (except perhaps for the first statement where x is unknown). In computing, this usage of "=" is called *assignment*. Above, all the statements except for the `print` are *assignment statements*.

In theoretical circles of computing language experts, some people consider the assignment statement to be a terrible mistake in the design of a programming language. It invites confusion, they say, because it makes programmers keep track of the meaning of names that change when a program runs. Indeed, some students stumble mentally when learning about assignment, while others find it a natural way to think about software. Some computing languages, like Haskell or Scheme, either do not have assignment statements or relegate them to rarely used features. One thing is for sure, Python (and `Java`, `C`, `C#`, etc.) do not have trouble evaluating and running assignment statements. Hence, the old-fashioned, not very helpful advice to students having difficulty was sometimes "learn to think like a computer." The reason for mentioning the debate among experts and pointing out the technical difference between different kinds of "=" is to motivate the reader to take some care, learn good technique for using assignment statements, and avoid certain tricky situations when writing software. Some advice in this and later chapters may help.

As to what is the value of x for the previous example, any answer will need to have some *temporal* qualification: more plainly put, we need to say *when*, as Python runs the script, x has a certain value and type. The value of x does vary as Python evaluates the script, so x is a variable. A surprising feature of Python is that *it has no language fea-*

```
def sqrt(x):
  return x**0.5
...
>>> sqrt(25)
5.0
>>> sqrt = 25
>>> sqrt(25)
TypeError: 'int' object is not callable
```

tures for naming constants. In fact, every symbolically named entity in Python is a *variable.* Even function names are technically variables! Disappointed? Disturbed? Perhaps you should be. Python allowed the name sqrt to be a function, but later sqrt became an integer, and it no longer worked for function application.

> ***Python has no named constants.***
> ***Python treats every name as a variable.***

To get some understanding of how Python processes scripts, it can be helpful to acquire a "mental model" of how Python works with variables. Here is the basic algorithm Python uses for managing names.

① When Python starts, it builds an empty dictionary to keep track of variables. The keys of this dictionary are variable names; corresponding to a key is a list containing the variable's type, its value, and other information Python needs for the variable.

② Python puts the standard built-in functions and other system variables into the dictionary.

③ For a script or an interactive session, Python modifies the dictionary whenever it evaluates a function definition or an assignment statement. If a variable's key already exists in the dictionary with the name of an assignment or definition, Python replaces the value component associated with that key; and if the key does not exist, it is added to the dictionary.

④ When Python evaluates an expression containing a variable, the dictionary is used to substitute a value or lookup a function definition, whichever is appropriate.

Steps ③ and ④ are repeated throughout the evaluation of a script or interactive session. Python's dir() function (and some others, such as locals()) enable you to inspect the variable dictionary, if you are curious.

Possibly this information is more than you wanted to know about how Python works; yet it is sometimes useful to realize that every time an assignment statement is evaluated, the variable dictionary is modified. The explanation ①–④ omits an important facet of Python: how does Python deal with function application, the binding of arguments to parameters, and assignment statements inside functions? This turns out to be a complicated mechanism. A later chapter partly describes how it works, though a full explanation is an advanced topic.

Assignment Syntax

It is possible with a single Python statement to assign several variables. There are two forms of multiple assignment, either giving several variables the same value or assigning several variables different values.

Multiple Assignment.   This kind of assignment is also valid in Java, C, and similar languages. The syntax is shown in the example on the right. The second statement assigns Avar, Kvar, and E all the same value, which is obtained by evaluating the expression R+2. It might seem that other reasonable variations of this form could work:

```
>>> R = 10
>>> Avar = Kvar = E = R + 2
>>> print(Avar,Kvar,E)
12 12 12
```

```
>>> a = 1 + b = c = 1
SyntaxError: can't assign to operator
```

The programmer's intent was to assign 2 to a and 1 to b and c, but Python is not happy with this attempted assignment. The only allowed form is to give all the variables the same value.

Tuple Assignment.   Python can assign different values to different variables within a single statement by using a *tuple* of variables on the left side of an assignment. This kind of assignment is called *tuple assignment*, sometimes also called *unpacking* or *unboxing*. An equivalent series of statements is:

```
>>> (a,b,c) = (1,2,3)
>>> print(a,b,c,b*c)
1 2 3 6
```

```
>>> a = 1
>>> b = 2
>>> c = 3
>>> print(a,b,c,b*c)
1 2 3 6
```

There are several ways this kind of assignment becomes quite handy for writing functions and scripts.

- Recall that, sometimes, a tuple can be formed without the enclosing parentheses. Tuple assignment is one instance where this works:

    ```
    >>> a, b, c = 45, 5>2, 12*3
    ```

- The number of items on the right side should be the same as the number of variables on the left side.

    ```
    >>> a, b = (False,"Hello",9)
    ValueError: too many values to unpack
    >>> a, b, c = 1,2
    ValueError: need more than 2 values to unpack
    ```

- You can use tuple assignment to "swap" the values of two variables:

```
>>> a, b = "one", "two"
>>> a, b = b, a
>>> print(a,b)
two one
```

- The right side of a tuple assignment can be any type of sequence.

```
>>> e, f, g, h - "help"
>>> print(e+h)
hp
>>> x,y,z = [5,6,7]
>>> print(x,y,z)
5 6 7
```

- When dealing with tuples that occur as arguments to a function, or tuples inside lists, it is sometimes nicer to use unpacking than indexing.

```
T = [(1.2,9.2),(4.0,7.3)]
R = T[1][0]-T[0][0] + T[1][1]-T[0][1]
print(R)
pointa, pointb = T
xa, ya = pointa
xb, yb = pointb
R = xb-xa + yb-ya
print (R)
```

Both `print` statements output the same value.

Augmented Assignment. Augmented assignment is common to several C-like languages, including `Java`, `C#`, and `C++`. The idea is to abbreviate assignment statements that update (change the value) a variable by one operator and an expression.

M += 1	equivalent to	M = M + 1
M -= 1	equivalent to	M = M - 1
M *= 2	equivalent to	M = M * 2
E /= 2.0	equivalent to	E = E / 2.0
w += g[4]-20	equivalent to	w = w + g[4] - 20
L += [True,False]	equivalent to	L = L + [True,False]
S += "end"	equivalent to	S = S + "end"

Augmented assignment saves keystrokes especially for long variable names, like `InvenQuantity`, where a simple operation can be done without needing to spell out the variable name twice in a statement. There are other augmented assignments in Python: for instance, `//=` is defined in Python3 (and even in later versions of Python2). The most common ones to remember are `+=`, `*=`, and `-=`,

List and Dictionary Item Assignment

```
PressureRec[5] = 2.507e3
NameTab["Bob"] += 3
R[3], R[7] = R[3]+1, R[0]*2
```

The assignment statement does not always replace a variable's value. For two types, list and dictionary, an assignment can replace the value for one, selected item. This is done by using indexing notation on the left side of the assignment. Typical assignment statements are shown in the shaded box. The values of items that are not mentioned on the left side of the "=" are unchanged by the assignment. To make the point clear, here is a table of "before" and "after" for variable A in some assignment statements.

before		after
`[5,0,6,1,8]`	`A[2] = True`	`[5,0,True,1,8]`
`[[1,2],"fast",[3,4]]`	`A[2][0] = 1`	`[[1,2],"fast",[1,4]]`
`{1:0, "xx":5, True:7}`	`A["xx"] = -1`	`{1:0, "xx":-1, True:7}`
`{1:0, "xx":5, True:7}`	`A[9] = 0`	`{1:0, "xx":5, True:7, 9:0}`

Some notes on indexing assignment help to explain the examples.

- Only dictionaries and lists permit indexed assignment; you *cannot* change a character in a string or an item of a tuple. This is further explained in Chapter 17.

- Dictionaries allow any string or number to be an index. Python will create a new item if necessary, and change the value for an item if the key already exists in the dictionary.

- Lists cannot have "holes" in the sequence of values. Consider this example:

```
>>> A = [9,8,4,3]
>>> A[99] = 0
IndexError: list assignment index out of range
>>> A[4] = 0
IndexError: list assignment index out of range
>>> A[-1] = 0
>>> A
[9,8,4,0]
```

If the goal is to use assignment to make a list longer by adding an item, there are other ways to do this, which are discussed in Chapter 17.

- One previous example combines tuple assignment with indexing. Generally, this can be confusing and lead to programming errors. The official Python reference documentation even has a warning about this, showing this example:

```
x = [0, 1]
i = 0
i, x[i] = 1, 2
print x
```

Can you guess what this prints? Most programmers do not have a good intuition about this kind of situation, so it is best not to mix tuple assignment with indexed assignment in such a way.

Deleting Variables and Items

```
>>> x, y, z = range(3)
>>> del y
>>> print x
0
>>> print y
NameError: name 'y' is not defined
>>> del y
NameError: name 'y' is not defined
>>> del x, z
>>> print x
NameError: name 'x' is not defined
```

Python does not have an "undo" for assignments the way that word processors do. When a program runs, millions or billions of assignments might take place per second; it is not practical for a computer to keep track of all changes so that they could be reversed. That being said, Python does have a statement to destroy a variable, which expunges the variable from the dictionary of names. The `del` statement causes a name to become undefined. What we see is the existence of variables in Python is transitory, they can come and go. (The above even works for Python3, where `range(3)` is not exactly a sequence, but behaves like a sequence.)

Indexed Delete. When the `del` statement is used for a particular item in a list or dictionary, that item is removed. This does not remove the variable, since the list or dictionary still exists, though in its changed form. The use of `del` for a dictionary is simple: the key and its associated value are removed from the dictionary. Thus, dictionaries can be like databases, where items are added or updated by indexed assignment and items are removed using `del`. For lists, the situation is a bit more complicated.

before		after
[5,0,6,1,8]	del A[2]	[5,0,1,8]
[1,2,3,4,5]	del A[0], A[-1]	[2,3,4]
[[1,2],[3,4]]	del A[1][0]	[[1,2], [4]]
[1,2,3,4,5]	del A[0], A[0]	[3,4,5]
[1,2,3,4,5]	del A[1], A[0]	[3,4,5]

The examples make it clear that Python deletes the items one at a time, processing the items from left to right. What is essential to understand is that indexing itself changes as the list shrinks. After removing an item $A[i]$, the indexing of every element $A[j]$ for $j > i$ is lowered by 1. Of course, for any item deletion, the index value has to be within range of the list:

```
>>> L = [0,1,2,3,4,5,6,7,8,9]
>>> del L[20]
IndexError: list assignment index out of range
```

Where Assignment Goes

You can use assignment statements and `del` statements in scripts, in functions, and in the body of an `if` (or `elif` or `else`) statement. The concept introduced earlier for *default* parameters in functions, or for keyword arguments when using functions, also uses the "=" symbol, but these earlier forms are *not* assignment statements. Unfortunately, Python has a limited range of symbols and they can be used with different meanings in different situations (much like natural languages such as English may use the same word with different meanings). You may also have noticed that "in" is both an operator to test whether an item is in a sequence *and* the "in" is used for custom lists—with a different meaning.

One place you *cannot* use assignment is within a list comprehension (a custom list). Watch what Python does when we try:

```
>>> E = 10*[True]
>>> [ E[i] = False for i in range(5) ]
SyntaxError:  invalid syntax
```

There is another way to effectively do what this expression attempts to do, which will be shown in Chapter 19.

Terminology Review

This chapter introduces jargon for variables, referring also to constants and symbolic names. The assignment statement (the single equal "=") can be to single variables or multiple variables; the tuple assignment provides a convenient way to unpack (or unbox) from sequences, which is handy for giving names to parts of a sequence. The `del` command removes a variable from Python's dictionary of symbolic names. The *scope* of a name is restricted by context, such as limiting access of a name to within a function's body.

Exercises

(1) What does the following script print?

```
a,b,c = range(10,40,10)
d = 100
print a*(b+c)-d
```

(2) What does the following script print?

```
a,b,c = "one", "two", "three"
if b>"four":
    b = "five"
c += "."
b = " " + b
print b+c
```

(Yes, it is allowable to use `if` in a script, even when not inside of a function.)

(3) What is the value for variable X after the following statements of a script run?

```
X = [9] + range(8) + [12,10]
X[4] = 0
del X[3]
del X[5]
```

(4) After these statements, what is the value of B?

```
B, C = '', list("toil")
B += C[0]
del C[0]
B += C[0]
del C[0]
B += C[0]
del C[0]
B += C[0]
```

(5) Same question, but a small change: after these statements, what is the value of B?

```
B, C = '', list("toil")
B = C[0] + B
del C[0]
B = C[0] + B
del C[0]
B = C[0] + B
del C[0]
B = C[0] + B
```

Chapter 16:   Functions and Variables

What happens in functions should stay in functions.

Perhaps the biggest obstacle for computing is complexity. Not everything that one can imagine is computable can actually be done. Unlike science fiction movies where the human protagonist commands the computer to calculate the odds, crack a security code, or find the identity of a suspect from slivers of evidence, the reality is that computing has its limits. The main theoretical limit is complexity: some things are inherently difficult to compute.

On a practical scale, complexity is a major impediment to the construction of software. A typical commercial aircraft has dozens if not hundreds of embedded computing devices; a telephone can have over a million statements from several computing languages. To help manage the complexity, there are several general themes. One theme mentioned in Chapter 9 is the Don't Repeat Yourself (DRY) principle. Another is the division of large software projects into chunks of manageable size, with the hope that the complexity of each chunk is relatively low.

Functions help manage complexity in several ways. First, the job of each function can be limited so that it does not need complicated logic. Second, even if what happens inside a function is based on some complex idea (possibly even some mathematical theory), the caller of a function can be unaware of how the function does its job, so interior complexity is hidden and users of the function are shielded from the complexity. And third, the variables used by the caller of a function can be protected from any of the function's statements, which sets up a boundary between variables of one software component (the calling program) and the variables used inside the function.

Scope of Variables

The notion of *scope* was introduced, informally, in Chapter 15. Here we first revisit the idea of scope for a script, rather than a function, to see the simple cases. The first case for scope is trivial. To show it, here is a script with some line numbers on the left (they are not part of the script, but just for reference in the discussion that follows).

```
1   X = 20
2   Y = int(X*1.5)
3   Z = (X+Y)/2
4   X += Y
5   print("value =",Z)
6   del Y, Z
7   print(X)
```

When the script runs, initially no variables (other than Python's built-in names) are defined. By the same token, when the script finishes, no variable is defined, because the memory of a Python program is *transient*, unlike the memory of data in a disk file, on CD, or on a flash drive. (In later chapters we shall see how to write to files, so that results can be *persistent* rather than transient.) Variable X becomes defined in line 1 of the script, and remains defined up to the end of the script. At line 4 we see that X is redefined, or *assigned* a new value. Variable Y is defined in line 2, and remains defined up to line 6, where it is deleted. The example illustrates that it matters **where**, within a script, that we look to decide whether a variable is defined or not. And, because the order of evaluation of lines in a script flows from the first line to the last line, it also matters **when** we consider the question of variable being defined or not.

The *scope* of a variable refers to the places and times that it is defined. When we say that a variable is "defined" we mean that it has a specific, unambiguous value. The value is fixed at the moment of *assignment*. In a script, the value of a variable is always its *most recent* assignment. Thus above, the value of X at lines 5, 6, and 7 is 50—because the assignment on line 4 redefines X to be the evaluation of X+Y at the moment that line 4 runs. To emphasize

```
1   A = "one"
2   B = "two " + A
3   A = "three"
4   print(B)
```

this behavior, consider this snippet of code. When it runs, the output is two one. The assignment to A in line 3 does not change the value of B, it only redefines A. The value of B was fixed in its most recent assignment, at line 2. One could imagine a programming language where definitions of one variable in terms of another would be "dynamic," changing when the underlying variables change (spreadsheets behave this way, for example). Python sets variables at the point of assignment by *value*, not by some definitional meaning.

Scope is not always trivial in a script. What happens when the code shown to the right runs? The scope of R is the entire script, from line 1 to line 5. The first line defines R as what some function "mystery()" returns (suppose we do not know exactly what this returns). Now, can you say what is the scope of variable C? Possibly, it is lines 3-5; but it may happen that mystery() does not return

```
1   R = mystery()
2   if type(R)==str:
3       C = R.split()
4   print("result")
5   print(C)
```

a string, in which case C will never be defined. Thus, it can be that the scope of a variable in a Python script can be unpredictable; it can be *dynamic* and depend on the values used and the conditional logic in the script.

Variables in Functions

Variables can freely be used inside functions. The scope of variables assigned within functions is limited to the body of the function and for the duration of a function application. The output of the script on the right is

```
def myfunction(S):
    x = S.split()
    y = ''.join(x)
    return len(x)-len(y)
def test():
    x = "one more time"
    y = "larger than a breadbox"
    print(myfunction(x))
    print(myfunction(y))
    print(x)
    print(y)
test()
```

2
3
one more time
larger than a breadbox

Seeing this output demonstrates that applying myfunction did not redefine variable x assigned in the body of test.

Somehow, when x is assigned within myfunction, the value of variables in test is unaffected. The technical reason is that the scope of a variable is limited to the function body where it is assigned. The way Python achieves this is roughly described by the following rules (later we talk about some exceptions to the rules).

① To aid the explanation, consider a function application `gfun(5,"it")` with the header of `gfun` being

$$\texttt{def gfun(a,b):}$$

When `gfun(5,"it")` is evaluated, Python first creates a new variable name dictionary, solely for this function application. At this point, there are thus *two* variable dictionaries, the one that already existed for the function's caller (which could be another function or perhaps a script), and the new one, the `gfun`-dictionary. The new `gfun`-dictionary is empty.

② Python next puts two items into the new dictionary, for parameter `a` and for parameter `b`. The values associated with these two items are obtained by evaluating the arguments of the function application, in this case, 5 and `"it"`. This step is called *binding arguments to parameter names*.

③ As Python evaluates statements of `gfun`, any assignment or expression evaluation uses the `gfun`-dictionary to find variables, create new variables, change variable values, or delete them.

④ When `gfun` returns, by a `return` statement, or if Python finishes evaluating all statements in `gfun` (perhaps because it has no `return` statement), then Python takes the value to be returned (or `None`), sets that aside, and destroys the `gfun`-dictionary.

⑤ Finally, Python substitutes whatever return value was obtained from the previous step into the expression where the `gfun(5,"it")` appears.

The rules explain how Python can avoid confusion over variable names during function evaluation. During the evaluation of `gfun(5,"it")`, there can safely be two different variables with the same name; but they have different scope, and therefore they are in different dictionaries. Python uses only one variable dictionary at a time, so there is no confusion. The only time the two dictionaries connect is when parameters bind to arguments, which may require getting values from the caller's dictionary. Each function application operates in a "private world" of variables, oblivious to the outside. A consequence of rule ④, which destroys the `gfun`-directory, is that a function cannot "remember" how many times it has been called, nor can it save some information between function applications. In Chapter 27 ("How Can a Function Remember?"), the problem of having a function remember previous calls is revisited.

Few programmers think about the work Python does to evaluate function application. This is probably a good thing. The example at the beginning of the chapter and the description of rules ①–⑤ mention the simple case of a single function application. In fact, Python can evaluate expressions such as `g(f(h(k(True))))`, which involves four functions: `f`, `g`, `h`, `k`. Technically, this means Python will need four dictionaries, one for the scope of each function. Each time Python evaluates function application, it *pushes down* the current set of dictionaries. The term "push down" is standard computing jargon, but a better way to describe this might be "put in background," referring to how applications launched on a software desktop open windows that cover up existing windows. The older windows move to the background; they will reappear once the current application finishes. To evaluate `g(f(h(k(True))))`, Python will push down `g`, then `f`, and then `h` before it finishes evaluating `k(True)`. In case you are curious, the opposite of "push down" is *pop up*: when function evaluation finishes, the previous dictionary of variable names and values that existed before evaluating the function "pops up" and becomes active.

An important consequence of pushing down and managing multiple dictionaries is that there can be *more than one variable with the same name*. However, at any moment during the run of a script of evaluation of a function, the question of scope is determined by the currently active dictionary of variable names and values.

Local and Global Scope

There are two exceptions to rules ①–⑤ above, which are "loopholes" in the scope restrictions on variables. One of these is an object reference mechanism, which is common to many programming languages, and is a topic of Chapter 17. The other is a way to bypass scoping rules for certain variables. The `global` statement allows functions to say that one or more variables created outside of the function can be used in expressions and assigned. When used

```
def Mfun(val):
    global acount
    r = val/2
    acount += 1
    return r*r
def top():
    global acount
    acount = 0
    v = max( [ Mfun(i) for i in range(10,18) ] )
    print "max is", v
    print "there were", acount, "function calls"
top()
```

in expressions, such *global variables* have their previous values, before the function was called. If a global variable is assigned within the function, the result of the assignment persists even after the function returns.

```
max is 64
there were 8 function calls
```

Running this script produces the output displayed to the left. In the example, variable `acount` belongs to two dictionaries, one for `top` and one for `Mfun`. The first time that `Mfun` is called, namely `Mfun(10)`, the value of `acount` is 0; the second time is `Mfun(11)`, and `acount` equals 1.

Superficially, it may seem that the `global` statement simplifies writing functions. It is a way to have some memory for how many times a function is called. Using `global` is a way that many functions could share information through variables they have in common to their name dictionaries. However, by the same token, there is some danger to using `global`. For one thing, the caller of a function that has a `global` statement may need to understand more about that function.

Suppose `Mfun` is defined as above, and an interactive Python session, shown on the right, tries a call `Mfun(0)`. The error occurs when `Mfun` tries to evaluate `acount += 1`, which is logically the same as `acount = acount`

```
>>> Mfun(0)
line 4, in Mfun
    acount += 1
NameError: global name 'acount' is not defined
```

+ 1. In order to evaluate this, Python first needs to get the current value of `acount`. But for the interactive session, variable `acount` was never assigned a value, so Python is unable to find a preexisting `acount` variable with a value, and prints the error message. Because the use of `global` means that the callers of functions need to understand more about what happens inside the function, i.e., that it depends on having the values of the global variables, this programming technique is generally considered to be poor practice. While there may be some circumstances that motivate `global`, nine times out of ten there is another, better way to achieve the same ends. The use of `global` may turn out to complicate software rather than simplify it.

Default Global

Even if you never use the `global` statement, it is worth knowing about. Here is why: Python automatically uses a "semi-global" way of evaluating variables inside of functions. To explain Python's behavior, rule ③ needs to be revised a bit:

> (Rule ③′) When Python starts function application, the statements of the function are examined to get the names of all variables that might be assigned. If some variable might be assigned (whether it is assigned or not may depend on conditional logic), but is not in a `global` statement, Python considers that variable name to be local. If a variable is not local by this criterion, then by default it is global.

Some program language experts are of the opinion that Python's "default global" behavior is a bug in the language design. Others like the way that functions refer to variables of the caller even though they are not parameters. In some ways, global variables, be they declared by `global` or be they default globals, are in effect secret parameters to a function—it is not enough to look at the function header, you have to read through the function body to figure out dependency on global variables. Secrecy may introduce more complexity, which is a danger to good software construction. To see why the default global behavior can be a danger, it is good to see a few examples.

Here is an example that uses no default global variables and has no surprises. The first statement in `Rfun`'s body establishes an initial value for `r`, which creates an entry in the `Rfun`'s local variable dictionary. One common mistake programmers make is forgetting to put some statement in a function; this can also happen because of a keystroke error in some editors, where a delete line might happen by pressing some key. The consequence is seen in the next example.

```
def Rfun(b):
    r = 2
    return b*r
...
>>> r = 7
>>> print Rfun(0), Rfun(8)
0 16
```

```
def Rfun(b):
    return b*r
...
>>> print Rfun(0), Rfun(8)
NameError: global name 'r' is not defined
```

The interaction here is good: Python actually detected that something is wrong in the definition of `Rfun`. The error message indicates that the local variable dictionary does not have the name `r` in it when it evaluated `b*r`, and Python could not find the name in any pushed down dictionary either. Sometimes, when a programmer forgets a statement in a program, Python will observe an error; however, this is not always the case.

This example confirms that Python uses the default global strategy of finding variable names and their values. The local dictionary takes priority, but will use a global approach when a variable is not assigned in the function body. But is this what the programmer intended? Just because Python did not complain does not mean the result is correct.

```
def Rfun(b):
  return b*r
...
>>> r = 7
>>> print Rfun(0), Rfun(8)
0 56
```

```
def Tfun(b):
  if not b:
    r = 5
  return r
...
>>> r = 7
>>> print Tfun(True)
UnboundLocalError: local variable 'r'
         referenced before assignment
```

In this last example, we observe that Python classified r in Tfun as a local variable, not a global one. A bug was thereby detected. Because r is *potentially assigned*, depending on whether b is True or False, Python conservatively estimates that r is a local variable. Therefore, in evaluating Tfun(b), the fact that r is 7 in the larger scope is missed, because Python only considers the local dictionary, where r is a local variable (which has not yet been assigned).

Terminology Review

Jargon used in this chapter includes: scope, global variable, binding arguments to parameters, default global variable, push-down, and pop-up.

Exercises

(1) What does the following script print?

```
def f(x):
   global f
   del f
   return 10*x
print f(10)
print f(100)
```

(2) This is an exercise to learn about two of the Python built-in functions, `locals()` and `globals()`. Try the script below. Which print statement generates the most output and which the least?

```
def f():
   S = globals()
   T = locals()
   print S.keys()
   print T.keys()
X = None
f()
```

(3) Why does this script get an error?

```
def f():
   del R
R = 0
f()
```

(4) What gets printed by this script?

```
def A(x,key=False):
   if key:
       return 2*x
   else:
       return x
def B(x,key=True):
   return A(x) + A(x,key)
key = False
print B(1,key)
print B(1)
```

(5) A programmer wrote the following code to test out a function `divisors(N)` that is supposed to return numbers that divide into N with no remainder (but not including 1 or N itself).

```
def divisors(N):
  D = [i for i in range(2,N/2) if N%j==0]
  return D
for j in range(20):
  print "Factors of", j, "are", divisors(j)
```

The program runs, but unfortunately, due to a typo (only one character is incorrect!) the program does not work correctly. What is the mistake?

Counter-Exception?

Here is an example that appears to defy the rule about default global variables presented earlier in the chapter.

```
X = {"red":3, "blue":4, "green":5}
M = [4,5]
def gremlin():
  M[2:] = [6,7]
  X["blue"] += 10
  return None
print X["blue"], M
gremlin()
print X["blue"], M
```

When run, this script first prints 4, [4,5] as one should expect. However, the second line it prints is 14, [4,5,6,7]. This is surprising, because the script was able to modify X and M by assignment, treating these as global variables, not local ones. Why is this so? Rule ③′ states that assignment to a variable makes it local to a function, unlike the result we see here. The difference to Python is that an assignment such as M[2:] = [6,7] *is not* an assignment to variable M, but instead it is an *item assignment* (actually it is a slice assignment). In the terminology of the next chapter, Chapter 17, the two assignments in the script are *mutations* to an existing variable. Had the script used an assignment like M = [0,1], then Python would make M a local variable. If you find these rules unintuitive, please consider any confusion yet another reason to be careful about using global variables. The behavior of Python concerning implicit global variables can be a source of trouble when one is trying to make simple, reliable software.

Chapter 17: Mutation

Mutants are not the ones mankind should fear.
— Dr. Jean Grey, *X-Men* (the Movie)

Imagine that the town where you live has decided to invite a visitor from a far-off, remote tribal land, which still has a hunter-gatherer society. Missionaries taught the visitor, named Mzlot'l, how to speak English, but he has no experience with modern civilization. When he arrives, the mayor throws a big party with lots of guests, who present Mzlot'l some gifts. He is amazed and delighted with some of these gifts, particularly enjoying a flashlight and a Swiss Army Knife, which he has to be shown how to open and use. However, when he is given a gift card for $100, nobody can explain why this is a good gift to him—he finds this gift to be worthless and stupid. He cannot understand "you can use it to buy stuff" because he has no experience with stores and transactions. As far as Mzlot'l is concerned, a good gift is something that has immediate, visible function and worth. The gift card is an abstract concept he does not fathom.

Money is a good example of an abstraction we use in everyday life. Money is the abstraction of value, especially paper money, which has very little intrinsic worth (it is just paper). Abstraction has merits and demerits. On the one hand, abstraction gives the freedom to substitute and manipulate quantities in many places. You can carry large amounts of money more easily than carrying raw goods, crops, lumber, or gold. On the other hand, to get something useful out of money you need to exchange it for what is actually useful. In that sense, money is an *indirect* marker of value, requiring the user to do something to exploit it. Also, you might need to have some concern about whether or not the money is valid, i.e., it is not counterfeit or worthless because of some government collapse.

Just as money is an abstraction and has some indirect character, it will be seen that some Python variables are based on indirect mechanisms. Largely, this feature of Python is hidden, and programmers may be unaware that variables may have *references* to values, rather than having values directly. This chapter exposes the use of indirection in certain Python data types, variables, methods, and operators.

The data types in Python fall into two categories, *mutable* and *immutable*. The mutable category includes lists, dictionaries, and sets. The other types introduced in Chapter 5 are all immutable types: `bool`, `int`, `float`, `tuple`, and `string`. It is the mutable types that use indirection in Python. These types are the subject of this chapter. Of the mutable types, the chapter concentrates on lists; working with dictionaries or sets has a similar flavor. The standard terms *mutable* and *immutable* are part of Python jargon, and used in the official reference manual for the language. In this chapter, the word *mutation* is used not to mean some biological, evolutionary process, but rather to form and reform data, like sculpting clay.

The technical matter of this chapter can be difficult to understand quickly. Different readers of this may comprehend some parts, but not others. The approach may seem tedious because the same idea is expressed in several ways and with many examples. Probably the most useful programming technique is slice assignment. The notion of indirection, as implemented for lists and dictionaries in Python, is a core idea in modern software. A patient reading of this chapter will give a solid foundation for Chapter 27 on object-oriented software design.

Mutation and Assignment

Recall that there are two ways to change a variable representing a list, either assignment to the variable or indexed assignment (and deletion), which specifies an item as the target of the assignment. There is significant, if invisible, difference between these two. Both assignments to A, to the right, give variable A a *reference* to a list; the first assignment creates A, and the second assignment replaces A's reference, so that A refers to a new list. By contrast, the assignment

```
>>> A = [0,1,2,3,4]
>>> print("A = ",A)
A = [0, 1, 2, 3, 4]
>>> A = "time after time",split()
>>> print("A = ",A)
A = ['time', 'after', 'time']
>>> A[2] = False
>>> print("A = ",A)
['time', 'after', False]
```

to A[2] **does not change** A's reference. Rather, it *mutates* the list referenced by A. These words may just seem like semantics, making some distinction that really has no practical consequence. Hold on. Later in the chapter, there are examples that will demonstrate these differences are important. For now, just be aware that there is some internal distinction between assigning without an index and assigning to an item.

Slice Assignment

An attractive syntax feature of Python is the ability to assign to a slice of a list. The syntax is simple once the concept of slices is understood: specify a slice on the left side of "=" and that slice is replaced by the expression on the right side. Note that the expression on the right side must be a sequence: since a slice itself is a sequence, Python needs to have a sequence to replace it. The example here shows that **False** cannot be assigned to a slice because **False** is

```
>>> X = [2,4,6,8,10,12,14,16]
>>> X[2:2+3] = ['a','b','c']
>>> X
[2, 4, 'a', 'b', 'c', 12, 14, 16]
>>> X[2:3] = False
TypeError: can only assign an iterable
>>> X[2:3] = 'x'
>>> X
[2, 4, 'x', 'b', 'c', 12, 14, 16]
```

not an iterable (consider the term **iterable**, for now, to be a sequence). So, even if the slice only has a single item, it is still a *list* of one item—a sequence is needed to replace it. By contrast, the assignment of **'x'** to the slice does not cause an error, because **'x'** is a sequence (strings are sequences). Types matter.

```
>>> X = [2,4,6,8,10,12,14,16]
>>> X[4:] = "1/2/3",split('/')
>>> X
[2, 4, 6, 8, '1', '2', '3']
>>> X[3:3+2] = []
>>> X
[2, 4, 6, '2', '3']
```

What makes slice assignment particularly useful is that the length of the slice and the length of the sequence on the right side of the assignment can differ. The first slice assignment, to X[4:], replaces a slice with four items by a sequence of length 3. Hence, slice assignment can delete items. This is shown more dramatically by the assignment to X[3:3+2], which obliterates two items.

```
>>> X = [2,4,6,8,10,12,14,16]
>>> X[2:2] = [True,False]
>>> X
[2, 4, True, False, 6, 8, 10, 12, 14, 16]
>>> X[0:0] = [100]
[100, 2, 4, True, False, 6, 8, 10, 12, 14, 16]
>>> X[0:len(X)] = [1,3,5]
>>> X
[1,3,5]
```

By the same logic, slice assignment can be used to insert items by replacing an empty slice. Two instances are shown here, the first inserting a sequence of two items just after the second item in X, and then a single-item list containing 100 is inserted before the first item in X. The final slice assignment of the example replaces the entire list; that

assignment could also have been written more concisely by "X[:] = [1,3,5]" with the same effect. This example is another illustration of the two kinds of assignment, variable replacement and mutation. The last slice assignment is mutation, because it replaces the list that X refers to, whereas the initial assignment at the start of the example gives X a new reference to a list. While it might seem like a meaningless distinction now, later in this chapter we see evidence that they are different.

Slice Deletion. The del statement can remove a range of items, as given by the slice notation:

```
>>> L = [5,6,7,8,9,10,11,12,13]
>>> del L[3:6]
>>> L
[5, 6, 7, 11, 12, 13]
>>> del L[2:2]
>>> L
[5, 6, 7, 11, 12, 13]
```

Observe that deleting an empty slice has no effect.

Mutating Methods

A number of sequence methods are *mutating methods*. A mutating method changes the list referenced by a variable, while leaving the reference unchanged. After we look at some built-in mutating methods here, we see in the following section how to write mutating functions. A mutating function can change containers (lists, dictionaries, sets, and similar things) referenced in variables that are arguments to the function.

sort. The sort() method rearranges the items of a list into increasing order. A quick example of this is shown to the right. It is possible to put keyword parameters to sort() and get a decreasing-order sort. Notice that,

```
>>> Y = [5,2,9,3,1,0,8]
>>> Y.sort()
>>> Y
[0,1,2,3,5,8,9]
```

A Functional Start to Computing with Python

unlike methods like `index()` and `count()`, the `sort()` method returns `None` this is why you do not see any output above after `Y.sort()`. Rather, `sort()` quietly does its job, which is to mutate the list into a sorted order.

> *Remark.* Python also has a built-in function `sorted()` which takes a sequence argument and returns a sorted copy of the sequence; function `sorted()` is non-mutating, whereas the `sort()` method is a mutator.

reverse. The `reverse()` method mutates a list by putting the items in reverse order. There is also a nonmutating, built-in function named `reversed()`. (You may recall that `reversed(S)` for a sequence returns the same as the expression `S[::-1]`.)

```
>>> Y = "let us go there".split()
>>> Y.reverse()
>>> Y
['there', 'go', 'us', 'let']
```

```
>>> Z = [5==5, 2>5, "RA", 7]
>>> Z.append(20)
>>> Z
[True, False, 'RA', 7, 20]
>>> Z.append([30])
>>> Z
[True, False, 'RA', 7, 20, [30]]
```

append. The `append()` method mutates a list by adding an item to the list. Note that the argument for `append()` is an item, which does not need to be a sequence. The last part of the example makes this clear, as it adds a list as the last item. A technical explanation for `append()` is that it does what slice assignment does:

`A.append(B)` is the same as `A[len(A):] = [B]`. If instead you want `A[len(A):] = B`, use the `extend()` method.

Other List-Mutating Methods. The Python reference manual describes several other mutating methods: `extend()`, `insert()`, `remove()`, and `pop()`. These are not essential to know, but it is likely you will see them and later use them as your familiarity with Python grows.

Mutation in Functions

The previous section on mutating methods presented a few methods and showed examples, but did not really explain how these methods can mutate a variable of type `list`. To get some idea of the programming techniques that a mutation method might use, this section shows how to write a *mutating function*. The interesting twist is how Python uses indirection to get around the limitation of variable scope. Mutating assignment can change the

```
def NewAppend(L,x):
    L[len(L):] = [x]
...
>>> V = [1,3,4]
>>> NewAppend(V,99)
>>> V
[1,3,4,99]
```

list of a variable of a function's caller, without using the `global` statement. Obviously from this example, a function is able to change a list given as a parameter. Does this contradict what Chapter 16 says about variable scope? The answer is no, but to understand why, we need to look a bit deeper at how Python does binding. When Python evaluates the function application `NewAppend(V,99)`, it creates a local dictionary for `NewAppend`, and puts two entries into this dictionary, one for `L` and one for `x`. The subtle point is that the value for `L` *is not* the list `[1,3,4]`; rather, it is a *reference* to that list. After the local dictionary has been created, but before the evaluation of the NewAppend completes, there are temporarily *two variables* that refer to the same list, L in NewAppend's scope, and V in the interactive session. When NewAppend does a mutating assignment, the list referenced by both variables changes. Ways that a function can mutate a list are index assignment, slice assignment, or the use of a list mutating method.

To reinforce the point about mutating assignment in a function, we make some small changes to the previous example. Each of the versions below makes two assignments to the argument L, but with different effects.

```
def NewAppend(L,x):
  L[len(L):] = [x]
  L = [True]
...
>>> V = [1,3,4]
>>> NewAppend(V,99)
>>> V
[1,3,4,99]
```

```
def NewAppend(L,x):
  L = [True]
  L[len(L):] = [x]
...
>>> V = [1,3,4]
>>> NewAppend(V,99)
>>> V
[1,3,4]
```

In the left version, the first assignment mutates L. The second assignment is nonmutating, so it gives L a reference to a new list. This reference to a new list does not change what V refers to, so the mutation to L is retained and accessible through V, whereas the second assignment has no effect on V. What about the version on the right? This time, before the mutating assignment was done, the reference of L had already been changed to something different from what V refers to. The point of the example is to prepare for the next sections, which build a mental model justifying Python's behavior for such programs.

⇨ web

Aliases

The previous examples and the discussion of mutation are some evidence that Python uses an indirect way of connecting variables to list values. The binding of a list variable to a parameter connects two variables to the same list, but there is a much simpler way to do this in Python. The assignment Kcopy = K creates variable Kcopy and gives it, as a value, a *reference* to the same list that K refers to. Therefore, when the list itself was mutated by index assignment, both K and Kcopy

```
>>> K = [6,2,9,4]
>>> Kcopy = K
>>> K[1] = True
>>> K
[6, True, 9, 4]
>>> Kcopy
[6, True, 9, 4]
```

refer to the same, mutated list. Another way to see the distinction is to use more than one list and the == comparison operator.

```
>>> J = [9,9,4]
>>> Jcopy = J
>>> W = [9,9,4]
>>> J == Jcopy, J == W, Jcopy == W
True, True, True
>>> Jcopy[2] = 'a'
>>> J == Jcopy, J == W, Jcopy == W
True, False, False
>>> J, W
[9, 9, 'a'], [9, 9, 4]
```

Two facts underly this example. First, even though the initial assignments to J and W give the same list value to each variable, it is clear from the later behavior that J and W do not refer to the *same* list. This is made clear when the Jcopy indexed assignment mutates the list that J references. Although J and W refer to different lists, the first comparison J == W evaluates to True, because the two lists have identical items.

One way to think about the previous example is to imagine Python has some table of names and values, like a dictionary. The table contains some hidden names, known only to Python, which are α and β. These hidden names have lists as their values, but the variable names do not. The variable names have hidden names for values. This is why we say mutable variables are *indirect* references to values. Though it is more

name	value
J	α
Jcopy	α
W	β
α	[9,9,4]
β	[9,9,4]

difficult to understand mutable than immutable types, the features of mutable variables are quite useful: there are mutating methods and ways to change lists passed as arguments to functions.

The concept of having multiple references to the same thing is an abstraction used widely in software. Probably the most familiar instance is how files and directories (folders) are organized. In Windows, you can create a *shortcut* to a file or application. A shortcut is not a copy of a file, because a copy would take up disk space; a shortcut is another name that can be used in place of the file and moved to the desktop or some other folder. The Linux/Unix term for this is a *link* to a file. The Python jargon for two variables that refer to the same list is *alias*. For the example above, `Jcopy` is an alias for the list that `J` references.

web

Equality of Reference. Two list variables can be equal, when compared by the == operator, even when they refer to different lists. Is there some way to see if two variables refer to the same list without mutating one of them, then checking that this mutation happened to the other one? Python has an operator just for this question. The is operator compares the *references* for two variables. It returns `True` only when the two variables refer to the same list. Above, `E is F` remains `True` up to the statement

```
>>> E = F = "tick tock clock".split()
>>> G = "tick tock clock".split()
>>> E == F, E == G, F == G
True, True, True
>>> E is F, E is G, F is G
True, False, False
>>> E[0] = 1.5
>>> E is F
True
>>> F = range(10)
>>> E is F
False
```

`F = range(10)`, which is a nonmutating assignment. The assignment to F gives it a new reference, different from E's.

Mutation and Augmented Assignment

The general rule for assignment, with regard to mutation, is that any kind of assignment except indexed or sliced assignment makes a new reference rather than mutating a list. It does not matter whether augmented assignment (e.g., `+=`) or tuple assignment is used, what matters is whether the variable on the left side of the assignment is indexed or sliced. There is one exception to the general rule.

Recall `append()` is a mutating method which adds an item to the end of a list. A similar method, `extend()`, inserts a list at the end of a list, seen by example to the right. The `extend()` method is thus a kind of concatenation method. The exception to the general rule is that Python translates "`+=`" for lists into a method call to `extend()`. The example on the left, below,

```
>>> A = B = [1,2]
>>> A.extend([3,4])
>>> B
[1, 2, 3, 4]
```

demonstrates this exception. However, in the example on the right, Python does not use `extend()` for what seems to be an equivalent way of concatenating. On the right, the second assignment to A gave it a new reference rather than mutate the list of the existing reference. You may never run into this particular oddity of Python's "+=" behavior, but if it catches you by surprise, debugging can be painful.

```
>>> A = B = [1,2]
>>> A += [3,4]
>>> A is B
True
>>> B
[1, 2, 3, 4]
```

```
>>> A = B = [1,2]
>>> A = A + [3,4]
>>> A is B
False
>>> B
[1, 2]
>>> A
[1, 2, 3, 4]
```

☆ ☆ ☆

Items as References

Previous examples demonstrate how different variables can be aliases to the same list (using a hidden name and indirect reference). The same idea also pertains to the items of sequences, e.g., lists, tuples, and dictionaries. Furthermore, an item *within* a list or dictionary can, in turn, be a reference to a sequence. The example here creates C to have a list for each item. The result looks surprising: the single assignment A[1] = 0 appears to have changed list C in two places. This is not a correct understanding: two items of list C actually refer to the same thing, the list initially defined by A. This example is well worth pondering: it shows both the power of allowing aliases as well as the confusion it might create when not used carefully.

```
>>> A = [1,2]
>>> B = A
>>> C = [A,[3,4],B]
>>> C
[[1,2], [3,4], [1,2]]
>>> C[2] is A
True
>>> C[0] is C[2]
True
>>> A[1] = 0
>>> C
[[1,0], [3,4], [1,0]]
```

Cloning

```
>>> A = [1,2]
>>> B = A
>>> del A
>>> B
[1, 2]
```

When you use a copy machine to reproduce a printed sheet of paper, you get a new sheet of paper, hopefully identical to the original for practical purposes. You can tear the copy, write on it, crumple it, and the original is unaffected. We have seen that B = A does not make a copy of a list, it makes another reference to a list. A nice illustration of this fact is shown on the left. After B = A, both variables refer to the same list. When variable A is deleted, the underlying list is not destroyed; there remains a reference B to the list. Python only destroys an actual list (and recycles memory) once all references to that list are gone.

Sometimes, making another reference to a list is exactly what is wanted. Parameter binding to list arguments makes another reference to a list, which is why functions can mutate list variables given in their arguments. In other situations, we may not want to make another reference, because a copy works better. A copy can be changed without changing the original. The easy way to make a copy is the trick shown here. Recall that `A[:]` *creates a new copy* of sequence `A`, not another reference to the existing sequence.

```
>>> A = [1,2]
>>> B = A[:]
>>> B == A
True
>>> B is A
False
>>> B[-1] = 99
>>> B
[1, 99]
>>> A
[1, 2]
```

```
>>> A = [1,[2,3],4]
>>> B = A[:]
>>> B[0] = 'x'
>>> B
['x', [2,3], 4]
>>> A
[1, [2,3], 4]
>>> B[1][0] = 'y'
>>> B
['x', ['y',3], 4]
>>> A
[1, ['y',3], 4]
```

Shallow versus Deep Copy.   One of the tricky topics this chapter has not covered is the issue of indirect references to lists when they are nested. Nested lists can be copied in several ways, with the extremes being *shallow copy* and *deep copy*. A shallow copy is simply `B = A[:]`. What more could one ask of copying? The example shows that although `B` is different from `A`, the second item of `B` is actually a reference to the same list that the second item of `A` references. A shallow copy only copies "one level" of a nested list. A *deep copy* would make copies at all levels of nesting. How to do a deep copy of a list is a topic beyond this chapter, but a simple example given next hints at how it can be done.

In the example on the right, `B` is defined twice, the first time as a shallow copy, and the second time as a deep copy. The key difference shows up in the alias test `B[1] is A[1]`: `True` for the shallow copy, but `False` for the deep copy. For some applications, the problem with the shallow copy is that a mutation of some item in a shallow copy could also change the value of the aliased original variable. With a deep copy, this is not a danger. Though the technique above for making a deep copy is specific to the particular example of `A`, the general technique is not too hard to imagine. There would need to be some nested way of cloning a list (or a dictionary) all the

```
>>> A = [1,[2,3],4]
>>> B = A[:]
>>> B is A
False
>>> B[1] is A[1]
True
>>> B == A
True
>>> B = [ A[0], A[1][:], A[2] ]
>>> B is A
False
>>> B[1] is A[1]
False
>>> B == A
True
```

way through the levels of nesting. Note, by the way, for a list containing only immutable items (numbers, strings, booleans), that there is no difference between shallow and deep copying. The Python standard library has a module `copy`, which makes deep copies of nested containers; Chapter 18 introduces the topic of modules in Python.

Terminology Review

Jargon in this chapter includes: mutable versus immutable types; mutating methods; aliases; references to lists; the `is` operator; cloning (shallow copy versus deep copy).

Exercises

These exercises use the Python2 style of the **print** statement and ask what will be printed. It is better to start with interactive (calculator mode) sessions and experiment with assignment before writing functions that mutate arguments.

(1) What will be the result of this interaction with Python?

```
>>> M,varX,varY,t = ("team",[],"sample",[True,False])
>>> print len(M)*len(varX) + len(varY)*len(t)
```

(2) What will Python print here?

```
>>> if = "el"
>>> if += "if"
>>> print if
```

(3) What is printed in this interactive session?

```
>>> t3,t4 = [50,2], "going going gone"
>>> t4 = t4.split()
>>> t3 += t4
>>> print t3
```

(4) What does Python print?

```
>>> a = b = "sub urban"
>>> a[3] = "-"
>>> print b
```

(5) For this question, first a function definition is given, then the interactive part follows. What does Python print?

```
def YR(z):
  z[0] *= 2

>>> X = Y = ["F","a","s","t"]
>>> YR(Y)
>>> print "".join(X+Y)
```

(6) What will Python print?

```
>>> A1 = {"A":9, "B":8, "C":7, "D":6}
>>> A2 = A1
>>> A2[0] = False
>>> print A1
>>> A2 = type(A2)
>>> print A1
```

(7) What will Python print?

```
>>> wall,table,lamp,desk = ("plane","K",[True,2,0],"neighbor")
>>> print len(table)*len(lamp)*len(desk)
```

(8) What will be printed?

```
>>> Camp = [True,True,77,88]
>>> Camp += 99
>>> print Camp
```

(9) What is the printed output for the following?

```
>>> t3,t4 = "going going gone", ["found","here"]
>>> t3 = t3.split()
>>> t3 += t4
>>> print t3
```

(10) What is printed?

```
>>> a = b = [4,3,5,2,1,6,7]
>>> a[-1:] = [False,False]
>>> print b
```

(11) For this question, first a function definition is given, then the interactive part follows.

```
def YR(z):
  if len(z[0])>0:
    z[0] = z[0].upper()

>>> X = Y = "easy beat for dancing".split()
>>> YR(Y)
>>> print " ".join(X+Y)
```

(12) What is printed here?

```
>>> A2 = {"A":9, "B":8, "C":7, "D":6}
>>> A1 = A2
>>> A2[0] = True
>>> print A1
>>> A2 = type(A2)
>>> print A1
```

Chapter 18:   Modules

Most imports come from outside of the country.
— George W. Bush

A text file containing Python statements can be run from a terminal with a command. This way of using Python is a *script*, which may contain function definitions, variable assignments, print statements, and more. Another way to organize Python statements is to distribute them among several files. One of these files can be a script we might designate as *the main program*, whereas others contain bits of Python that the main program uses.

The terminology for a file that is not an independent script, but contains Python statements, is a *module*. A module is nothing more than a file containing Python statements, function definitions, and variable assignments. The way that a (main) program uses the contents of a module is to "include" or "import" it. Python has special statements to import modules. Typically, a Python program imports the modules it needs near the beginning of the program. Without having an import statement, a program cannot use a module.

Roughly speaking, there are three kinds of modules. (*i*) Standard library modules, which are distributed along with Python—these modules are always available to use, and the official Python manual and supporting documents explain what these modules offer. Examples of such modules are ones that have mathematical functions, communication network facilities, and time/date formatting and conversion tools. (*ii*) Externally provided modules have been written by volunteers and by many organizations. Examples of these are game-building kits, graphical display managers, web development frameworks, and scientific libraries. (*iii*) Local modules are things that you, or persons in some local department in an organization, write. Even beginners can find it useful to arrange functions into different modules.

Type (*ii*), modules external to the standard library, are for many (if not most) people, the real attraction of Python. At the end of this chapter is a section named *treasure*, describing some of the better known software packages and modules that contribute to Python's popularity as a computing platform. Unfortunately, installing externally available modules is not always simple and perhaps not even possible with both Python2 and Python3. This book generally (with the exception of one drawing tool) avoids depending on external modules for introducing computing with Python.

Import Statements

Let's say you have a main program in a file named `myprog.py` and a module named `myutil.py`, as shown in Figure 18.1, with `myprog.py` on the left and `myutil.py` on the right. The syntax of the *import statement* in the figure is "`from myutil import *`."

```
from myutil import *                    def times(x,y):
T = [6,20,13] + range(1,4)                  return x*y
print product(T)                        def product(V):
                                            return reduce(times,V)
```

Figure 18.1: Main program and module it uses.

Running `myprog.py` is seen on the right. The main program `myprog.py` was able to use the function defined in the module `myutil.py`. Note that there is nothing special about the contents of `myutil.py`: Python will even allow you to use the

```
$ python myprog.py
9360
```

file as a main program sometimes and as a module at other times. Thus, being a module is a *role* for a file containing Python definitions. If you use an import statement to bring in the definitions from another file, then that other file is considered to be a module. Note also that the filename's suffix ".py" is *not* given in the import statement. Python automatically assumes that the module name is a file that has suffix ".py."

```
>>> from math import *
>>> log(50)
3.912023005428146
>>> pi
3.1415926535897931
>>> sin(pi)
1.2246063538223773e-16
```

Modules can also be used in interactive sessions. A common instance of this is the standard `math` module. The `math` module defines many mathematical functions as well as certain variables (`pi` and `e`). Observe that `sin(pi)` returned a very small number (rather than the true mathematical value zero) because floating point arithmetic only approximates real arithmetic. Somewhere in Python's software libraries there needs to be a file named `math.py`; the question of where `math.py`

can be found, what it contains, and how it is documented will be explained later.

Selective Import

```
from B import *
from C import *
```

Import can be used within modules as well as in the main program. The main program could be `A.py`, which has an import statement "`from B import *`," implying there is a file `B.py`. The file `B.py` could also have an import statement, such as "`from C import *`," to bring definitions in from `C.py`. Alternatively, a different main program might import both `B.py` and `C.py`: the first two lines in the main program could be those shown in the box above. After these two lines, the main program can use functions defined in `B.py` and functions defined in `C.py`.

There is a potential problem, however, when importing from two or more modules. What if two modules define the same function? For example, it could be that `B.py` defines a function `raxor`, and also `C.py` defines a function named `raxor` that does something completely different from the one inside `B.py`. Which one will the importing program get to use? The general answer is that the second module to be imported overwrites the definitions of the first module that was imported. An import statement "`from C import *`" overwrites any defined functions or variables that have the same names as the ones in `C.py`. This fact means one should take care using this kind of statement.

```
from B import *
from C import capit
```

Most often, the people who write programs importing modules do not know all the function names inside a module, and really are only interested in a few things. Python offers a more refined way of importing. To illustrate, suppose that a main program only needs a function `capit` from `C.py`. The first two lines of the main program could be those in the shaded box. Now, even if `C.py` has a `raxor` function that would overwrite the one `B.py` has defined, there is no conflict: only the function `capit` is brought in from `C.py`.

The same technique can be used to import multiple definitions. This example selectively imports just three things from `math`; because *only* the named variables and functions are imported, other things from `math`, like `cos`, `log`, and `exp`, are not available to the importing program.

```
>>> from math import pi, e, sin
>>> sin(e**pi)
-0.91257759866927624
```

Namespaces

```
>>> import math
>>> math.sin(2*math.pi)
-2.4492127076447545e-16
>>> pi
NameError: name 'pi' is not defined
>>> math.pi
3.1415926535897931
>>> math.ki
AttributeError: 'module' object has
              no attribute 'ki'
```

Python offers an entirely different idea for managing name conflicts, that is, conflicts between existing function or variable names and those imported from modules. The idea is to retain the module name as part of the function names. The Python statement to accomplish this is "import," shown by this example. The simple "import math" makes the functions and variables of the `math` module accessible, but they need an extra *qualifier* as part of the name. The Python jargon for "`math.pi`" labels the part before the period, `math`, as the qualifier or module name, and the part following the period is called the *attribute*. Above, both `sin` and `pi` are used as attributes. The last line of the example shows Python complaining that "`math.ki`" is an error, because there is no function or variable `ki` in the `math` module; in other words, Python cannot find the *attribute* named `ki` within `math.py`.

Typically, we may think of modules brought in by an `import` statement in a way similar to how function bodies deal with variable names. Recall that within a function, as it runs, Python sets up a new name dictionary for evaluating the function's statements and expressions. For modules, Python adds to the current name dictionary, enlarging the "space" of names. Since each imported module has its own qualifier (using the module's name), we can think of separate *namespaces*, one for each module. The qualified name "`math.sin`" refers to the name "sin" within the namespace of `math`.

```
import A
import B
import C
print ( A.foo(), B.foo(), C.foo() )
```

With this style of importing, a script could use two functions named `foo()` found in different modules. For example, there could be modules `A`, `B`, `C` imported in a script. The `print` can refer to the three different `foo` functions without any name conflict, thanks to the qualifiers and separate namespaces.

Many Python modules and main programs use `import` statements for more than one module. A typical example, shown here, imports typical modules from the standard library. The example shows that four modules are imported, though perhaps more are imported indirectly, behind the scene, because modules may import modules. The same example could be more concisely expressed as

```
import sys
import os
import csv
import time
```

```
import sys, os
import csv, time
```

Or, using just one line `import sys, os, csv, time`. All of these forms of using `import` get the same result.

Name Queries

Python has a built-in function to query the namespace for modules (and for other things as well). The function `dir()` can be used interactively to see what names are currently used. The example shows that after starting Python, `dir()` returns a list of three names. These un-

```
$ python
Python 2.5.2
>>> dir()
['__builtins__', '__doc__', '__name__']
```

usual names are the "hidden" internal namespaces of Python. To see something more understandable, we continue the example by importing `math`:

```
>>> import math
>>> dir()
['__builtins__', '__doc__', '__name__', 'math']
>>> type(math)
<type 'module'>
```

The `dir()` function now returns a list containing a new namespace, reflecting the fact that `math` has been imported. Observe also that Python identifies the type of "math" to be a module. What if you now would like to list the names *inside* of a namespace?

```
>>> dir(math)
['__doc__', '__file__', '__name__', 'acos', 'asin',
'atan', 'atan2', 'ceil', 'cos', 'cosh', 'degrees',
'e', 'exp', 'fabs', 'floor', 'fmod', 'frexp', 'hypot',
'ldexp', 'log', 'log10', 'modf', 'pi', 'pow', 'radians',
'sin', 'sinh', 'sqrt', 'tan', 'tanh']
>>> type(math.degrees)
<type 'builtin_function_or_method'>
>>> type(math.e)
<type 'float'>
```

You can see that the namespace for the `math` module has an assortment of things. More can be learned about the names using Python's `type()` function.

Module Help

Python standard modules, like `math`, `time`, `sys`, `os`, `csv`, and hundreds more, have some limited documentation. You can see this documentation using Python's built-in `help()` function. For example:

```
$ python
Python 2.5.2
>>> import math
>>> help(math)
NAME
    math
FILE
    /usr/lib/python2.5/lib-dynload/math.so
MODULE DOCS
    /usr/doc/python-2.5.2/html/module-math.html
DESCRIPTION
    This module is always available.  It provides access
    to the mathematical functions defined by the C standard.
FUNCTIONS
    acos(...)
        acos(x)

        Return the arc cosine (measured in radians) of x.
```

This documentation continues for many screens full of text; you might need to press the space bar many times to go through it all interactively.

Python Standard Library

Increasingly, useful Python programs cannot be written without use of modules from the standard library, which comes with all Python distributions, and extra modules such as described later in this chapter. Consult `http://docs.python.org/library/` to see a catalog of the modules in the standard library. The main Web page for Python has the caption, for this catalog, "keep this under your pillow." There are many modules covering different application domains, but a few that merit highlighting here are:

> `functools`, `itertools`, `operator` modules are mentioned in Chapters 13 and 14. Some useful data types are found in the `collections` module.

> `random`, `time`, `sys`, `os` are covered in Chapter 28; the `subprocess` module is illustrated in Chapter 27. Chapter 26 uses several network-oriented modules. For detailed parsing of Web pages (that contain HTML), there are parsing modules in the standard library.

> The `csv` module is quite useful for parsing comma-separated files, commonly exported from spreadsheet applications.

> Chapter 29 shows examples using the `Tkinter` module, for interactive window programs.

Some of these modules are either exercises at the end of the chapter or are used in later chapters (the `doctest` module was introduced earlier, in "Exercise: Unit Testing and Online Supplement" after Chapter 10).

Module Placement

When you write your own modules, they will probably be placed in the same directory (folder) as the main program. When Python encounters an `import` statement (or a `from` statement), it *searches* for a corresponding ".py" file in the current directory (folder) where the program is being run. Can modules be placed elsewhere? Yes, but the rules for what is allowed and how Python searches for modules are complex due to the various different operating systems (Windows, Unix, etc.), which have their own individually tailored organization of files and directories. For example, there can be a `PYTHONPATH` variable set in operating system configurations, which tells Python where to search for modules.

The standard modules that are distributed with an installation of Python, like `math`, `sys`, `time`, and so on, have been highly optimized for efficiency. Many of these modules are in fact mostly written in `C` or another language to take advantage of hardware features or to use memory more efficiently. Other standard modules are written in Python, for example `unittest.py` is a module for unit testing. The standard modules are placed in a directory that is automatically searched no matter where a main program being run is located. The location of this special Python directory depends on the operating system. If you are curious, you can find this directory and explore the code that implements modules.

Third-party modules are ones not distributed with an installation of Python; they are typically added to a system by downloading a "kit" or package via the Internet and then following some installation instructions. Python has a special directory for such added software, typically containing subdirectories (subfolders) for each package. The third-party modules are typically put in these directories, and Python will automatically search for modules in these places. Some packages give the user an option, during the installation process, to place the modules in a directory specified by the person doing the installation.

Optimization and Byte-Code. When you initially start using your own modules, you will possibly be surprised to see new files appearing in the same directory of the modules. When Python imports a module, it first *compiles* the module into a form that is easier to run (but impossible for human viewing). Thus, for a module `abc.py`, Python creates a file `abc.pyc` containing the compiled, or *byte-code* version of the module. It is called *byte-code* because it contains instructions for a virtual machine that executes code particular to Python.

Name Abbreviation

Python modules are proliferating, making all kinds of special features and computing platforms accessible through Python programming. One consequence of this proliferation is that we have run out of simple, intuitive names for modules. Increasingly, modules are being organized into directories (folders) and possibly even subdirectories. In Python2, for example, the shell command `python -m SimpleHTTPServer` runs the module named `SimpleHTTPServer`, which is part of the standard Python library, as a main program (this starts a Web server). However, in Python3, to better organize modules, this has been changed to `python3 -m http.server`, because there is now a directory named `http` in the standard library, which has a module named `server` in that directory. The period (".") here is syntax for a path: the statement `import x.y.z` would bring in module `z`, found in subdirectory `y` of directory `x`.

The use of directories and generally having longer module names can make it cumbersome to use a simple `import` statement. It is inconvenient to write `Acme.CRM.site.foo(m)` to invoke a function `foo`. To streamline such cases, Python provides the `as` keyword for importing modules. Instead of writing `import Acme.CRM.site` and then using the full name for invoking functions in the module, one can write this:

```
import Acme.CRM.site as Ac
```

After this, `Ac` works as an abbreviation for the full name of the module: `Ac.foo(m)` can be used to call `foo` with argument `m`. The use of "`as`" for abbreviation can also be used with function names in statements such as `from Acme.CRM.site import foo as f`, after which `f(m)` calls the `foo` function from the module.

Learning More

Online resources and examples are the best source for learning about modules. The Python documentation (available at `www.python.org`) lists all the standard modules, their functions, methods, and variables, with a few small examples. Generally, the official Python documentation assumes you already know most of the Python language and concepts, and even skips over simple facts (like adding qualifiers to the names, using the import statements, and so on). It is better for beginners to find some tutorial that uses a module and learn how to use it. The official Python documentation is useful as a catalog, to learn what kinds of modules are offered and what features have been added with new versions of Python.

APIs, SDKs, Frameworks

Many software systems have their own ways of interacting with users, displaying and managing data. Yet, there could be additional features that designers did not build into the system. Some systems provide an *application programmer interface* (API) so that users who know how to program can interact with the system using some defined functions and data layouts. There can be a library of API calls, which enable users to enhance and manage the software system in novel ways. Beyond APIs, some systems and products have a *software development kit* (SDK), which can include tools, software, and hardware, in addition to an API library. Using an SDK, a developer can extend a system's capabilities and interfaces and even allow for a distributed value-enhanced version of the original product.

Related to APIs and SDKs is the concept of a *framework*. Whereas a software system might be completely usable without needing to tinker with an API or SDK, the intent of a framework is software that is incomplete, yet designed to be completed and customized by the framework's user. A typical instance of a framework is a Web server. It is up to the user to configure, write code, and use tools to make a Web server usable. Frameworks can have API calls and SDK-like features, but usually have more powerful ways to control and manipulate the system. In some frameworks, the framework user writes a function that the framework calls to guide decisions and control the look-and-feel of output and input.

The World of Packages

A *package* is typically a collection of modules, but can also include documentation, extra files, and even code written in languages other than Python. External modules are usually added to a Python library using some package installation technique. Search engines can help one find modules, examples, or working applications based on Python. Before trying external packages, it is wise to check whether the new modules will be compatible with the current Python version, and whether the new modules require yet other software in order to work. Indeed, for some externally provided modules, there may be a "laundry list" of things to do, other software to install first, licenses to review, and decisions to be made about where libraries should reside.

Library Placement

Where does an externally provided module go when it is added to a system? The usual answer, assumed by nearly all installation procedures, is to put the new module in the "site-packages" of the current Python distribution directory (if a system has been set up with multiple Python versions, this becomes more difficult). On a Unix system, this directory is typically in an area that requires privileges for writing: so installing a new module would require more than ordinary privileges. It is possible, but more work, to install new modules to a subdirectory of a user's area; then some additional work would be needed to specify the subdirectory and set up some path information so that Python knows where to look for the new modules (which can be done by establishing a PYTHONPATH environmental variable or by an additional parameter on a command line). It is usually preferred to put new modules in the site-packages directory. Keep in mind that if a new version of Python is installed, the site-packages directory may be overwritten (emptied) or it may not be compatible with the new version of Python.

Automatic Installation

The easiest kind of software installation is one that automates all the steps. For this to be possible, someone else has done the hard work of writing installation scripts that discover the kind of computer, its operating system, versions of software previously installed, and perhaps hundreds of other crucial details, to know how the software should properly be installed. Professionally packaged software often has automatic ways to install packages; however, Python modules found through search engines may not be professionally packaged (sometimes you get what you pay for) and then more work has to be done.

"Easy" Install

A popular way to install Python modules is based on a package of modules called setuptools. Once this package has been installed, an "easy install" script, which runs as a command easy_install, can process "egg" files containing the material for new modules. The bootstrap process for using such Python eggs is to first, using a more manual procedure, install the setup tools. After that, other module installation becomes nearly automatic. The easy-install script will check for module dependencies, complaining if a module needs yet another module to be installed first, in order for everything to work properly. Here are some imagined examples of using easy-install:

```
$ easy_install http://www.acme.org/software/wondermod.tar.gz
$ easy_install --upgrade WonderMod
$ easy_install Downloads/wondermod-12.3.egg
```

Like more professional software tools, the easy-install command does try to automatically find dependencies and download them to complete a correct installation of new modules. Note that the setuptools package is not currently part of the official Python distribution or documentation, though it is well documented online. Recently, a newer mechanism for installing Python packages, pip, has been introduced as a replacement for `easy_install`; `pip` further automates the process of installing a package with dependencies (see `www.pip-installer.org`).

Setup Script

More primitive than easy-install/pip is the `distutils` package of Python. This is supported and documented by the official Python distribution. The recommended procedure is to download a compressed directory containing the new modules, unpack it, and find a `setup.py` script in the directory. Then, the shell command

```
$ python setup.py install
```

attempts to install the modules to Python's `site-packages` directory (needing administrative privileges to do so). There is an option to install the new modules to another directory,

```
$ python setup.py install --home=/home/user/py-lib
```

(adjust the name of the alternate directory as needed, remembering also to set up the Python search path for modules appropriately). On a Windows system, the procedure for using `setup.py` is similar. See the section on *Installing Python Modules* of the official Python documentation for more details.

Treasure

A list of popular and tested packages of Python modules and scripts can be viewed at

$$\text{http://pypi.python.org/pypi}$$

Packages continue to be improved, new packages supersede others, and the state of the art evolves: it is difficult to know what is best for your needs, let alone keep up with the torrent of packages being updated or added to such a list. In some cases, the best packages offer modules that are improvements over the Python standard library (particularly for networking modules). In other cases, the external modules might have some glitches, limitations, or depend on particular Python versions. Below, we have a list of some influential, popular, or useful packages. In addition to those listed, Python can be used in other contexts, like CGI scripts (e.g., called by an Apache Web server to respond to a browser request) and communication with Web services, social network apps, and database environments. Increasingly, Web-based software offers programming interfaces (usually APIs, or Application Programming Interfaces) to Python.

Numeric and Scientific Interests

A variety of packages support numerical methods, statistical analysis of data, advanced mathematical algorithms, and data visualization to explore results of calculations. Use the `NumPy` package for its numerical methods (another option is `Blaze`) and `SciPy` for libraries of scientific functions. The `matplotlib` library can graph and display data in simple up to complex visualization styles. Instead of installing each of these packages individually, many users now opt to obtain an all-in-one, commercial distribution of Python (see `http://www.python.org/getit/` for a list of available Python distributions).

For data analysis, the starting point is often to use built-in modules like `csv` and `re` to rearrange and convert data; then for analysis, the `pandas` package supplies many modules and functions for statistical models of data.

Less well known, but interesting to students, might be the `SymPy` package, which can do things like symbolic integration, solving equations and other math tasks, all by manipulating symbols rather than computing with values.

Games, Media, and Images

`Pygame` is the best-known game development package. It includes a media player and other tools for working with sounds, animation, and images, but there are also specialized packages outside of `PyGame` that manipulate media, such as `pyglet` or `pillow`, for working on images.

Natural Language and Text

For processing natural language, there is the Natural Language TookKit (`www.nltk.org`). There are packages for working with fonts, PDF files, PostScript, and some other formats for text. Related, but not natural language, are packages and modules geared to spreadsheets and `CSV` formats (Python's standard library has a module for `CSV`).

Data Mining and Machine Learning

A number of packages implement machine learning algorithms either in Python, or make available nonPython code through Python interfaces. Data mining of web-hosted information is chiefly done through packages that dig beneath markup languages to get at data; examples are `Scrapy` and `BeautifulSoup`. Other packages assist in data analysis, notably `pandas` and `databrewery`. For working with databases, there are too many packages to mention here; most database software installations have Python interfaces.

Web Frameworks

Let's say you would like to develop a Web site that goes beyond what Python's standard library has. A *Web framework* has features that automate data persistence (either by using files or working with a database), organize templates and page styles, and facilitate browser processing (using `HTML5`, `CSS`, Javascript, jQuery, or other technology). These frameworks have become sophisticated collections of packages, configuration files that take some effort to fully master. The Python is the "glue" to customize those parts of the framework that can give a Web site an individualized look-and-feel. `Django` is one of the best-known Python-based frameworks; many interesting Web sites have been built using the `Django` framework. Lighter weight, so-called micro-frameworks `Flask` and `Bottle` might be suited for small Web servers. There are also Wiki-oriented projects like `MoinMoin`.

Networking

The Google search engine was originally programming in Python, though to scale up, it had to be rewritten in more efficient languages. Python is still a valid choice for many networking tasks, including special-purpose servers and clients. On the server side, the `Tornado` framework and `Twisted` framework have better concurrency performance than the simple servers found in Python's standard library. On the client side, the `requests` package aims to be a more modern and reliable set of functions than what Python's standard library offers. For learning about how Web servers and browsers communicate, an "HTTP Proxy" server is quite valuable—there are several written in Python.

Desktop Windowing

If you are writing an application that has a graphical user interface, and you would like the interface to use the same look-and-feel as other applications on your system, then you will probably wish to go beyond what Python's standard library offers (Tk, see Chapter 29). The most widely used packages for GUI programming are WxWidgets and PyGTK. It can be simpler to avoid GUI programming altogether and use a combination of Web browser and Python-based server or a Web framework. However, for highly interactive applications with advanced graphics or multimedia work, windowing packages are the usual choice (PyGame depends on using such a package).

Exercises

The best way to do these exercises is to use online material, typically some example or tutorial page, that explains with examples how the module should be used. Such tutorial pages will probably refer to features of Python you do not know about, but you may be able to copy their examples and try them.

(1) Write a function numa(w) that takes a string w as parameter. The function should use the standard Python urllib module to read the Web page given by w and count the number of times the letter "a" occurs in the Web page. For example,

```
>>> numa("http://www.google.com/index.html")
393
```

(2) Use the standard Python calendar module to print an image of the current month, for instance, you could print this with a single print statement using the prmonth method.

```
        May 2011
Su Mo Tu We Th Fr Sa
 1  2  3  4  5  6  7
 8  9 10 11 12 13 14
15 16 17 18 19 20 21
22 23 24 25 26 27 28
29 30 31
```

(3) Read the documentation on the sys module, specifically the sys.argv variable. Write a script using that module, which prints the command line arguments when the script is run from a command prompt. For instance,

```
> python myscript.py 1 X 99
arguments are:  1, 'X', 99
```

would be an example of running such a script. (For more advanced parsing of command line options, the argparse, getopt and optparse modules are in the library.)

(4) Try the subprocess module in a script to execute a system command. After importing subprocess, a Python script should be able to list the current directory with a statement such as

```
subprocess.call("dir",shell=True)
```

(The `subprocess` command is also capable of returning a response from a command as a string, so that the Python script can extract information from the string; a later exercise in Chapter 27 has response processing.)

(5) Python cannot represent real numbers with infinite precision. However, there is a `Fraction` type in the standard library, available through the `fractions` module.

```
from fractions import Fraction
```

Experiment with the `Fraction` type. Other alternative numeric types and functions are found in the `decimal` module, also worth knowing about.

(6) An advanced exercise is to learn how Python libraries and packages work by exploring the code behind the standard libraries. To do this, you'll need to have Python installed on a machine where you can access system files (usually not the case when running Python from a browser in the "cloud") and where there is some way to search for files. Two starting points for such an exercise are:

- Locate the file `pprint.py`, which should be in the directory containing many of Python's standard library modules (`pprint` was introduced in the box "Pretty Printing" in Chapter 8). Use an editor to open the file and see what variables and functions are defined. You can try the same with other modules you see in the library. Many of the programming techniques are explained in later chapters (classes and objects come in Chapter 27). Some standard python modules, such as the `array` module, do not have Python source code. For the sake of efficiency, such modules are written in C or another low-level language.

- Find and read Python documentation on modules, which has a section on packages (a good place to start is `docs.python.org/tutorial`, which has a "packages" section). Several conventions of interest explained there are the `__init__.py` file, the `__all__` variable, and the notion of the `__main__` module.

Within Python modules, you may find that many variables start with an underscore character (`_`). This is a convention, which you can also look up, about so-called *private variables* (or class-local variables).

Chapter 19:   Repetition

Me and recursion don't get along.
— Computer Science Student

Automation is a hallmark of the Industrial Age. During the industrial revolution, repetitive tasks formerly done by people and horses came to be implemented by steam-powered machines; initially the machines were used selectively for the manufacture of clothing. Subsequently, transportation networks and a power infrastructure emerged, eventually moving to electricity for power. Transport networks connected natural resources to manufacturing facilities and to markets, and so the industrial age made machinery ubiquitous.

A story similar to the industrial revolution took place more recently in the Information Age, which has its roots in the automation of repetitive tasks like counting, summing, tabulating, and indexing. Initially, a limited range of calculators and computers could automate for local needs. Applications for these devices was limited to manufacturing, finance, and some specialized areas requiring calculation. Later, communication networks and an industry of low-cost switching devices connected computing globally, enabling nearly free information flow across countries and organizational boundaries. Thanks to the buildup of this infrastructure, the range of applications that automate information tasks expanded to entertainment, journalism, agriculture, and health sciences, to name a few areas.

The final frontier for computing is the automation of automation. This is still very much a research topic, with little progress to show. Roughly speaking, this goal of computing science is to put computer programming out of business. The holy grail is to create computing systems that automatically synthesize their own software. This vision needs far more than what programming languages offer. Nonetheless, we can look to programming languages to see how they help reduce repetition in many algorithms and for common application needs.

This chapter introduces the concepts of iteration and recursion, which are crucial ideas in computing. Some students find these ideas to be major stumbling blocks toward a deeper understanding of software. Indeed, learning about how to handle repetition in a programming language is a hurdle that must be passed to get on to more interesting things. Take your time; practice; do not be afraid to admit this is difficult material. The goal of the chapter is *only* to introduce Python's language features for repetition. It is not expected that you will know how to use these features from what is presented here. The objective is to show how Python interprets the statements.

Repeating Statements

We begin with a personal task of automation, making some address labels. A Python script to print a label could be the two **print** statements on the right. It turns out that the paper for printing labels is a special paper

```
print("123 Main Street")
print("Mytown, Oregon")
```

with a sticky side, and to be economical it would be best to print the label at least five times on one sheet. One way to do this is to make a script that repeats the **print** statements above five times. Some editors make this easy using copy-and-paste. This way of automating repetitive programming is *bad software practice*. If everyone used this technique, programs would be bloated, boring, and possibly difficult to maintain. For instance, if the address needs to be changed, one would have to use an editor to find-and-replace in all the places where the needed change occurs. There is a better way.

Some programming languages have a special statement of the form "do 5 times" which can be put in front of the print commands, which does exactly what we want. Unfortunately, Python does not have such a statement. Rather, Python offers the **for** statement, which has syn-

```
for c in "xxxxx":
    print("123 Main Street")
    print("Mytown, Oregon")
```

tax like **def** and **if**, needing a colon and indentation. We have seen **for** in Chapter 13 under the topic of list comprehension (custom lists). There, the **for** qualifies a variable with "in" specifying a sequence over which the variable ranges. The same holds for the **for** statement as well: The two **print** statements have to be indented by the same amount of whitespace, so that they align on the left. This indented part is the *body* of the **for** statement; the indented statements are sometimes called a *block* of statements (blocks of statements occur in function bodies, **if** statements, and other Python syntax). The odd thing is the syntax of the **for** statement above, which specifies that a variable c ranges over a string of five x characters; the variable c is not used in the body.

We could get exactly the same behavior another way. The **range(5)** acts as a sequence of five items. For either version, Python will repeat the running of both **print** statements in the body for each item of the sequence; the only fact that matters is the length of the sequence. You

```
for c in range(5):
    print("123 Main Street")
    print("Mytown, Oregon")
```

might wonder why this is any better than using an editor to copy-and-paste five times the same **print** commands. The answer is simple to show.

```
def PrintMany(n):
  for c in range(n):
    print("123 Main Street")
    print("Mytown, Oregon")
```

Here, inside the PrintMany function, the for statement will cause the print statements in its body to be run n times, where the value of n might *not be known* at the time of using an editor to write the Python statements. It could be that the value of n is determined when the script runs, by asking the user at the keyboard.

Informally, a repetition such as the for statement (or later, the while statement) is called a *loop*. Loop statements are central to all programming languages save the most primitive (assembly language may not have a loop statement). The body of the loop is the part (block of statements) that repeats in each cycle through the repetition.

For-Loops with Variables

```
print 0
print 2
print 4
print 6
print 8
```

Most often, repetition in software is not literally the same thing over and over, but a similar thing repeated with a slight variation. Consider the script shown here. Each line is different from any other, but there is definitely a repetitive pattern. What is needed is a way to "parameterize" the repetitive pattern so that a template of the pattern can be set up once and then repeated, with variation, for some number of times.

```
for i in range(0,9,2):
  print i
```

The for statement captures this pattern. This script and the previous one have equivalent output, but this one is preferable for programming purposes. It makes the program smaller and easier to understand, easier to work with and debug. Sometimes patterns are not as easy to see, and it takes some experience to recognize that a for statement can do the job.

To the right, we see an exception in the pattern, but it is limited to a single instance (the number 400). Python has just the feature needed to take care of exceptions in the logic of programming; if, else, and elif statements. The idea is to change the behavior of the script when the *loop variable* i takes on a certain value in the body of the for loop. Implicitly, when the script runs, the loop variable i is assigned the next value each time the body of the loop runs.

```
print 0
print 2
print 400
print 6
print 8
```

```
for i in range(0,9,2):
  if i == 4:
    print 400
  else:
    print i
```

The for loop above does the job of printing, on five lines, the numbers 0, 2, 400, 6, and 8. The if statement in the body of the loop causes the regular logic of "print i" to deviate when i is 4.

Understanding

Pause

This is right, take a moment to ask yourself. Do you *really* understand the for statement? The last section showed some examples, flatly asserting that the for statement produces something equivalent to repeating some Python statements. The students who claim to understand this upon first sight are most probably the ones who already know a programming language such as Java, C#, javascript, and so on. But if you do not have such experience, then it is unlikely you really understand how for works. Books and documents are poor media for explaining the for statement because the way Python treats for is a dynamic process. A better way to learn about repetition in a programming language would be some interactive game, or to experiment with for and build your own mental model of what is happening.

In spite of the inadequacies of the printed page, the following is an attempt to show how for works, in "slow motion." We start with the simple loop shown to the right. This loop will print the letters of "Hello," one at a time, on five lines.

```
for c in "Hello":
    print c
```

When Python encounters this loop, it will internally expand them into something like the Python statements shown to the left. This expanded view of how Python processes a for statement shows that nothing very complex or sophisticated is going on. Before each print c, the loop variable c is assigned the value that will be used by the body of the loop, in this case one print statement. The thing to remember when you see a for statement is that a repetitive series of assignments, one for each item in the sequence before the colon, will be interleaved with the repetition of the loop body.

```
c = 'H'
print c
c = 'e'
print c
c = 'l'
print c
c = 'l'
print c
c = 'o'
print c
```

Another example shown here expands both the for loop and the xrange function (recall that xrange is a generator in Python2, equivalent to range in Python3). Python stops the looping when another i = i + 2 would put i over the limit value 9 in the xrange sequence.

As a test of your understanding, what do you suppose is the last thing that would be printed (after At end) in the following script?

```
for i in range(0,9,2):
    print i
print "At end", i
```

```
for i in xrange(0,9,2):
    print i
```
———————————————
```
i = 0
print i
i = i + 2
print i
i = i + 2
print i
i = i + 2
print i
i = i + 2
print i
```

Loops on Condition: While Statements

Python has a statement for repetition that is more primitive than the `for` statement. It repeats the evaluation of its body so long as some condition holds. The `while` statement demands that a condition be given rather than a variable and a sequence. This is a primitive kind of repetition statement, resembling assembly language or other lower level computing languages. Without trying to explain it first, let's examine the "expanded view," which is the series of actions Python would do, expressed as statements.

```
v = 5
while v>0:
    print v*v*v
    v -= 1
```

```
v = 5
if v>0:
    print v*v*v
    v = v - 1
    if v>0:
        print v*v*v
        v = v - 1
        if v>0:
            print v*v*v
            v = v - 1
            if v>0:
                print v*v*v
                v = v - 1
                if v>0:
                    print v*v*v
                    v = v - 1
                    if v>0:
                        print v*v*v
                        v = v -1
```

(Let's stop here; most probably you get the idea.) In principle, the indentation and repetition could continue *ad infinitum*. To make things simpler, we show the same thing but with some of the expressions evaluated:

```
v = 5
if v>0:
    print 5*5*5
    v = 4
    if v>0:
        print 4*4*4
        v = 3
        if v>0:
            print 3*3*3
            v = 2
            if v>0:
                print 2*2*2
                v = 1
                if v>0:
                    print 1*1*1
                    v = 0
                    if v>0:
```

Here we can stop. The final `if` condition will evaluate to `False`, so it is fruitless to continue any longer.

The mechanism of Python's `while` statement should now be clear. The block of statements indented after the `while`, called the *body* of the `while` loop, will be repeated until the condition is evaluated to be `False`.

Using `while` has good and bad aspects. For some applications, it is not possible to know in advance how many times something should be repeated: the condition for halting repetition might be discovered during the course of repeating whatever is being done. In these cases, `for` will not do the job, and we need `while`. On the negative side, using `while` can accidentally result in the dreaded *infinite loop*, where the repetition goes on forever, because the condition of the `while` never becomes `False`.[1] The jargon term *loop* is generally used for repetition: "while loop" and "for loop" are common names for this kind of syntax in programming languages. Another one is a "do loop," because some programming languages have another syntax with a `do` statement. Still other widely used terminology is the term *iteration* in place of repetition.

As a final example on the `while` statement, recall the earlier `for` loop shown again here, to the right. Because `while` is more primitive than `for`, it is no surprise that we can express the same repetition using `while` as this `for` loop.

```
for i in range(0,9,2):
    print i
```

```
i = 0
while i<9:
  print i
  i = i + 2
i = 8
```

Why the `i = 8` at the end? Whereas `range(0,9,2)` represents the list `[0,2,4,6,8]`, the `while` statement above would actually put variable `i` up to the value `10` before finding out that `i<9` is `False`. Of course, putting `i` up to `10` goes too far, hence the assignment after the loop assigns it to the value it would have after the equivalent `for` loop.

Practice

Few people grasp all the consequences, let alone how to properly control loops with `for` and `while` upon first seeing them. Rather than explore all the ways loops can be used here, two later chapters, Chapters 22 and 23, are devoted to common patterns of loops found in practice. By studying these patterns and trying some exercises using these patterns, deeper understanding of loops should follow. The remainder of this chapter shows alternative ways of thinking about repetition using analogies and revisiting recursion (the earlier Chapter 14 focused on tail recursion).

---

[1]Technically, there is no such thing in practice as an infinite loop, because sooner or later someone will turn off the power.

Feedback Control

How do systems, be they engineered systems like aircraft on autopilot or biological systems, regulate their behavior? The answer is *feedback*. A simple temperature control system in a building samples the temperature inside, and if it is too cold, starts up a boiler or furnace. In contrast to engineered control systems, natural systems have evolved feedback mechanisms.

A classic example of feedback in nature is the relationship between predator and prey, sometimes shown by simulation (on the right is a typical simulation by the Lotka-Volterra equations). As the population of prey (e.g., rabbits) increases, the population of the predator (e.g., foxes) increases due to the increased food supply. The graph shows that increase is not immediate, because it takes time for the predators to reproduce. What happens is typical of many feedback systems: the predator increases beyond the available food supply, which is dwindling under pressure from the high level of predation.

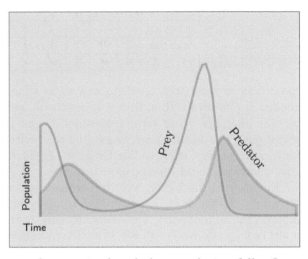

Eventually, the predator population cannot be sustained and the population falls. Once this happens to a sufficient degree, the prey can once again rebound. Our takeaway, for purposes of this chapter, is that a characteristic of feedback is a delay, or lag, between control actions and the system under control.

```
minval, minind, i = V[0], 0, 0
while i<len(V):
    if V[i]<minval:
        minval, minind = V[i], i
    i = i + 1
```

Something similar to the lag associated with feedback can be seen also in a Python `for`-loop. The loop shown here assigns `minval` to be the minimum value of a sequence V and also assigns `minind` to be the index of this minimum value in V. The loop has an interesting property when it runs. The body of the loop has three statements, the last being an increment to variable i. Immediately after Python performs an increment to i, the next statement will be the test of the `while` condition, to see whether or not further iterations are needed. Between finishing the increment to i and testing this condition, a special property is satisfied: `minval` is equal to the minimum of the slice `V[:i]`. This fact is not immediately obvious, so it is worth elaborating a bit. Let $\mathcal{P}$ be a symbol representing the property that `minval` equals `min(V[i:])`. Now consider what happens when the loop first starts: if `minval` is not smaller than the next item `V[i]`, then `minval` is wrong for property $\mathcal{P}$ once i is again incremented—in which case, `minval` has to be corrected. Technically, each iteration of the loop might "break" property $\mathcal{P}$, followed by a correction to repair the situation. The reason the loop works is that $\mathcal{P}$ implies `minval` is the smallest value in V once i increments up to `len(V)` (because `V[:len(V)]` is V itself).

The lag between statements that temporarily disrupt a goal (like property $\mathcal{P}$), followed by a statement or a block of statements that again establish the goal, resembles the lag between prey and predator seen in the graph above. It is typical of feedback, and of programs with loops, that they make progress in discrete, sometimes abrupt steps. Probably over 99% of programmers never formalize their thinking to realize there is some property like $\mathcal{P}$ lurking behind a loop, however, something like this (technically called an *invariant* property) is fundamental to advanced computer science.

To illustrate $\mathcal{P}$ concretely, suppose V is the list `[9,4,8,2,3]`. Below is a table with rows for the variables that change when the loop runs, plus an extra row for $\mathcal{P}$ showing whether it is satisfactory (✔) or not (✘). The top row is a step number, where we number the two assignment statements in the loop—we number two steps in each iteration (ignoring the internal steps Python takes to evaluate conditions for `while` and `if`).

step	1	2	3	4	5	6	7	8	9	10
i	0	1	1	2	2	3	3	4	4	5
minval	9	9	4	4	4	4	2	2	2	2
minind	0	0	1	1	1	1	3	3	3	3
$\mathcal{P}$	✘	✔	✘	✔	✔	✔	✘	✔	✔	✔

Let's look at time step 3, where `minval` is assigned 4 and `i` is 1. Right after this step, condition $\mathcal{P}$ is invalidated, since 4 is not the minimum of `V[:1]` (which has minimum value 9); but after one more step, `i` becomes 2, and then $\mathcal{P}$ is OK. If this kind of reasoning seems overly detailed, please be assured that software construction more often depends on pattern matching: after reading Chapters 22–23 and working through exercises there, loop constructions should become more intuitive.

Engineering disciplines have a more analytic view of feedback, again related to loops. Recall the flowchart in Figure 11.1, in Chapter 11. The flowchart depicts a loop that accumulates the sum of a list. The diamond shape in the flowchart is effectively the condition of a `while` loop. Control engineers often diagram feedback control systems with boxes and arrows representing different organizational units and flow of communication between them. Figure 19.1 shows a simplified diagram of a control loop (which often have many more organizational units than just the three shown here).

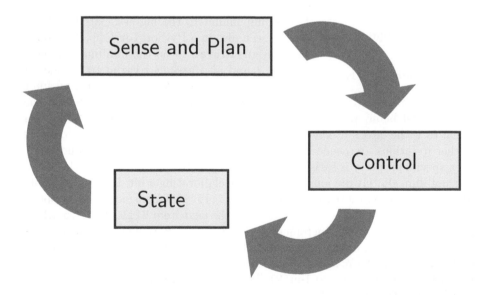

Figure 19.1: Simplified control loop.

The control loop of the figure consists of the *state*, which represents all the variables of the system to be controlled by feedback. For a building system, the variables might include temperature and air pressure (flow). The *sense and plan* block in the diagram reads sensors that sample some of the state variables; this part of the system then calculates the difference perceived between the sample and where the system should ideally be, in terms of state variables. The *control* block then gets signals to turn on heat, fans, and so on. Notice that the sense and plan component cannot simply change the actual state of the building: it can only indirectly change it by turning things on and off. This creates a lag and possibly also overshoots in temperature control. Software regulating communication networks builds on the model of a control loop. Sensing consists of measuring communication rates, level of traffic, delay, and other "variables" of the network (whether in fact these are program variables or not). If traffic is congested in some places, a control action can be to reroute communication on alternate paths.

What about `for` and `while` loops in Python? In software, the values of the variables constitute the state. While it is true that variables can be changed by assignment, it is generally not easy or advisable to change all variables in a single line of a program. Unlike list comprehensions, which appear to instantaneously calculate using all items of a list, `for` and `while` loops reflect the more primitive nature of computing, by handling data a little at a time, perhaps one item in each iteration. For software, it is this level of detail, namely that many calculations may be needed to complete an iteration, which introduces something akin to lag in a control system. For beginners, the confusion arises because each iteration may *write over* the state, that is, the state changes by assignments to variables. Thus, the variables at the start of the loop become "input" to the next iteration, which then "outputs" new values into these same variables. This is why we can think of loops as feedback. Each iteration takes values from the previous one, calculates new values, and these are fed into the next iteration.

Recursion

Recursion was introduced in Chapter 14, but for the functional style of computing (perhaps you skipped that chapter, so this may be the first introduction of the topic). Remarkably, it is possible to express any computing idea without having any syntax for iteration; without any `for`, `while`, or similar feature, repetition can still be done. Repetition is expressible using *function recursion*. Put simply, recursion refers to functions that may contain expressions wherein they invoke themselves. Upon first glance, this notion seems nonsense. Careful logical thinkers do not define words in terms of themselves. A dictionary definition of the noun *set*, for instance, should not use the word "set" in it. We would reject a definition like

> *a set is any concept referring to a set-like thing.*

The problem is that you have to know what a set is before being able to read this definition.

How can Python allow functions to be self-referential, defining them in terms of themselves? Let's look at an example. On the right, a function for multiply uses `multiply` sometimes to return its result. The idea of the function is simple: multiplication of integers is just repeated addition. There are special cases for multiplying by 0 or by 1, and the function handles those cases. It is the function's final statement that is in question. Here is the clever idea behind this function's last line: if you want the product `x*y` and you know `y>1`, then you can reason:

```
def multiply(x,y):
    if y == 0:
        return 0
    if y == 1:
        return x
    return (x + multiply(x,y-1))
```

$$x \times y \quad = \quad x \times (1 + (y-1)) \quad = \quad x + x \times (y-1)$$

This observation is exactly what the last line of `multiply` expresses. However, to understand how Python deals with recursion, we need to study an example. The following is the series of steps that Python takes to evaluate `multiply(5,3)`.

1. `multiply(5,3)`   *function application*
    (x binds to 5, y binds to 3)
2. `5 + multiply(x,y-1)`   *return expression*
3. `multiply(5,2)`   *evaluation needed*

At step 2, the addition cannot be completed without knowing the evaluation of `multiply(5,2)`, which is the reason for step 3. At such a juncture, Python is stuck. What it does is to save the current situation in memory, similar to what a human does (or should do) when interrupted in the midst of doing some activity when the phone rings. Handle the phone call, and when done, return back to the activity where it was left off. We show the next steps with an additional level of indenting, plus a star (✮) meaning that there will be further work when these steps are done.

✮   4. `multiply(5,2)`   *function application*
        (x binds to 5, y binds to 2)
✮   5. `5 + multiply(x,y-1)`   *return expression*
✮   6. `multiply(5,1)`   *evaluation needed*

Again, Python is stuck here. It cannot add up numbers in step 5 without having the evaluation of `multiply(5,1)`. So, once again, Python has to remember exactly where it is stuck, take a sidetracked path, and do the necessary evaluation.

   As the story of evaluation continues, two ✮ symbols are shown before step to indicate that Python actually has two pending evaluations to complete.

✮ ✮   7. `multiply(5,1)`   *function application*
            (x binds to 5, y binds to 1)
✮ ✮   8. `y == 1, so return x`   *return expression*
✮ ✮   9. `5`   *evaluation complete*

Finally, Python has finished a function evaluation. Where were we? Oh, yes, the value from the function evaluation allows the most recent suspended work to continue.

✮   10. `5 + 5`   *substituting returned value*
✮   11. `10`   *evaluation complete*

Step 10 is really just going back to step 5 (notice both of these steps have a single ✮), now that the result of `multiply(5,1)` is known. Step 11 finishes the evaluation of `multiply(5,2)`, so Python can get back to where it had left off previously at steps 2-3. The suspended work remaining continues.

12. `5 + 10`   *substituting returned value*
13. `15`   *evaluation complete*

In this way, Python calculates that `multiply(5,3)` evaluates to 15. This way of working seems nonintuitive to some people, because humans often make mistakes when interrupted and having to stop work and get back to it later. However, computers have no trouble doing the bookkeeping. In most cases, recursion can be just as efficient as using `while` or `for`.

Previous Example. One more example is helpful to give some evidence that recursion can do anything that a `for` or `while` statement could do. Once again, we recall the example shown to the right. In order to express the same idea using recursion, a function `priRang` will be defined. The function has a recursive definition. Below, the left side shows the Python and the right side shows the output when it is run.

```
for i in range(0,9,2):
    print i
```

```
def priRang(n):
    if n < 9:
        print n
        priRang(n+2)
priRang(0)
i = 8
```
```
0
2
4
6
8
```

The `priRang` function has one parameter, which it promptly prints, before another function application. Following the function definition, there are two Python statements. The first evaluation by Python is for the function application `priRang(0)`. This will bind 0 to `n`, and start a similar series of evaluation, temporary suspension of work, and recursive evaluation, just like the previous example. After printing 8, there will be an evaluation of `priRang(10)`, for which there is no recursion. The final assignment `i = 8` is just to be very exact in reproducing all the same results as the `for` statement, since it ends up with `i` being 8.

If you find recursion to be a natural idea, simple to understand, congratulations. Most people find this concept strange and not easy to use. For instance, if the function definition is changed just a bit, reversing the order of two statements:

```
def priRang(n):
    if n < 9:
        priRang(n+2)
        print n
priRang(0)
i = 8
```
```
8
6
4
2
0
```

The explanation of the reversed order in output is simple. The `print` statement comes *after* the recursive call in the body of the `if` statement. That means Python will continue to put aside what it is doing, evaluation of the recursion, and will not even get back to *any* `print` statement until it evaluates `priRang(10)`, which is a dead end as far as recursion is concerned (at which time the binding `n = 8` is in effect).

Terminology Review

Jargon introduced in this chapter includes: block of statements, loop, infinite loop, `for` loop, `while` loop, iteration, and recursion.

Exercises

(1) In the code below, determine what should replace "?" to get the printed output shown.

```
def R():
    for c in ?:
        print("d"+c+"t")

>>> R()
dat
det
dit
dot
```

(2) Two statements in the code below have "?" that should be changed so that the script will print as seen below. How should these statements be changed?

```
def K(m):
  e = ?
  while e>1:
    print e*e
    ?

>>> K(5)
25
16
9
4
```

(3) Something not illustrated in this chapter (discussed later in Chapter 23) is the possibility of putting a loop inside of a loop. What does the following script print?

```
for term in "large game whole".split():
  for suffix in "st ly -size".split():
    print(term+suffix)
```

(4) Here is the printed output from a function `gen()`:

```
1
1
2
3
2
2
4
6
3
3
6
9
```

Write a definition of function `gen()` that has only two `print` statements. *Hint:* First write a function that uses a loop to print 1, 2, 3—then modify the function to have another loop within the body of the first loop (like problem [3], above) which prints the other output lines.

(5) The word "iterate" has a larger meaning for the business of software and product development. Find and read the article "On Language: Iterate," which appeared in the *New York Times*, June 7, 2010 (the language column by Ben Zimmer).

(6) The term "unrolling a loop" means rewriting a loop so that the body of the loop is repeated manually (typing in the same statement or nearly the same statement multiple times). Here is a simple loop to print numbers 1–8:

```
for i in range(1,9):
  print(i)
```

The loop above goes through 8 iterations. Rewrite this as a loop that only goes through 4 iterations, has a body with two `print` statements, yet prints the same output as the loop shown above.

(7) A standard beginner exercise is to show how a mathematical function, such as factorial, can be computed using the different repetition facilities of a programming language. The factorial function *fact*(*n*) is typically defined by

$$fact(n) \quad = \quad n \cdot (n-1) \cdot (n-2) \cdots 3 \cdot 2 \cdot 1$$

Thus, $fact(5) = 5 \cdot 4 \cdot 3 \cdot 2 \cdot 1 = 120$. The exercise is to write a Python `fact(n)` function that returns the factorial of parameter `n`.

(a) Use a `for` loop to calculate factorial. Before the `for` statement, assign a variable `S = 1`; then, within the body of the `for` loop, use an augmented assignment to give `S` a new value in each iteration. When the iteration is done, `S` will be the value of the factorial.

(b) Use a `while` loop to calculate factorial. Before the `while` loop, assign two variables:

```
L, S = range(1,n+1), 1
```

Within the body of the `while` loop, use the `pop` method to simultaneously extract an item from `L` and remove that item from `L`. Here is an interactive example of how the `pop` method works:

```
>>> D = [9,200,True,5]
>>> x = D.pop()
>>> x
5
>>> D
[9, 200, True]
```

(c) The recursive technique for computing factorial is based on an alternative mathematical definition, which is equivalent to the one shown above:

$$fact(n) \quad = \quad \begin{cases} 1 & \text{if } n < 2 \\ n \cdot fact(n-1) & \text{otherwise} \end{cases}$$

Translating this recursive mathematical to a Python function definition is mostly straightforward; remember to put the `return` statements in the definition. During debugging, it can be helpful to put in some `print` statements.

☆(8) Write a recursive function `whittle(A,i)` which returns `A[i]`, where `A` is a sequence and `i` is a number in the range `0<=i<len(A)`. So that the problem is not trivial (and to make it interesting), you are only allowed to use 0 and `len(A)/2` (or `len(A)//2` for Python3) as the values in any index or split expression. To give some idea of how `whittle` would work, observe that if `A` is the string `"abcd,"` then an expression for `whittle(A,2)` is `"abcd"[len(A)/2:][0]`. However, this little `"abcd"` example is not general for all values of `i` and does not show the recursive nature of the problem (which is important for much longer sequences than four character strings). For the recursive definition, you need to split `A` into left and right halves, but use recursion just on one of the halves.

(9) A beginning programmer wrote the following function, which was intended to print numbers from a list in two parts, first the even numbers, then the odd numbers. But the function has a bug. Can you find the bug?

```
def evenodd(somelist):
    evens = odds = []
```

```
for item in somelist:
  if item%2==0:
      evens.append(item)
  else:
      odds.append(item)
for item in evens:
  print item
for item in odds:
  print item
```

☆(10) Suppose a positive number n is given, and the problem is to find nonnegative integers x and y so that $x \cdot 5 + y \cdot 8 == n$. This is a kind of search problem, searching through various alternatives to see what works for a conjectured pair (x, y) of integers. One way to solve the problem is to use comprehensions. Observe, for example, that we know $x \leq n/5$ and $y \leq n/8$, because larger values of x or y would cause any sum to be larger than n. So, a comprehension like this produces all the possibilities:

```
[ (x,y) for x in range(n/5) for y in range(n/8)
        if x*5 + y*8 == n ]
```

Using this list comprehension, Python searches through *all* possible pairs (x, y). The exercise here is to use recursion for a somewhat different search strategy. The observation for the recursive search is this: if $x \cdot 5 + y \cdot 8 == n$ and $x > 0$, then $(x - 1) \cdot 5 + y \cdot 8 == (n - 5)$; similarly if $y > 0$, then $x \cdot 5 + (y - 1) \cdot 8 == (n - 8)$. The significance of this observation is this: provided there is (recursive) solution to finding a pair of values (a, b) so that $a \cdot 5 + b \cdot 8 == (n - 5)$, the answer to the original problems is easy: $x = a + 1$ and $y = b$. So, it should not be too difficult to make a recursive search. Define a function `factor(N)` that uses recursion to find a pair `(x,y)` that are integers making `x*5+y*8==N`. In your answer, note that for some values of N there may be no solution: `factor(2)` should return `(None,None)` to indicate that no pair can be found. Thus, a recursive call like `factor(N-5)` *might* return `(None,None)`, the body of `factor` will need to test for such an outcome from a recursive call.

Interlude: Game Cycle

An early computer game, before the advent of powerful hardware for graphics, was based on a maze of rooms and passageways between the rooms. This game had a text-based interface where the player navigated the maze through keyboard commands. This later evolved into role-playing scenarios, eventually motivating many well-known immersive game experiences. Here we introduce the *game cycle* for a generic maze-like game. So long as the game is in progress, the control algorithm effectively boils down to a `while` repetition of table lookup. This turns out to be a deeply significant pattern in computing: the way that nearly all computer processing units (the CPUs) work is the same, consisting of an endless repetition of table-lookup operations. Software, too, exploits this pattern under the hood of many modules and libraries.

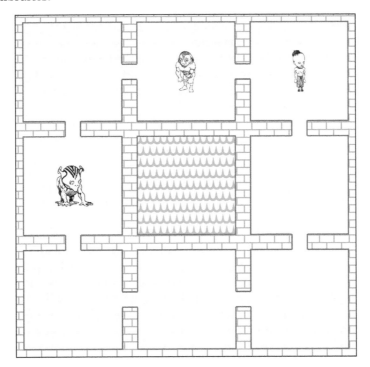

The simple map above shows eight rooms with passageways. Three of the rooms have creatures, just to add some fun to the game. To distinguish rooms, we give them names for the sake of Python representation: let "NW" for NorthWest be the upper left room; let "N" for North be the upper center room, and so on. Our goal is not to fully develop a game; we only show the mechanics of moving from one game situation to another, and how this is done by table lookup. Such things as game strategy, or how to make it interesting and fun are more advanced questions.

Before looking at Python code for a game, you may recall from the box "Syntactic Sugar" in Chapter 11, how a dictionary lookup can substitute for an `if` statement. What we do for a game is avoid writing many complicated `if`–`elif` statements. Instead, we can build a table (as a dictionary) of all the game moves and outcomes. Most of the planning goes into the table, which may simplify the logic of the program.

Suppose the game has one player, who moves by tossing virtual coin. Chapter 28 shows an easy way to simulate coin tossing, using a random selection function, which we use here. Let `room` be a variable that names the current location of the player, and let `D` be a dictionary describing where to move after a coin toss. The game cycle is the `while` loop shown to the right. This is not much of a game: it never ends, there are no points, and the player moves around aimlessly by a coin toss decision. It does show the central point, that movement is guided by table lookup. The dictionary `D` has keys for all possible combinations of coin toss and location. If this script

```
import random
Head,Tail = 1,0
D = {("NW",Head):"N",("N",Head):"NE",
    ("NE",Head):"E",("E",Head):"SE",
    ("SE",Head):"S",("S",Head):"SW",
    ("SW",Head):"W",("W",Head):"NW",
    ("NW",Tail):"W",("W",Tail):"SW",
    ("SW",Tail):"S",("S",Tail):"SE",
    ("SE",Tail):"E",("E",Tail):"NE",
    ("NE",Tail):"N",("N",Tail):"NW"}
room = "SE" # initial location

while True:
    cointoss = random.select([Head,Tail])
    room = D[(room,cointoss)]
    print "moving to", room
```

started and the first three iterations of the `while` loop got `Head, Head, Tail` as the values for `cointoss`, then the first three locations printed would be `S`, `SW`, and `S` (the dictionary has been set up for `Head` to move clockwise around the rooms and `Tail` to move the opposite way).

```
Head,Tail = 1,0
R,L = 1,0
D = {("NW",Head):"N",("N",Head):"NE",
    ...} # same as before
room = "SE" # initial location

while True:
    print "You are in room", room
    next = input("Please enter R or L: ")
    room = D[(room,next)]
```

As a first improvement, let's have the player decide which way to move, L or R (for Left and Right), instead of using a simulated coin toss. To do this, we borrow the technique of asking a player for keyboard input from the Python console, described in Chapter 25. In this revised version of the game, the player is asked to type which move to make, which then becomes part of the lookup key in the dictionary. The game is still pointless, because the player never wins or loses. However, even without an initial map of the rooms, a player could experiment with L and R inputs, interacting with the program, and discover the names of all the rooms. The flow of data in the game cycle is depicted in the diagram below: `room` helps select the next `room` value.

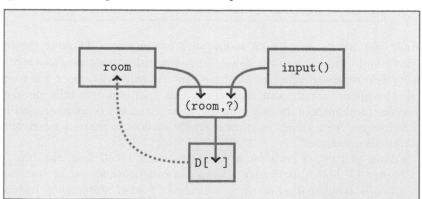

The point of the diagram is that dictionary `D` behaves like a function with two parameters, though represented as a tuple, which is the key for the dictionary lookup. Whenever we have a function with quite simple logic, for example, returning different values only depending on various cases for what the arguments are, it is worth considering whether a table lookup using a dictionary might simplify the programming.

skiffen

kelbdud

rœdle

What about the creatures? Let's have the player interact with the creatures and either gain or lose points at random, and winning or losing based on the number of points. The dictionary C has keys for rooms where the creatures are, with the associated value being the creature's name and list of points to be won or lost. In this third version, there are two dictionaries, C and D; also, there are two variables that change as the game proceeds, `room` and `points`. The player types L or R, moves from place to place, encountering the creatures and by random selection, the point total shrinks or grows. The game ends when the number of points exceeds 200 or goes to zero (or negative). One can imagine further improvements to the game. For example, at each turn, the

```
import random
Head,Tail,R,L = 1,0,1,0
D = {("NW",Head):"N",("N",Head):"NE",
    ...} # same as before
C = {"W":("skiffen",[-30,50]),
    "N":("kelbdud",[-50,40]),
    "NE":("roodle",[-25,60])}
room,points = "SE",100

while 0<points<200:
    print "You are in room", room
    if room in C:
        print C[room][0], "is in here"
        points += random.select(C[room][1])
        print "points now:", points
    next = input("Please enter R or L: ")
    room = D[(room,next)]
print "Game over!"
```

creatures could randomly move to another room or stay put; more exotic features could be added, like collecting magic potions or solving puzzles to gain points when meeting a particular creature. Our purpose here, however, is not to perfect the game, but to extract the pattern of the basic game cycle and see how it is more broadly useful in computing.

State Machine. The version of the game above has two variables that change during the game; suppose creatures moved also, then there would be three changing variables; `room`, `points`, and C. It is useful to aggregate all these variables into a single entity called `state`. The word "state" is meant to stand for all dynamic status and attribute concepts associated with the application—the game; the sense of "state" is similar to what one means in phrases like "state of the economy" or "state of the world." The aggregation to define `state` could be as simple as `state = [room, points, C]`. Then in the game code, changing some portion of the state would be by assignment: `state[1] += 20` adds 20 points to the player's point total. As a further elaboration, we might have multiple players of the game, accomplished by letting room and point components be lists. Then to add 20 points to player 3's total, it would be `state[1][3] += 20`.

```
D = define tables, constants, etc.
state = define initial state
while notDone(state):
    state = nextState(state,D)
```

The code shown to the left represents a *state machine*, which is the essential logic of the game cycle. A state machine boils down to an iteration that changes the **state** variable in each cycle of the loop. Two functions mentioned in the code may be implemented as table lookup, using dictionaries, and also inject some printing, soliciting input from files or users, invoking random choice, and so on. The code shows an assignment to change the state, **state = nextState(state,D)**; however, if **state** is a mutable type (list or dictionary), this statement would just be "**nextState(state,D)**" instead, putting the code that changes **state** inside the body of **nextState**.

Looking ahead to Chapter 27, where Python classes and objects are introduced, a better way to manage state would use methods rather than functions. The code here shows how a **state** object could be equipped with methods to check for game termination (the **done** method) and to

```
D = define tables, constants, etc.
state = define initial state object
while not state.done():
    state.next(D)
```

compute the state after one more turn (the **next** method). Superficially, this seems just a small syntax change, but there is more involved to setting up classes and objects, explained in Chapter 27. One advantage to using an object representation is the flexibility of naming components. It is somewhat nicer to let "**state.players**" refer to the list of the game's players than to use list notation "**state[1]**" or dictionary notation "**state["players"]**"—objects defined appropriately allow named attributes that are easier to remember and make code more understandable.

Game Cycle and Regular Expressions

One of the jewels of computing is the discovery of a fundamental connection between the state machine way of writing programs and the patterns found in regular expressions, a topic mentioned in "Regular Expressions" in Chapter 14 and later in Chapter 27. Python's `re` module can search through strings for patterns of characters: `re.compile("ab+a")` produces a regular expression object, which can be used to match or search text read from a file. The object that `re.compile("ab+a")` returns will match a character string which starts with `a`, then has one or more `b`'s, followed by another `a`. Examples of this pattern are `aba`, `abba`, `abbba`, and so on. A state machine that can *recognize* this pattern is derived from the diagram below.

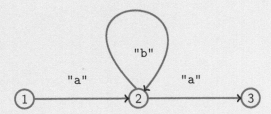

The circled numbers in the diagram are the states of the state machine. Seen as a game, the starting point is state 1; to get from state 1 to state 2, an input character `a` is needed. Once at state 2, getting an input `b` leads back to state 2. To end the game, state 3 is reached from state 2 by reading input character `a`. This state machine is implemented in Python by a dictionary `D = {(1,"a"):2, (2,"b"):2, (2,"a"):3}`. If a combination of state and input character does not occur in the dictionary, say `(1,"r")`, then the pattern `ab+a` is not matched. With a little imagination, you can see the relation between a game board of rooms and creatures, and this abstract diagram representing the `ab+a` pattern. The state machine idea serves both to run a game cycle and to recognize a pattern.

The state machine idea has an even wider application in software that controls or monitors communication, either between machines or between users and machines. In a crude way, the pattern `ab+a` might signify the buttons that control a display panel. The "a" button turns on the power, the "b" button refreshes information on the panel, and when the "a" button is pressed again, the panel powers off. It is even possible to put functions in the table used by the state machine and have these functions called whenever the machine changes state. For example, let `D = {(1,"a"):(2,f), (2,"b"):(2,g), (2,"a"):(3,h)}`, where f, g, and h are functions. Upon looking up `D[(1,"a")]`, the state machine learns not only that 2 is the next state, but that function `f` is supposed to be called (perhaps `f()` turns on the panel's power).

The idea of using table lookup via the state machine algorithm is quite powerful for recognizing textual patterns. What `re.compile("ab+a")` creates could include a dictionary like `D`, among other things. For more information about the theory that connects such things as state machines and textual patterns, you can research the term *deterministic finite automaton* online using a search engine. State machines are so prevalent in software that most compilers and interpreters of computing languages, including Python, use them to parse the programs we write and decide whether or not they have syntax errors.

Chapter 20:   Documentation

Ink is better than the best memory.
— Chinese proverb

It seems obvious that computing languages would not exist if computers did not exist. Yet the concept of an algorithm predates computers by at least a thousand years. The *idea* of computing is independent of automatic machinery. Even without actual computers, a number of complicated algorithms were devised to compute numeric results, help construct buildings, tune musical instruments, and prepare medicinal remedies. Some of these algorithms have iterative or recursive structure and take some explaining to communicate their details. Thus, even without computers, there is some need to *document*, or explain algorithms, the functions they use and define, and the nature of their inputs and outputs.

All computing languages provide syntax so that, along with the instructions and program statements, some documentation and explanation can be carried along with such things as function definitions, variable assignments, loops, and other statements. The documentation is typically just natural language (English, Swahili, German, etc.), and the only syntax needed in a computing language is a way to avoid confusion between the documentation and the program statements to be run on a computer.

For some motivation, recall the cryptic C program shown in Chapter 5. In fact, this kind of inscrutable program can even be written in Python. The program shown below on the left, by Jeff Preshing[1] is (incredibly) a valid Python program. Technically, this program can be put on two, rather long lines of Python, using tricks of extending a logical line (see Chapter 30 for more about this). When it runs, it produces the high-resolution image shown on the right.

```
                                  =   (
                               255,
                             lambda
               V           ,B,c
             :c    and Y(V*V+B,B,  c
               -1)if(abs(V)<6)else
     (                 2+c-4*abs(V)**-0.4)/i
       )  ;v,      x=1500,1000;C=range(v*x
        );import   struct;P=struct.pack;M,\
    j  ='<QIIHHHH',open('M.bmp','wb').write
for X in j('BM'+P(M,v*x*3+26,26,12,v,x,1,24))or C:
    i  ,Y=_;j(P('BBB',*(lambda T:(T*80+T**9
       *i-950*T  **99,T*70-880*T**18+701*
      T  **9    ,T*i**(1-T**45*2)))(sum(
      [           Y(0,(A%3/3.+X%v+(X/v+
                  A/3/3.-x/2)/1j)*2.5
               /x   -2.7,i)**2 for  \
               A      in C
                    [:9]])
                    /9)
                    )  )
```

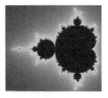

This is not good programming style! Trying to explain or understand such a program would not be enjoyable for most people. Our goal should be to write software that is understandable, easy to work with, and to use. (Notice that the text of this program has been formatted to resemble its output. The term *quine*, in the lore of computing, refers to a program that outputs itself.)

---

[1]http://preshing.com/20110926/high-resolution-mandlebrot-in-obfuscated-python

Comments in Programs

The Python language uses the "#" symbol as a mechanism to add non-Python text to scripts, functions, modules, and so on. Anywhere you like, you can add some text to a line of Python, provided it is preceded by the #- character, and Python will ignore what follows on that line. Here is an interactive example:

```
>>> 2 + 2 == 4 # wouldn't it be nice to get 5 ?
True
```

Python ignored the text starting with #, as if it were invisible. There really is no reason to add text in an interactive session. However, in a script, you can use such text, called a *program comment*, as a note to yourself, so that you remember things later. For instance, consider this function:

```
def product(X):
    # probably this function should first
    # have some validation that X is a list of numbers
    p = 1.0
    for a in X:
      p *= a
    return p
```

The extra lines beginning with # will be ignored by Python, but are notes by the author of the **product** function, admitting that the function has a potential bug: it will have errors if the parameter X does not represent a list of numbers. Perhaps the author will edit the function someday and change it to deal with cases where X is not a list of numbers.

Docstrings

One unusual feature of Python, Java, C, and similar languages is that a line can have an expression that will be evaluated, but then ignored. For example, we can write the **product** function this way:

```
def product(X):
    p = 1.0
    40 + len( "the right decision".split() )
    for a in X:
      p *= a
    return p
```

What is that line starting with 40 doing? Python will evaluate it (calculating 43), but then there is no variable assigned, no **return** statement, so some extra work is being done but for no purpose. Python allows this—there is no error generated. Similarly, we could rewrite **product** this way:

```
def product(X):
    "product(X) computes X[0]*X[1]*...*X[len(X)-1]"
    p = 1.0
    for a in X:
      p *= a
    return p
```

In this version, the first line is evaluated by Python (it is just a string), but then nothing is done with the result. *However,* this is a convenient trick for making a comment by a programmer. More often, it is done with long string notation.

```
def product(X):
    '''the product(X) function computes
        X[0]*X[1]*...*X[k]
      where k is len(X).  Special cases:
        if len(X) is 0, product(X) -> 1.0
        if len(X) is 1, product(X) is X[0]
    '''
    p = 1.0
    for a in X:
      p *= a
    return p
```

Now the comment is *documentation*, explaining to anyone who might want to use the `product` function what it is supposed to do. Python has special terminology for a string put as the first line in the body of a function: it is called the function's *docstring*. Suppose we put `product`'s definition in a file, say `stuff.py`, and start an interactive session in the same directory as the file. Consider this example:

```
>>> import stuff
>>> print(stuff.product.__doc__)
the product(X) function computes
   X[0]*X[1]*...*X[k]
where k is len(X).  Special cases:
   if len(X) is 0, product(X) -> 1.0
   if len(X) is 1, product(X) is X[0]
>>>
```

Yes, the unusual syntax is intentional: the underscore characters reveal how Python uses special names for certain features of its infrastructure. The name "`__doc__`" is used like a variable to refer to a function's docstring. Above, the first line of the example imports `stuff.py` as a module (see Chapter 18). The second line prints the docstring of the `product` function in the module. It could be that `stuff.py` has other functions: each of these functions can have its own docstring, which can be printed or manipulated like any other string. In addition, if the first line of a module is a string (usually a long string), it can be a comment covering the entire module. For instance, `stuff.py` might start like this:

```
'''
   The stuff module is something I wrote to
   have a product function, a streverse function,
   and a stdev function.  See their docstrings
   for further info.
'''
def product(X):
    '''the product(X) function computes
        X[0]*X[1]*...*X[k]
    ...
```

With this as background, an interactive session using `stuff.py` might be:

```
>>> import stuff
>>> print(stuff.__doc__)
  The stuff module is something I wrote to
  have a product function, a streverse function,
  and a stdev function.  See their docstrings
  for further info.
>>>
```

Interactive Help

In an interactive session, you can use the built-in `help` function to see docstrings (which was introduced in Chapter 18). Example:

```
>>> import stuff
>>> help(stuff)
NAME
    stuff
FILE
    /home/user/Desktop/Demo/stuff.py
DESCRIPTION
  The stuff module is something I wrote to
  have a product function, a streverse function,
...
```

Much more is printed, showing all the functions, their docstrings, and more. Most all Python modules have docstrings and can be explored using the `help` function.

Motivations for Documentation

Why add comments to Python programs? There is no right answer to this question. In fact, there is (sometimes spirited) debate about what comments should and should not be included in code. Overall, the rationale for comments—which are targeted to a human audience rather than a compiler or the computer that runs the program—is that programs should be made understandable for other programmers and even for the authors of the programs. This issue of making programs understandable to others can be crucial for effective team software development. Most software has to be changed in response to user demands, sometimes long after the software was first written. Trying to figure out how programs work can be quite frustrating without some guide or hints on how decisions were made during the software development.

Comments might help, and might hurt understanding of a program. Often, the best way to make a program understandable is *not* with the comments, but rather by structuring it to be simple. If the functions are simple and straightforward, if there are no "tricks" in how it manipulates types, methods, variables, and other syntactic elements, then it is hopefully easier to understand. Here follows a list of the conventional reasons for having comments.

1. Remembrances, notes to self: The nature of these comments is to jog the memory of the author. Typical are statements about future plans, limitations, or explanations of why some code was written, why an earlier version failed, and perhaps even links (`http` references) to further documents.

2. Notes to coworkers: In a team, these notes help others understand parts of the code they did not author. Also, when one person changes code written by another team member, it can be helpful to point out where and why the change(s) were made. In a larger organization, some of these comments might also refer to other software written by other teams, refer to organizational documents, mission statements, and so forth.

3. Explanation of technique: Perhaps a function or a family of functions implement some sophisticated mechanism that is not easy to understand from the program statements alone. Then, it can be helpful to explain in English what is being done, what is the basic approach, and how it was carried out in the actual program. This type of comment could be useful for students submitting homework, in case the program is incomplete.

4. History of development: If you look at most industrial strength software, including open-source software, there is usually some record of how the software was developed, which features were added (including date, authorship, testing details) as new versions of the software were built up over time. Though much of the history of development is typically maintained in databases or conventional versioning systems, comments are valuable in programs because they place the log at the location of where things changed.

5. Intellectual property claims, legal disclaimers, organizational standard statements. Virtually all distributed software has some kind of standard language in comments to claim copyright or to (attempt) claims about liability, something like a EULA (End User License Agreement); some military or government software might have statements about the level of confidentiality.

6. Credits, citations, and attributions: If the author(s) copied ideas from someplace, then there may be thanks given, or a reference to an article, or a link to where the ideas originate. This is not only polite, but can be a valuable way to track down a reference that more fully explains things (like a Wikipedia article). Another example of this is network software that uses a standard protocol documented in some official repository, where there is full, formal specification of the ideas.

7. User documentation: The purpose of some software is to provide a library of functions, subroutines, procedures, and methods to other programmers. What is needed for the *users* of such software is not the full understanding of how the functions work. It is likely enough to understand the *interfaces* so that the software will be usable. As an example, it might be that a module provides some functions to display a map, allowing for the map to be scaled, colored, be annotated, and to merge in some online data searches on objects included in the map. For this, a user does not need to know all the details: what the user wants is to know how to "tune" the map, turning the knobs and controls on the map under application control. How can the user know this? Perhaps the docstring can explain parameters to functions, can explain the purpose of each function, and so on. While it can be argued that such documentation should belong in a separate user manual, it is traditional to have some level of this documentation in comments, especially during software development.

Yet more items could well be added to the list above. The main takeaway from seeing this list is that there are many reasons for having comments and several different readers (audiences) for the comments in a program. In the old days, it could have been said that programming languages were "write-only" languages (because nobody ever read what is in a program, they only run it on the computer). But we can see now that it is useful to add comments to programs.

Cruft, Clarity, and Style

Above, it was mentioned that comments can actually *hurt* the understanding of a program. This is usually because what the comments state is at odds with what the program actually does or expects for input. One source of such bad comments is *cruft*. The term "cruft" is often experienced visiting Web pages. On a Web page, there can be a link that either leads nowhere or leads to an errant Web page. Usually this is because, over time, Web pages change yet the links to them do not change: these are *crufty links*. Similarly, when a program has been documented with comments, they can initially be accurate descriptions of the logic of the functions and variables. Later, when a program is modified to fix bugs, make it more efficient, add new features, and so forth, the old comments might be left in the code. The old comments thereby become false statements: they are cruft in the program.

Clarity of Expression

Adding comments may help others understand how a function, module, or script works, but there are other practical steps outside of comments to improve code readability. The issue of making code clear to others is particularly important when organizations use teams of developers who share in the creating and maintenance of software. When one person is not around and a coworker has to take over the responsibility for some component of a system, documentation and readability are crucial. What can one do to make life easier for others working with program code?

1. Spacing: A few blank lines, keeping lines short, indenting blocks of code (Python allows you to indent by a single space, but further indenting can make things more readable).

2. Limited nesting: Python and other programming languages allow for arbitrary nesting. Hence, one can write `if`-statements within `if`-statements within yet other `if`-statements, and so on, making the logic quite complicated. Often, just placing code in a new function and describing that function with comments can simplify the appearance. Putting some limits on the degree of nesting (of `if`, of `for`, of expressions) relieves some mental load for the reader; similarly, limiting the number of statements in a function can structure the program to make it simpler.

3. Avoid tricky expressions. The following is legal Python code, but not easy to understand:

   ```
   if (a<b)<=False:
   ```

   One should avoid tricky use of expressions, even if they work.

4. Choose descriptive, memorable variable names. Here are examples of such names:

   ```
   VecTotal, Mean, TabControl = 0.0, 0.0, ''
   ```

   Here are some poor choices:

   ```
   II1ILILIL = 2.5
   I1IIILILL = 0.0
   LastYearOveralProjectdQuartrlyEarnings = ''
   ```

   There really is no "right way" to name variables. Some famous software gurus have, from time to time, expressed their opinions on guidelines for variable names. One well-known discipline of naming is **camel case** (which you can look up on any Web search engine); Charles Simonyi promoted the so-called "Hungarian notation" for variable naming.

The Pass Statement

It can be helpful to document programs even before they are entirely written. Your plans and intentions for functions can be set down early, so that each time you return to the implementation task, remembering what needs to be done is easy. One Python

```
def HandleInput(line,D):
    if line.startswith(">"):
        pass # store line into D
    else:
        return "invalid line"
```

statement that can be handy for this is the **pass** statement. The **pass** statement does nothing, though it is technically not a comment. A reason for using **pass** is that Python does require at least *some* valid statement for each indented block, whether for a function definition, an **if**, or other similar situations. In the example seen here, the intent of the programmer was to write code that obtained information from the **line** parameter, storing that into a dictionary D; at present, the code is missing, though the function **HandleInput** could be tested for invalid lines, since there is a statement (just **pass**) associated with the case of a valid line. Later chapters introduce other situations where it is useful to have the **pass** statement.

Assertions

Although Python ignores comments, there is a special statement in Python and most modern languages that is like a comment, but does influence program behavior. The **assert** statement causes an error to arise if a particular condition—a condition invented by the author of the function or program— is violated. Suppose there is a function **product(X)** that is supposed to calculate the product of a list of integers. The author uses the **assert** statement to declare that the input to the function, parameter X, should be a nonempty list of integers, as follows:

```
def product(X):
    assert type(X)==list and len(X)>0
    r = 1.0
    for t in X:
        assert type(t)==int
        r *= t
    return r
```

Above, the **assert** is like a technical comment: the first **assert** is a requirement that X should be a list and that it should have at least one item in it. The **assert** in the body of the loop states the requirement that each item in the list should be an integer. When the **product** function is used later, in some script or other function, Python will check the conditions given in these **assert** statements; if the conditions are not satisfied by the data, then Python will halt the program and generate an error.

Style

Master programmers (especially very opinionated ones) develop their own style preferences for how many comments a program should have, what should be in the comments, and so on. Few of these people agree on style preferences. The style guidelines expressed by Guido van Rossum, the inventor of Python, are described in the document found via this link:

http://www.python.org/dev/peps/pep-0008/ (search for PEP 8 Style Guide
for Python Code if this link does not work)

The list of style guidelines is extensive. A few gems from this list are:

- Comments that contradict the code are worse than no comments. Always make a
  priority of keeping the comments up-to-date when the code changes!

- Comments should be complete sentences. If a comment is a phrase or sentence, its
  first word should be capitalized, unless it is an identifier that begins with a lowercase
  letter (never alter the case of identifiers!).

- Use inline comments sparingly. An inline comment is a comment on the same line
  as a statement. Inline comments should be separated by at least two spaces from
  the statement. They should start with a # and a single space. Inline comments are
  unnecessary and in fact distracting if they state the obvious. Do not do this:

```
x = x + 1                       # Increment x
```

But sometimes, this is useful:

```
x = x + 1                       # Compensate for border
```

Formalized Comments

The syntax for comments was originally invented for human readers: Python ignores the
text inside of comments. Later, some software developers started adding special formatting
conventions to their comments. For example, one might see this in a comment:

```
# The second parameter <b>X</b> to this function must be
```

For anyone familiar with HTML, the language for marking up Web pages, this may look
familiar. The comment is using HTML to **make bold** the text between "" and "."
After adding these extra formatting specifiers to the text, developers wrote other programs
that extracted the comments from scripts and modules (ignoring the Python code) and
made them into Web pages. This makes for some nice online documentation of programs,
however, it burdens the programmer with writing fancy HTML to document the code.

Pseudocode

Pseudocode is any high-level description of a program or algorithm using human-readable
language, but put in a format that approximates how some programming language might
appear. Pseudocode for a sort function might be something like this:

```
sort(X) function (X is a list of ints)
   make a new list L, initially empty
   make a copy of X, call it Y
   while Y has items,
      move smallest item in Y to L,
      removing it from Y
   finished result is in L
```

Many times textbooks describe algorithms with pseudocode, and software developers may write pseudocode of programs on whiteboards in meetings, during discussions. After planning sessions, the pseudocode and other notes can become comments included in the finished programs. It is good practice to begin your own work by writing pseudocode.

Keep in mind that the intent of pseudocode is to convey the technical ideas of an algorithm or program, without being constrained by the exact syntax. The goal is to communicate the idea to another team member, or even to yourself (or your instructor). You can be somewhat free from the language details. After the pseudocode looks reasonably complete and detailed, you can convert it into actual Python statements.

Terminology Review

Jargon introduced in this chapter includes: program comments, docstrings, documentation, cruft, assertions (and the `assert` statement), pseudocode.

Exercises

All but the last exercise here ask you to look at pseudocode and translate it into working Python code. This is similar to "Exercises: Unit Testing and Online Supplement" after Chapter 10, except that here the idea of the solution is given to you. If problem solving in Python does not come naturally, translating pseudocode can be a useful exercise. Another similar kind of exercise for beginners is to take working Python functions and modify them to add new features or change some aspect of their behavior. Generally, these exercises depend on knowing more about loops (and in some cases, using input/output) than has been shown in previous chapters. So it is best to first learn material from Chapters 22–25 before solving these problems.

(**1**) This first problem has quite detailed pseudocode; usually pseudocode describes problem solving with higher-level concepts. Write a function `plusrev(E,F)` that itemwise concatenates sequence E with the reverse of sequence F. Two examples are seen

```
>>> plusrev([1,2,3],[10,20,30])
[31, 22, 13]
>>> plusrev("one two three four".split(),
            "1 2 3 4".split())
["one4", "two3", "three2", "four1"]
```

to the right. Your implementation of `plusrev(E,F)` should correspond to the pseudocode sketched by the numbered list here.

① Assert that parameters E and F have the same type as each other.

② Assert that E and F have the same length.

③ Let t be the length of E.

④ Setting up the accumulation pattern, let R be the empty list.

⑤ Let i iterate from zero up to t-1, with the body of the loop doing the following: stick on to the right end of R the "+" of the i-th item of E and the t-(i+1)-th item of F. (Maybe another idea is to use negative indexing on F; do whatever is easier.)

⑥ At end of loop, do not forget to return R.

(**2**) A function is needed that "cleans up" a dictionary by removing key-value items where the value is None, while leaving all other items alone. This function, cleanone(D), thus has to modify dictionary D. The function does not need to return anything, just change D by possibly removing some items.

① Let K be an empty list.

② In an accumulation loop, go through D and find each item which has None as the value, putting the key into the list K.

③ Finally, iterate through K, removing whatever item of D has the key listed in K.

(**3**) Write a function merge(A,B) that merges two sorted lists into a single list. How merge should work is suggested by the example on the right. Pseudocode for merge follows.

```
>>> merge([29,58,61,82],[7,45,49,58,90,93])
[7, 29, 45, 49, 58, 58, 61, 82, 90, 93]
```

- Let i and j be variables that are respectively used to go through index values for the two input lists A and B. Initially, let both of these variables be zero.

- Let C be a variable to be returned when the function is done; initially let C be zero.

- Repeat the following steps until C is returned:

  ① If i is as big as the number of items in A, append to C all items of B starting from index j, and then return C.

  ② If j is as big as the number of items in B, append to C all of A starting from index i, and then return C.

  ③ Otherwise, let m be the minimum of the i-th item of A and the j-th item of B.

  ④ If m came from A, add one to i and concatenate m onto C.

  ⑤ Else, m came from B; so add one to j and concatenate m onto C.

(**4**) Write diag(X,j) that returns a list of the j-th "diagonal" of a *square table*. A square table, or square matrix, has the same number of rows and columns. A three-row, three-column square matrix of numbers is on the right. A diagonal goes through items along a slanted row. For this example, diagonal

$$X \;=\; \begin{pmatrix} 100 & 200 & 300 \\ 5 & 10 & 15 \\ 9 & 90 & 900 \end{pmatrix}$$

0 is [9], diagonal 1 is [5, 90], diagonal 2 is [100, 10, 900], diagonal 3 is [200, 15], and diagonal 4 is [300].

① Let n be the number of rows of X.

② Assert that X has the same number of rows and columns.

③ Assert that j is at least zero and at most 2*(n-1).

④ If j specifies a diagonal starting along the first column compute the following:

- let k be the row number to start listing the diagonal (this would be n-1 if j is zero, etc.).

- let p be the number of items in the diagonal j; there is a simple formula to calculate this; figure that out on some scratch paper first.

⑤ Else, j specifies a diagonal starting on the top row, but not at the first column; then calculate the following:

- let k be the column number in the first row to start listing the diagonal (this would be 1 if j is n, etc.).
- let p be the number of items in the diagonal j; there is another simple formula to calculate this; figure that out on some scratch paper first.

⑥ For each of the two above cases, the list to return can be stated as a list comprehension, using k, p, and double indexing (like X [?] [??] by putting in the right things for the question marks).

(5) At an interactive Python session, try the following:

```
import this
print ( this.s )
```

Can you figure out the result?

Chapter 21:   Debugging

Confidence is what you have before you understand the problem.
— Woody Allen

Mistakes are an inevitable and practical part of using computer languages. Some bugs are syntax errors, reported by Python even before it runs the program. Others may only show up when a combination of input values drives the program to go through a particular sequence of statements. This chapter surveys some of the standard methods and tools used to track down bugs. The novel *Anna Karenina* by Tolstoy begins with "Happy families are all alike; every unhappy family is unhappy in its own way." So it seems also with incorrect programs. There are myriad ways a program can fail. Moreover, a program can have numerous flaws, such that fixing one eventually reveals another.

Why is designing software difficult, and why is it that debugging cannot be fully automatic? Fully capable languages allow for programming any kind of behavior. It is not hard to write a program that counts 1, 2, 3, ..., 8927105, 8927107, ...—it counts perfectly until reaching a certain number, then skips the next number. Software can do crazy things, and computing systems cannot distinguish between what is correct and what is considered to be a bug, unless we go to considerable effort to specify very precisely and in full detail the difference between correct and incorrect behavior. More often, identifying a bug is a case of "I know one when I see one." Debugging, then, consists of replaying a behavior and searching for the errant code.

Kinds of Bugs

Terminology distinguishing bugs is helpful to say what techniques are needed to search for them. Sometimes the classification is uncertain because, when a bug is observed, all the circumstances may not be known without further tests.

Crashes. The easiest to identify are bugs that stop a program with an error message. Figure 21.1 shows typical *traceback* from running a Python script that has a bug. Only the last two lines relate directly to the error: the kind of error is `IndexError` and the line number in the script is shown. The other lines indicate that the error was within a nesting of evaluations; Chapter 26 explains how errors in Python "percolate" up through pending function evaluations. The traceback messages in Figure 21.1 indicate the sequence of events leading up to the crash:

$$\text{print reportgen}(\dots) \rightarrow \text{m = topmonth}(\dots) \rightarrow \text{crash in sorted}(\dots)$$

Here, the main thing of interest is where the bug happened, on line 141 of the script, an error raised by `sorted`. It takes a bit of practice getting used to traceback messages, and it helps to use an editor that numbers the lines of a script (so you can see which lines the traceback messages refer to).

With luck, finding the line of the script where the program crashed is enough to figure out the cause of a bug.

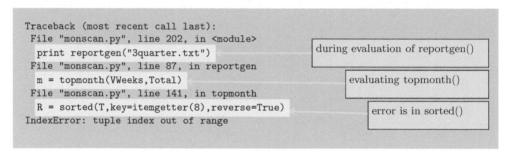

Figure 21.1: Traceback report of an error.

Traceback error messages are not always enough to diagnose a bug. It can be that a program gets a `ZeroDivisionError`, but when you look at the program, the reason why one of the numbers was zero is not obvious. Sometimes, when a program crashes, you need to see how the condition triggering the crash came to be. Debugging a program can be like crime scene investigation, where the causes that lead to the actual error need some detective work. Later in this chapter we see some methods for tracking down bugs.

Repeatable Errors. Ideally, all bugs are repeatable on demand. The worst situation for finding bugs is an unrepeatable error. For example, suppose you have a Web server that crashes very rarely, and only when a particular user and browser combination connects to the server. If we do not know who is the user and what the user did, we might see messages for the crash, but neither understand the cause nor have the ability to recreate the bug and devise experiments to track it down. Fortunately for beginners, nearly all errors are repeatable. The techniques described in this chapter generally presume that bugs are repeatable.

Incorrect Results. Even programs that do not crash can have bugs. A program may have an infinite loop—it would run forever unless we stop it. Other kinds of incorrect programs finish and write output, but the results might be nonsense. Beyond these examples, software used for interactive graphics or networking can misbehave in too many ways to enumerate. While there is no fully comprehensive way to identify bugs in programs relative to how we expect them to behave, this is more often a shortcoming of the way we humans describe (or fail to describe) our expectations. Later in the chapter we hint at computing research areas that address the problem of verifying and validating software.

Advanced Bug Types

Unrepeatable bugs are rare in commonplace programs. The situation of a bug that is not easily reproduced is usually due to timing of parallel or concurrent computing (an unlikely specialty area for beginners to be using).

Heisenbugs are oddities in the theory of debugging. A bug is called a *Heisenbug* if it disappears when you try to debug it: attempts to use debugging tools, adding extra statements to trace execution, or other changes that are normally helpful to track down bugs do not work for Heisenbugs. Fortunately, such bugs are very uncommon.

Methods of Debugging

Two metaphors motivate the methods for tracking down bugs. First, it is a process of search, so general ideas about searching can be helpful in locating problems. Second, hunches are sometimes shortcuts in the search. The search metaphor motivates "binary search" in debugging, explained below. The hunch metaphor can be more elegantly called abductive reasoning (this is what Sherlock Holmes used), which consists of making a hypothesis about the cause of a bug, and then devising experiments to reject or accept the hypothesis. Debugging is usually a combination of these metaphors.

Tracing Execution

Since a bug is a deviation from expected program behavior, it is sensible to have tools that examine behavior. Considering that program statements might run at the rate of well over a million per second, we have two alternatives: either slow down the rate of Python's statement evaluation so that we can watch it a step at a time, or record the evaluation somehow to a log of events for later scrutiny. Both of these alternatives are valuable.

Step-Through Debuggers. Some Integrated Development Environments (IDEs) have debuggers that let you control the rate of statement evaluation. Typical options for debuggers are single-step evaluations controlled interactively, by clicking a button, possibly allowing you to see variable values with each (next) statement that runs. This can become tedious, so debuggers may also have a *breakpoint* facility. The idea is to mark one or more program statements as "breakpoints," then launch the program to run at normal speed *until* a breakpoint is reached; then the program stops, allowing interactive inspection of variables and resumption of execution.

Figure 21.2 shows an example of stepping through a program, but without breakpoints. On the left, the program is shown with the next line to be evaluated shaded. On the right of the figure, values for variables are shown. Unfortunately, standard Python does not have a graphical debugger; one has to find an IDE or other interactive tool elsewhere in the Python software world for this facility. Python's standard library does have an interactive debugger, the `pdb` module. However, the interface to `pdb` is text-based and not so intuitive for beginners. At the end of the chapter, we look at `pdb`; we consider first alternative ways to inspect program behavior.

```
def tempis(T):
  n = len(T)
  R = n*[None]
  for i in range(n):
    t = T[i]
    if t<10:
      R[i] = "cold"
    elif 10<t<20:
      R[i] = "warm"
    elif 20<t<100:
      R[i] = "hot"
  return R
V = [15,29,72,5,20,22]
W = ','.join(tempis(V))
print W
```

```
now on step 27 of program

Current variables

i → 3

R → [ 'warm' 'hot' 'hot' None None None ]

t → 5

T → [ 15 29 72 5 20 22 ]

n → 6
Background variables:

tempis → function

V → [ 15 29 72 5 20 22 ]
```

execution stats: 41 steps to run; 0 total lines of output

Forward   Backward   Edit

Figure 21.2: Stepping through a program.

```
def tempis(T):
  n = len(T)
  R = n*[None]
  for i in range(n):
    t = T[i]
    if t<10:
      R[i] = "cold"
    elif 10<t<20:
      R[i] = "warm"
    elif 20<t<100:
      R[i] = "hot"
  return R
V = [15,29,72,5,20,22]
W = ",".join(tempis(V))
print W
```

Papering Over. The script shown to the left (the same as shown in Figure 21.2) consists of a function and a small test of the function. The function tempis(T) is supposed to take a list of temperature values and return a list classifying them as cold, warm, or hot. To test the function, the script assigns W to be a comma-separated string of temperature classifications for a sample list of numbers. When it runs, the script crashes with a **TypeError**, where Python complains that instead of a list of strings, which join expects, the list given to join on the assignment to W had a **None** value. To make a point, let's suppose an inexperienced programmer ran the script and saw the error message. The programmer might first think, how can I eliminate the error? One idea is "papering over" the error, which is to make the error go away by changing the script, hoping that fixes the bug.

Code on the right shows how the programmer attempted to fix the bug. After noticing that the `join` failed because of a `None` value, and that the `return R` statement at the end of `tempis(T)` might include a `None` because R is initially created as a list of n `None` values, the obvious fix is to change the third line of the script so that R is initially a list of empty strings. That way, no matter what `tempis(T)` returns, the `join` of the resulting list will work, because everything in R will be a string. What does the script do after this change? The printed output of the script is `warm,hot,hot,cold,,hot`. Although the new script does not crash, the output is not correct.

```
def tempis(T):
  n = len(T)
  R = n*[""]
  for i in range(n):
    t = T[i]
    if t<10:
      R[i] = "cold"
    elif 10<t<20:
      R[i] = "warm"
    elif 20<t<100:
      R[i] = "hot"
  return R
V = [15,29,72,5,20,22]
W = ",".join(tempis(V))
print W p
```

It is not enough simply to prevent a crash—that is like treating a symptom rather than finding a cure. In fact, a crash is *preferable* to incorrect output in many situations, because it makes the existence of a bug obvious.

Visibility through Printing. Instead of trying to paper over the bug, it is better to understand the root cause of the error. The trouble is, with a behavior such as a running program, the error can be detected long after the initial cause leading to the crash. Though a step-through debugger might be nice to study the program behavior leading up to the error, we can also use simple print statements to give us the visibility needed for debugging. Figure 21.3 shows another modification to the `tempis(T)` function, one that has an extra print statement inserted. The code is shown on the left in Figure 21.3, with corresponding output shown on the right.

```
def tempis(T):
  n = len(T)
  R = n*[None]
  for i in range(n):
    t = T[i]
    if t<10:
      R[i] = "cold"
    elif 10<t<20:
      R[i] = "warm"
    elif 20<t<100:
      R[i] = "hot"
    print "**", T[i], R[i]
  return R
V = [15,29,72,5,20,22]
W = ','.join(tempis(V))
print W
```

```
** 15 warm
** 29 hot
** 72 hot
** 5 cold
** 20 None
** 22 hot
Traceback (most recent call last):
  File "bug01.py", line 15, in <module>
    W = ','.join(tempis(V))
TypeError: sequence item 4:
  expected string, NoneType found
```

Figure 21.3: After adding a print statement for debugging.

The print statement is the last line in the body of the `for` loop of `tempis`. It prints "`**`" to make it obvious this printing is only for debugging; once the bug is fixed, any extra debugging print statements will be removed (or converted into comments). Running this modified script makes it clear just where the `None` value originates: the value 20 is not classified as either warm, hot, or cold. The crash still occurs, but seeing the values of T and R at each iteration is enough to understand the bug. One of the `elif` conditions should be changed, either `10<t<=20` or `20<=t<100` will classify 20. The correct choice is up to the application needs for temperature classification.

Binary Search. Adding temporary print statements to debug a program can be very useful, but it takes some experience to do this efficiently. Here are a few tips: (*i*) it can help to add more than one debugging print statement to give more visibility into buggy behavior; (*ii*) if you have more than one debugging print in a program, start each print with some different string (e.g., "**", "==", "++", etc.) to make it clear when you look at the output which print statement is responsible for the output; (*iii*) if there are complex expressions in the code, such as `R.split().index(T[f(j)])`, then consider breaking up the expression into several statements that assign intermediate values to variables that can be printed (to make them visible in debugging runs); (*iv*) if you have no hypothesis on where the bug might be, use *binary search* to find the problem. The idea of binary search is simple: if there is a single bug, then it is either in the first half or the second half of the program. Therefore, try putting a print statement about halfway through the code and run the program. If the resulting output indicates there is some problem with variables, then the bug is in the first half of the program—then repeat this debugging by putting a print statement somewhere near quarter-way in the code. However, if no problem is indicated with the print halfway through, try moving the print to about the three-quarters point in the code and retry. Binary search is faster than *linear search*, which is to move a debugging print one statement at a time in each retry of the program. Of course, in practice, the idea of binary search or linear search must be adapted to the program structure, taking into account the functions, loops, and expressions.

Logging. Tracing program execution by adding debugging print statements is useful not only for programs that crash, but also for software that does not crash and has incorrect behavior. Particularly for programs that do not crash, there are situations where a standard print statement cannot be used. In certain environments, such a graphical user interfaces (Chapter 29) or some kinds of network programs, Python that is called by a Web server to handle a request from a browser, and even some IDEs prevent viewing the output of print statements as a program runs. Two ideas for overcoming such a limitation on using print are logging debugging output to files or modifying the print statements to send the output somewhere other than to the console. For logging debugging output, Python has a `logging` module; details on using that are beyond the scope of this book. As to redirecting the output from a print statement, Chapter 25 explains how this can be done. Another idea can be to use Python's file and writing features, also explained in Chapter 25, to record values into a file for debugging.

Assertions and Testing

Whereas crashes (program termination with an error message) makes it clear that a bug may exist, incorrect behavior is a "silent" bug. Silent bugs, or latent bugs (which may only show up in rare cases of input), are not only challenges for writing programs, they are dangerous for improving and maintaining software. With each new version of a software system, a new feature added to a program may introduce errors in older, existing features. The suggestion of many software professionals, to meet such challenges, is (*i*) to ensure that incorrect behavior results in a crash (some kind of identifiable error like `IndexError`), and (*ii*) to create a test suite of sample inputs to the functions in a program to test their behaviors. Chapter 20 introduces the `assert` statement, which provides what is needed for (*i*); the unit testing facility explained in "Test Suites" ("Exercises: Unit Testing and Online Supplement" after Chapter 10) is one of Python's facilities addressing (*ii*).

An `assert` statement can assist debugging by converting incorrect behavior into a crash. If some argument x is supposed to be a nonempty list, then the statement `assert` `type(x)==list` and `len(x)>0` will raise an `AssertionError` if x does not satisfy the stated property. An advantage of using `assert` over debugging print statements is that the `assert` can remain in a program even after debugging is finished, whereas print statements for debugging are not useful (and become annoying) after the program is debugged. Later, if the program is changed to add new features, an `assert` statement will continue to check that variables or arguments satisfy the `assert` conditions.

The unit testing facility described "Exercises: Unit Testing and Online Supplement" after Chapter 10, is most useful when debugging modules. The unit tests are only comments, and are not used, unless the module is run as a script; when the module is imported, the unit testing is skipped. Each time a suite of modules is changed to add new features in a software development cycle, the unit tests can be rerun to validate that modules still satisfy all the tests. This policy of verifying that software continues to satisfy a test suite is called *regression testing*. Use of regression testing can accelerate the detection of bugs in software development. Python cannot currently generate the unit tests automatically; it is up to programmers to write the unit test cases in ways that hopefully stress test or cover the edge/corner cases of how functions can be called, in order to increase the likelihood of finding any bugs.

Using pdb

```
import pdb
def tempis(T):
  n = len(T)
  R = n*[None]
  for i in range(n):
    t = T[i]
    if t<10:
      R[i] = "cold"
    elif 10<t<20:
      R[i] = "warm"
    elif 20<t<100:
      R[i] = "hot"
    if R[i] == None:
      pdb.set_trace()
  return R
V = [15,29,72,5,20,22]
W = ",".join(tempis(V))
print W
```

Python's `pdb` module is a text-based, interactive debugger. The idea is to start a script, usually at the command line, and wait for the script to pause at a breakpoint. The first breakpoint occurs after the statement `pdb.set_trace()` runs. The code to the left shows the example from earlier in the chapter, modified to put the breakpoint when `R[i]` is `None` at the end of the `for`-loop iteration. Presumably, a programmer put this breakpoint in because of seeing the error in the `join`. A transcript of running the modified script is shown below. The shaded areas are the parts where a programmer interacts with `pdb` when the script runs. The breakpoint is reported by "`temptest.py(5)`" to occur on line 5 of the script. The programmer is then prompted to enter some `pdb` command—the prompts are the "(PDB)" lines. The programmer typed an interactive `print` statement to display the current values of i, `R[i]`, and `T[i]`. Here, the programmer sees that the error is likely associated with 20 as the value of `T[i]`. Normally, inspecting the variables at the breakpoint is enough to understand the bug, from which the programmer can change the program, fix the bug, or try another experiment. However, `pdb` has other commands (see Python documentation for the full set of `pdb` commands). For example, the programmer could enter the command `next` to continue the script's next line. By repeatedly entering `next` (abbreviated as `n`), the programmer can watch the script a line at a time. At any point, the `print` statement can be entered to view values of variables.

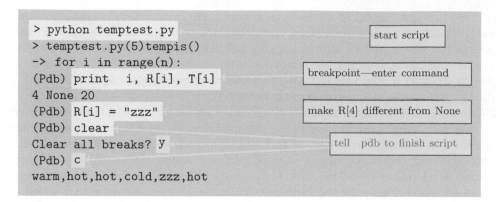

```
> python temptest.py                                              start script
> temptest.py(5)tempis()
-> for i in range(n):                                    breakpoint—enter command
(Pdb) print   i, R[i], T[i]
4 None 20
(Pdb) R[i] = "zzz"                                       make R[4] different from None
(Pdb) clear
Clear all breaks? y                                      tell   pdb to finish script
(Pdb) c
warm,hot,hot,cold,zzz,hot
```

In the transcript above, the programmer made an unusual choice. Instead of letting the script continue with a `pdb` command, the programmer assigned `R[i]` = `"zzz,"` which changed `R[4]` from `None` to the string `zzz`. The next command, `clear`, removed breakpoints, and the command `continue` (abbreviated as `c`) ran the script to its conclusion.

The `pdb` module is not a user-friendly way to debug, depending on knowing special PDB commands and changing scripts to include `pdb.set_trace()` for setting a breakpoint. Nonetheless, it is worth seeing how a debugger can display and even change information during program execution.

Verification and Validation

It is no secret that Python's built-in debugging facilities leave a lot to be desired. Other programming languages have IDEs with breakpoints and other helpful features, such as monitoring every change to a particular variable or object. Industrial and academic researchers have devised many tools and programming techniques to assist in debugging, testing, automatic verification, and bug prevention. On the testing side, there are tools that automatically generate test suites which force every combination of control flow through `if`, `elif`, `else`, `while`, and so on, in a function; such test suites can exhaustively check for crash-bugs. Some tools even warn of suspicious behavior, which is likely incorrect behavior.

To verify that a program has no incorrect behavior, researchers have tools and compilers for automatically, or semiautomatically, exploring all the behaviors of a program, comparing these behaviors against a specification of what are the desired correct behaviors. The caveat for using such tools is that one first has to specify, in perfect detail, what are the correct behaviors. This is usually done using a *specification language*, which is different from the programming language. Roughly speaking, the idea resembles double-entry bookkeeping (which is sometimes cited as one of the most transformative inventions in civilization, dating at least to the 15th century). The method of double-entry bookkeeping has an inherently redundant way of tracking the flow of goods and money; this redundancy significantly increases the odds of finding accounting mistakes. With software, having distinct ways to specify behavior, one in a specification language and another in a programming language, offers a similar hope of finding mistakes. If the behavior of the specification and the behavior of the program differ, one of them has to be mistaken.

Even approximations to the idea of a complete behavior specification can be useful. A few verification projects manage to weave specification and program into a single source file; sometimes these specifications only cover a portion of the correct behavior, but may still serve to uncover mistakes and potential bugs using verification tools. The only feature of Python that might be thought of as a specification is the `assert` statement. If one is careful to write `assert` statements about all the parameters to a function, which state all the expected properties of the parameters, then the quality of the code may be improved by preventing bugs or exposing incorrect calls to the function. However, unlike the research tools, Python has no way to automatically verify all the behaviors of a function.

Chapter 22:   Accumulation Loop Patterns

Biologically the species is the accumulation of the experiments
of all its successful individuals since the beginning.
— H. G. Wells

One hallmark of master crafters, at least to the outsider, is how they make things look easy. The same can be said of some graceful athletes, musicians, and cartoonists, that they make what they do look natural and effortless. Yet what we view when watching these individuals is most likely the product of years of learning and practice. One cannot really learn a craft only by watching the masters; learning a craft requires participation and practice ourselves. Similarly, learning how to write Python functions that use repetition constructs (`for` loops) or recursion is best done by practice.

There are many techniques for learning how to write loops. Some simple problems naturally suggest loop-based solutions. A sequence of problems, graded from relatively easy to more complex, make for good training exercises. Other useful exercises present function definitions that are incomplete (like "fill in the blank" problems), which limits the work needed to find a solution. Another indispensable learning technique is to go through a catalog of *patterns* that have been found in programs containing loops. Such patterns are sometimes called *idioms* of programming; others call these patterns *computing paradigms* because they are standard forms for programs found useful in practice. This chapter features some of the principal kinds of idioms used in Python loops.

Loop synthesis refers to the mental process of writing `for` or `while` loops. The usual way one learns how to write loops is to study many examples, and learn either directly or by intuition the patterns that others have found. Just learning the patterns is quite helpful in becoming comfortable with loops. However, there are other cues that help to write loops; for instance, from the kind of technical problems one faces in devising programs, there can be hints on which patterns might be useful. If the programming problem is an information search, then it makes sense to consider patterns that others have used for searching. If the programming problem works with scientific applications, then another set of patterns would likely be relevant. In some cases, the idioms and patterns presented in this chapter are accompanied by observations about problem characteristics that would suggest using a particular pattern.

The content of this chapter repeats patterns already shown in Chapter 14, but here the same ideas are shown in an imperative style rather than a functional style. Whereas functional patterns for accumulation either rely on `reduce` or using tail recursion, the imperative style directly programs accumulation using `for` loops.

Block Repetition

The simplest form of repetition is to collapse a statement repeated a constant number of times. Chapter 19 explains simple repetition and repetition with variation. Loop synthesis is nearly trivial for problems that call for simple repetition. We repeat some themes from Chapter 19, but with added commentary about efficiency and no-

```
def printwow():
    print("Wow")
    print("Wow")
    print("Wow")
```

tation. Rather than writing the code shown here, we can write either of the three versions below, though for the third version, an argument 3 needs to be bound to parameter `n` in the `printwow()` function.

```
def printwow():
    for i in [0,0,0]:
        print("Wow")
```

```
def printwow():
    for i in 3*[0]:
        print("Wow")
```

```
def printwow(n):
    for i in range(n):
        print("Wow")
```

The next step up in making things more complicated is to use the loop variable in the body of the loop: there should be some expression using the loop variable. Often a

```
def sumsquares(n):  # will return 0 + 1 + 2 + ... + n
    SumSquare = 0
    for loopvariable in range(n):
        SumSquare += loopvariable
    return SumSquare
```

loop variable that takes on the values in a `range` expression is used as an index value in a sequence, as seen in several examples in Chapter 19.

One surprise that Python syntax offers is that unboxing (tuple assignment) can be used in `for` loops. Here is a small example. After this code runs, variable `Comb` will have the value

```
Vector = [(21,105),(204,38),
          (150,242),(63,12)]
Comb = 0
for (x,y) in Vector:
    Comb += x*y
```

calculated from $21 \cdot 105 + 204 \cdot 38 + 150 \cdot 242 + 63 \cdot 12$. In the example's first iteration `x,y = 21,105`, and in the second iteration `x,y = 204,38`. Thus, in each iteration of the loop, `(x,y)` refers to one tuple in `Vector`. The parentheses in the `for` statement above are optional; the statement can also be written as "`for x,y in Vector:`" because Python will interpret "`x,y`" as being a tuple. This kind of `for` loop is useful for graphics programs that deal with drawing points and lines based on (x, y)-type coordinates.

To fully understand how the `for` statement works in Python, one needs to understand the evaluation of the general form

$$\text{for} \quad \textit{loopvars} \quad \text{in} \quad \textit{loopiter}:$$

In this general form, "*loopvars*" is either the name of a single variable or a multiple variable comprising a tuple, as illustrated above; and "*loopiter*" is either a sequence, an iterator, a generator, or a sequence-like object (such as a dictionary or Python3's `range` object).

```
S = [4,2,5,0,9,7,6]
for m in range(len(S)):
    if S[m]%2==1:
        del S[m]
print(S)
```

To show that the understanding of the form of `for` is not trivial, consider the Python code shown here. The idea of this code is to remove all the odd numbers from list S, and one might expect it to print `[4,2,0,6]`. However, when it runs, Python reports an `IndexError`, which halts the run. The problem is that m will take on the values 0, 1, 2, ..., 6, because S contains seven items after the first assignment, and this is what determines the evaluation of `range(len(S))`. After five iterations are completed, two items are removed from S, which makes the length of the list five rather than seven: thus `S[m]` becomes undefined when m is greater than 4. That explains why Python encounters the `IndexError`.

A similar phenomenon occurs with dictionaries. Code here shows a loop through the keys of a dictionary. The `for` loop's *loopiter* expression uses a method for the dictionary type, the `keys()` method, which returns a list of the keys in the dictionary. When this code runs, it prints `zrwk` (the order of the keys is mixed up by Python)—the new dictionary item added during the run, `D[8] = "x"`, is not

```
D = {7:"k", 2:"w", -8:"z", 0:"r"}
AllChars = ""
for key in D.keys():
    if D[key]<0:
        D[-key] = "x"
    AllChars += D[key]
print(AllChars)
```

printed because the `for` loop determined the *loopiter* expression: `D.keys()` evaluates to the list `[-8,0,2,7]`, and these are the values that `key` will take on during the iterations.

The Accumulation Pattern

The *accumulation pattern* is one of the most basic idioms of computing with sequences. It is a generalization of summation (Python's built in `reduce` function expresses the accumulation pattern, but only to a limited extent), but can go well beyond what `sum` can do. The accumulation pattern has several forms, one of which is seen here:

```
Accum = NullValue
for loopvar in loopiter :
    Accum = expr( Accum, loopvar )
```

The italicized names above, *NullValue*, *loopvar*, *loopiter*, and *expr* will vary considerably when the accumulation pattern is put into practice. The *expr* should be seen as some Python expression (combination of operators, functions, methods, etc.) that has both `Accum` and `loopvar` in it. In more elaborate cases, the body of the loop could be more than a single assignment to `Accum`: it could have `if` statements and multiple assignments. The remainder of this section on the accumulation pattern presents a series of examples, gradually increasing the complexity.

Numeric Accumulation

sum, product, and so on. The most direct cases of accumulation are sums, products, and related notions. The accumulation pattern for a product of a list of numbers is illustrated on the right. Here, *NullValue* is 1, and the *expr* of the pattern is `Accum * item` (however, written concisely by augmented assignment). The same pattern can work for all the mathematical operators (`* + - / // ** %`), though it rarely makes sense except for `+` and `*`.

```
def product(somelist):
    Accum = 1
    for item in somelist:
        Accum *= item
    return Accum
```

```
def allmin(somelist):
    Accum = somelist[0]
    for item in somelist:
        Accum = min(Accum,item)
    return Accum
```

min, max, and so on. For accumulation, we can use any function f that (i) takes two numeric arguments and (ii) returns a numeric argument. The body of the loop, in general, would be `Accum = ` $f($ `Accum`, *item*$)$. The example here finds the minimum value in a list. The most difficult task in writing this code is the selection of *NullValue*, in this case `somelist[0]`. Ideally, the best choice for *NullValue* is arguably some number known to be larger than any item in the list: the `min` function would then lower the value of `Accum` in the first iteration. A nice choice for *NullValue* might be ∞, but this choice is unavailable in Python.

The code of `allmin` can equivalently be the definition here. This rewriting shows how the accumulation pattern can use a block of statements in the loop to give a possibly new value to `Accum`. Writing `allmin` this way is nothing more than realizing that the built-in function `min` could be defined by

```
def allmin(somelist):
    Accum = somelist[0]
    for item in somelist:
        if item < Accum:
            Accum = item
    return Accum
```

```
def min(a,b):
    if a < b:
        return a
    return b
```

Substituting this `min` definition into the accumulation pattern yields the rewritten version.

Sum of Gaps. This is a more advanced example than the previous ones. The goal is to write a function that will total up the differences between consecutive items in a list of numbers. If the input is `[1,1,1,1]` then the total is 0, because there is no difference between consecutive items; if the input is `[1,1,2,2]` then the total is -1, because the only difference is 1-2 ➜ -1.

```
def sumgaps(R):
    Accum = 0
    limit = len(R)-1          # see below why we subtract 1
    for i in range(limit):    # i goes over [0,1,...,len(R)-2]
        Accum += R[i+1]-R[i]   # danger: we have i+1 as index,
                               # so loop better stop before len(R)-1
    return Accum
```

Boolean Accumulation

The accumulation pattern for boolean types is covered by Python's built-in `all` and `any` functions. Here we show that these ideas can be programmed by accumulation because there are cases (see the "Exercises" at the end of the chapter) where boolean accumulation is preferable to using `all` or `any`. The example here is a defini-

```
def all(M):  # M is a list of booleans
    Accum = True
    for value in M:
        Accum = Accum and value
    return Accum
```

tion of the `all` function. The function `any` can similarly be defined, with `False` as *NullValue*, and having "Accum = Accum or value" as the body of the loop. Another equivalent way to write `all` would be:

```
def all(M):  # M is a list of booleans
    Accum = True
    for value in M:
        if value:  # makes sense because value is a boolean
            pass
        else:  # value is False
            Accum = False
    return Accum
```

Note: The `pass` statement is used for the `if` block, only because there is nothing to be done with `Accum` where `value` is `True`, yet Python insists on having some statement indented following any `if` statement.

The reason this second version of **all** works correctly is that the basic boolean **and** operator is so simple, the same result can be done by **if/else** logic. It is quite a simple exercise, for instance, to define a function that does the same thing as "**and**" using just "**if**" statements in the function (plus a **return** at the end of the function).

String Accumulation

As a demonstration (because it is rarely used in practice), we show how *NullValue* and *expr* can be adapted to the string type. Here is an example to collect all the vowels in a string, returning the result as a string. When this code runs, **eaeeuaeiaiaiouio** is printed.

```
Input = "Prepare the surface with a mild acid solution"
Vowels = "aeiouAEIOU"
Accum = ''
for character in Input:
    if character in Vowels:
        Accum = Accum + character
print(Accum)
```

List Accumulation

List accumulation is useful for many applications. Generally, *NullValue* is the empty list and *expr* is some form of concatenation, either using the + operator, the += augmented assignment, or a list method such as **append**, **extend**, or **insert** (slice assignment could be substituted for any of these methods).

An equivalent of Python's **map** function can be done using list accumulation. The example here illustrates how **map(len,wordlist)** might be accomplished using a loop. In each iterate, **Accum** concatenates a new item, namely the length of the next word of Z. Better style than this would be to use "**Accum.append(len(item))**," but we present this version to emphasize the accumulation pattern. The printed output of this example is **[3,5,4,3,6,9,4,3,3]**.

```
def wordlengths(wordlist):
    Accum = []
    for item in Alist:
        Accum = Accum + [len(item)]
    return Accum
Z = '''The river kept its finest
spectacle till the end'''.split()
print( wordlengths(Z) )
```

```
def reversed(Alist):
    Accum = []
    for item in Alist:
        Accum = [item] + Accum
    return Accum
```

Here is a definition of **reversed** (which happens to be a built-in function in Python). The result of evaluating **reversed([1,2,3])** is **[3,2,1]**. The order of concatenation above is crucial. It would be a mistake to have **Accum = Accum + [item]** for the body of the loop, because the result of **reversed([1,2,3])** would then be **[1,2,3]**.

Python's **zip** is a built-in function that combines two or more lists into a single list of tuples. The accumulation pattern can also build an output list of tuples given two lists as the input parameters. The function is written to accommodate the shorter of the two input

```
def zip(Alist,Blist):
    Accum = []
    OutSize = min(len(Alist),len(Blist))
    for i in range(OutSize):
        v = ( Alist[i], Blist[i] )
        Accum.append(v)
    return Accum
```

lists. This example of accumulation uses the index notation (`Alist[i]` and `Blist[i]`) referencing the input list items, in contrast to earlier examples that directly use items supplied by the `for ... in` statement. Whether it is better to use indexing or to directly loop through items of a sequence is a matter of personal style. However, for some problems, there is no choice but to use indexing. Processing two or more input lists in tandem is such a problem, because the `for` statement does not have a way to go through multiple lists in parallel. The only choice is to loop over a range of index values and use indexing, as the example shows.

To get the equivalent of the `filter` function, an `if` statement is needed. This example shows how a filtering idea works on a list of strings. The function `bigwords` extracts a list of the words longer than eight characters by only appending to `Accum` the "big" words. Selective filtering in a loop, like this example, can also be used to implement searching algorithms; a topic that is explained further in Chapter 23.

```
def bigwords(sentence):
    Accum = []
    for word in sentence.split():
        if len(word)>8:
            Accum.append(word)
    return Accum
```

While the `bigwords` function does return the list of big words in a string, the resulting list might contain duplicates; perhaps this is what is needed, perhaps not. What if we do not want the resulting list to have duplicate words? Two new versions are shown below. On the left, to make the list get only unique words, the code avoids adding a word to `Accum` when it is already in the list. Python offers another way to write `not (word in Accum)`. Using the `not in` operator, the code on the left is rewritten to be the version on the right.

```
def bigwords(sentence):
    Accum = []
    for word in sentence.split():
        if len(word)>8 and not (word in Accum):
            Accum.append(word)
    return Accum
```

```
def bigwords(sentence):
    Accum = []
    for word in sentence.split():
        if len(word)>8 and word not in Accum:
            Accum.append(word)
    return Accum
```

Dictionary Accumulation

The patterns of accumulation seen thus far include `Accum` types that are numeric, boolean, or list. These are sufficient for most applications, but dictionaries are well suited to applications of classification or statistics. Furthermore, even where a list might be used, dictionaries are far more efficient than lists when the data to be processed is quite large.

To illustrate the pattern, suppose `Book` is a list of all the words in some novel, in the order they occur. Further simplifying the problem, assume that all punctuation has been removed (periods, commas, semicolons, and so on) and all the words are lowercase. The goal is to make a table of each word in `Book` along with the number of times that word appears. Most likely, common words "the," "an," and "a" will have the highest counts. A solution to the problem is shown to the right.

```
Accum = { }
for word in Book:
    if word not in Accum:
        Accum[word] = 0
    Accum[word] += 1
# now display the table
for word in Accum:
    print(word,Accum[word])
```

The dictionary accumulation example has a trick worth noting. The *NullValue* for the accumulation pattern is an empty dictionary, but accumulation step is not so straightforward. It would be nice if the body of the accumulation loop consisted of the single line such as `Accum[word] += 1`, with the simple intent of incrementing the count for a particular word. Unfortunately, `word` may not be in the dictionary (there is a first time for every word). Therefore, there is an `if` statement that adds a new word to the dictionary if it is not already present. The initial count for the new word is zero because it will be incremented by the next statement, making the count equal to 1.

This kind of issue with dictionaries, needing to initialize a count when a value is first seen, comes up often enough that many prefer using the dictionary `get` method instead of indexing by key. As an example, suppose `v = D["box"]` would get an error because `"box"` is not a key in dictionary D. The assignment `v = D.get("box",9)` will succeed, making `v` equal to 9 (the second argument to the `get` method specifies what to return if the key is not found in the dictionary).

Alternatively, suppose `D["box"]` has the value 120. When the key is present in the dictionary, the `get` method looks up the value and returns that: so `v = D.get("box",9)` assigns 120 to `v`, since `"box"` is a key in D. Thus, the script to count all the words in `Book` can be written more simply, shown here on the right. The first time a word is encountered, the `get()` method

```
Accum = { }
for word in Book:
    Accum[word] = Accum.get(word,0) + 1
# now display the table
for word in Accum:
    print(word,Accum[word])
```

returns zero, so the first assignment to `Accum[word]` will be 1; any assignments in subsequent iterations will increment to the count for that word. Another idea is to use a standard library module which provides a tool just to address this issue; if you are curious, look up `defaultdict` in Python's `collections` module.

Because dictionaries tolerate numbers, booleans, tuples, and strings as keys, the same code can count frequencies of numbers in a sequence. For instance, if `Book` is the list of numbers `[1,1,2,5,6,2,1]`, then the output consists of the four lines shown on the right.

```
1 3
2 2
5 1
6 1
```

Loops Using *Iterables* and Generators

You may encounter an error message like "object is not an iterable" trying to write a for loop or using some sequence methods. Chapter 13 informally describes iterators (and the associated term *iterable*) with generators. In fact, Python automatically creates an iterator (if one is not already available) in order to perform a for loop. Technically, an *iterator* is a Python type, like other data types (boolean, string, list, and so on), which has several methods. The next() method is the one related to loops. Writing a loop with code such as "for letter in "fast":" is equivalent to the following:

```
g = (c for c in "fast")
while True:
    try:
        letter = g.next()
        (here would be statements for the body of the loop)
    except StopIteration:
        break
```

This while repetition with a True condition—is an infinite loop. However, when the generator is exhausted (recall from Chapter 13 that generators get "used up"), the next() method will trigger a runtime error, similar to a divide-by-zero error. This error is named StopIteration and would cause the program to fail were it not for the "try" statement. The try and except statements are explained later, in Chapter 26. These statements cause the while loop to terminate normally (via the break, explained in Chapter 23) after all the generator's items have been processed by the loop.

After seeing the above and reading some explanation of how iterators work with loops, you may appreciate the simpler syntax of for loops. The fact that for loops work generally with iterators (and not just sequences) is quite useful. Chapter 25 introduces input and output using files, and file-like objects (which include networking concepts and some computer graphics devices); file-like objects are also iterables, which means we can use simple for-loop syntax to work with them.

Generator Loops

We have seen how loops can *use* generators that supply items for the loop variable, but what about *creating* a generator? Chapter 13 introduces the comprehension syntax for defining a generator, but it is rather limited. It turns out that making a generator with imperative syntax is as easy as using the keyword `yield` in place of `return` in a function. The script here defines a generator `mr()` equivalent to `range()`:

```
def mr(limit):
    i = 0
    while i<limit:
        yield i
        i += 1


for k in mr(5):
    print k
```

When this script runs, it prints 0, 1, 2, 3, 4, because the `for` loop's iteration variable k gets incremented values from `mr(5)` with each iteration. How does this work? One way to think about `yield` is that it returns a value, yet leaves the function `mr()` in a kind of suspended animation, where it will resume the next time it is called. Technically, Python evaluates `mr(5)` and instead of getting an integer value or a list, `mr(5)` is a generator. Python makes this evaluation because a `yield` statement was found within the function's body. Then, for each application of the `next()` method, the code of the generator is activated until a `yield` statement provides a value. Of course, you do not see a `next()` method invocation above; the previous box in this chapter explains how, behind the scenes, this is actually happening.

Python's syntax for generators is yet more powerful than the example shows. It is possible for code using a generator g to use the `g.send(v)` method to "send" a value v into the loop of the generator code (though, to make this work, there should be a statement like `x = yield i` so that x is assigned the value v). This fancier kind of generator syntax is well beyond this chapter, but good to know about if you plan to be an expert in computing (another example is part of "Interlude Signal Processing" after Chapter 27). The idea of sending values into a generator and getting other values back is called a *coroutine*. The use of complicated control design, such as coroutines and "callback" logic in programming is common in certain object-oriented system design patterns.

Going Further

Examples in this chapter are simple, processing little lists and strings. In practice, the accumulation pattern is used to process files. The pattern can be nested and have more elaborate conditions. Also, because `for` loops may process sequence-like objects such as generators, accumulation is often connected with procedures and algorithms that generate data. The two boxes on previous pages briefly explain how generators are related to iteration.

Terminology Review

This chapter introduced the accumulation pattern, presented many examples showing it with different data types, operators, and expressions in the loops. The chapter also demonstrated that removing items from a list can interfere with a `for` loop. Some jargon used in this chapter includes: computing paradigms, programming idioms, loop synthesis, and the accumulation pattern.

Excrcises

All of the exercises from Chapter 13 could be exercises here, using loops instead of list concatenation to define functions. Similarly, all of the problems that follow could be solved without using loops (exploiting many of Python's built-in functions, which do looping already in how they work). The intent is to exercise the patterns.

(1) The problem is to write a function `divsum(xlist,ylist)` where the two arguments are lists of numbers and the two lists have the same length.

```
xlist[0]/ylist[0] + xlist[1]/ylist[1] + xlist[2]/ylist[2] + ...
```

(summing such fractions up to the end of the lists).

(2) Function `strange(numlist)` returns a string that is the concatenation (gluing together) of the `str(item)` for all items in `numlist`. Here are some interactive examples showing how the function should work:

```
>>> strange( [1,2,3,4] )
'1234'
>>> strange( range(5) )
'01234'
>>> strange( range(100,110) )
'100101102103104105106107108109'
```

(3) Write a function `allodd` that returns `True` if all numbers in a list are odd numbers. The pattern for the solution is boolean accumulation, adapting the body of the loop to checking each item for being odd or even.

(4) The function `isDouble(X)` returns a boolean (`True` or `False`). The idea of `isDouble(X)` is to return `True` only if X is the same sequence repeated twice. For example, `isDouble([0,1,0,1])` returns `True`, whereas `isDouble([1,2,3,4])` returns `False`; also `isDouble("wayway")` returns `True`. Obviously, `len(X)` needs to be an even number. The recommended way to write `isDouble` is to use boolean accumulation, in each iteration comparing `X[i]==X[2*i]`, where loop variable i steps through `range(len(X)/2)`.

(5) Function `isPrefix` has three parameters: `isPrefix(prefix,stem,candidate)`. The idea is to return `True` if there is a value n so that

```
prefix + stem[:n]   == candidate
```

is `True`. The solution can be formulated as a search problem, searching for the value n, by trying the integers found in `range(len(stem))` or some similar range of numbers.

(6) The function `sumgaps` shown in this chapter adds up all the "gaps" in a list of numbers. Write a similar function that determines what is the smallest gap (possibly a negative number) between any two items in a list of numbers.

(7) Define a function `base7(numlist)`. The parameter (`numlist`) is a list of numbers; assume each item in `numlist` is a digit in `[0,1,2,3,4,5,6]`. The content of `numlist` should be viewed as a "base 7" numeral, for example: `[2,5,6]` is 139 in decimal, because

$$2 \times 7^2 + 5 \times 7^1 + 6 \times 7^0 \quad = \quad 2 \times 49 + 5 \times 7 + 6 \times 1 \quad = \quad 139$$

The result of evaluating `base7([2,5,6])` would be 139. Use the accumulation pattern to write the `base7` function.

(8) The function `maxdist(P,ref)` is described here:

1. Parameter P is a list of (x, y) pairs, which represent points in 2D-space. Think of P as a list of points on the plane.

2. Parameter `ref` is also a point, that is, `ref` is an (x, y) pair.

3. The function should return the maximum distance between `ref` and any point in P.

4. The *distance* between two points, say (x_1, y_1) and (x_2, y_2), is

$$\sqrt{(x_1 - x_2)^2 + (y_1 - y_2)^2}$$

(9) The *integer logarithm (base 2) of* x, denoted by $\lfloor \lg_2 x \rfloor$, is the smallest number n such that $x/2/2/2 \cdots 2$ (n times dividing by two) is less than 2. For instance,

$$9/2/2/2 \quad = \quad 4.5/2/2 \quad = \quad 2.25/2 \quad = \quad 1.125$$

Hence, the integer logarithm of 9 is 3. Write a function using a `while` loop that calculates the integer logarithm. The pattern is accumulation, where each iteration divides the current number by 2.0 and increments `Accum`, to keep track of the number of divisions done. The condition on the `while` loop checks whether the current number is less than 2.

(10) Can you explain Python's behavior for the following script?

```
X = [True,False]
X.append(X)
X[-1].reverse()
del X[0][0][0][0]
print X
```

(11) Suppose variable `Text` is a list of words (character strings) each beginning with a lowercase letter. Write a single `for` loop that makes 26 counts, one for each letter that a word may start with. For example, when the loop finishes, some variable `Count` will have all the counters; perhaps `Count[2]` ("c" is the third letter in the alphabet) or `Count["c"]` will be the number of words in `Text` beginning with "c."

Chapter 23: Search Loop Patterns

for item in sequence: if interesting(item): break

He who would search for pearls must dive below.
— John Dryden

Sequential Search

Loops are often used to search sequences for particular values. The result of the search might be boolean (`True` if the desired value was present), which is what the `in` operator does, or it might be that the search returns the location of the value, which is what Python's `index` method can do. Observe first that the accumulation pattern

```
def findval(T):
    for i in range(len(T)):
        if 2<T[i]<7:
            return i
    return len(T)  # failed to find
```

can search for *all* the places where a value occurs and accumulate these places into a list.

However, if we are only interested in finding the first place where a value occurs, then accumulation would be overkill (less efficient). Suppose a list T contains numbers and the problem is to find the first location, if any, where a value between 2 and 7 occurs. The findval(T) function shown here can search for the value.

```
def findval(T,interval):
  a,b = interval # a tuple like (2,7)
  for i in range(len(T)):
    if a<T[i]<b:
      return i
  return len(T)  # failed to find
```

findval(T) will return an integer less than the length of the list T if a value between 2 and 7 is found, but otherwise it will return the length of T. Instead of fixing the criterion in the function ("hard coding" 2 and 7), we can let the caller of findval specify these numbers, shown in the version to the left.

Here is a thought question: How many iterations does the function use to find a suitable value? For instance, the list T might have a thousand integers; the particular invocation of findval could be findval(T,(1,3))—this is just a search for the first instance of the number 2. If the value 2 happens to be the first item in T, then findval will return 0 by the first iteration, and it will not go through the 999 other items of T. If the value 2 first occurs around the middle of T, then findval would go through about 500 items in T before returning.

One point of the thought question above is that the search idiom, called *sequential search*, is unlike the accumulation pattern in that it does not always iterate over the entire input sequence. The trick is that the **return** statement, if it runs within a loop, stops the function evaluation immediately. A name for this trick is *early return*, because the function does not go through all of its statements in every run: depending on the input data, the function may "return early" under control of some conditional logic.

Break and Continue

The idea of early return within a loop was so popular for programming languages that new syntax features were added to many languages, Python included. Two special statements, **break** and **continue**, alter the way that loops run. The **break** statement ends a loop early. The **search** function shown here uses **break**. What you see to the right contains two instances of the search pattern, one for parameter Alist and the other for parameter Blist. When the loop finds parameter value in

```
def search(Alist,Blist,value):
  '''search both Alist and Blist for value
     returning a tuple of the places in both
     where value was found, or otherwise
     returning None (value not found in both)'''
  for i in range(len(Alist)):
    if Alist[i]==value:
      break
  if Alist[i]!=value:
    return None
  for k in range(len(Blist)):
    if Blist[k]==value:
      break
  if Blist[k]!=value:
    return None
  return (i,k)
```

Alist, the **break** statement ends the loop right away. The **break** statement does not exit the **search** function, it just ends the currently running loop. In case value is not found in Alist, the **break** statement for that loop will not be used, and the loop will run over the entirety of Alist. This is why there is the if Alist[i]!=value following the loop. Maybe the loop ends early due to **break**, but maybe the loop does not end early. In that case, it could be that the loop failed to find any item of Alist equal to value—so this if statement will check for that possibility and return None.

Pause

If you have not seen `break` or `continue` before, it is worth thinking carefully about the example above. Whereas a `return` statement causes the work of a function to immediately stop, not so for `break`. Unlike `return`, the work of the function containing the loop is not finished by `break`. It is just the *current loop* that is done. If there is another statement in the function after the loop, then the function should proceed by evaluating this statement after the loop. Mentally, however, when you see `break` you should be aware that the `break` only takes effect when the `if` condition is `True`.

The `break` is quite often used in `while` loops, illustrated by a small example. Suppose there is a list of positive integers, which represent weights of parts to be shipped. All the parts need to be shipped, but they need to be put into boxes. More than one part can be put into a box, so long as the total weight in a box is under 640 grams. Here is a function `pack` that takes the input list

```
def pack(parts):
    Total = 0
    # assume any part is under 640 grams
    while len(parts)>0:
        if parts[0]+Total > 640:
            break
        Total += parts[0]  # pack this part
        del parts[0]
    return Total
```

`parts` and returns the weight of the *first* box that will be shipped (the more advanced problem would be to give weights of all the boxes). The `while` loop will end early (by `break`) if the total of the parts considered to be in the box would go over 640 grams by adding the next part in the input list. However, it is possible that one box might have all parts in the input list, in which case the loop will not end early.

In contrast to `break`, the `continue` statement *does not* end the loop early. Instead, the `continue` statement ends *the current iteration* early. An illustrative example is this `for` loop. This loop prints `[1,3,5,7,9,11,13,15,17,19]`. The reason is that the loop skips appending even numbers to `Accum`, because an iteration where `x` is an even number ends when the

```
Accum = []
for x in range(20):
    if x%2==0:
        continue
    Accum.append(x)
print(Accum)
```

`continue` statement runs. However, the loop does not stop: it picks up with the next value of `x` out of `range(20)`.

Generally, if you have doubts about how `break` and `continue` work, it may be helpful to try small examples that have `prints` put within the body of the loop and outside of the loop. This will allow you to "trace" what Python does when the loop runs, so you can deduce what Python must be doing in the evaluation process.

Break and Continue Summary

- The break statement causes an immediate "jump" to the first statement after the loop.

- break ends the loop early.

- The continue statement causes an immediate jump back to the start of the loop (picking up the next value of the iteration variable).

- continue ends the *current iteration* early.

- continue does not end the loop.

Break versus Return

An easy way to end a loop, when inside a function, is simply to use **return**. Here is a function that sums numbers of a list so long as the sum does not exceed 100. As soon as the sum would go over 100, the function returns the accumulated sum up to that point. This brings up the question, why would one ever use **break**, when the **return** statement exits the function (and hence stops the loop) right away? There are two answers to this. First, it

```
def limitSum(M):
    Accum = 0
    for item in M:
        if Accum+item > 100:
            return Accum
        Accum += item
```

could be that a loop is done in a script outside of a function; a **return** statement is only valid within a function. Second, within a function, it might be that there is more work to do after the loop finishes, even if it ends early.

```
def strange(M):
    Accum = 0
    for item in M:
        if Accum+item > 100:
            break
        Accum += item
    for item in M:
        if Accum % item == 0:
            return item
```

This second example again calculates the sum up to where further additions would exceed 100, but then does more. It returns the first item in the list such that the sum is divisible by that item. To do this, it is necessary to have a second loop, one that searches for the satisfactory item. The **break** ends the first loop, to get the sum, so that the second loop can begin. A **return** instead of **break** in the first loop would be a mistake. Although this example is rather artificial, there are many occasions in practice where scripts or functions use multiple loops in succession, which motivate using **break** rather than **return**.

Consider the problem of detecting whether a string's first double letter (like the phrase "exceed expectation") also has that letter later on in the string (the answer would be `False` for "battle plan"). To make a point, we solve this using a loop:

```
def HasTwoAndLater(astr):
    for i in range(len(astr)-1) # one less than normal, so that astr[i+1] works
        if astr[i]==astr[i+1]:    # first double-letter in the string
            break
    # now, out of the loop; astr[i] is the double letter
    for j in range(i+2,len(astr)):  # j starts after the double letter
        if astr[j]==astr[i]        # astr[j] is later
            return True
    return False
```

In this code, replacing the `break` by `return` would not give the correct result.

Nested Loops

Most examples in this chapter deal with lists of numbers or lists of strings. Many applications require more sophisticated kinds of lists, where items of a list might themselves be lists, dictionaries, or tuples. A classic example of this is an array, typically shown in mathematics texts in tabular form:

14	20	31	88	70	12	15	21
5	90	44	45	37	65	12	0
73	20	39	86	91	55	25	52
15	38	12	21	83	51	70	40

This array has four rows and eight columns. A Python representation of this concept would typically be something like the following:

```
M = []
M.append( [14,20,31,88,70,12,15,21] )
M.append( [5,90,44,45,37,65,12,0] )
M.append( [73,20,39,86,91,55,25,52] )
M.append( [15,38,12,21,83,51,70,40] )
```

These statements result in M being a list of four items; each item of M is itself a list of eight numbers. A simple accumulation problem is to sum all the numbers in the array, which is done here by the accumu-

```
Accum = 0
for i in range(len(M)):  # loops over 4 rows
    for j in range(len(M[i])):  # loop over 8 columns
        Accum += M[i][j]
```

lation pattern and a nested loop. Initially, this kind of nested loop—especially when it uses indexes and `range`, looks confusing. Indeed, it takes some practice getting used to this style of programming (which is common in scientific applications). To understand it, observe first that `M[0]`, `M[1]`, `M[2]`, `M[3]` are each lists (see `append` methods above). Thus, the data type of `M[i]` is a list. Consequently, the notation `(M[i])[j]` or just `M[i][j]` refers to a number: column `j` within row `i` of the array.

With only a small change, the summation of the matrix items is changed here to a search. In this case, the code searches for the first even number found in the matrix, saving the value of the item in variable **search**. An exercise at the end of the chapter asks to

```
search = None
for i in range(len(M)):
  for j in range(len(M[i])):
    if search == None and M[i][j]%2 == 0:
      search = M[i][j]
```

further modify this program so that it need not go through all the iterations of the loops; it should be able to stop as soon as the first even number is found. The challenge in doing this is the way **break** works in Python. When there are nested loops, the **break** statement only applies to the loop body where the **break** runs. Thus, if an "inner loop" (more deeply nested) encounters a **break**, Python will immediately stop this inner loop, but continue with the outer loop. Similarly, the scope of **continue** applies to the loop body where it is found.

Recursive Data

Chapter 14 introduced recursion and recursive structuring of data, such as lists within lists. We revisit the topic in this chapter to consider how such cases can be handled using the imperative style of programming. First, a recursive strategy is described (in case you missed Chapter 14), then a method using **while** is discussed.

Lists of numbers, list of words, even arrays represented as lists of lists have a kind of "data regularity" about them. The items have the same type, or in the case of lists of lists, there is a similarity between items. However, there are many naturally occurring problems that have a kind of irregularity. Consider this list Q:

Q = [[2,1,9],3,[[6,7],0],[12,[5,[1,1],4],17],9]

Some items of Q are numbers, some are lists; one item is a list of numbers, another is a list containing numbers and lists. Suppose we need to sum up all the numbers in Q; what should be done with this irregularity? First, we look at recursion to solve the problem. To fully appreciate how **recursum** works, printed text is insufficient: you really

```
def recursum(List):
    Accum = 0
    for item in List:
        if type(item)==int:
            Accum += item
            continue
        # if the program gets here, item is a list
        Accum += recursum(item)
    return Accum
```

need to use a debugger, or add some print statements and watch as Python runs the program. Intuitively, the loop will be the ordinary accumulation pattern alone when the list only contains integers. However, when an item turns out to be a list, then we take a "leap of faith" that **recursum(item)** will calculate the sum of all numbers within **item**. An example, in some tedious detail, of how **recursum** would be evaluated is shown in Figure 23.1. Do not be put off by this level of detail: programmers *do not* need to think about all these operations, since that is the job of computers. A programmer need only concentrate on the first level of evaluation, trusting that recursion can go all the way to the bottom in doing the evaluation.

Just as a minor modification to summing items of a matrix turned accumulation into a search, the same can be done for a recursive data structure. All that is needed is to initialize some variable, say **search**, to be a value that is *not* in the data, then use recursion or iteration to go through the items. When the matching item is found, it can be saved in the `search` variable. This is straightforward with iteration, though the pattern calls for some explanation (given on the next page). What if recursion is used? The problem with recursion is that assigning to a variable `search` inside of a recursive call will not work: variable assignments inside functions change only *local* (not global) variables. Chapter 17 shows how to circumvent this restriction: let `search` be a list, initially empty, and when a matching item is found, append it to list `search`. Mutating a variable is compatible with recursion.

```
recursum([[2,1,9],3,[[6,7],0]])   →
recursum(0 ✦ [2,1,9],3,[[6,7],0])   →
recursum(0 ✦ recursum([2,1,9]) ; [3,[[6,7],0]])   →
recursum(0 ✦ recursum(0 ✦ [2,1,9]) ; [3,[[6,7],0]])   →
recursum(0 ✦ recursum(2 ✦ [1,9]) ; [3,[[6,7],0]])   →
recursum(0 ✦ recursum(3 ✦ [9]) ; [3,[[6,7],0]])   →
recursum(0 ✦ recursum(12 ✦ []) ; [3,[[6,7],0]])   →
recursum(0 ✦ 12 ; [3,[[6,7],0]]   →
recursum(12 ✦ ; [3,[6,7],0])   →
recursum(15 ✦ recursum([[6,7],0]))   →
recursum(15 ✦ recursum(0 ✦ [[6,7],0]))   →
recursum(15 ✦ recursum(0 ✦ [recursum([6,7]),0])   →
recursum(15 ✦ recursum(0 ✦ [recursum(0 ✦ [6,7]),0])   →
recursum(15 ✦ recursum(0 ✦ [recursum(6 ✦ [7]),0])   →
recursum(15 ✦ recursum(0 ✦ [recursum(13 ✦ []),0])   →
recursum(15 ✦ recursum(0 ✦ [13,0])   →
recursum(15 ✦ recursum(13 ✦ [0])   →
recursum(15 ✦ recursum(13 ✦ [])   →
recursum(15 ✦ 13)   →
28
```

Figure 23.1: Example of a `recursum` evaluation: the ✦-symbol separates the current value of the `Accum` variable from the remainder of the work to be done; notice that recursion creates different levels of `recursum` evaluation, each with its own `Accum` variable.

A classic question of computer science is whether the technique of recursion is actually necessary to process recursive data structures. The answer is no, thanks to a device known as a *queue*. A queue is nothing more than a list manipulated by indexing and slicing in a certain way. Here is a nonrecursive solution to the problem. Two equivalent versions are shown below, but the one on the right makes better use of Python list methods.

```
def loopsum(List):
    Accum, Queue = 0,List[:]
    # initial Queue is copy of List
    while len(Queue)>0:
        head = Queue[0]
        del Queue[0]
        if type(head) == int:
            Accum += head
        else:  # head is a list
          for item in head:
              Queue.append(item)
    return Accum
```

```
def loopsum(List):
    Accum, Queue = 0,List[:]
    while len(Queue)>0:
        head = Queue.pop(0)
        if type(head) == int:
            Accum += head
        else:  # head is a list
            Queue.extend(head)
    return Accum
```

A queue is just a list that is mutated in only two possible ways: either more items are added to the end, or the first item of the list is removed from the list. The `pop(0)` method removes the first item and also returns it, so that `head = Queue.pop(0)` simultaneously gets the first item from `Queue` and deletes that item.

The intuition of using the queue is this. As the `for` loop goes through the items of `List`, each will either be an `int` or a `list`. The items that are of type `int` can be dealt with immediately, by adding to `Accum` (the accumulation pattern). But if the item is a list, then summing of this item is postponed: the item is concatenated to the end of the queue, which represents work to be done later. The final trick is the initialization before the loop, which makes `Accum` zero and makes `Queue` be a copy of the original `List`. If you manually go through an example, being careful to put postponed work on the end of `Queue` (using the `extend` method), you observe how the postponed work inevitably gets added to `Accum`.

There is one more way to write `recursum` that is not recursive—it is a Python trick, that rarely works, and it is **not considered good practice**. The code is shown on the left, with an example sequence of data transformations shown to the right.

```
def recursum(L):
    S = str(L)
    for char in "[,]":
        S = S.replace(char,' ')
    return sum(map(int,S.split()))
```

```
[[2,1,9],3,[[6,7],0]      →
"[[2,1,9],3,[[6,7],0]"     →
" 2,1,9],3, 6,7],0]"       →
" 2 1 9] 3 6 7] 0]"        →
" 2 1 9 3 6 7 0"           →
["2","1","9","3","6","7","0"]  →
[2,1,9,3,6,7,0]            →
28
```

This definition might seem appealing because it avoids recursion. However, it does not respect the recursive nature of the data structure, and only works because of the way Python represents lists when formatting (*via* the `str` conversion).

Tools

Most searching boils down to pattern matching. For numeric problems, it can be that a certain pattern of values is of interest: looking through equity prices to see when a stock price exceeded its 200-day moving average, or looking at voltage measurements to find a spike. Other patterns are character or byte arrangements. Chapter 27 shows an example using Python's `re` module, which can search through text for patterns given by regular expressions. An-

```
<?xml version="1.0" encoding="UTF-8"?>
<!DOCTYPE html
PUBLIC "-//W3C//DTD XHTML 1.0 Transitional//EN"
"DTD/xhtml1-transitional.dtd">
<html xmlns="http://www.w3.org/1999/xhtml"
xml:lang="en" lang="en">
<head><title>Most Excellent Page</title>
</head>
<body bgcolor="white" link="blue" text="red">
<p>This will be a great page.</p>
</body>
</html>
```

other similar case is scanning the content of Web pages looking for special "tags" that mark text areas. Above is the source of a Web page, written in the HTML language. Below, we show an example of searching through this source to extract the title of the page. This is just one example of using a tool to make search simpler; there are many such tools for different problem domains.

```
from pyquery import PyQuery
root = PyQuery(source)
print root('title').text()
```

Let's say we want to read the XHTML source of a page as a string, and then extract from that string just the title of the page. The title is enclosed between `<title>` and `</title>` tags. It is certainly possible to write Python code to search for the tags and then pull out the title, but it can be worth learning about tools that simplify the job. One tool to consider is pyquery, which is a module similar to Javascript's `jQuery` library for navigating through elements of an HTML document (see `http://packages.python.org/pyquery/`). Though pyquery is not part of the standard library, it is worth the effort to install this package if you plan on frequently searching through a Web page source. For the HTML example shown above, put into a string variable `source`, the three lines shown here and find the page title and print it. The output from these lines is `Most Excellent Page`. Note that if the page did not have a title field, this code would have failed, raising a Python error. Recovering from such errors within a Python program is a topic of Chapter 26.

Terminology Review

This chapter introduced the `break` and `continue` statements, discussed early return, how to exit loops or skip iterations, and some sequential search patterns. The possibility of nested loops, including inner loop and outer loop ideas, shows how loops can be combined. Recursive data structures, also found in the tree examples in Chapter 14, can use either recursion or loops for searching or accumulation.

Exercises

(1) The problem is to write a loop searching for the *last* even number in a list of numbers. This is a simple exercise, using for example `range(len(V)-1,-1,-1)`, which will allow the search to proceed from back to front. Instead, replace the ? below to get the result (do not use a comprehension expression).

```
def FindLastEven(V):
    for e in ? :
        if e%2==0:
            return e
```

(2) Write a version of `find` that searches a matrix (a list of lists of integers) for the first even number that either returns that number or returns `None` if the matrix has no even number. Your code should use `break` so that all iterations end as soon as the first even number is found.

(3) Let X be a list of numbers. Write a function `sp(X)` that returns `True` if there is an item `X[k]` for k>0 which equals `sum(X[:k])`. Do not use `sum` in your definition of `sp`.

(4) Given a list of strings, which of these strings are also found within all the previous items of the list?

(5) Find an item of a list that is an alias of another item in the list.

(6) The problem is to define `inside(Points)` which returns `True` if at least one item in `Points` is within the rectangle with corners at (0,0), (2,0), (2,1), (0,1). The sequence `Points` has pairs of numbers as its items (each item represents an (x, y) point on the plane).

Loopy Data

Can you explain the following interactive Python session?

```
>>> X = [1,2,3]
>>> X.append(X)
>>> X
[1, 2, 3, [...]]
>>> X is X[3]
True
>>> X.insert(1,X)
>>> X
[1, [...], 2, 3, [...]]
>>> (X is X[1]) and (X is X[4])
True
```

In this session, variable `X` is truly a *recursive data structure*—the line "`X.append(X)`" tells Python to add the list `X` to itself, which would make the list `X` contain itself. Does this even make sense? You can see that Python tolerates this sort of behavior. Using the terminology of Chapter 17, `X` and `X[3]` turn out to be aliases of the same list. After the insertion "`X.insert(1,X)`," all three of `X`, `X[1]`, and `X[4]` are aliases of the same list: apparently, `X` contains itself twice!

In the history of philosophy, this situation borders on what is called an *antinomy*, a paradox of sorts. Over a century ago, Bertrand Russell wondered if the notion of a set of all sets could be reasonable. Would a set of all sets contain itself? There is no way to prove the answer or disprove it—this question is called Russell's Paradox.

In computer science, many very useful data structures can have self-references. Above, the list `X` contains two references to `X`, one at index 1 and another at index 4. Such "loopy" lists are valuable because they can represent things like organizational charts where the relationships between parts of an organization are naturally complex, with communication lines between the different parts represented in any way we desire. Lists that allow any kind of reference (even self-reference) give us just the flexibility needed. However, the algorithms that compute using such lists need to be careful to avoid infinite loops: some extra checks in the `while` loops or recursive functions need to detect when self-reference may occur.

Chapter 24:   Drawing

> *Sci-fi films are the epic films of the day because we can no longer put 10,000 extras in the scene, but we can draw thousands of aliens with computers.*
> — William Shatner

Many introductions to computing begin with graphics. Drawing and related ideas, like shading, coloring, animation, and special effects are intuitive and appear deceptively simple to produce. Remember, even humans could draw and appreciate figures long before reading, writing, and calculation were on the scene. It comes then as a surprise that graphics is rather complicated for computers, requiring many layers of software and hardware to do well. It is far simpler to program a computer to search millions of items than it is to draw a realistic scene. Thus, it should not be so strange to find that Python lacks any built-in features for graphics.

In order to access graphical hardware, Python needs to use software packages that are external to the language. Even the choice of what package to use is not obvious. If Python controls the screen on a small mobile device, there is likely a particular package optimized for that device. The techniques for graphics vary depending on the hardware drivers (possibly vendor specific), the operating system, and maybe the type of browser plugins if the graphics is portrayed over a network. One of the most widely implemented, if somewhat crude, graphics packages is something called `Tk`, a so-called *framework* for graphical user interfaces. As an outgrowth of some robotics research and later some projects with educating schoolchildren in computing, a package for Python called `turtle` was developed. More modern software for drawing is available outside of the Python standard library of modules. This chapter also describes the `teken` module, which was written for this book, to introduce drawing shapes using HTML5, which most modern Web browsers can render in high quality.

Turtle Drawing

We show first an interactive example of the `turtle` module. Figure 24.1 shows an interactive session on the left and the output on the right. What cannot be seen from the figure is the interactive nature of the drawing. After each command, a small change became visible on the output area (Python creates a new window to show the drawing).

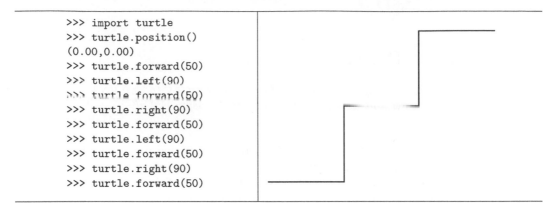

```
>>> import turtle
>>> turtle.position()
(0.00,0.00)
>>> turtle.forward(50)
>>> turtle.left(90)
>>> turtle.forward(50)
>>> turtle.right(90)
>>> turtle.forward(50)
>>> turtle.left(90)
>>> turtle.forward(50)
>>> turtle.right(90)
>>> turtle.forward(50)
```

Figure 24.1: Interactive Python using `turtle`.

The session begins by importing the `turtle` module. The first statement thereafter calls `turtle`'s `position()` function, which reports the (x, y) location of "the turtle," which is a name for a virtual pen that does the drawing. Most function calls in the `turtle` module either report on the turtle's status, command the turtle to move or change some attribute (like the color of the pen), or in the case of real-time graphics, delay before doing some action. In the figure, the turtle is at $(0, 0)$ initially, shown as a pair of `floats`, in what `position()` returns. At any moment, we think of the turtle as oriented (we might think of the turtle as pointing south, north, east, west, and so on). The next series of function calls move the turtle in the direction of its current orientation or change the orientation. The `forward(50)` function tells the turtle to move 50 units forward; the `left(90)` tells the turtle to reorient 90 degrees counterclockwise; the `right(90)` tells the turtle to reorient 90 degrees clockwise from its current orientation. Each time the turtle moves, it drags a pen, leaving a trail. The model of drawing using a turtle is intuitive, like steering a vehicle.

Another example using a low-level line drawing is this illustration of applied trigonometry, using a module named `teken`, developed for this textbook. The code on the left renders the figure on the right:

```
import math, teken
'''
This program adapts the first example from the article
"Plotting the Spirograph Equations with Gnuplot", by Victor
Luana, Linux Gazette #133, December 2006.
'''
T,R,r,p = 200, 100.0, 2.0, 80.0
linepoints = [ ]
for i in range(T):
    t = float(i)
    x = (R-r)*math.cos(t) + p*math.cos((R-r)*t/r)
    y = (R-r)*math.sin(t) + p*math.sin((R-r)*t/r)
    x,y = int(200+x), int(200+y)
    point = (int(x), int(y))
    linepoints.append(point)

teken.polyline(points=linepoints,color="blue")
teken.show()
```

Drawing by Shapes

More modern drawing software libraries offer the developer catalogs of shapes, fonts, animation, shading, and patterns for complicated visual displays, including the inclusion of photographs and artwork. Figure 24.2 shows a script using the **teken** module and the resulting drawing on the right. There are several features of this script that contrast with the **turtle**-style of drawing. Instead of a virtual pen, and commands to move the pen, change direction, and go forward, the commands of the **teken** module draw in some defined shapes, lines, or text areas (called labels).

```
import teken

teken.rectangle(start=(50,20),color="cyan",
    fill="palegreen",height=200,width=200)

teken.circle(start=(120,120),radius=60,
    color="yellow",fill="white")

spec = "yellow orange red purple blue green"
for i,c in enumerate(spec.split()):
  teken.line(start=(150,0),
            end=(50+20*i,140),color=c)

teken.label(start=(150,150),angle=45,
        text="Draw",color="darkviolet")

teken.show()
```

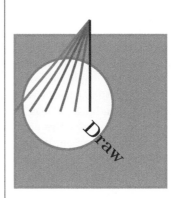

Figure 24.2: Drawing shapes with **teken**.

Things to notice about the script in Figure 24.2 are the following points:

- The picture area, called the *canvas*, is addressed by (x, y) coordinates; by default, **teken** supposes this to be a 400×400 area. The x-coordinate addresses the canvas horizontally, with $x = 0$ being the leftmost and $x = 399$ as the rightmost point in the area (although the browser may clip the visible area, depending on the window parameters). However, *unlike mathematical texts*, the y coordinate addresses the canvas with $y = 0$ at the top and $y = 399$ at the bottom—the reverse of what we expect in traditional mathematics. This way of using canvas coordinates is typical of several graphical software interfaces.

- The **teken** functions may not be interactive (this depends on the particular circumstances of browser rendering of the HTML5 canvas commands). The last line in the script, **teken.show()**, forces all the previous calls that draw shapes to become visible. This is also typical of many graphical software packages, which virtually draw figures offscreen and only later move them to the display area.

- One shape (or line or label) draws on top of previously drawn shapes. Hence, a drawing is built up by a number of function calls using **teken**.

Coordinate Drawing versus Relative Placement

Drawing shapes beyond lines, rectangles, ellipses, and so on, can take some planning, because **teken** is based on coordinates. Some scripts in this chapter use trigonometry to calculate coordinates for drawing a complicated sequence of line segments. Instead of drawing shapes and text at particular coordinates, there is another way (but not available using `teken`). Some software offers functions for *relative placement* of shapes. The suite of software used to design Web pages, for example, is based on HTML, CSS, Javascript, JQuery, and other packages to flexibly design the placement of objects on a page. This can be done in qualitative terms such as "center" or relative terms such as "above," "left of," and so on. Chapter 27 describes a graphical user interface, which leaves the details of how objects are placed up to algorithms to determine. Of course, for really fine control of placement, the coordinate way to specifying where shapes go may still be needed.

Graphing Data

There are many other ways of drawing in Python using modules and extra libraries designed for graphical or richer media experiences. One important specialty is portraying quantitative information. The topic of data presentation has grown to be its own domain of expertise for which Python packages (not usually distributed with standard Python) can be used. Though the standard Python distribution includes the Tk library for interactive widgets, drawing, and plotting—the `turtle` and the `tkinter` modules use Tk—there are much nicer packages for data presentation.

matplotlib. The example shown here uses `matplotlib`, which is a presentation library of modules typically used in scientific or statistical Python applications. Two simple examples and their outputs are shown below, but they barely scratch the surface. To get a better idea of what this package can do, it is best to visit the gallery on the `matplotlib` Web site.

```
import math, random, matplotlib.pyplot as plt
theta, r = [], []
for i in range(1,101):
    angle = 2*math.pi * (i/100.0)
    theta.append(angle)
    r.append(1.0 - math.sin(3*angle))
plt.polar(theta,r)
plt.show()
```

```
pointsY = [5*math.sin(5*math.pi*i/100)
                    for i in range(100)]
pointsW = [random.choice(range(-5,6))
                    for i in range(30)]
plt.ylabel("sin and random list")
plt.xlabel("trial number")
plt.plot(pointsY)
plt.plot(pointsW)
plt.show()
```

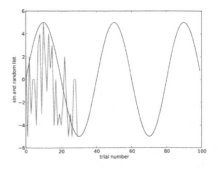

Interlude: Animation Design

Computer graphics begins with low-level considerations for drawing lines, polygons, and even setting the color of pixels on a display, but quickly the designs become more ambitious, going far beyond what this text can describe. Realistic scene rendering depends on knowing about shading, shadows, reflections, and other optical properties. Special effects can make objects transparent or luminous. Though the finer points of computer graphics can be complex, one element of graphical display is easy to understand: animation.

Animation by computer graphics consists of playing a sequence of frames, like a movie. The frames are viewed sequentially, over time, to give us the illusion of movement. Animation is thus *a behavior*: the software has to produce values (the drawings) as a function of time (or frame number). If the animation is part of an interactive game, then the software-controlled behavior will depend on inputs from users, making programming more complicated. Careful design decreases the complexity of software.

For the simplest case of animation, a general design in pseudocode looks like this:

```
for n in range(numberFrames):
    frame = some code that draws frame n
    output frame
```

The question is how to get details about "*some code that draws frame*" above. It may seem like a straightforward process, designing code to draw the contents of a frame, but it is worth thinking about how to minimize the complexity of the design—we do not want to end up with a messy program that is difficult to understand.

Example. The simple example illustrates a design choice. The animation displays a stick-figure rotating and shrinking, while a cat creeps along below. Using **teken**, a ten-frame animation can be this (with the first four frames shown below):

```
import teken
for i in range(10):
    theta, mag, creepx = 10+15*i, 1-0.1*i, 50 + 25*i
    teken.image(name="stickfig.gif",start=(250,50),
        width=120,height=250,angle=theta,scale=mag)
    teken.image(name="cat.gif",start=(creepx,200),
        width=98,height=72)
    teken.show()
    teken.clear()
```

Alternative Design. With just two images, the stick-figure and the cat, a simple loop body can do everything and the program is understandable. But what if the animation contained hundreds of moving parts? Then a straightforward design might lead to a loop body with many hundreds of lines of code. Instead of directly writing Python statements for each image in the loop, we could use a list of figures and the associated functions that draw them.

```
import teken

def drawStickFig(t):  # t is "time" in the animation
    theta, mag = 10+15*t, 1-0.1*t
    teken.image(name="stickfig.gif",start=(250,50),
        width=120,height=250,angle=theta,scale=mag)

def drawCat(t):
    x = 50 + 25*t
    teken.image(name="cat.gif",start=(x,200),
        width=98,height=72)

figures = {"stickFigure":drawStickFig, "cat":drawCat}

for i in range(10):
    for item in figures:
        drawFunction = figures[item]
        drawFunction(i)
    teken.show()
    teken.clear()
```

In this alternative design, every figure has its own drawing function. The main animation loop now conveys the logic of the animation without needing to show the details of how each figure is drawn. Changes to such a program might be more localized so that a programmer can work on a particular function without needing to think about other functions. One can imagine this kind of design becoming more elaborate: perhaps the drawing of some figures should be skipped depending on user inputs to the program (like a game); or more parameters to the drawing functions could customize how figures are drawn.

Beyond this alternative design using a dictionary of names and functions, Chapter 27 offers another tool from Python's catalog: objects and classes. Roughly speaking, by letting each figure be an *object*, we can define functions that "remember" things between successive calls. For example, the function invoked by `drawCat(5)` could look at variables assigned during the evaluation of `drawCat(4)` (or whatever an earlier call to `drawCat` was). This can simplify sophisticated programs because these "memory variables" do not have to be known to the caller of `drawCat`. The `Cat` object has its own private, enduring memory as well as providing a function. The syntax of objects, explained in Chapter 27, for the `Cat` object could be `p.draw(5)`, where `p` is a variable equal to the `Cat` object. This syntax should look familiar: it is the same syntax seen in string expressions like `"--".join(T)`; it turns out that the data structures of Python, be they lists, strings, or dictionaries, are secretly objects.

Chapter 25:   Input and Output

Data is not information, information is not knowledge,
knowledge is not understanding, understanding is not wisdom.
— Clifford Stoll

The field of computing grew out of applications characterized by input-output problems. Businesses tabulate sales and inventory figures, producing quarterly reports. Scientific applications process experimental data, generating statistical summaries, graphs, and charts. Recent computing needs transcend simple reports: they require interactive, mobile, and dynamic data sharing. That said, the basics of how most software works depends on some form of handling input datasets and creating results in desired, standard formats. Though new formats for output include video or 3D descriptions (there are now so-called 3D printers that manufacture objects from software designs), it is still a good idea to learn simple character formats using ASCII, which is what this chapter offers.

The starting concepts for this chapter are input from keyboard, output to the console, and file i/o (reading and writing files that are on persistent storage, like disk or flash memory). Along the way, there are dependent concepts that turn out to be useful later for other purposes: Python has a formatting "mini-language" for precise control of how numbers and strings are placed; there are different options for conversion of input data from character form to internal data types. The plan of this chapter is to begin with the simple case of input from the keyboard and output to a console. Although this should be simple, this is an area where Python2 and Python3 significantly differ; the discussion has a number of examples showing language features for the two versions of Python. The remainder of the chapter thereafter deals with files.

Console and Keyboard Input

Python2 has two built-in functions that solicit text input from a user at the keyboard. These two functions, called `input()` and `raw_input()`, have in common that they suspend a running function or script indefinitely, waiting

```
>>> x = input("Type a number here --> ")
Type a number here --> 7
>>> x
7
```

until a user types in some character data and presses Enter on the keyboard. The box above contains a simple demonstration of `input()`, done in an interactive Python2 session. What you cannot see in the box is the pause waiting for user input. The line "Type a number here --> 7" was partly made by Python2 and partly made by the user. Python2 printed the text `Type a number here -->` and put the cursor just after this text, waiting for the user to enter something. The string argument to `input()` is called the *prompt*, and it is displayed just before where you expect the user to type in some text. The prompt is optional; if you do not supply a prompt, Python2 will wait for user input on a new, blank line. The prompt is a nice way to indicate that something is expected from the user (otherwise, Python2 would wait forever, or until the window is closed).

```
a = input("number please: ")
b = input("another one please: ")
print("you entered", a, b)
print("types of a,b are", type(a), type(b))
```

The `input()` function is usually called from a script or some function within a script. The script on the left looks simple, The `input()` function is called twice, saving the first value in variable `a` and the second in `b`. Suppose this script is put into a file named `demo.py`. Examples in the following paragraphs run `demo.py` to show there is more to `input()` than one might first think. Below are two examples of running `demo.py` from a Linux terminal:

```
> python demo.py
number please: 201.5
another one please: -40
you entered 201.5 -40
types of a,b are <class 'float'> <class 'int'>
>
```

```
> python demo.py
number please: 12*60
another one please: a/4 + 22
you entered 720 182
types of a,b are <class 'int'> <class 'int'>
>
```

The example on the left is straightforward. The one on the right demonstrates that variable `a`, assigned from the first `input()` call, can be typed by the user in the response to the second `input()`. Initially, this might seem like a clever feature of Python. The surprise here is that Python2 will accept an expression as the value that the user enters via keyboard, which can be any expression of the kind that might appear in normal Python2 statements. However, it has to be an expression: functions, methods, and operators are allowed; but assignment statements, `if`, `for`, and so on, are *not* allowed. Above, the input text "a/4 + 22" references variable `a`, which was assigned 720 by the previous statement.

A somewhat strange example is shown here, where the user entered a Python slice expression of a string instead of a number. Though this method of getting input from a user is quite flexible, it opens the door to many mistakes.

```
> python demo.py
number please: [x**2 for x in range(5)]
another one please: "fabricate"[:4]
you entered [0, 1, 4, 9, 16] fabri
types of a,b are <class 'list'> <class 'str'>
>
```

```
> python demo.py
number please: one
NameError: name 'one' is not defined
>
```

The input `one` caused the script to stop with an error, because Python could not evaluate the string "one" and get a value (if the input had been `"one,"` quotes included, then Python2 would at least get a string). Worse even than input that causes a script to stop with an error could be input of an expression containing mutating method calls: when Python2 evaluates `somelist.reverse()` it *changes* what is in the variable `somelist`. Therefore, some people consider the `input()` function to be a security problem, because it can allow the user to crash a program, trick it into giving bad results, and so on.

PyTwo's `raw_input()` function does not suffer from such security problems. Scripts do not crash and users cannot do more than supply characters for input to the script. To the right is a rewriting of `demo.py` using

```
a = raw_input("number please: ")
b = raw_input("another one please: ")
print("you entered", a, b)
print("types of a,b are", type(a), type(b))
```

`raw_input()`. An example running the revised script, which uses `raw_input()`, follows, and it purposefully has some input that would be illegal for the `input()` function:

```
> python demo.py
number please: 1 plus 2
another one please: seven
you entered 1 plus 2 seven
types of a,b are <class 'str'> <class 'str'>
>
```

You see why `raw_input()` does not run into trouble: the result of calling `raw_input()` is always a string. Python will not interpret this string as an expression, so there is no danger of causing the script to fail with an error.

Python3. In Python3, the `input()` was removed, and `raw_input()` renamed to `input()`; in other words, Python3's `input()` function behaves the way Python2's `raw_input()` does.

Input Conversion and Validation

On the one hand, Python2's `raw_input()` (or Python3's `input()`) does not fail, no matter what a user enters from the keyboard. On the other hand, getting a string may not be what is needed. Therefore, using `raw_input()` often calls for some data

```
mass = raw_input("Enter mass: ")
velocity = raw_input("Enter velocity: ")
mass = int(mass)
velocity = int(velocity)
print("mv =", mass*velocity)
```

conversion, from string to some other data type. Suppose we would like to make small Python2 script `demo.py` that gets two numbers from the keyboard, as shown here. Below are two sample runs of the script. On the left is a normal run of the script, and on the right the user made a mistake in the response to the input prompt.

```
> python demo.py
Enter mass: 10
Enter velocity: 30
mv = 300
>
```

```
> python demo.py
Enter mass: 10.
Enter velocity: 30
    mass = int(mass)
ValueError: invalid literal for int(): '10.'
```

Python's `int()` function converts a string to an `int`, but causes trouble if the string contains characters not expected for integers. If we want a script that tolerates user mistakes, and generally has a more "robust" behavior, then some kind of input validation is needed.

For conversion from a string to an integer, Python requires that the string contain only numeric digits whereas the keyboard input contained a period (Python is actually more flexible: the result of `int("-0095")` is 95, for instance). It may seem, therefore, that `raw_input()` is no better than Python2's `input()` for dealing with user mistakes. However, there are other steps one can add to the `demo.py` to *validate* the user input before attempting conversion:

```python
def valid(numstring):
    if len(numstring)<1:
        return False
    for char in numstring:
        if char not in "0123456789":
            return False
    return True

def getinput(varname):
    while True:
        R = raw_input("Enter " + varname + ": ")
        if valid(R):
            return R
        print("Please retry - input must be digits only")

mass = int( getinput("mass") )
velocity = int( getinput("velocity") )
print("mv =", mass*velocity)
```

The `valid()` function will only return `True` if the argument is a string that `int()` would convert without error. The `getinput()` function will ask the user to retry, and retry again (with no limit on retries) until what the user keys in is valid—which is why this way of handling input is called *input validation*.

It is relatively easy to validate a string that should consist only of numeric digits. But many input formats are considerably more complex: dates, times, and scientific numbers with exponents are not easy to validate. In a later chapter, we will revisit the topic of input validation and see a more powerful technique that Python offers for this purpose.

Output Formatting

Python's `print()` function (Python3) or the `print` statement (Python2) convert various Python types such as strings, lists, integers, and dictionaries to some standard format for display. Whereas strings need no conversion (`print` only has to interpret control sequences like \n for proper output), all the other types first need conversion to strings. For instance,

```
>>> print( [1,2,3] )
[1, 2, 3]
```

shows that `print` first converted the list `[1,2,3]` into a string, and then displayed that string. We can also see the same conversion interactively:

```
>>> str( [1,2,3] )
'[1, 2, 3]'
>>> repr( [1,2,3] )
'[1, 2, 3]'
```

The built-in `repr()` function is the preferred way to convert a type into a string, though `str()` works as well. One crucial advantage of `repr()` is seen in the interactive experiments with a string:

```
>>> str("abc")
'abc'
>>> repr("abc")
"'abc'"
```

For a string, `repr()` creates a string that, when printed, would show how Python encodes a string (do not worry if this makes little sense right now, since our goal for `repr()` is mainly to convert lists, dictionaries, and other more complex types). What if `repr`'s conversion of a list into a string is not exactly what is desired? Here is a simple way to get a conversion that does not introduce blanks:

```
>>> repr( [1,2,3] ).replace(' ','')
'[1,2,3]'
```

The trick of using string methods, or even functions you may write, lets you take the string that `repr` produces and change it as you like.

Templates

The idea of a text *template* is familiar to anyone who has received form letters.

> *Dear* ——————— ,
>   *Good news! We have added* ———— *value points to your account. And
> if you purchase an upgrade to your current package,* ...

A program fills in the blanks before sending the form letter, putting a customer name in the first blank and an amount in the second blank. Python3 and later versions of Python2 support a built-in string method `format()` that implements the idea of a template. A simple example of this, shown as an interactive session, is:

```
>>> "starting time {0}, ending time {1}".format(1200,1930)
'starting time 1200, ending time 1930'
>>> "W{0}{1}t {0} wh{1}l{2}".format('a','i','e.')
'Wait a while.'
```

The `format` method's template contains special areas such as `{0}` that will be replaced by arguments to the method. We call the special areas `{0}`, `{1}`, ..., *pattern fields* in the template. The first argument (1200 and `'a'` above) replaces `{0}` wherever this pattern field occurs, the second argument replaces `{1}`, and so on. The *template*, or *pattern string*, is shown as a string above, but typically would be a variable of type `str`; such a variable could be thousands of characters, representing many lines of text.

The `format()` goes far beyond replacing pattern fields. The `format()` method *substitutes* for the text in the pattern field, guided by information from the arguments and from instructions in the special areas themselves. A full enumeration of `format`'s power is beyond this chapter, though the main features are worth mention:

- `format()` converts its arguments to strings during substitution.

- `format()` can either use positional arguments (where `{0}` refers to the first argument, `{1}` the second argument, and so on), or `format()` may use a dictionary as its argument, in which case substitution is driven by the names of keys in the dictionary (which are given within the pattern fields).

- When numbers are converted to strings, the pattern field can say whether the number should be left-justified, right-justified, printed in decimal, hexadecimal, using exponent notation, the number of significant digits, and other formatting details.

Taking full advantage of `format()` is not simple. Indeed, the official Python documentation has a section entitled "Format Specification Mini-Language," indicating that `format()` actually uses a specialized data language describing how arguments substitute for text in a string. The following table shows just a few examples and what they intend, for pattern fields.

`{4:30}`	→	use fifth argument, format in 30 characters
`{1:>30}`	→	use second argument, right align in 30 chars
`{0:^30}`	→	use first argument, center in 30 chars
`{0:-^30}`	→	use first argument, center in 30 chars, dash fill
`{:f}`	→	use fixed decimal notation
`{:e}`	→	use exponent notation
`{:8.5f}`	→	format in 8 chars, with 5 digits after decimal
`{:,}`	→	format as human-readable thousands using comma

To understand this small table, it is helpful to show some examples. The first example shows that the argument index can be omitted, and Python will simply substitute pattern fields in the order they occur:

```
>>> "{:12}aaaaaa{:e}".format("hi",2345.6789)
'hi          aaaaaa2.345679e+03'
>>> "{1:-^10.2f} and {0:,} ok".format(235111982,1.5)
'---1.50--- and 235,111,982 ok'
```

Experienced Python programmers do not typically memorize the full formatting mini-language (what can be put into pattern fields); rather, they learn to locate the documentation on the language themselves, then experiment perhaps interactively to be sure that what they have put into the pattern fields gets the right results.

Python2 Substitution. Before `format()` was introduced into the Python language, there was another template operator. This older operator is still supported in Python2, though it is not available in Python3. We mention it here in case you happen to look at older scripts or have need to work with an older version of Python2, such as version 2.4. Recall that Python has a remainder operator, "%" often used to test whether an integer is even or odd. The remainder operator is only defined for integers. Taking advantage of this known limitation, Python used % for another purpose, with strings. This example shows how the operator handled substitution in templates:

```
>>> "M is %d and V is %5.2f in the equation" % (100,12.5)
'M is 100 and V is 12.50 in the equation'
```

For the older-style % operator, pattern fields were identified by the % character, and a mini-language of formatting controlled some details of number conversion to strings.

Reading Files

The functions, scripts, and examples of this section suppose that `ex.txt` is a file containing these five lines:

```
A flea and a fly in a flue
Were imprisoned, so what could they do?
Said the fly, "let us flee!"
"Let us fly!" said the flea.
So they flew through a flaw in the flue.
```

The file `ex.txt` would be located in some directory, which determines its "full address" for technical purposes. For instance, on a Linux system, it might be `/home/user/Desktop/ex.txt` whereas on a Windows system it could be `C:\Users\Robert\Desktop\ex.txt`. When you see the file through a windowing system with folders and icons, the file might just appear with the name `ex`, because the window system may hide the ".txt" suffix: window systems are designed for users, not for software developers. Whatever the situation, you will probably need to know the full address and work with directories (folders), possibly changing the "working directory" (using the `cd` command under Windows or Linux) to use files with Python.

We start with some interactive exercises that read from a file. The first concept to know about is a *file object*, which has the type `file` in Python. For reading files, there are three basic operations, `open`, `close`, and `read` (there are a few others as well, for more advanced work).

```
>>> F = open("ex.txt",'r')
>>> G = open("ex.txt")
>>> print(type(F),type(G))
<class 'file'> <class 'file'>
```

The interactive example creates two file objects; each of these file objects does the same as the other, it serves as a basis for reading the file `ex.txt`—this only works without the full address because this interactive exercise was done in the same directory as where `ex.txt` resides. There is no reason to create two file objects to read a file. The exercise just demonstrates four different ways to do the same thing. The argument `'r'` in two cases above tells Python that the file should be prepared for reading (not writing). If left out, this argument defaults to `'r'` anyway.

> **Note for Python2:** Another built-in called `file()` can be used as well as `open()`, but `file()` is not valid in Python3.

Let's assume F has the file object for ex.txt, obtained by the assignment F = open("ex.txt"). To work with file F, the read() method returns the content of the file as a string, in this example, assigned to variable text. Looking at the example, one sees that the file contains 166 characters and 5 newline characters (one at the end

```
>>> text = F.read()
>>> len(text)
166
>>> text.count('\n')
5
```

of each line). Now, suppose we need to process the text in the file. The following script puts the ideas above together with a loop to print the three most frequently occurring words in the file.

```
F = open("ex.txt")
text = F.read()
wordlist = text.split()
countable = { } # will be dictionary words & counts
for word in wordlist:
    if word not in countable:
        countable[word] = 0
    countable[word] += 1
# next, make a list of (count,word) tuples
freqlist = []
for word in countable:
    new = (countable[word],word)
    freqlist.append(new)
# sort the list by increasing order of count values
freqlist.sort()
# print highest three instances
print(freqlist[-1],freqlist[-2],freqlist[-3])
```

When the script runs, it prints

```
('the', 3) ('a', 3) ('us', 2)
```

You may notice some deficiencies in this script. One could argue that the count for 'a' should be 4, not 3; but the script counted A and a as different words. Also, the script included punctuation marks in the words. A more careful version of this script would overcome these deficiencies.

Note for Python3

The read() function may not work for files that contain nontext characters. If myfile.dat contains some data in binary (not text), then to read from the file, Python has to be informed, when the file is being opened, to treat the file as a binary file. Here is an example:

```
F = open("myfile.dat","rb") # "b" means binary
data = F.read()
```

As a result of these two statements, variable data contains the file, however, the type of data is a new (Python3) type called bytes. It is beyond this chapter to fully explain the bytes type, which is much like a string, but for binary values. The conversion between string and bytes types is by methods,

$$A.encode() \quad \text{for str A, returns a bytes copy}$$
$$B.decode() \quad \text{for bytes B, returns a str copy}$$

Reading Lines and Bytes

Quite often, the data in text files is organized into lines, which are separated by \n, or in the case of Windows, by \r\n strings. For many applications, it is natural to process the input line by line. Here is a script to make print a list of the line lengths in ex.txt:

```
F = open("ex.txt")
text = F.read()
linelist = text.split('\n')
lengths = []
for line in linelist:
    lengths.append(len(line))
print(lengths)
```

The output from this script may surprise you:

```
[26, 39, 28, 28, 40, 0]
```

(To understand why there is a 0 at the end of the list, you may need to review how the split method works in Chapter 12.) This way of processing lines, by reading in the whole file to a string, then using split, is considered poor style for two reasons:

1. The split('\n') technique alone may not be what you want, as the example above indicates; also, it will leave in the \r characters if the text file has Windows file encoding, but not have these characters under Linux systems. This makes life more complicated than it should be.

2. Reading in the entire file to a string may not be practical for very long files. It would be better to read such a file a bit at a time. Fortunately, Python has several ways to do this.

Rather than use read(), there is another, somewhat "intuitive" way to read the lines of a file:

```
F = open("ex.txt")
lengths = []
for line in F:
    lengths.append(len(line))
print(lengths)
```

The output from this is:

```
[27, 40, 29, 29, 41]
```

Notice here that an ordinary for loop can use a file object as though it were a sequence. Doing so, the *loopiter* variable takes on a new string, the contents of a line in the file, in each iteration. Also, in each iteration, the line variable contains the full line, including the ending \n character (which explains why the lengths of the lines are one larger than in the earlier, similar example).

One cautionary note on using a `for` loop to process the lines in a file: unlike `for` loops over ordinary sequences, a `for` iteration over lines of a file only works once:

```
F = open("ex.txt")
firstlinecount = 0
for line in F:
    firstlinecount += 1
secondlinecount = 0
for line in F:  # attempt second time
    secondlinecount += 1
print([firstlinecount,secondlinecount])
```

This script prints [5, 0]. The file object behaves as though a single iteration over its lines "deplete it," so that it has no more lines for another loop. However, a simple change makes a difference:

```
F = open("ex.txt")
firstlinecount = 0
for line in F:
    firstlinecount += 1
F.close()
F = open("ex.txt")
secondlinecount = 0
for line in F:  # attempt second time
    secondlinecount += 1
print([firstlinecount,secondlinecount])
```

Now it prints [5, 5]. The `close()` method tells Python that a file object is finished, and will not be read further. However, the line following creates a new file object and assigns it to `F` (it happens to be for the same input file), so the loop following works as expected.

Reading Bytes

It makes sense to read lines of a file that is text. The same does not hold for many other kinds of file, including MP3 files, image files (gif, jpg, etc.), or raw data from scientific instruments. These are considered *binary files* as opposed to text files. Python can read binary files into a string, using the `read()` method, but again this is impractical for large files. The technique for reading binary files is to read them in *chunks*, a bit at a time, processing the input as bytes of data. The way to do this is to supply an argument for the `read` method, which tells Python how many bytes from the

```
F = open("ex.txt")
scount = 0
while True:
    char = F.read(1)
    if len(char)<1:
        break
    if char=='s':
        scount += 1
print(scount)
```

file to read. As an illustration, the script above treats `ex.txt` as though it were a binary file, counting the number of characters equal to `'s'`: This script sets up what looks like an infinite loop; the rationale for this is that we may not know, at the outset, how many bytes the file contains. Each assignment `char = F.read(1)` is essentially a request, to Python, to read the next byte from the file and put that into variable `char`. However, at the end of the file, this request will fail: as a result, `char` will be an empty string at the end. This is why the following `if` statement checks the length of `char`, to see whether the end of the file has been reached—this terminates the `while` loop. The choice of using `read(1)` was motivated by the goal, looking at one character at a time in a loop. Other applications might read four bytes in each iteration, in which case the method would be `read(4)` to request the next four bytes.

There is much more to reading and interpreting the bytes of a binary file than the example above would suggest. Typically, another module `struct` is used to convert bytes into integers, floating point numbers, and so forth. You can read about `struct` online if you encounter the need to process binary files in some application (also relevant may be `binhex` and `binascii` modules).

Standard Input and Standard Output

Another criticism of the examples above is that they "hard code" the file name. That is, the name of the file `ex.txt` is written into the Python code. What you would like to use is the same script one time for `ex.txt`, another time for `june.txt`, and so forth? It would be nice to do this without having to change the Python code. Linux has a convention to allow just this capability, called *redirection*.

STDIN.   Long ago, in the early days of operating systems, most programs were simple: they would read input, typically from punched cards, magnetic tape, or paper tape, and print output results on paper. The input device, whether a card reader or a tape reader, had a symbolic name like STDIN or SYSIN. Later, as computing media progressed from cards and

```
import sys
linecount = 0
for line in sys.stdin:
    linecount += 1
print(linecount)
```

tape to other forms, this notion persisted. Programs were supplied, automatically, with an input file named `stdin` or something similar. Python can use this `stdin` feature, shown here in a script.

```
> python linecount.py < ex.txt
5
```

The `sys` module has many functions and variables related to the operating system support of Python, including the `stdin` file. Suppose this script is put into `linecount.py`, and we would like to count the lines in `ex.txt`. The part of the command specifying the input file, that is, the part with tells which file will be used for `sys.stdin`, is the "< ex.txt." This is a convention of the operating system (shell language of system commands), to *redirect* where a program will look for `stdin` input. Note: if this is omitted, and if a program tries to read from `stdin`, then the input will be expected from the user at the keyboard.

A test is shown on the right, where the redirection is omitted. What happens is that, in response to "python linecount.py," the cursor blinks on the next line, waiting for user input (which will be treated as the stdin file). The user typed one, and the script asked for more input; the user typed two, and again the script waited for input. The user tried to get out of this, typing stop, then exit, and so on. Actually, this goes on and on with more lines, because the user has no way to tell the program that

```
> python linecount.py
one
two
stop
exit
quit
help, get me out!
```

stdin has ended via the keyboard device. The moral of the story is that it is better to use input() and validation if keyboard input is appropriate; otherwise, use redirection to associate sys.stdin with some file. The following interaction at a Linux shell prompt illustrates why redirection is handy:

```
> python linecount.py < monday.txt
3128
> python linecount.py < tuesday.txt
405
> python linecount.py < tuesday.txt
11218
```

The linecount.py script was invoked three times on three different files, without having to make any change to the script.

Multiple Files

There is no limit in Python to the number of files that a program can use. An example below shows a loop through two files. One thing to keep in mind is that there is some memory overhead for each file. Large programs that read many files may benefit from reducing the overhead. The memory overhead for such large programs is not the total number of files they read, but rather the number of *open* files at any time during the run. To reduce this overhead, it is wise to close each file when it is no longer needed, for instance

```
F = open("ex.txt","r")
for line in F:
  myprocess(line)
F.close()  # done with file F
...
```

Some function myprocess() looks at each line of the file; after the loop terminates, it is a good idea to close the file.

readline.   Consider the task of merging two files `ex1.txt` and `ex2.txt`. There could be many ways to merge two files, including a back-to-back merge, a line after line merge, and so on. As an example, the following program takes a pair of lines, one from each file, and prints the concatenation of these two lines, in a loop. The example introduces another method for file objects, the `readline` method. Each use of `readline` returns the next line in the file. At the end of the file, `readline` returns the empty string.

```
F, G = open("ex1.txt"), open("ex2.txt")
while True:
    line1 = F.readline()
    line2 = G.readline()
    if line1=='' and line2=='':
        break  # end of both files
    outputline = line1 + line2
    print(outputline)
F.close()
G.close()
```

When the script runs, it may be that one of the two input files has fewer lines than the other. In such an event, the `while` loop will get empty strings from `readline()` of the shorter file as it continues to read lines from the longer file. Python also has a `readlines()` method: it returns a list of all the lines in a file (unlike `read()`, which returns the entire file contents as a string).

Writing to Files

Python offers a `write()` method that adds strings to a file. To use `write()`, the file object needs to be prepared for output. A statement to create a file object for output is

```
F = open("out.txt","w")
```

The second argument (the `"w"`) tells Python that the file object will be used for writing (and if the second argument is omitted, the default is reading).

The `write()` method is deceptively simple to use: `F.write("hello")` adds the string `hello` to the file represented by file object `F`. The underlying behavior of Python, and the operating system, add some wrinkles to this simple interpretation. Reading and writing differ significantly in *timing* of data transfer. When a program has a statement `R = F.readline()`, the assignment of a string to variable `R` actually takes some amount of time to perform (under a millisecond). Though this amount of time is not humanly perceptible, it does cause Python to wait until the data is transferred

```
T = "hello"
F.write(T)
print("done")
```

from the file to `R`. In contrast, the script shown above may not transfer `hello` to the file before printing `done`.

As far as using methods `read`, `readline`, or `readlines`, the only thing we need to know is that these methods fetch some data when the method is called. However, for the `write` method, the situation is not so simple. For reasons of efficiency, the `write` method *does not instantly transfer data*. Instead, the `write` method "schedules" the actual transfer of data to the file at some future time. There are several motivations for scheduling future data transfer. It can be that the file media (flash, disc, etc.) is rather slow compared to program steps, so it would be less efficient to make the program slow down for each `write` call; it can be that the file media uses less power (energy) when multiple file transfers are "bundled" together into larger size blocks of data.

Flushing Buffers

Two file object methods can be used to *force* the transfer of data that previous `write` calls have scheduled: they are `flush()` and `close()`. The `flush()` method can be called at any time after a file object has been prepared for output, up to the point where the `close()` method has been called. The `close()` method not only finishes and schedules data transfer, but it also releases any memory resources entailed by the file object. After the `close()` method has been called, the file object is no longer available for `write` operations.

Why does this matter? Suppose a program generates a large output, writing to a file that will be many gigabytes when the program finishes. Now imagine that the program does not finish because of a power outage that crashes the computer. What will be in the file after the power goes out? Hard to say. However, if the program occasionally uses the `flush()` method, then at least some of the scheduled data transfer will likely be added to the output file. Such a program could run for hours or days before it closes the output file, and using `flush()` is therefore sensible. In the small exercises of this chapter, using `flush()` will not be justified. Just remember that a program writing to a file should use `close()` before the program finishes. In fact, when a Python program does finish, the operating system automatically closes any open files. Yet the habit of using `close()` is valuable. Consider a Python program that acts as a Web server, responding to network requests and recording something related to those requests in files. This program might run for weeks or months, handling millions of network requests. For this program, it would be essential to use `close()` to finish scheduled data transfer so that the output files have all the data they should (so that these files could be used for other needs, including analysis, report generation, and so on).

Please use `close()` when finished writing.

With Context Manager

If you look at Python code found in library modules, you may encounter the "`with`" statement, usually in connection with files. Python's **with** statement is typically followed by a block of statements using a file, but omitting `close` on the file. This is because **with** automatically closes the file, whether it was opened and read, written, or not. A brief example follows.

```
S = list()
with open("forex.txt") as F:
    for line in F:
        if line.startswith("--"):
            S.append(line)
# S is now list of lines having "--" at beginning
```

As a beginner, you should not need to use **with**. The **with** statement is associated with a *context manager* in Python, a concept you likely will not need to understand or use.

String Preparation

The argument of the `write()` method must be a string.
Here is a demonstration of the fact:

```
F = open("out.txt",'w')
for x in range(20):
    s = repr(x)
    F.write(s)
F.close()
```

```
>>> F = open("out.txt",'w')
>>> F.write(1.5)
TypeError: must be string, not float
```

If only a string can be written, but one would like to write numbers, then some kind of conversion to a string is needed, as seen in the script above. The script writes integers converted to strings, using the built-in `repr()` function described earlier in this chapter. After running this script, the file `out.txt` consists of the single line:

```
012345678910111213141516171819
```

This result may not be what one would hope for. Unlike `print`, the `write()` method does not automatically insert spaces or newline (\n) characters. This is where formatting comes handy. Below, the left script uses the `format` method on the template string `"{}\n"` to ensure that each number is not only converted to a string, but a newline comes after that. Instead of using `format`, an assignment such as "s = repr(x)+"\n"" would also work for the same purpose. The content of `out.txt` after the script runs is shown below on the right.

```
F = open("out.txt",'w')
for x in range(10,16):
    s = "{}\n".format(x)
    F.write(s)
F.close()
```

```
10
11
12
13
14
15
```

Reading and Writing

Python has additional methods for file objects so that the same file can be both read from and written to in the same program. Databases consist of files that are *updated*, meaning that data is read from the file, changed in memory, and then written back over the original values. Python is capable of doing this, but it is an advanced topic, beyond this chapter. Another feature worth mentioning is that on most operating systems where Python runs, an output file can be opened in *append mode*: when a file object is created with append mode, the data written to the file does not replace what the file already may have—new data written to the file is concatenated to what is already in the file. Append mode is frequently used for logging events, audit trails, or other applications where many scripts write output to the same file, and the result is a file with the output of all of them.

Printing to Files

The `print` statement in Python2, or the `print` function in Python3, is implemented internally within Python using the `write()` method. By default, Python directs printed output to a file object `sys.stdout`. Usually, the operating system

```
for value in range(3,8):
    print(value)
```

sends anything intended for standard output (`sys.stdout`) to the console, as seen during interactive Python sessions. As with the standard input `sys.stdin`, it is possible to redirect where standard output goes. Consider the basic script shown above. Suppose this two-line script is in a file `basic.py`, and the following command is run at a Linux shell prompt:

```
> python basic.py > out.txt
>
```

The ">" at the beginning of the two lines above is a marker for the command prompt, whereas the ">" before `out.txt` tells Linux to *redirect* standard output from the console to a file named `out.txt`. This is why you see no output from the script on the console. However, if you use some editor to look at `out.txt` after the script has run, the content will be the lines shown to the right. Both input redirection and output redirection can be used on the same script run.

```
3
4
5
6
7
```

```
> python countlines.py < myfile.txt > count.txt
```

The example runs the `countlines.py` script, taking standard input from the file `myfile.txt`, and sending anything printed to a file `count.txt`.

Python2 print to File Object. A strange syntax is used in Python2 for printing to a file object other than to standard output (fortunately abandoned in Python3). Generally, you can use the `print` statement to place output into any file that has been created for output using

```
F = open("newout.txt","w")
for W in range(50):
    print >> F, W, W**2, W**3
F.close()
```

">>" syntax. Here is an example printing to a file `newout.txt`. Unlike the `write()` method, the `print` statement will put spaces between the items printed and add a newline character at the end of the line.

Python3 print to File Object. For Python3, there is no `print` statement, there is the `print()` function. It has a keyword parameter `file` that defaults to `sys.stdout`. For any `print()` function call, the `file` argument can specify a file object for output. The `print()` function

```
F = open("newout.txt","w")
for W in range(50):
    print(W, W**2, W**3, file=F)
F.close()
```

will put spaces between the items and add a newline (\n). The `print()` function has other keyword parameters that can change some details of behavior, including the spacing between items printed and whether the newline character is inserted at the end.

Terminology Review

Python2 has two techniques for getting input from the keyboard, `input()` and `raw_input()`, whereas Python3 has only `input()`. The `format` method and the formatting mini-language use a template to control how output strings convert other types into readable form. This chapter introduced *file objects* and methods `read()`, `write()`, `readline()`, `close()`, plus functions to create file objects, `open()` and `file()`. Standard input, standard output, and redirection (for both input and output) have names and special notation (`sys.stdin`, `sys.stdout`, with "<" and ">" in a Linux command console). A new kind of `for` loop was introduced in this chapter, which is used to iterate over the lines of a file. The `repr()` built-in function was introduced, and the Python3 `bytes` type was mentioned, for which there are methods `decode()` and `encode()`.

Exercises

(1) Consider the classic problem of solving simultaneous equations, often specified by values $a_1, b_1, c_1, a_2, b_2, c_2$ in the equations

$$a_1 \cdot x + b_1 \cdot y = c_1$$
$$a_2 \cdot x + b_2 \cdot y = c_2$$

Write a Python script that asks the user for six numbers corresponding to the values in these equations and then either outputs what are x and y or reports that no solution can be calculated.

(2) Write a script that takes a text file, perhaps containing a news article or some short story, and makes a version of the same file in which all punctuation characters $(., ; : ' " ? -)$ have been removed, as well as numeric digits (0123456789) and other nonalphabetic characters $(\$\%\string^\&*()[]@!'\string~<>\string\, \text{etc.})$. Furthermore, the script should convert uppercase to lowercase. Thus, the output file should only contain whitespace characters and letters $(a–z)$, but have the same number of lines as the input file and the same number of "words."

(3) Write a script that produces a table with two columns, words and counts. The input for the script is a text file containing simple words, like the output file from problem (2). For each word in the input file, there should be a row in the table with that word and the number of times it occurs in the input file, so there should be as many rows in the table as there are different (distinct) words in the input file. The table's two columns should line up, so that all words start at the beginning of the line, and all numbers line up in the same column.

(4) Write a script that sums values in the third column of CSV file. You may do this either by reading each line of the file, splitting by commas and converting list items to numbers, or you may research how to use Python's csv module.

Interlude: File Indexing

As a case study, this section develops programs for searching a directory of text files. Informally, what we would like to create is a command like "`findfiles seahorse`" and see a list printed of all the files containing the word "`seahorse.`" Many systems already have such a command or perhaps an application that searches through files for a pattern. But in this case study, the aim is something similar to a search engine. In contrast to an active search of Web sites, a search engine works in two phases: (*i*) first scan the web, building a catalog of the words in pages and where they are found; (*ii*) in response to a search request, look through the catalog built in phase (*i*) and report on the search hits. Hence, the structure of this case study is to first develop a program to build a catalog of all the text files in a directory. This catalog is called the *index* of the files, inspired by indices at the end of books.

Building an Index

Before we get going, a bit of research is in order. The first interlude of this book ("Interlude: An Inventory Problem"), examined the problem of how to represent the data (tables) of Acme Perfume. There are different ways to represent inventory, each worthy of consideration. Similarly, one of the first design choices for constructing an index is deciding on how to represent information in the index. What will the index be used for? The only purpose here is a `findfiles` program, which searches or uses lookup to find a word within the index. Python already has the ideal data structure for this purpose, the dictionary. We can have the index be a dictionary, with all the words in all the files, as keys in the dictionary.

If words are the keys in the dictionary, what are the values associated with those keys? The obvious answer is to have a list of filenames as the value for a key. We will follow this simple design, but later find better ideas because of the need for *persistent data*. Unlike all the scripts and functions elsewhere in this book, the project of this section is one where results must *persist* after the program finishes. Once all files are read and their words put in a dictionary, the first phase is done. The output of the first phase is a dictionary, which has to be saved somewhere for later queries.

Another research task is to figure out how the first phase will get the name of a directory of files, learn how to list all the files therein, and how to save the output (dictionary) for later use by the second phase. After one does some Web searches, reads Python manuals, and tries interactive testing, two valuable techniques are discovered. First, the name of the directory can be a command line argument, so that `sys.argv[0]` will be a string containing the directory name. Second, the `os.listdir()` function returns a

```
import sys, os
wordindex = dict() # empty
def addwords(D,F):
  # function will read F
  # and add words to D
filelist = os.listdir(sys.argv[0])
for file in filelist:
  addwords(wordindex,file)
output = open("windex.txt",'w')
output.write(repr(wordindex))
output.close()
```

list of files and subdirectories within a directory, which is what we need. Third, to save the dictionary the program can either print it (and we then capture `stdout` by redirection) or write it to a file. The sketched program shown here writes the dictionary to a file `windex.txt`, after converting it to a string form using the `repr()` built-in.

It is a good idea to pause here, before any more program development, and think through the consequences of the design so far. If all goes well, the first phase will be a program that goes through a bunch of files in a directory and writes a file `windex.txt`. Let's say the command to run

```
{"a":["prog.txt","memo.txt",
"first.py"], "and":["memo.txt",
"first.py","other.py"], "any":
...
```

the first phase is "`python indexor.py HomeWorks`" where `Homeworks` is a directory. What will `windex.txt` look like after this? Just a tiny fragment of what we imagine is shown here. The result is essentially the same as what is seen printing a dictionary. This output of `indexor.py` will later become the input of `findfiles.py`, so the second phase will have to read `windex.txt` and recreate the dictionary. How does a program read a file, which is the printed image of a dictionary, and get back the dictionary from this? With integers, a simple conversion like `int("12")` returns the number 12, but not so with a dictionary. There is no conversion such as `dict("{'a':3}")` which returns the dictionary `{"a":3}`. So, the choice made so far of simply converting a dictionary to a string using `repr()`, turns out to be a burden on the design of `findfiles.py`.

Chapter 26 introduces Python's `eval()` function, which is capable of evaluating a string that has a valid Python expression and returning a value. Function `eval()` could reconstitute the dictionary with an assignment such as this:

```
wordindex = eval(open("windex.txt").read())
```

However, as Chapter 26 observes, the use of `eval()` can be dangerous and is also difficult to debug if things go awry. Another idea is to use Python's `pickle` module. The `pickle` module is Python's implementation of the concept called *serialization* (actually it is Java terminology). Serialization entails having two library facilities, one for converting data structures or objects into a form suitable for writing to a file or transmitting over a network, and another facility for doing the reverse conversion back into a data structure or object. The `pickle` module has functions for both kinds of conversion. We could use `pickle` instead of using `repr`, write the pickled data to `windex.txt`, and then let `findfiles.py` read `windex.txt` and use "unpickle" to get dictionary `wordindex`. Yet another choice would be to find, and learn how to use, modules that convert Python data structures to JSON or XML, which are standard ways of representing data in text files. The bottom line is that we have many choices in the design. However, for illustrative purposes, this case study uses a simple design that makes the job of `findfiles.py` easy.

Instead of writing `repr(wordindex)` to `windex.txt`, a design that simplifies processing is shown here. On one line, a word is written, and on the next line the files which have that word are written as a string, separated by commas (we assume that filenames do not contain commas). The corresponding code which reads

```
output = open("windex.txt",'w')
for key,value in wordindex.items():
    output.write(key+"\n") # word
    fl = ','.join(value)
    output.write(fl+"\n")
output.close()
```

`windex.txt` and recreates the dictionary is straightforward, and is shown in the next paragraph.

The code here reads the file two lines at a time, using a `for` loop, and adds (key,value) pairs to the dictionary with a nested loop. In computing jargon, a nested loop such as this is sometimes called *the inner loop*. The code here would best be encapsulated into a function and tested during the debugging of `findfiles.py`. Two observations about this code explain some details. First, recall that a `for` loop reading a text file will get the newline (`'\n'`) character at the end of each line; the code uses whitespace split to

```
dsource = open("windex.txt")
wordindex = dict()
for line in dsource:
    # read word and remove '\n'
    word = line.split()[0]
    wordindex[word] = list()
    nextline = dsource.next()
    fl = line.split()[0]
    for filename in fl.split(','):
        wordindex[word].append(filename)
dsource.close()
```

eliminate the newline, followed by indexing to pull out the first string from the list that `split()` returns. Second, this code shows a way to deal with the situation where we need to process *two lines* of input in each iteration of the loop. Because our first phase writes a word on one line and the list of files on the following line, we need to read lines in pairs here. The `for` loop cannot read two lines at once, so the assignment `nextline = dsource.next()` reads a line using the `next()` method (which is what `for` does behind the scenes, see the box "Loops Using *Iterables* and Generators" in Chapter 22).

A remaining issue is the `addwords(D,F)` function, which was not defined earlier. With `D` being the dictionary under construction and `F` being a filename, this function should mutate `D` for each word in `F` so that `findfiles.py` will later report this. The design of `addwords` is simple. Using a `for` loop, we can read lines of the file, split each line, and with an inner loop, make sure the words are in the dictionary and associated with the file named by `F`. In the following code, some extra tricks have been inserted, such as removing trailing punctuation, converting hyphens into spaces, and using the lowercase version of the word.

```
def cleanword(W):
    "return a cleaned-up version of word W"
    from string import punctuation
    C = W
    while len(C)>0 and C[-1] in punctuation:
        C = C[:-1]
    return C.lower()
def addwords(D,F):
    '''Mutate D for each word in F so that D[word]
       refers to a list that contains F (as a filename)'''
    fileF = open(F)
    for line in fileF:
        line = line.replace("-"," ") # handle hypenated words
        words = line.split()
        for word in words:
            word = cleanword(word)
            if len(word)==0:
                continue # in case cleaned up word is empty
            if word not in D:
                D[word] = list()
            if F not in D[word]:
                D[word].append(F)
    fileF.close()
```

The `addwords()` function makes use of another function, `cleanword()`. By what rationale was this new function added to the design? The basic theme in much software function is overcoming library deficiency. The idea behind our improvement to the `indexor.py` program is to make it easy for `findfiles.py` to automatically find words without regard to being upper- or lowercase words. Further, we would like "stop" and "stop." to be indexed the same. Therefore, what we *wish* Python had built in was some kind of word regularizer, which converted to lowercase, removed punctuation, took care of hyphenation, and more. Python does not have a built-in function for that. So, to make up for this lack in Python, we write our own function. Many functions in programs exist because the designer had a wish list of features that the programming language or system did not already have. So, this is one rationale for creating `cleanword()`. But, some readers might object, why define a function if it is only going to be called once? Why not instead just take the code in `cleanword()` and merge it into the code for `addwords()`? The reasons are program readability and testing. If we move the code of `cleanword()` directly into the inner loop of `addwords()`, then we end up having a triply nested loop, which makes the program more difficult to read. As a general rule, one should aim to write Python code that does not have more than a few levels of indenting. That will make the code easier to comprehend and debug. The other reason to keep `cleanword()` as a separate function is testing. The `cleanword()` function can be tested separately from the rest of the program; unit tests can even validate that it works correctly. A final observation about `cleanword()` is its use of Python's **string** module. This module has a variable **punctuation**, which is nothing more than a string of all the punctuation characters found in the ASCII character set (period, comma, semicolon, question mark, etc.).

The basic design of the first phase of the case study is in place. The missing part, shown here, is the `findfile.py` script, which reconstitutes the dictionary built by `indexor.py` and uses it to search for a word. Though this completes the basic design, there is much to be done to make this design robust. For one thing, either of these phases could encounter errors due to missing files, getting some kind of error when attempting to read a file with binary data, or attempting to read a subdirectory (which `os.listdir()` can return in its list) as a file. Chapter 26 introduces

```
import sys, pprint
def getdict():
    # code was sketched earlier
    ...
tofind = sys.argv[0]
wordindex = getdict()
if tofind not in wordindex:
    print "word not found"
else:
    print "word in files:"
    fl = wordindex[tofind]
    pprint.pprint(fl)
```

Python's **try .. except** syntax whereby a program can catch an error and take some remedial action, recovering from the error instead of crashing. In fact, most well-designed programs have error-recovery as part of their design. A second concern about the simple design of the case study is performance. Though Python is not the most efficient language, proper design can sometimes dramatically improve running time of programs.

☆   ☆   ☆

Refining the Index

In what way might the performance of `indexor.py` and `findfiles.py` be improved? Here are two ideas. First, one could think about a design of `indexor.py` that *incrementally* mutates the index of words for a directory. Search engines build indices incrementally rather than all in one run. Perhaps `indexor.py` could run from time to time, only changing the dictionary in `windex.txt` when a file of the directory has changed. With an incremental design, the running time for `indexor.py` might be significantly smaller (even negligible time when no files have changed since the last run). A second performance improvement would be to change `findfiles.py` so that instead of reading all of `windex.txt` and rebuilding `wordindex`, maybe just some small portion of `windex.txt` could be read. That would speed up searching for a word in a file. There are many other ways one could think of improving the design, not all related to running time performance. Another idea might be to change the dictionary so that the location (line number, column number) of words within files is retained. Such a new feature might enable searching for phrases as well as words.

Of the ideas for improvement, this case study investigates the second improvement idea, which is to read just a portion of `windex.txt`. By exploring this idea, we also glimpse a little of the way dictionaries work "under the hood" in Python. Again, in order to pursue the improvement, some initial research is a good idea. How can a program read just a portion of a file? How can it be known which part of a file to read? Answers to these questions are the first order of business.

Most persistent media, like hard disk or flash memory, makes random access possible. This should make one suspect that files have methods beyond `read()` and `write()` that somehow enable reading and writing to start at different points within a file. If we search Python's documentation (or just use a search engine), the `seek()` method's description is found. The `seek()` method takes an integer argument and *positions* the file object so that the next `read()` or `write()` starts from that offset. For example, given file object `F`, after `F.seek(100)` the next `F.read()` will access data 100 bytes into the file. There are some caveats about `seek()` noted in the documentation, but it will satisfy needs of this case study.

Another research question is this: how can we know *where*, in a file, to look for a particular word, say the word `famous`? To answer this, we dig into the internals of Python that enable dictionaries to fetch values by keys. The magic that makes dictionaries work is the concept called *hash tables*, which is beyond this book. A hash table has the two very useful characteristics: (*i*) it can be indexed, like a sequence type (list, tuple, string) very fast, using a number as the index; (*ii*) there is a *hash function* that turns a key value, such as a string, into a number.

```
>>> dir(str)
['__add__', '__class__', ...
'__hash__', '__init__', ...
'join', 'replace', ... ]
>>> "famous".__hash__()
868660305
```

Using property (*ii*), Python figures out where a (`key,value`) pair belongs in the dictionary by first using the hash function to get a number, and then using property (*i*) to know the right place in the table for storing or reading the `value` associated with a `key`. It is not necessary to fully understand this, though it is revealing to look at how Python does this. To the left, in an interactive script, some internal methods are exposed: The response to `dir(str)` is a list of all the methods and attributes of the string (`str`) type; there are far too many to show here, and most are omitted (hence the "..."). Two of the methods we recognize, `join()` and `replace()`; most of them are unfamiliar. One especially of interest is the `__hash__()` method—it is this method that calculates the number used by dictionaries to find the location for a key. The example concludes by showing the value of the hash function (that is, the `__hash__()` method) for the word `famous`. Any type used as a key in a dictionary, be it a string, tuple, or numeric type, secretly has a _hash_() method. We will use Python's hash method to figure out where, in a file, to find information for the word famous.

Imagine that the indexing file, window.txt, contains 10,000 total characters. Let us consider a simple plan on where a word and its list of filenames will be placed in window.txt: either the first or second half. If famous is in the second half, then a method call like F.seek(5000) skips over the first half of window.txt, and subsequent reading from file object F can search for the line containing the word famous. How can it be known whether famous is in the first or second half? The answer is found from the expression "famous"._hash_()%2. This expression will evaluate to 0 or to 1, depending on whether the hash function result for famous is even or odd. Thus, if the hash value for famous is odd, then famous will be in the second half of window.txt. Of course, to ensure that this works, we have to arrange that indexor.py puts famous and its list of filenames in the second half, but this is possible since indexor.py can use the same hash function (the _hash_() method) that findfiles.py does.

The performance improvement by just reading half of window.txt is not very impressive, but the idea can be tweaked to get much better performance. Instead of using odd or even, we make the expression to determine location "famous"._hash_()%k where k is a larger number, say 172. This effectively divides window.txt into 172 chunks of equal size, and some clever value in seek() will skip right to the chunk that has famous. Though many details remain, this is the basis for the improvement (and, incidentally, a powerful strategy in modern design of efficient databases). One more modification to the idea is helpful. Instead of fixing the number of chunks to be some number like 172, we let the k be tuned by indexor.py. Similarly, the number of bytes in a chunk, say p bytes, will be tuned by indexor.py. The data, coming from indexor.py's dictionary of words and filenames, will determine the number of chunks k and the value of p.

```
import sys
F = open("window.txt")
k = int(F.read(8))
p = int(F.read(8))
word = sys.argv[0]
chunk = word.__hash__()%k
F.seek(p*chunk)
area = F.read(p).split('\n')
lines = iter(area)
for text in lines:
  if word == text:
    print lines.next()
    break
```

A crude script for the revised findfiles.py is shown here. It reads the first eight bytes of window.txt to learn the value k, the next eight bytes to get the value p, and thus the size of the chunk and the number of chunks is known. The chunk that should have the word being sought is calculated using the hash function. This chunk is read, split by newline into a list of strings, and then an iterator line is created. Python's built-in iter function does the equivalent of making a generator such as (e for e in area); this allows us to use the next() method in the for loop going through the lines that comprise the chunk. Once the loop hits the matching word, it prints the next line and quits the loop. This script has a number of bugs, does not print output nicely, and does not show a message when the word is not found. It does illustrate, quite concisely, how the hash function idea could significantly improve performance.

The hard part of the job is revising `indexor.py` so that it puts words and corresponding file lists into the correct chunks, plus determining the values for `p`, `k`, and writing those into the first 16 bytes. What should determine `k` and `p`? The value of `k` must be large enough so that the number of words for which `word.__hash__()%k` have the same value (meaning they will go into the same chunk) does not exceed `p` bytes. This is the hardest part of the problem. Once we know values for `k` and `p`, the `seek()` method can be used to write the data into the appropriate chunk. After `k` is known, it will be simple to create a list of `k` dictionaries, one for each chunk. Then each word of the dictionary built by the `addwords()` function (earlier in this chapter) can be copied to one of `k` new dictionaries. Writing the contents of a dictionary to a chunk can be like the code given on the opening page of Chapter 5.

To understand how `p` and `k` might be found, a bit of computing research terminology is helpful. When a hash function calculates the same value for two different words, we call that a *collision*. Depending on the quality of the hash function, collisions may happen frequently (many words get the same hash value) or not at all (a so-called *perfect* hash function). Python's built-in `__hash__()` is high-quality, but not perfect. Collisions can happen. To limit collisions so that too many words do not end up in the same chunk, we may experiment with `p` and `k`. A useful observation of computing researchers is that the quality of the hash function will improve the larger `k` is; and for our design, we observe that the larger `p` is, the more collisions we can allow yet ensure the chunk does not overflow with words. So, on the one hand, using large values for `k` and `p` will overcome the collision problem, but on the other hand, these large values will make the `windex.txt` file become big. Below, we offer a primitive design that increases both `k` and `p` until all words fit into their hash-computed chunks. This is not an exact science, but it is the nature of the problem.

To organize all the tasks of revising `indexor.py`, here is a "wish list" for helpful functions. These are functions we wish Python already had in some module.

- `EntSize(W)`. We wish there were a function that would tell us how many bytes total are in the two lines of `windex.txt` for the word `W`.

- `MaxEnt(D)`. Let's say `D` is the dictionary that is created by running `addwords(D,F)` on every file object `F` in the directory. We wish there were a function `MaxEnt(D)` that returns the maximum of `EntSize(W)` for any word `W` in dictionary `D`.

- `Collisions(k,D)`. We would like a function that tells us, for a given `k`, how many words maximum, from `D`, can get the same chunk number.

- `allow(k,p,D)`. The `allow` function should return a boolean telling us whether or not a file with `k` chunks each of size `p` bytes will prevent any chunk from overflowing with words due to collisions.

- `Buckets(k,D)`. It would be nice to have a function that takes `D` and returns a new list of `k` dictionaries, one for each chunk, with the words and filenames put into these new dictionaries.

- `writeBucket(i,B)`. This function takes a dictionary `B` (one item of the list that `Buckets` builds) and writes it to chunk `i` of `windex.txt`.

- `writekp()`. Let there be a function that writes values of `k` and `p` in the first 16 bytes of `windex.txt`.

Perhaps this wish list is incomplete, but it can be a starting point to sketching a revised `indexor.py`.

A rough version of `indexor.py` is the script shown here. It is missing a function `setup()`, which includes code creating a dictionary, running `addwords()` for each file in a specified directory, and returning that completed dictionary. In other words, `setup()` builds D for us. The other functions have been informally described in the wish list. The strategy for finding k and p is simple: starting with estimates for each, the `allow()` function checks whether or not they will

```
k, p, D = 32, 1024, setup()
while not allow(k,p,D):
    k, p = 2*k, 2*p
L = Buckets(k,D)
F = open("windex.txt",'w')
for i,B in enumerate(L):
    writeBucket(i,B,F)
writekp(k,p,F)
F.close()
```

work; if not, the values for k and p are doubled and the test repeated. Once allowable values are found, file `windex.txt` can be written using other functions in the wish list. When testing an implementation of this code, we may find that doubling k and p was too drastic (and that `windex.txt` would be too large). In that case, other ideas for increasing these values could be explored.

Here we have a somewhat pessimistic, though simple implementation of `allow()`. If we conservatively estimate that every word will consume `MaxEnt(D)` bytes when written to `windex.txt`, and if there can be `Collisions(k,D)` words in a chunk, then p will need to be at least `m*t` bytes.

```
def allow(k,p,D):
    m = MaxEnt(D)
    t = Collisions(k,D)
    return p >= m*t
```

```
def Collisions(k,D):
    allhash = [ w.__hash__()%k for
                    w in D.keys() ]
    V = { i:0 for i in range(k) }
    for x in allhash:
        V[x] += 1
    return max(V.values())
```

The `Collisions()` function reports the most number of words that would go by hashing to the same chunk. The logic here may seem curious. First, `allhash` is a list of all the chunk numbers for all words in D. Then a new dictionary V is created with chunk numbers as keys and zero as the value for every chunk. The chunks are tabulated by V, so that `V[x]` will be the total number of words which would end up in chunk x. The function returns the maximum value over all items in V. This implementation of `Collisions()` is a reminder that even with an imperative style of programming, the pythonic way of using comprehensions can make for elegant, simple code.

```
def Buckets(k,D):
    L = [ dict() for i in range(k) ]
    for key in D:
        j = key.__hash__()%k # chunk
        N = L[j]
        N[key] = D[key]
    return L
```

Rather than fleshing out all the functions on the wish list, we end this case study by showing just one of them. The logic of `Buckets()` is simple enough. After creating k new dictionaries with a list comprehension, the keys of D are examined in a loop. For each key, the chunk number is calculated and the new dictionary for that chunk is referenced by N, which is then mutated to copy the key and value from D.

This mutation, because of aliasing, changes the appropriate dictionary in list L.

Chapter 26:   Network Programs

> *Societies have always been shaped more by the nature of the media*
> *by which [they] communicate than by the content of the communication.*
> — Marshall McLuhan

Communication networks are familiar to all of us: e-mail, the Web, video over cable, and thousands of smartphone applications are essential components of our lives. Less familiar, yet no less important, are hidden data networks. Computing has grown to be pervasive in modern infrastructure. Although most infrastructure computing is confined to microprocessors with limited functions (heating systems in buildings, fuel monitors in vehicles, traffic control systems, devices that track packages, alarm systems, etc.) these functions gain considerable value to the extent that they are networked, even if such networking is hidden from casual observation.

The standard Python library has a suite of modules for networking, all of them oriented to Internet protocols (other modules specific to cellular networks or low-level hardware networks are currently outside of the standard library). One feature of networking sets it apart from most other computing application: failures are part of normal life in networks. A path through the Internet may involve hundreds of computers, routing switches, fiber optic cables, and wireless communication susceptible to electromagnetic noise. In such situations, the probability of some communication outage or just some message being lost is significant enough to warrant some precaution by application programs. Another source of worry is that networks can be overloaded by peak data traffic, which again disrupts service temporarily.

The goal of this chapter is to introduce some of Python's standard network modules and also to show how errors can be handled by scripts, functions, and modules. The error-handling uses **try** and **except** statements, which are widely used for many purposes (beyond networking) in Python programming.

Reading a Web Page

The technical steps involved in getting a Web page from a server are complex: The server name has to be resolved into hardware addresses, messages are broken into data units suitable to the network medium (wire, wireless, or fiber), the server has to process the request to serve up particular page, and so forth. Fortunately, all of this has been packaged up into a simple interface. After putting all of the complexity into modules, it is as easy as opening a file object and then using techniques from Chapter 25 to do the rest. The examples that follow use a **for** loop to process the file object, however, **read()** could just as well have been used.

Python2's `urllib2.urlopen()`. The script here writes a copy of a Web page to a local file. Two file objects are used, **UF** for reading the Web page and **PageFile** for saving the page. The `urlopen()` function will fail if there is no Internet connection or if the URL does not correspond to a Web page.

```
import urllib2
UF = urllib2.urlopen("http://www.nist.gov")
PageFile = file("Web page.txt",'w')
for line in UF:
    PageFile.write(line)
PageFile.close()
```

Python3's `urllib.request.urlopen()`. A script to do the same as the one above, but for Python3, is given here. Notice in the version for Python3 that a different module is used (`urllib.request`) and that the lines of the Web page are treated as binary: a Web page *could* contain binary values, hence the conditional

```
import urllib.request
UF = urllib.request.urlopen("http://www.nist.gov")
PageFile = open("Web page.txt",'w')
for line in UF:
    if type(line)==bytes:
        line = line.decode()
    PageFile.write(line)
PageFile.close()
```

logic converts the `bytes` type into a string. The reason for this is that the ordinary `write()` method on a file expects its argument to be a string, not something of type `bytes`.

The Try and Except Statements

Suppose one of the examples above is changed to introduce an error, but the error is not a syntax error, just a mistake in the name of the Web page. In that case, Python will get some kind of internal error in a system or network function, which will be reflected to a script. Here is an example (from Python2) showing an error message:

```
Traceback (most recent call last):
  File "fetch.py", line 2, in <module>
    UF = urllib2.urlopen("http://www.nist.cov")
  File "/usr/lib/python2.7/urllib2.py", line 126, in urlopen
    return _opener.open(url, data, timeout)
  File "/usr/lib/python2.7/urllib2.py", line 391, in open
    response = self._open(req, data)
  File "/usr/lib/python2.7/urllib2.py", line 409, in _open
    '_open', req)
  File "/usr/lib/python2.7/urllib2.py", line 369, in _call_chain
    result = func(*args)
  File "/usr/lib/python2.7/urllib2.py", line 1173, in http_open
    return self.do_open(httplib.HTTPConnection, req)
  File "/usr/lib/python2.7/urllib2.py", line 1148, in do_open
    raise URLError(err)
urllib2.URLError: <urlopen error [Errno -2] Name or service not known>
```

Nearly all of this information is of no use to most Python programs except the last line, which may indicate the type of error and could provide enough text for some investigation using a search engine.

Python and many other languages provide syntax to detect errors when they occur, *within the program*, so that a function or a script can take corrective steps without having to completely fail. A user may not even be aware of errors that a program catches and corrects on its own.

Catching Errors

```
A = [1,2,0,5]
for num in A:
    print(1.0/float(num))
```

Before we address errors of networks, consider this simple example of a script that stops with an error. This script fails due to a ZeroDivisionError because the third item in list A is zero. Python has **try** and **except** statements which can catch such errors. A revised script is shown below, with the output of the script on the right. Both **try** and **except** statements expect an indented block of statements (perhaps just one statement) to follow.

```
A = [1,2,0,5]
for num in A:
    try:
        print(1.0/float(num))
    except ZeroDivisionError:
        print("ouch!")
```

```
1.0
0.5
ouch!
0.2
```

The **try** statement's block can be any number of statements, and an error might occur anywhere in this block; if an error does occur, then the **try**'s block of statements run instead of halting the entire program with an error message.

The **except** statement in the example above names the kind of error that is anticipated. Here is a similar example showing how this works in more detail.

```
A = [1,2,0,5]
for i in [0,1,2,3,4]:
    try:
        print(1.0/float(A[i]))
    except ZeroDivisionError:
        print("ouch!")
```

```
1.0
0.5
ouch!
0.2
IndexError: list index out of range
```

Though the bug is easy to find (the *loopiter* variable i will have the value 4 in the last iteration), it can also be caught by an **except** statement. Several ways to do this are shown below on the left, by adding another **except** statement, and on the right, by specifying multiple kinds of errors to be caught.

```
A = [1,2,0,5]
for i in [0,1,2,3,4]:
    try:
        print(1.0/float(A[i]))
    except ZeroDivisionError:
        print("ouch!")
    except IndexError:
        print("ouch!")
```

```
A = [1,2,0,5]
for i in [0,1,2,3,4]:
    try:
        print(1.0/float(A[i]))
    except (ZeroDivisionError, IndexError):
        print("ouch!")
```

For beginners, the easiest way to catch errors is to be lazy and omit naming an error. Python does permit this. When an `except` statement does not name any error, it will catch any kind of error. Where it is a division by zero error, an index error, a missing file error, an `except` without a specific named error will catch it.

```
A = [1,2,0,5]
for i in [0,1,2,3,4]:
    try:
        print(1.0/float(A[i]))
    except:
        print("ouch!")
```

> **Note:** The full syntax of `try ... except` is considerably more complicated than the examples above; there are optional `else` and `finally` clauses, and more.

Although the `except` statement works without naming any particular kind of error (such as `IndexError`), **this is possibly dangerous** programming practice. The reason is that if one is lazy and simply uses `except` without naming any error, debugging becomes more difficult. Instead of knowing *why* the block of statements under the `try` failed, all that is known is some kind of failure occurred. For example, in fetching a Web page, there can be different kinds of error: the URL is incorrect, or maybe the network is not available, or perhaps if the Web page should be written to a file, it could be that writing to a file fails because there is not enough storage. Without naming the error type anticipated, there is no way for someone using the Python program to determine the cause of the error and correct the situation: debugging is then more difficult.

Raising Errors

```
def scan(M):
    if type(M) != list:
        raise ValueError
    for item in M:
        if type(item) != int:
            raise ValueError
```

Python permits functions and scripts to generate their own errors, halting the entire program immediately with an error message. It is as simple as using the `raise` statement. Technically, all the normal Python errors (`IndexError`, `TypeError`, etc.) are known as *exceptions*. The example here is a function `scan(M)` that halts with a `ValueError` if the argument is not a list of integers. Our choice of `ValueError` in this example is arbitrary; we might just as well have used `IndexError` or any other standard error name (there are about 20 of them).

The logic of error generation (using `raise`) and the `try ... except` combination control how and where errors are caught within programs. Suppose we have a script, which starts with the definition of `scan(M)` above, and then continues with the code presented here. This script fails due to a `ValueError` in the evaluation of `scan(X)`, because X will at one point be the last "row" of M. It is useful to go over *error propagation* during a Python run of a script. The error is *generated* by the `raise` statement in the `scan` function. This error causes the evaluation of `scan(X)` in the first line of `product(X)` to get

```
def product(X):
    scan(X) # make sure X is list of int
    P = 1
    for item in X:
        P *= item
    return P
def sumprods(Array):
    S = 0
    for row in Array:
        S += product(row)
    return S
M = [ [1,2,3], [4,5,6], [2.5,9,8] ]
print(sumprods(M))
```

a `ValueError`; since the `product` function does not have a `try ... except` combination of statements, the `product(X)` function fails. In turn, the statement of `sumprods(Array)` "S += product(row)" will fail with a `ValueError`, because that is the kind of error that causes `product(row)` to fail. Thus, what we see is a "cascade of errors," where the caller of a function that fails also fails; then the caller of the caller fails; and so on. This is why the error messages printed by Python are often so verbose: they show the whole chain of error propagation, with line numbers in each function of the cascade of errors.

Now we show how using `try ... except` might deal with the situation of `scan(M)` raising an exception. The revised definition puts the `try ... except` in the `sumprods` function, substituting zero for the product in case of an error. Could the `try ... except` have been put instead in the `product` function? Yes. This is a design decision that depends on needs of the application.

```
def sumprods(Array):
    S = 0
    for row in Array:
        try:
            x = product(row)
        except ValueError:
            x = 0
        S += x
    return S
M = [ [1,2,3], [4,5,6], [2.5,9,8] ]
print(sumprods(M))
```

The `raise` statement can also have an argument with an explanation, which might be helpful to users who see the error. Repeating the example earlier, we add some explanatory strings:

```
def scan(M):
    if type(M) != list:
        raise ValueError("scan argument not a list")
    for item in M:
        if type(item) != int:
            raise ValueError("scan list item not an integer")
```

An `except ValueError` statement would catch either of the two `ValueError`s, but if this error is seen on a console, the extra explanation from the `ValueError` argument can be used to help the user understand the problem. For instance,

```
>>> scan(True)
ValueError: scan argument not a list
```

Input Conversion

This is a topic that actually belongs to Chapter 25, but it makes sense to reconsider the topic in light of `try ... except`. Recall that Python2's `input` function can fail due to invalid input. Though it is generally not a good idea to use this `input` function, a program can catch errors using `try ... except`, for instance:

```
while True:
    try:
        X = input("Enter a number: ")
    except:  # remember, this is Python 2
        print "Bad input, please retry"
        continue
    print "Your number squared: ", X*X
```

This script can tolerate a bad input such as 5o9, tell the user, and ask again. (However, the script can still fail because a user could enter [True], which will not trigger an error in `input()`, but later in the multiplication.)

Python's Evaluation Function. What about Python3, whose `input()` function behaves like the `raw_input()` of Python2? There are times that Python2's `input()` function is handy; say a program needs to get a list, like `[1,True,2.5]`— from a string `"[1,  True,  2.5]."` This type of conversion is easy using the built-in `eval()`: the result of

```
X = eval("[1, True, 2.5]")
```

is that X is the list `[1,True,2.5]`. All the dangers that were mentioned in Chapter 25 for the Python2 `input()` function are dangers for `eval()` as well. It is wise to have some validation before trying `eval()`, and then to use `try ... except` to catch errors in converting from a string containing a Python expression to a Python value.

Catching Network Errors

Now we put together the preceding topics into a larger purpose: A script that takes a file containing URLs visits many Web pages (skipping the ones that have trouble) and reports the average size of a Web page. The input file is `urls.txt`. The first line of `urls.txt` might be `www.nist.gov`, the second line might be `www.usps.com`, and so forth. Here is the script, a Python3 program:

```
import urllib, urllib.request
URLFile = open("urls.txt")
S = n = 0  # S for sum of bytes, n for number of pages
for line in URLFile:
    tofetch = "http://" + line
    tofetch = tofetch.strip() # remove '\n'
    try:
        F = urllib.request.urlopen(tofetch)
        V = F.read()
        S += len(V)
        n += 1
        F.close()
    except urllib.error.URLError:
        pass # ignore failures
# at end of loop, use S and n to get average
T = "Average page size = {0}".format(S//n)
print(T)
```

(The specific kind of error, here `urllib.error.URLError`, was found by reading the Python3 documentation for the `urllib` module.) When writing such a script, which reads a file and also fetches a Web page, it would be reasonable to add extra `print()`'s so that you can watch progress while the script is running. For example, within the block of statements for the `try`, the script could print some message about the URL about to be fetched.

Making a Web Server

The previous section showed that it is relatively simple, in Python, to fetch a Web page. Technically, this is accomplished by a *network protocol* called HTTP. A protocol is usually some established standard (accepted by industry groups and government authorities) for the nature of messages, what they should contain, their format and data encoding, and other details. The HTTP protocol (the "P" stands for Protocol) is the protocol used for a dialog between a *client* and a *server*. The client-server terminology refers to the fact that there are two programs (both could be Python scripts) in which one party, the client, asks for something from the other party, the server. The server is often a program that answers to requests of thousands, if not millions, of clients. For HTTP, the client is nearly always a Web browser. In response to clicking on a link or typing a URL into the request box, the browser finds the server and sends it a request for a page. The server then "serves up" a Web page in response.

The earlier examples showed how one half of the situation can be done in Python, the *client side*. Now we look at how Python can do the other half, the *server side*. As it is for the client, there are differences in how the modules for Python2 and Python3 work, so an example is shown for each.

Python2 HTTP Server

The simplest HTTP server, shown below, uses syntax that goes beyond what has been seen thus far in previous chapters; it relies on *class* definition, which is covered in a later chapter. For the present, just accept that there is some mysterious new syntax, to be explained later. The following script is in a file `webserver.py`:

```python
import BaseHTTPServer
class MyHandler(BaseHTTPServer.BaseHTTPRequestHandler):
    def do_GET(self):
        try:
            self.send_response(200)
            self.send_header('Content-type','text/html')
            self.end_headers()
            self.wfile.write("<html><body><h2>Hi There</h2></body></html>")
            return
        except:
            return
# main program is here
try:
    server = BaseHTTPServer.HTTPServer(('',8000), MyHandler)
    print 'started httpserver...'
    server.serve_forever()
except KeyboardInterrupt:
    print '^C received, shutting down server'
    server.socket.close()
```

The organization of the code above is partly explained by these remarks:

- The Python2 module for HTTP servers is `BaseHTTPServer`, imported on the first line. It is called "base" because other, more complex HTTP servers are built on top of this module.

- The line starting with `class` declares that a server (or even more than one server) will be customized using the "base" server of the module. The syntax of `class` implies that some *methods* will be defined. We have seen already methods for strings and lists (recall the methods like `replace()`, `index()`, etc.). Here is an example of user-defined methods.

- The `do_GET()` method will automatically be called by the base HTTP server when a browser request arrives. The block of statements in the body of `do_GET()` say what will happen with a request. There can be conditional logic, error codes, even `print` statements here.

- There is a file object `self.wfile`, which is the place to build a response to a request. Since this is a file object, the `write()` method is used for creating the response to a browser request. Notice that the argument in the example above is a string, and you may observe that this string is HTML, to be interpreted by the browser.

- The main part of the script is a `try ... except` statement. The error it catches is a user entering a CTL+c (Ctrl and c simultaneously) to stop the server.

- Within the `try` block of statements, a server is created with "port" number 8000. This number is somewhat arbitrary, but must be different from the number of any other server on the same computer (in student exercises, it is wise to change this from 8000 to 8045 or some other distinct value).

Now, to launch this Web server, the command (under Linux) could be the following:

```
> python webserver.py
started httpserver...
localhost - - [10/Aug/2010 16:53:23] "GET / HTTP/1.1" 200 -
^C^C received, shutting down server
>
```

The response to starting the script was the first printed message, `started httpserver`. However, what we cannot see above is that a browser was then used to request a page. In the browser's URL area, the following was entered:

```
http://localhost:8000
```

This unusual URL (quite different from something like `http://www.nist.gov`) has two components, `localhost` and the number 8000, which is the port number the server uses. The name `localhost` is standard terminology for bypassing the Internet and directly using a server on the same computer where the browser runs. For testing purposes, `localhost` is quite handy. After entering this URL, the browser displayed a simple page with **Hi There**, as directed by the HTML written in the script.

This very simple example misses some useful features that `BaseHTTPServer` offers. For instance, the `do_GET()` method can inspect a string sent by the browser, looking for particular information about which "page" to return (in reality, "page" is just jargon, and the server can return any kind of string). If the string sent by the browser contains `index.html`, then the server logic could have an `if` statement and a block of code to create a page for that.

Python3 HTTP Server

The base HTTP server for Python3 is nearly the same as the one for Python2, the main difference being a reorganization of the library code into different module names.

```
import http.server
class MyHandler(http.server.BaseHTTPRequestHandler):
    def do_GET(self):
        try:
            self.send_response(200)
            self.send_header('Content-type','text/html')
            self.end_headers()
            response = "<html><body><h2>Hi There</h2></body></html>"
            self.wfile.write(response.encode())
            return
        except:
            return

try:
  server = http.server.HTTPServer(('',8000), MyHandler)
  print('started httpserver...')
  server.serve_forever()
except KeyboardInterrupt:
  print('^C received, shutting down server')
  server.socket.close()
```

The only changes in the script for Python3 are the module name, `http.server`, using `print()` as a function rather than as a command, and having to write `bytes` rather than a string to the `self.wfile` file object. The `encode` method does the conversion from string to the `bytes` type.

Client and Server

Once a server has been started, say by the command "`python webserver.py`," any number of browser requests can be entered, and each will return a Web page. In fact, Web page requests could come from different browsers or even a client written with a simple Python program. Below is an example of a script that could be run in another window (command shell) on the same computer where `webserver.py` runs. The script name for the following is `webclient.py`. The example uses Python2 (the Python3 version would be similar):

```
import urllib2
UF = urllib2.urlopen("http://localhost:8000")
print UF.read()
```

Supposing that `webserver.py` is running in another window, the following shows the result of running `webclient.py`.

```
> python webclient.py
<html><body><h2>Hi There</h2></body></html>
>
```

The result is no surprise—the client gets just what the server wrote as a response. Unlike a browser, this elementary client does not process the HTML tags (`<html>`, `<body>`, etc.).

General Client-Server Interaction. Going beyond this example, most scenarios of client and server programs have a continuing dialog between the two parties. A client contacts the server, which responds, and the client then sends another request to the server. This request/response kind of dialog can transfer the contents of a file, query a database, execute some financial transaction, and even have function calls on the client side to draw or control devices. These scenarios are the subject of specialized texts on network programming. It is worth noting that influential systems like Google and BitTorrent originated as Python scripts. One good thing about networks is that standards for communication do not vary across operating systems, versions of languages, and platforms. The server could be running Python3, and the client Python2, and communication would work properly

Serving Multiple Pages

The basic example of the previous section always returns the same "page," regardless of the request. It is more interesting when the server can respond to different page requests with different pages. The following is a fragment of a Python2 script, just showing the `do_GET(self)` method definition used earlier in the chapter (for Python3, strings would have to be converted to the `bytes` type before writing them).

```python
def do_GET(self):
  try:
    if self.path.endswith("/index.html"):
      f = open("index.html")
      self.send_response(200)
      self.send_header('Content-type','text/html')
      self.end_headers()
      self.wfile.write(f.read())
      f.close()
      return
    elif self.path.endswith("/show.html"):
      f = open("show.html")
      s = f.read()
      f.close()
      s = s.format(self.path,self.client_address)
      self.send_response(200)
      self.send_header('Content-type','text/html')
      self.end_headers()
      self.wfile.write(s)
      return
    else:
      f = open("404.html")
      self.send_response(404)
      self.send_header('Content-type','text/html')
      self.end_headers()
      self.wfile.write(f.read())
      f.close()
      return
  except:
      pass
```

Does this code seem repetitive? Yes, it would likely be improved using functions that encapsulate some repeated statements. The code does show how the server might return three different Web pages, one for `index.html`, one for `show.html`, and another for any other request. All Web pages are HTML stored in files. The one interesting case is `show.html`, which might contain the following lines:

```
<html><body> <p>
Your request for <font color="red">{0}</font>
</p><p>
originated from <font color="red">{1}</font>
</p></body></html>
```

The file is essentially a template with the formatting codes {0} and {1} that will be substituted by `self.path` and `self.client_address` when the server responds with the Web page. This shows that pages can be *dynamic*, changing content of what is in the page depending on the client or other factors. A typical value for `self.path` would be /show.html if the client URL was `http://localhost:8000/show.html`. Thus, the server can look at the string in `self.path` to customize the response it returns. The variable `self.client_address` is a tuple (an IP address and a port), identifying the client's network location.

Terminology Review

This chapter uses the `try ... except` statement, which is helpful for network applications, but has many other uses. The notions of client and server programs, examples of HTTP and HTML, and customizing a library module (the base HTTP server) are covered as well.

Exercises

The best source of exercises is the Internet, using a search engine, to find Python Web servers, clients, and network tutorials; you can learn from them, change the code, and experiment with your own ideas, and go on from there. As a warm-up, we offer some simple exercises here.

(1) Write a Python program that gets a URL from the user, using `input()` (Python3) or `raw_input()` (Python2) and then fetches the Web page and counts the number of lowercase j's that are in the response.

(2) Write a Python script that reports whether a URL is a valid Web site, using the `try .. except` to decide whether the URL functioned or not.

(3) The `self.path` variable in the `do_GET(self)` method can contain lots of information; a URL could be something like

>   `http://localhost:8432/goto/www.nist.gov`

so that the `self.path` would contain /goto/www.nist.gov. See if you can write a server that creates a URL out of the contents of `self.path` and then use that URL to fetch a page from another server (like `www.nist.gov`); the goal is to return that page back to the client.

(4) Use a search engine to find a tutorial on how to use Python's `socket` module, which gives access to the lowest level of networking. Write a script that transmits the content of a file to another Python program (you will need to write two scripts, one is a "server" to receive the file, and the other is the "client" that sends the file). You may also use Python's `socketserver` module if it is helpful.

Chapter 27: Objects, Classes, and Inheritance

Mathematicians do not study objects,
but relations between objects.
— Henri Poincare

Object-oriented programming is one of those buzzwords which is difficult to nail down precisely. Reading an explanation of this in, say Wikipedia, quickly opens up more buzzwords and abstractions until it seems like going around in circles. Why all the fuss? To understand what objects (and classes) mean for a programming language, it helps to look briefly at the history of how languages treat data with higher-level operations than manipulating bits and bytes. However, even after learning of this history, there is still the question of why it is important to learn about objects. The simple answer is that, for better or worse, most modern software and their libraries of modules now depend on using objects. So, to use much of the useful software out there (and there is a vast amount of great software), one needs to understand objects and associated concepts.

A Bit of History. Back in Chapter 5, there is justification for Python types beyond simple numbers and bits. Python tuples and lists can have any kind of item, including strings, dictionaries, and lists. Other languages do not have so much freedom. Typically, the other programming languages have arrays, or something like lists, which only permit one kind of item (a list only of numbers or only of strings). There is one practical concern for any language, which is the problem of representing data given by the application, be it business, entertainment, or scientific purpose. Often the data is naturally seen as either a table or a list of records. In a table, there are rows, which resemble records. A spreadsheet is a natural example. Records are common in business and government, where records correspond to individuals (taxpayers), companies, or manufactured appliances (inventory). A feature of a record is that it has *fields*. Usually, each field has a name (somewhat like a column heading in a table), and an application "type" such as a date, a monetary value, a quantity, checkmarks (paid/unpaid), and so forth. Using Python, it is easy to represent a record as using the `list` type, but in designing applications one might also need to think about how a record would be stored on some permanent media. A low-level language such as assembler or C enables programmers to precisely lay out a record in terms of the bytes of memory and the placement of fields in memory. The C language uses a concept of a *data structure*, called a `struct` in C. Similarly, arrays have a precise layout in memory in C.

The simple view of data as records only goes so far to help us represent application information. In a genealogy application, family trees have to be represented; some family trees are large, some are small, so putting a family tree in a single record does not seem practical. If each member of the family tree has a record, then there needs to be some way to relate the records (father, mother, sibling) and group the records (different family names). If records are deleted or arbitrarily modified, the family tree might not make sense. In an effort to avoid making a mess of everything just using records, some theorists proposed *abstract data types* (ADTs) that not only structure data, but define all the operations that are allowed to read, write, delete, and create items of the ADT.

Beyond even abstract data types comes the realization that there are common patterns of applications and computing systems. Two business applications might be quite similar up to a certain level of detail, so it would be sensible to use a common base for their software. Graphical applications often use ideas based around geometry and hardware ideas (pixels, shading). Even if two graphical applications are quite different, certain aspects of them will be alike enough to warrant using the same basic ADTs and algorithms, though customized for efficiency and particular quirks. This is the fundamental realization behind object-oriented programming: the syntax of a programming language can help automate the reuse and customization of ADTs. One principal idea is that of a *class hierarchy*, wherein all the ADTs in the universe of programming are categorized into various branches, viewed as an evolutionary tree of data structures and operations on them. Different languages have their own hierarchies (Java has its standard library, Microsoft has defined a hierarchy in the .NET framework).

Classes, Instances, Objects, Attributes

This section is quite abstract and may be hard to understand in a single reading. It may help to scan the terminology, go on to the next section, and then come back to this section after seeing a few examples.

Python has syntax allowing a program (module or script) to define a *class*, which is similar in spirit to a new data type. You can define as many classes (i.e., new data types) as needed. Once a class has been defined, a program can create *instances* of that class. The situation is similar to the `list` type in Python. A program can create as many lists as needed, and each will have `list` as its type. Another term for an instance of a class is *object*: every object is an instance of a class.

Objects are essentially packages of data. In most object-oriented languages the data within an object can only be viewed or changed using *methods* defined for the object. The definitions of the methods are found in the class from which the object comes (remember, an object is an instance of a class). Python has a less strict interpretation of objects and classes. Objects belong to classes, however, objects are completely mutable: the data *should* be viewed and manipulated using methods, however, ordinary assignment statements can read and write data of objects as well.

Inside an object, the data items are typically ordinary basic things such as numbers, characters, strings, or other simple data. Each of the items in the object is a variable named in the class definition for that object. Most object-oriented programming languages call the variables and methods of a class *members* of that class; in Python these are often called *attributes* rather than members.

The collected experience of writing software with classes shows that some classes strongly resemble others: the methods are similar, and perhaps the data of objects in the respective classes looks about the same. To take advantage of this observation, programming languages enable a new class to be defined in terms of an existing one. Roughly speaking, the idea is to say "define class X to be like class Y, with a few exceptions." This notion of defining one class to be like another is called *inheritance*. Classes can thereby have a parent-child relation. Class X could have class Y as a parent class. The conventional name for a parent class is *superclass*, whereas the conventional name for a child class is *subclass*. In most object-oriented programming languages, a parent can have many children, but a child can only have one parent; Python actually does allow a child class to have multiple parent classes (that goes well beyond what this chapter covers). The practical consequence of a parent-child relation is that, by default, class X will have all the attributes (variables and methods) of class Y. There are ways for the definition of class X to *override* what are Y's members, if that is what is needed in customizing X.

Elementary Objects in Python

The simplest example of creating an object, letting g refer to the object, and showing its Python type is:

```
>>> g = object()
>>> type(g)
<type 'object'>
```

Unfortunately, there is not much that can be done with such a simple object: it is an instance of class that has no attributes. To make a more meaningful object, we first need to define a class. The simplest definition of a class, here given the name "point," is:

```
class point():
    pass
```

The `pass` statement does nothing; it is only put there because Python expects to have at least one statement within any class definition (otherwise there would be a syntax error). Here is an interactive example of creating an instance of the class `point`:

```
>>> g = point()
>>> type(g)
<type 'instance'>
>>> g.x = 50
>>> g.y = 200
>>> h = g
>>> h is g
True
>>> h.x
50
>>> h.x + g.y
250
```

The first line creates a `point` object and lets variable g refer to this new object. The assignment `g.x = 50` creates an attribute x of the object. The subsequent lines that assign to h and refer to attributes show that objects are treated like other mutables (lists and dictionaries), as described in Chapter 17. Above, h is an alias of g: they both refer to the same object.

Methods Are Functions

Methods are functions defined within a class. This section shows different methods for class `point`; suppose p is an instance of `point`. To *call* a method, a program would use this syntax:

```
r = p.mean()
```

This assigns the result of invoking method `mean` for object p. Within class `point` there needs to be a definition of the `mean` method. For instance,

```
class point():
    def mean(self):
        return (self.x + self.y)/2.0
```

The definition of `mean` is unusual: there is a parameter `self`, but the expression `p.mean()` has no argument. The explanation is that `self` represents the object in question, `p` in this case. Though the variable name `p` precedes the method `mean()` in the expression `p.mean()`, Python treats this as if `mean(p)` were the expression matching up arguments to the method definition. Another example shows a method requiring an argument:

```
class point():
  def mean(self):
    return (self.x + self.y)/2.0
  def right(self,amount):
    self.x += amount
    return
```

Using this version of `point`, the expression `p.right()` would be an error, because `self` would be `p`, but there is nothing to match up with `amount` in the definition. Proper would be `p.right(20)`, which will let parameter `amount` bind with the number 20. You might also notice that methods can *change* the values of the variables within an object: `p.right(20)` increases `p.x` by 20.

The Init Method

One method name with special significance is the "`__init__`" method. Nearly all class definitions are written to have such a method.

```
class point():
  def __init__(self,a,b):
    self.x, self.y = a, b
  def right(self,amount):
    self.x += amount
```

Here is an interactive example using the class `point`.

```
>>> p = point(30,80)
>>> p.x
30
>>> p.y
80
>>> p.right(20)
>>> p.x
50
```

In the first line, `point(30,80)` creates an instance of `point`, letting `p` be a reference to this new object. The arguments 30, 80 match up to parameters of the `__init__` method, so that the `x` and `y` variables of the new object have the desired initial values. General terminology for an initializing method is *object constructor*, since the purpose is to construct a new instance of the class and set up various attributes for later use.

Containment

Object attributes can be variables, and these variables could in fact be references to other objects. As a warmup to illustrating this potential of objects, here is a small example showing that a list can have objects as items.

```
>>> p = point(0,100)
>>> Triangle = [ point(-50,0), point(50,0), p ]
>>> point1 = Triangle[0]
>>> point1.x
-50
>>> point1 is Triangle[0]
True
>>> Triangle[2].y
100
```

The assignment to `Triangle` above shows that creation of an object can be within expressions, which put the object inside a list. A reference to an object behaves like a reference to the other mutable types in Python, dictionaries, and lists.

Line Objects. In geometry, a line is defined by two (distinct) points. A Python class to make a line could be:

```
class Line():
  def __init__(self,a,b):
    self.point1, self.point2 = a,b
    if a.x==b.x and a.y==b.y:
      raise ValueError
  def length(self):
    dx = self.point2.x-self.point1.x
    dy = self.point2.y-self.point1.y
    return (dx*dx + dy*dy)**0.5
```

The constructor method `__init__` for `Line` needs two arguments, both of them point objects. Since a line cannot be defined with a single (x, y) point, the constructor raises an error if both arguments refer to the same (x, y) point. The `length` method calculates the distance between the two points defining the line. Other methods like `slope` and `intercept` could easily be defined as well. Using the `Line` class is straightforward:

```
>>> L = Line(point(1,1),point(8,-5))
>>> L.point2.y
-5
>>> L.length()
9.2195445729
```

The way that Python evaluates `L.point2.y` is left-to-right: the `point2` attribute of object L is itself a `point` object, which has a y attribute. An equivalent way to write this would be `(L.point2).y`.

Subclasses

This chapter's exposition of classes and objects is limited; the example here just shows some elementary syntax for class inheritance.

```
class ColoredLine(Line):
    def setColor(self,newcolor):
      self.color = newcolor
    def getColor(self):
      try:
        return self.color
      except:
        return None
```

The example defines a class `ColoredLine` that inherits the attributes of its parent class, named in the definition: the `Line` class. The `ColoredLine` class possesses the `Line` attributes plus new attributes, `color`, `setColor`, and `getColor`.

```
>>> L = Line(point(0,0),point(5,1))
>>> L.getColor()
AttributeError: Line instance has no attribute 'getcolor'
>>> M = ColoredLine(point(0,0),point(5,1))
>>> print(M.getColor())
None
>>> M.setColor(27)
>>> M.getColor()
27
```

Only a `ColoredLine` instance has methods `setColor` and `getColor`.

In Python2, defining a class that inherits from `object` effectively creates a new type; in Python3, all defined classes are types. Moreover, you can define your own class that is a subclass of any Python type.

Going Further

The syntax for inheritance (defining a new class in terms of an existing parent class) is more complex than the simple example above might suggest. Some difficulties arise from having constructor methods in both parent and child classes; we do not explain this any further—the only reason to show it is that you may come across this syntax while looking at Python programs you encounter. Built-in functions `super()`, `isinstance()`, and `issubclass()` assist in the definition of hierarchical classes. The built-in `type()` function, only seen in this book as a way to inspect the type of a variable or expression, also has a three-argument functionality that can dynamically create a class or type. For further information about these functions and the general topic of class hierarchies in Python, a more complete and advanced text should be studied. The only need for hierarchy in this chapter is to exploit some features in the Python library of modules: some of them require that you define a new class in terms of a class defined in a module. Chapter 26 has an example of this: The `MyHandler` class is defined as a subclass of the `BaseHTTPRequestHandler` class, so that it can customize behavior of a standard HTTP server.

Period Syntax

Consider all the uses of the period (dot, ".") in Python:

- The decimal point is part of `float` notation: 2.5, 1.305e-7, etc.

- Method syntax, which is a kind of function invocation, uses the dot: `''.join(X)`, `Evar.index("ing")`, `M.sort()`, etc.

- Names of variables, classes, and functions in modules imported using the `import` statement require a period to qualify the name. (And in Python3, a period can be used to refer to directory and subdirectory relation where a module is located.) Examples of this are `math.pi`, `math.sqrt()`, `random.choice()`.

- Attributes of objects use the `p.x` notation.

When periods occur in expressions, recall that the default rule for Python syntax is left-to-right evaluation. As Python evaluates such an expression, the type of the term under evaluation determines what is expected next. If Python determines that `R` is a module name in evaluating `R.t`, then `t` had better be some variable, function, or class within module `R`. Similarly, if `x` is an object reference in the expression `x.a`, then `a` must be an attribute of `x`. Technically, this holds for an expression like `''.join(V)` because the empty string `''` is an instance of the "string" class, and the method `join` is defined in the string class, so `''.join` is an attribute:

```
>>> type(''.join)
<type 'builtin_function_or_method'>
```

In expression `M.e.b`, it could be that `M` is a module, `e` is an object reference inside of the module, and `b` is an attribute of `e`. Even more complicated expressions are allowed by Python, so long as they follow the syntax rules and make sense in terms of the types and the rules for using dot listed above.

```
(Tref[i][j]).(Ftab("S",k)).summary(V.y[b:b+8])
```

In parsing this rather messy expression, Python could first determine that `Tref[i][j]` refers to a module, then determine that `Ftab("S",k)` returns an object reference within that module, and that `summary` is a method of the object—so the expression would make sense. Of course, this complicated way of expressing an idea is not recommended.

Example: Date/Time Objects

The Python `datetime` module is based on objects. As with all Python modules, the only reliable documentation is that found at `www.python.org`; it is somewhat cryptic documentation, however, with knowledge of objects and Python syntax, and perhaps some examples found with a bit of searching, these modules are very useful. The following script is an exercise using `datetime` objects.

```
import datetime
import date
DayBirth = datetime.date(1992,8,4) # date of birth
WeekDays = "Mon Tue Wed Thu Fri Sat Sun".split()
day = WeekDays[ DayBirth.weekday() ]
S = "born on a {0}.".format(day)
print(S)
Now = datetime.date.today() # current date/time
Age = Now - DayBirth # creates timedelta object
S = "current age in days since birth is {0}."
```

```
S = S.format(Age.days)
print(S)
```

One interesting feature shown above is the calculation of age, `Age = Now - DayBirth`. The `datetime` module actually extends Python's minus operator ("–") so that objects can be subtracted (in this case, two `date` objects). The result creates a `timedelta` object. This hints at how Python can define classes and instances that essentially behave as new data types for the language.

Example: Regular Expressions

> *Some people, when confronted with a problem, think*
> *"I know, I'll use regular expressions." Now they have two problems.*
> — Jamie Zawinski

The concept of *regular expressions* is fundamental to much of the day-to-day work in information technology and the software industry. The essential idea is easy to grasp: consoles, or command shells, typically allow one to see all the files that begin with "T" by entering

```
> ls T*
T.pl Tcpserv.py Token.bak Tankfill.tgz Transactor TAX.doc
```

The "*" is a *wildcard* character, meaning that it can stand for any string of characters. Hence, filenames like `Temp.txt` and `Tomorrow.data` would be listed, whereas files that do not begin with `T` would not be shown. Many search engines allow similar syntax to limit and tailor search results.

Regular expressions are supported by libraries or modules in most programming languages. Some programming languages even incorporate regular expressions into the syntax of the language itself, notably Perl, where using regular expressions is a way of life, so to speak. Regular expressions go well beyond "*," typically using many special characters (`+`, `[`, `]`, `*`, `(`, `)`, `?`, and others) to control how text to be searched will match up with some pattern expression. On the one hand, regular expressions enable very concise, flexible and powerful matching of patterns to text data, which is quite useful for tasks of searching, data extraction, conversion, and general preparation of information. On the other hand, the notation and conventions of regular expressions are a mini-language that is easy to forget, can differ slightly from one programming language to the next, and has a very cryptic appearance. Whatever one might conclude about regular expression usage, it is an important programming idiom in current software systems and worth knowing about.

The official Python documentation includes a "Regular Expression HOWTO," which should be consulted for those planning to use this feature in Python. What follows is just one example of the power of regular expressions. The task in the example is to read a file `dorian.txt` and find all strings in the file consisting of lowercase characters, starting with "a" and ending with "ly," making a list of these.

```
import re
T = open("dorian.txt").read()
regobject = re.compile("a[a-z]*ly")
matches = regobject.findall(T)
print(matches)
```

The pattern for searching through the file text above is the string `"a[a-z]*ly,"` which stands for anything that begins with **a**, followed by any number of characters in the lowercase alphabet (a–z), followed by `ly`. The output of the example is too lengthy to reproduce here (the file `dorian.txt` contains over 75,000 words). The first few lines of the output are:

```
['adly', 'ally', 'ardly', 'arily', 'anguidly', 'ainly',
'ally', 'ally', 'ally', 'absolutely', 'ally', 'awfully',
'absolutely', 'asionally', 'ally', 'ally', 'ainly', 'angely',
```

The script is quite short, yet able to match a generic pattern to many forms of string matching the pattern. Methods other than `findall` return "match objects," from which the index of a match within the file text can be extracted.

Example: HTML Processing

Network programs may fetch Web pages, which use HTML, a language to mark up text for display and browser interaction. While it is possible to write Python functions that scan HTML and extract meaning from the data, it is usually easier to use a Python module to do this. The following example is a script that processes HTML in a string (alternatively it could be in a file object, as shown in Chapter 26). The script uses the Python2 version of HTML processing, but Python3's version is nearly the same.

```python
import HTMLParser
class LinkParser(HTMLParser.HTMLParser):
  def handle_starttag(self,tag,attrs):
    if tag == 'a':
      linktuple = attrs[0]
      href, url = linktuple
      self.mylinks.append(url)

T = '''<html><body bgcolor="gray">
<h1>My Title</h1><p>Welcome to Webpage.
The <a href="http://www.python.org">Python
Link</a> is a good resource.  Sometimes
the <A href="http://en.wikipedia.org">
Wikipedia page</a> is helpful.
</body></html>'''

# create a parser object
p = LinkParser()
p.mylinks = [ ] # collect links
p.feed(T)
for url in p.mylinks:
  print(url)
```

Observe that to use the `HTMLParser`, a script must define a class that inherits from the `HTMLParser` class, customizing a method that is called repeatedly during a scan of some HTML input. The input is "fed" to a parser object, which is created first (above, it is variable p). Thanks to Python's flexibility, the script adds a new attribute `mylinks`, a list to collect all the URLs in a Web page. Object-oriented software purists would not write the script this way: a purist would instead create the `mylinks` attribute inside the `__init__` method, however, doing so would entail using **super()**, which goes beyond what this chapter covers. The output of the script above is

```
http://www.python.org
http://en.wikipedia.org
```

Terminology Review

Object-oriented programming is rich with jargon. Motivations start with records, fields within records, structured data, and abstract data types. The notion of classes and instances of classes, commonly called objects, incorporates inheritance so that classes can form a hierarchy, in which a class may have parent and child classes (superclass and subclass). Within a class, there are members, which could be data or methods; Python notation uses a period (dot) after an object reference for an attribute; an attribute may be a variable or may be a method. When one class inherits from another, all the members automatically carry over from the parent, unless the definition of the child overrides them. Most standard Python modules use class/object techniques; some modules require that applications using them define subclasses, which override methods to customize their behavior.

Exercises

(1) Find and read documentation of Python's `webbrowser` module. Then try the following, interactively:

```
>>> import webbrowser
>>> T = webbrowser.get()
>>> T.open("http://www.python.org")
```

This should cause a Web browser to start and display a Web page. Above, the variable T is a reference to a browser "controller" object. Write a script that launches a Web browser and opens several tabs with different pages.

(2) Python's `list` class defines the methods and operators of lists. At an interactive Python session, you can see the hidden methods of `list` by the command `help(list)`. Write a new class `mylist` that inherits the methods of `list`. The following should work after your class definition:

```
>>> R = mylist("one two three".split())
>>> R[0]
'one'
>>> len(R)
3
```

Now revise your definition of `mylist` so that it has a method `middle()`, which returns the "middle" item of the sequence it contains. Continuing the example above, `R.middle()` should return `"two."` One more thing to try with the definition of `mylist`, change the length method so that `len(R)` returns double what the number of items has, that is, six instead of three.

(3) Write a definition of a class named `Box` that has three methods, a `__init__(self)` method, a `register(self)` method, and a `isRegistered(self)` method. The behavior of the latter two should be as follows:

```
>>> p = Box()  # create a Box object
>>> p.isRegistered()  # has p been registered?
False
>>> p.isRegistered()  # now has p been registered?
False
>>> p.register()
>>> p.isRegistered()  # has p been registered?
True
>>> p.isRegistered()  # is p still registered?
True
```

(4) This script is supposed to print the number of letters in common to two words. The words "entangle" and "legal" have 4 letters in common (a, e, g, l), so the script should print 4 as the result. Instead the script has some errors. Even after correcting the syntax errors, it still does not work correctly, because the way it calculates the result is wrong. What are the errors and how can it be made to work correctly?

```
class Word():
    def init(self,value)
        self.text = value
```

```
    def common(OtherWord)
        n = 0
        for letter in Otherword.text:
            n += self.text.count(letter)
        return n

A = Word("entangle")
B = Word("legal")
print A.common(B)
```

(5) This exercise is for Unix/Linux systems only (might work on a Mac OS, too). The module for the exercise is `subprocess`, which enables a Python script to issue typical commands like `ls` (list directory), `tail` (get the last lines of a file), `mv` (move or rename a file or directory), and hundreds more. The commands can even be new ones that you invent. The `subprocess` not only lets you issue the commands within Python, but any number of parameters to these commands can be given as a list of strings, and the response from the command will be captured as a string, where the Python script can extract information. This kind of facility to call up system commands, get responses, and process data approaches the real meaning of *script*—it can automate what people might have to otherwise do manually, but which is a regular enough activity to merit automation. Here is an example using `subprocess`:

```
import sys, subprocess
subprocess.call("date",shell=True)
subprocess.call("date -u",shell=True)
```

The script runs `date` commands as though they had been typed in from a shell prompt; the output goes back to the console. What if we would like the output to be returned to the Python script? The next example has another method of `subprocess`, which enables the output from a command to be returned in an object.

```
import sys
import subprocess
# create a Popen object, which runs the unix command
#          ls -l /opt
# listing what's in the /opt directory.
P = subprocess.Popen(["ls","-l","/opt"],stdout=subprocess.PIPE)
# run the Popen object and wait until it's done:  the
# communicate() method returns a tuple (A,B) where both
# A and B are strings, with A being the command's normal
# output and B having error messages, if any
out,error = P.communicate()
# go through lines in out, and nicely format them
for line in out.split('\n'):
    sys.stdout.write("\t" + line + '\n')
sys.stdout.write("----------------------\n")   # make marker at end
```

Modify this second example so that it changes options on the `ls` command (you can read about the options by reading a manual page on `ls`, searching online). Another experiment could be to extract just some information from the string in `out` and summarize that.

Interlude: Signal Processing

Most of the data generated in the world of embedded computers, in social networking, in the realm of commerce, is a kind of *flow* of information. For example, in finance there is a continuous stream of trading events, and in commerce we see transactions in large volumes. A typical embedded computer situation is found in large aircraft, which are equipped with vibration and strain sensors, generating terabytes of readings in each flight. Though most of this kind of data ends up not being useful at the level of each and every bit, the general volume, "velocity," and trending of events and readings can signify important trends. Here, we consider a simplified problem typical of this domain of computing.

Suppose we have a sensor that measures relative movement using an *accelerometer*, which produces a reading corresponding to movement (actually, acceleration) in physical space, at the rate of 120 readings every second. The accelerometer is embedded in a vehicle, connected to a computer with a radio, so that the radio might be used to send a distress message if the vehicle is in some kind of danger. It turns out not worthwhile to record all of the accelerometer data; experts dealing with the accelerometer tell us that a change of 10% in a stream of readings likely means the vehicle needs attention due to some accident or malfunction. Furthermore, there can sometimes be false readings due to electrical noise in the system, so the engineers recommend that the 10% change detection be with respect to the average of several previous readings.

The nearly pseudocode design of what we would like to implement is simple, seen on the right. The `Accelorometer()` function produces one reading from the sensor device, and `sendWarning(x)` transmits a distress message.

```
while True:
    x = Accelerometer()
    if not normal(x):
        sendWarning(x)
```

It is the `normal(x)` function that is of interest here. That function needs to return a boolean depending on how x relates to previous iterations of the `while` loop. The problem is, how can the function `normal(x)` refer to the last several readings, in order to return `False` if x represents a 10% change? In Python, there is not an obvious answer to this. Instead, most people would rewrite the code as shown on the right, below.

Though this change will enable `normal` to see the last five previous readings via the `history` argument, it clutters up the logic and puts the responsibility of keeping an appropriate amount of history in the main program, not inside `normal`. (Maybe the choice of the number 5 will need to be changed later, as the engineers tune their warning logic.) So we return to the real question.

```
history = []
while True:
    x = Accelerometer()
    if not normal(x,history):
        sendWarning(x)
    if len(history) < 5:
        history.append(x)
    else:
        history = history[1:] + [x]
```

How Can a Python Function Remember?

In the paragraphs that follow, several advanced Python techniques show different ways of answering this kind of question.

Global Variables

The first idea that may come to mind is to record the history of previous readings in a global variable. Then, a statement such as `global history` would presumably allow `normal(x)` to change the variable `history` to include `x`, and that way the body of `normal(x)` might use the previous readings to test for a 10% change. Unfortunately, the statement `global history` encounters the error `NameError: global name 'history' is not defined`. To make this idea work, the main program would have to first assign to a `history` variable so that it would exist when `normal(x)` is called. Since the goal was to have `normal(x)` completely take care of maintaining history itself, without any extra statements outside of `normal(x)`, we would rather not have to first create the `history` variable. Though there are some ways around this situation (for instance, by inspecting the names that Python returns from the `globals()` function), the code would not be easy to understand by doing things this way. Let us look for another idea.

Use Classes and Objects

The whole idea of a function "remembering" previous calls, or having some kind of durable information between calls, is part of the motivation of classes, objects, and methods. It is fairly straightforward, using notions from Chapter 27, to revise the code to use an object, seen by the

```
G = WarnClass()
while True:
    x = Accelerometer()
    if not G.normal(x):
        sendWarning(x)
```

example to the right. The new variable `G` is an instance of a new class `WarnClass`, which has a method `normal(self,x)`. Within the definition of `normal`, the code could freely use any kind of attributes, perhaps going beyond just `self.history`, so the main program does not need to worry about how `normal` does its checking for the 10% threshold.

```
normal = WarnClass()
while True:
    x = Accelerometer()
    if not normal(x):
        sendWarning(x)
```

If only to show off another Python feature, the revised version on the left uses another trick. In this code, `normal` is an object of `WarnClass`; the curious thing here is that `normal(x)` looks like a function call, which is strange since we normally associate methods, not functions, with objects.

The trick is that the definition of class `WarnClass` defines a method `__call__(self,x)`. Just as the `__init__(self)` method is invoked whenever an object is created, one may also define a `__call__` method that will be invoked each time a statement tries to use the object with function-calling syntax. This is a somewhat obscure trick, not recommended for common practice. It is shown here mainly to reveal some of the under-the-hood mechanisms that Python is capable of exposing.

Hidden Mutable in Keyword Parameter

The design based on classes and objects is the standard recommendation of most programming practice. However, Python does have a curious treatment of mutables when specified as default values in keyword parameters. An example is seen to the right. The header of `normal` now in-

```
def normal(x,history=[]):
    history.append(x)
    if len(history)>5:
        del history[0]
    ... # code for 10% detection
```

cludes a keyword parameter for `history`, initially with the empty list as the default value. The curious aspect of Python is that this default value actually changes with each mutation to `history`. After five calls to `normal`, say `normal(70)`, `normal(73)`, `normal(75)`, `normal(74)`, `normal(76)`, `history` will be the list `[70,73,75,74,76]`. It is a matter of some debate whether or not this behavior of Python is a good or bad feature. Technically, using it does precisely satisfy the objective of having a function remember values between calls. For this technique to work properly, the caller of `normal` *should not* specify a `history` argument, since that would override the default parameter value. This is why we refer to `history` as a "hidden" keyword parameter—it is not something to be advertised to callers of the function (though nothing prevents the caller from doing so). Most beginners find this behavior of functions surprising; for further information, try a Web search on default parameter values in Python. (One other interesting trick, suggested in the "Trivia" section in Chapter 30, is to use a *function attribute* to the same purpose as the hidden keyword parameter.)

Coroutine Processing

The most exotic way for a function to remember values between calls is simply to let the function run forever. That idea seems puzzling: if a function never uses `return`, how can a caller get back a result from the function call? Python's answer exploits generators, specifically generator loops (see the box "Loops Using *Iterables* and Generators" in Chapter 22). Within a generator loop, the `yield` statement can both transmit a value, such as the boolean result of a 10% threshold test inside of `normal`, and get the next value of x. In the main program, instead of using `next()` to get the result from `normal`, the main program uses `send(x)`. Sample code is shown below.

```
def normal():
    history = []
    x = yield  # yield with no value just to get first x
    while True:
        history.append(x)  # history[-1] is x
        r = False  # warning is false by default
        if len(history)>5:
            mean = sum(history[:-1]) / 5.0
            if abs(history[-1] - mean) >= 0.1*mean:
                r = True
            del history[0]
        x = yield r     # "return" r, and get next x value


# main program
T = normal()  # create generator (like an object)
T.send(None)  # initialize the generator by sending None
while True:
    x = Accelerometer()
    v = T.send(x)  # give normal the next x & get result
    if v:
        sendWarning(x)
```

In a sense, organizing a program this way, where the main program is a loop that "calls" a generator using the `send()` method, resembles parallel processing. The program behavior roughly is like two concurrently running entities, the main program and `normal`, each running a loop. They meet up for communication using `send()` and `yield`. This view of two entities concurrently running loops and exchanging information is called the *coroutine* pattern of programming. It is an advanced programming technique not advised for beginners. We show it here to give some idea of how computer scientists organize systems using concepts of concurrency or parallelism in designs.

Chapter 28:   Randomness, Time, and System Modules

> *Creativity is the ability to introduce order into the randomness of nature.*
> — Eric Hoffer

> *Now the whole point about machines is they are designed not to be random. When you call up a word processing program on your computer, you don't want it to be different every time you call it up. You want it to stay the same.*
> — Rupert Sheldrake

A list of the top five most useful modules in the Python library would probably include `math`, `sys`, `random`, `time`, and `os`. The `math` module has been seen in earlier chapters; the goal of this chapter is to briefly introduce the other most useful modules.

The Random Module

The `random` module is a collection of methods for generating random numbers, ideal statistical distributions (Gaussian, uniform, exponential, Pareto, and more), and some useful sampling and selection methods. We touch on just a few of the methods here; online Python documentation lists all the methods and describes what they do. The methods and their explanations follow, describing the methods as though they are functions from the `random` module; then an example script is presented. Later, it is shown that these really are methods and a class/object is associated with them.

Of course, the idea behavior of any simulation of randomness would be unpredictable—free from any patterns. Each time that a random method gets called, it could return something different from the last time (though, of course, it is not so easy, since even the behavior of always being different is too predictable). It turns out, however, that computers are incapable of generating, through software, truly random numbers. The best that can be done is to generate *pseudorandom* numbers, which look like random values for practical purposes. The technique for generating random numbers or random operations is based on the notion of a *seed value*, explained later in this chapter. Paradoxically, this technique enables program behavior to be perfectly repeatable and predictable, yet have seemingly random properties.

Methods

`uniform(a,b)` returns a number randomly selected (with equal or uniform probability) from all numbers between a and b. Example:

```
>>> import random
>>> random.uniform(0.0,1.0)
0.5127619674301888
```

`randint(a,b)` returns an integer x randomly chosen to satisfy $a \leq x \leq b$. Example:

```
>>> from random import *
>>> randint(-5,5), randint(-5,5), randint(-5,5)
(-1, -5, 2)
```

`choice(M)` returns a randomly chosen item from sequence M. Example:

351

```
>>> import random
>>> random.choice("minority")
't'
>>> random.choice("minority")
'm'
```

`shuffle(M)` scrambles list M randomly (mutating M). Example:

```
>>> import random
>>> T = "the design from months to days".split()
>>> random.shuffle(T)
>>> ['to', 'the', 'days', 'from', 'design', 'months']
```

Case Study: The Monte Hall Problem

This puzzle is a popular question about randomness, information, and choice. The game show presents the contestant three curtains, and it is known that a big prize awaits behind one curtain, but which? You initially choose one curtain, but before it is opened, Monte Hall (the game show host) raises *another* curtain and reveals that one does not have the big prize. You still have a chance to win! Now Monte asks, would you like to switch to the other remaining curtain, or stay put with your first choice? What is the best strategy here? Rather than launch into some mathematical argument, let's write a script that simulates the game 10,000 times with each strategy: switching curtains or staying put. We should observe a difference between the strategies.

```
def StayPut():
    curtains = [None,None,None]
    prize = random.choice( [0,1,2] )
    curtains[prize] = "Win"
    contestant = random.choice( [0,1,2] )
    return curtains[contestant]=="Win"
```

Before planning a 10,000 trial experiment, we need to have the technique for a single experiment, which is one run of the game show. Let the curtains be numbered 0, 1, 2; the location of the big prize will be random (using the `random.choice` method). Then, let the contestant choose a curtain at random. Now comes the reveal by Monte of a nonprize curtain, followed by the contestant's strategy. Above is this idea realized as a function for the nonswitching strategy, the `StayPut()` function.

The `StayPut()` function will sometimes return `True`, sometimes return `False`, depending on whether the simulated contestant chose the winning curtain. There is nothing about simulating Monte opening a curtain, since the strategy here is to stay put no matter what. The other strategy is to switch, shown here. Running 10,000 trials of these strategies is a simple iteration, accumulating the number of times that a contestant wins. On the top of the next page, code for the `Switch()` function is presented, with a script for a simulation comparing `StayPut()` and `Switch()` below.

```
def Switch():
  curtains = [None,None,None]
  prize = random.choice( [0,1,2] )  # hidden prize
  curtains[prize] = "Win"
  contestant = random.choice( [0,1,2] )  # simulated choice
  reveal = [0,1,2]      # these are the curtains, but
  reveal.remove(prize) # only consider nonprize curtain
  if contestant in reveal:     # see if contestant chose nonprize
     reveal.remove(contestant) # remove prize & contestant choice
  raisecurtain = random.choice(reveal)   # raise nonprize curtain
  finalchoice = [0,1,2]
  finalchoice.remove(raisecurtain)
  finalchoice.remove(contestant)
  finalchoice = finalchoice[0] # switch and see - is it a win?
  return curtains[finalchoice]=="Win"
```

```
StayCount = 0
SwitchCount = 0
countmap = { True:1, False: 0 }
for n in range(10000): # try both strategies 10,000 times
    StayCount += countmap[StayPut()]
    SwitchCount += countmap[Switch()]

# now report which strategy got the most wins
template = "Staying put got {0} wins, switching got {1} wins"
print( template.format(StayCount, SwitchCount) )
```

We leave the reader in suspense over the outcome of the simulation (run it if you like). The point of this case study is that, rather than the mathematical approach of deriving probability values and formulas to answer a question, simulation can be a simple way to study decision strategies.

 web

Random Objects

Random number generation is extremely useful in simulations, games (to add some variety in behaviors), and for statistical experiments. There is an unexpected side effect of using randomness: it may be that a program has a bug, but the bug shows up very rarely because it depends on what the **random** methods do. This can be quite frustrating if a bug happens but is not easily repeatable for debugging purposes. Fortunately, software random number generation is not actually random in the true sense of the word. Random number generators have an initial *seed* value, which determines how it will behave. The **seed(x)** method sets the seed value to **x**. Here is a small demonstration:

```
>>> import random
>>> random.seed(5)
>>> [random.randint(0,1000) for t in range(10)]
[623, 742, 795, 943, 740, 923, 29, 466, 944, 649]
>>> [random.randint(0,1000) for t in range(10)]
[901, 113, 469, 246, 544, 574, 13, 216, 279, 917]
>>> random.seed(5)
>>> [random.randint(0,1000) for t in range(10)]
[623, 742, 795, 943, 740, 923, 29, 466, 944, 649]
```

```
>>> import random
>>> V = random.Random()
>>> V.seed(231)
>>> V.choice("one two three".split())
'three'
```

Above, after setting the seed value to 5, a list of ten random numbers is generated, then another list. Then the seed is set back again to 5, and it is evident that the next list is identical to the earlier one generated after the same seed value. What is seen to the left is based on the **Random** class defined in the **random** module; the **import random** statement creates an instance (object) of this class, and the methods in all earlier examples of this chapter use this object. The seed value is an attribute (integer variable within the object), which the **seed()** method assigns. In fact, each method of **random** that does some random number generation takes the current seed, uses it somehow to make some "random" choice, and then changes the seed to a new value. If needed, the **Random** class can be used directly.

Two points of interest are worth knowing about the **random** module. First, there is a connection between pseudorandom number generation and the concept of a hash table, mentioned "Refining the Index" in "Interlude: File Indexing," in connection with file indexing. Python has a **__hash__** method for the nonmutable types (string, tuple, numbers), which is internally used in implementing dictionaries. When **"abc".__hash__()** is evaluated, an integer is returned. The **__hash__** method has been carefully designed so that the likelihood that different strings get the same hash result is quite low.

```
class Random():
  def cycle(self): # get next seed
    self.seed *= 1103515245
    self.seed += 12345
    self.seed &= 0x7fffffff
  def __init__(self,seed=None):
    if seed == None:
      import time
      self.seed = int(time.time())
  def random(self):
    import math
    self.cycle()
    m,e = math.frexp(float(self.seed))
    return 2.0*(m-0.5)
```

In some sense, what **__hash__** does is similar to what the **random** module does. The other point of interest is how **random** works. The code shown above is a primitive implementation of a pseudorandom number generator. The logic is a bit mysterious, yet the operations are simple.

The Time Module

Python's `time` module is a collection of variables and functions to format, measure, and control time. Several of the functions are useful for getting the current time, formatting it for display, and measuring elapsed time. The `time` module is sometimes used in conjunction with the `datetime` and `calendar` modules for displaying chronological data. The display functions are documented in the online Python manual; this section does not describe them. The emphasis here is measurement and control functions.

```python
import random, time
def countlist(M):
  "count number of unique items in list M"
  L = []
  for item in M:
    if item not in L:
      L.append(item)
  return len(L)
def countdict(M):
  "count number of unique items in list M"
  D = { }
  for item in M:
    D[item] = True
  return len(D)

biglist = [random.randint(0,1000) for x in range(1000000)]
start = time.clock()
countlist(biglist)
end = time.clock()
print("using list: {0} seconds".format(end-start))
start = time.clock()
countdict(biglist)
end = time.clock()
print("using dictionary: {0} seconds".format(end-start))
```

Typical result running this program:

```
using list: 22.49 seconds
using dictionary: 0.34 seconds
```

Figure 28.1: Timing measurement comparing `list` and `dict` types.

`time()` returns a `float`, which is supposed to be the number of elapsed seconds since January 1, 1970. However, it is only as accurate as the setting of the clock on the computer and the hardware support for timekeeping. A typical example could be (shown in Python3):

```python
import urllib.request, time
start = time.time()
page = urllib.request.urlopen("http://www.nist.gov")
end = time.time()
print("elapsed time = {0}".format(end-start))
```

The example measures the time taken to fetch a Web page.

`clock()` returns a `float`, which is supposed to be the amount of time that the computer's processor (the *Central Processing Unit*, or CPU) spent running the current Python session or program since it started. This is usually quite accurate, though it becomes less accurate over very small amounts of time. The `clock()` function can be useful for efficiency experiments to compare different ways of looping or comparing different algorithms to see which runs faster. An example of this is shown in Figure 28.1. The dictionary clearly wins the contest of efficiency here.

`sleep(amt)` is used to suspend the running Python program and wait for `amt` seconds before resuming. The `amt` argument can be a `float` for fractions of a second. For instance, `time.sleep(1.5)` causes the program to pause for one and a half seconds. The sleeping could be interrupted by an exception, say a `CTL-c` from the keyboard; in that case, the sleeping ends prematurely, and the program resumes.

The Sys Module

The `sys` module gives programs access to facilities of the underlying infrastructure of Python, which is the interface between the operating system and the running of Python language programs. Chapter 25 discusses two of the `sys` module's object, `stdin` and `stdout`. Two more are listed here.

`argv` is a list of strings, usually made by splitting the shell command that launched the current Python session. An example of this could be a two-line script `myscript.py`:

```
import sys
print(sys.argv)
```

Running this script with a couple of examples shows how `argv` reflects shell commands:

```
$ python myscript.py
['myscript.py']
$ python myscript.py yada blah -hello x=5
['myscript.py', 'yada', 'blah', '-hello', 'x=5']
```

The `argv` list is, in a sense, the input argument to running a Python script: the program can examine the command line, extract values from the `argv` list, and use these values to decide which file to open, what functions to call, how to format the output, and so on. The extra strings following `myscript.py` in the example above are sometimes called *command line options*, since they are put on a shell command and may control optional behavior of the script, depending on how the program uses the `argv` information.

`sys.exit(rc)` is a function that halts program execution, closing files, cleaning up memory, and terminating all Python activities. The value `rc` is an integer, which may (or may not) be significant to the operating system shell, presumably as an indication from the program as to why it quit. Typically, an `rc` value of zero means that the exit is a normal completion of the program, whereas other values indicate some kind of error condition.

There are many other `sys` functions and variables which give detailed information about the resources used by Python, the location of module libraries, and more.

The OS Module

The `OS` module makes some standard operating system functions and commands into Python functions. This module differs from others because it may not work the same for different operating systems. The official online documentation should be consulted to fully comprehend the limitation. Here are a few of the os functions and variables, concentrating on directory and file *paths*, which are strings that designate the location of entities in the system's file system.

getcwd() returns a path, the *current working directory*, likely the directory where the command to launch the Python program initially launched.

listdir(path) returns a list of all the files and directories present in the specified path. For instance,

```
>>> import os
>>> os.listdir("/opt")
['safe', 'allf.py', 'Adobe', 'ibm', 'sun', 'java', 'inven.txt']
```

Note that some of the strings in the returned list might be names of files, and others names of subdirectories. Thus, to use listdir to explore all files under a directory, recursion might be needed. Alternatively, use the walk function described below.

stat(path) returns a "stat" object for the path. This object has attributes for the most recent access time, most recent update time, size (of file), and many other details about the file or directory named by the path. See the online documentation for a comprehensive list of the attributes.

path.abspath(path) returns a fully qualified path for the given path. The path argument could be a simple file name, like 'test.py,' which would make sense in the context of the current working directory; but the "full address" of the path could be

/home/user/jrane/progs/test.py

which is what path.abspath() would return.

path.isdir(path) returns True if the named path is a directory.

path.isfile(path) returns True if the named path is a file.

path.walk(top,func,arg) is a function typical of the object-oriented or functional styles of programming. (**Note** for Python3: the path.walk function is replaced by walk, so instead of using os.path.walk, use os.walk in Python3.) To use this, you need first to create a function (the func parameter). This will be a function that gets called for each subdirectory under a given path, going down each subdirectory, sub-subdirectory, and so on, recursively. The top parameter is the starting path for the recursive "walk" through all subdirectories; the arg parameter can be anything, and it will be passed along to the function named by func (it could be used to avoid using global as a way to access other objects you create for saving results). The head for the func function is:

def func(arg,dirname,fnames):

where dirname is the path of a subdirectory and fnames is a list of all the entities (files and subdirectories) within that subdirectory, similar to what listdir() returns.

The OS module has so many functions for system interfaces that it would likely be possible to write a shell interpreter in Python. Figure 28.2 shows an example using various functions from os to total up the number of bytes in all the Python scripts under the opt directory. The script in Figure 28.2 uses two details from os not explained above. First, the st_size attribute from a stat object is the size, in bytes, of a file. Second, the full path of a file

```
import os

class Counter():
  def __init__(self):
    self.total = 0
  def add(self,val):
    self.total += val

def sizepy(count,place):
  if ( os.path.isfile(place) and
       place.endswith(".py") ):
       size = os.stat(place).st_size
       count.add(int(size))

def accumsizes(count,dirname,fnames):
  for name in fnames:
     fullname = dirname + os.sep + name
     sizepy(count,fullname)

C = Counter()
os.path.walk("opt",accumsizes,C)
print C.total
```

Figure 28.2: Recursive directory exploration using os module.

is made by concatenating the name of a directory with the name of a file, using `os.sep` between these two. The reason is that Linux (Mac or Unix) systems use "/" to separate names in a path, whereas Windows uses "\" as the separator. The `os.sep` will reflect the choice of the underlying operating system. Note that this script will fail, as will other `os` functions, if the user running the program does not have sufficient permissions to access the files or directories. Though this may be overcome using `try .. except` statements, we showed the simpler, failure-free case here.

Terminology Review

Jargon worth remembering from this chapter includes random number generation, pseudo-random, random seed, CPU time, `argv`, and (file/directory) path.

Exercises

(1) Use Python to solve the following problem—do not use some mathematical analysis to compute the answer. In some imaginary country, the government has a strict policy on how families grow. Each family is allowed to have at most one daughter, but can have as many sons as they wish. For purposes of calculation, assume the odds of having a son or daughter are equally likely (like a coin toss), and that a family will continue to have children until a daughter is born. Also, there are no twins, triplets, or other outlier events. What will be the proportion of males to females in this country?

(2) Consider a die (single of dice) that is tossed repeatedly. Each toss gets a number between 1 and 6, with equal likelihood. The problem is to see how often there are two of the same number in a row, three of the same number in a row, four in a row, and so on. For instance, if the sequence of tosses has these values:

> 3 4 2 1 5 5 4 2 3 3 3 2 6 4 6 5 1 1 2 4 6

Then there are two times that a number is repeated exactly twice (5 5 and 1 1) and one time that a number is repeated exactly three times (3 3 3). Simulate the tossing of a die a million times, and report on the number of times that a number is repeated exactly k times in a row, for $k = 2, 3, 4, \ldots$.

(3) Modify the directory walk example to build a list of all files that have all uppercase names. *Hint:* Accumulate such files in a list, which can be an attribute of an object, similar to the object C in the walk example.

(4) Which is faster, summing a list of a million random numbers using `sum`, using a `for` loop with the accumulation pattern, or using recursion? To answer this question, use `clock` to measure the amount of CPU time each of these consume. Make sure in your tests that you do not count the time of generating the list of random numbers.

Chapter 29:   Graphical User Interfaces

*Software suppliers are trying to make their software packages more
"user-friendly." Their best approach, so far, has been to take all the
old brochures, and stamp the words, "user-friendly" on the cover.*
— Bill Gates

Visual display of information is older than any language. Graphical display of data, particularly quantities, is more recent. Accurate maps portray distance and land mass sizes. A rope connecting a float, pulley, and counterweight may show current water level. A sundial casts a shadow indicating the hour. The later invention of clocks with dials was inspired by the sundial's circular shadow motion. Common to these historical points is that information flow is in one direction: the user sees, but cannot control the phenomena giving rise to the data by the display mechanism.

Interaction with graphical display is a comparatively recent innovation. Some interaction reverses information flow: the user changes a graphic of a data value, and this change effects some control of the underlying phenomenon (some alarm clocks and thermostats have this property). Other interactions control the graphical display, set parameters to software, and guide system behavior. The invention of modern *graphical user interface* (GUI) systems, especially the general form of using rectangular windows, keyboard, and mouse, is credited to Alan Kay, working at Xerox Parc in the 1980s. This combination of hardware, software, and presentation subsequently moved to Apple, then Microsoft Windows and Unix platforms.

A major challenge for the implementation of GUIs is the software architecture. What are the best languages, the most suitable patterns and disciplined design strategies? While there is no best answer to such a question, the community of software experts has settled on some common principles and terminology. The basis for design is commonality in the styles of presentation and user interface patterns. Windows generally have control boxes at corners, can be resized by dragging, there are pull-down menus, cut-and-paste operations, slider bars, checkboxes, and so on. At a higher level of design, applications use metaphors for what windows and controls represent: dashboards on vehicles, folders, scrollable lists, text input/output areas, and similar familiar concepts. Designs composed of these elements of windows and application metaphors have promoted so-called *GUI Frameworks*, which are "programming kits" for building GUI applications. This chapter illustrates the framework approach in Python, using the Tk framework.

Before interaction with software, programs were nearly always elaborations of input-output functions: the program would dictate when input was used and when output was returned. With GUI systems, there is a "paradigm shift" to another style of programming, *event-driven* control of programs. The fundamental difference is that the program does not dictate the exact sequence of inputs. Nearly all event-driven programs are organized around indefinite loops (like a `while` loop), where most of the time the program is waiting for events. In Tk and other GUI frameworks, this loop is implicit: the application invokes a particular method, which does not return. The event loop is inside that method, hidden from view of the programmer. The application just needs to set up some objects whose methods will be called when events occur. Thus, GUI applications are "reactive" programs that react to events.

Learning about GUI software can be frustrating: the problem is that there are so many GUI frameworks, each with its own quirks and version dependencies. Most of the frameworks are designed to be independent of the programming language, so that a variety of programming languages can be used for the same framework. Python has no inherent GUI facility. The one used in this chapter, Tk, is usually part of a Python installation, which is why we choose it as a learning platform. However, Tk is relatively old, not as convenient to use as newer alternatives, and does not take advantage of some newer native windowing functions available under Apple, Microsoft, and Linux desktop software. For Python there are many independent GUI frameworks (gtk, WxWindows, native GUI for Windows, etc.) that are superior to Tk, though requiring significant training to fully exploit. Specialized GUI frameworks for smartphones (Android, iPhone) may also support Python programming. Another method of interaction is *via* Web browser languages (Javascript, HTML5), browser plugins that have their own programming languages (Flash, Silverlight). One such technique puts Python programs on the server side, which respond to a URL request for a page by returning text that includes both HTML and Javascript: the Python program then uses templates to customize the Javascript program that will control browser interaction with the user. This theme is typical of modern software, where programs generate yet other programs (Python which generates Javascript), a topic more advanced than this chapter explores.

GUI Concepts: Widgets, Layouts, Actions

Everyone who has used a Web browser or desktop software recognizes common GUI patterns. The individual patterns that are employed repeatedly are components of GUI frameworks. Examples of these components are pull-down menus, buttons, slider bars, file selectors, text entry boxes, and popup alerts. For each of these components, which are common to numerous applications, a GUI framework defines a *widget*. A typical application may use the button widget dozens of times, in different places, on the screen. Naturally, the programming for widgets is captured by object-oriented design. GUI frameworks provide a button (widget) class, and each button on a screen is an instance of the button class. The button class has methods for setting color, text, font style, and behavior associated with the button.

Widgets are not just for low-level components like buttons. More sophisticated repeatable patterns such as calendar/date selectors and color choosers may also be represented by widget-style classes. These higher-level widgets are assemblies of lower-level widgets: a calendar widget could be composed of many button widgets, label widgets, and a slider widget, arranged into the familiar calendar appearance. In fact, GUI frameworks are the best advertisement for object-oriented design. GUI programs draw from libraries of widgets and other repeatable components (files, database access, networking) by instantiating objects, which are customized instances of the library classes.

To deliver an attractive and easy-to-use feel, an application needs to control the placement of widgets on the screen. It is straightforward to place widgets on the screen using (x, y) coordinates. Coordinates may be given in standard units of size (centimeters) or number of pixels (the smallest displayable area on a screen). The dimensions, width and height, of a widget can be similarly specified in standard size units. Complications to this straightforward approach occur when the same application has to contend with varying hardware displays. Screens vary in size, aspect ratio, and number of pixels. Some applications even prepare for both desktop use and mobile device displays that have small screens. Input hardware can also vary: touchscreens, mice, or gesture recognizers could be inputs to the same application, depending on where it is deployed. To manage such complications, GUI frameworks provide *geometry managers*. A geometry manager enables applications to place widgets in relative terms, like left, right, top, bottom, northeast, south, and so forth. In action, the geometry manager calculates coordinates depending on the actual size of the window (which could even be resized dynamically by the user), attempting to fit the relative locations of the widgets while rendering the output so that things are legible and usable. Geometry managers are usually implemented in methods of *container widgets*; an application may create a container widget first, give it some preferred dimension (width and height), then pack smaller widgets into the container. Typical names for containers with geometry managers are `Frame` and `GridLayout`. Applications with many widgets typically use container widgets recursively. The entire application window may be subdivided into different areas, so that each area has its own container. A geometry manager might be tasked with placing a widget that itself hosts several subwidgets.

Some widgets are only for display purposes, showing titles, items in a table, graphical images (`jpg`, `gif`, `png`), or video boxes. Other widgets are intended for user interaction. The type of user interaction is controlled by the application. The application can say what happens when the widget is clicked, double-clicked, or when the mouse moves over the widget. GUI frameworks permit applications to *bind* a widget *handler* with an event—but this is not the same meaning of "bind" as Python uses for parameters and arguments explained in Chapter 10. Rather, the GUI framework predefines some kinds of user *events*, including mouse clicks, keyboard entry, and mouse movement (with and without button pressed). An element of the framework is a *controller*, which constantly monitors input devices and the state of the screen to detect events. When an event occurs, the controller finds all appropriate widgets related to the event and determines whether or not the application has bound a handler to this event. If so, the controller *dispatches* the handler, meaning that it invokes the handler in the same way that programs call functions. The function of the handler is to "handle" (take care of) the event. In an object-oriented context, handlers are nearly always methods of classes which the application defines. Rather than defining such a class afresh, the programmer defines a subclass of something in the GUI framework.

What can a handler do? For debugging or demonstration purposes, a handler might just have a few `print` statements. Usually handlers contain calls to the GUI framework functions, read and write files, or do nothing. A typical action of a handler would be to change the color of a widget or copy data that is logically associated with a widget to some variable and do some small calculation, perhaps adding a new widget to the current display. In this way, one user event triggers a change to what appears on the screen.

This way of programming an application by creating widgets, placing them with a geometry manager, then arranging handlers to deal with events, tends to give application programs a chaotic appearance. If we ignore all the code related to the GUI framework, the part of the application for calculations, network communication, file reading, and printing is scattered about, with pieces in handlers, object constructors, and in functions defined by the programmer. Instead of a simple, straightforward flow of control—discussed in Chapter 11—the logic of the program is hard to see. Indeed, what happens when the program runs depends on what the user does. In some sense, each GUI program is a game between two players, the application and the user. The user generates events, the application redraws the screen, the user responds, and so on. In contrast, using the `raw_input()` function is simple because a script or function stops and waits while the user responds with input. For a GUI application, the application could be in the midst of doing some calculation or reading a file at the same instant that a user clicks on a widget. The whole idea of GUI applications is to make life easy for the user, not the programmer. The application may get events *asynchronously*, meaning that user events may not be synchronized to the pace or order of operations done by the application. The GUI controller does background bookkeeping for events, calling the handler(s) for events and updating displays of widgets as they change. Most GUI controllers also try to take advantage of low-level hardware features for drawing pixels and text; a typical optimization feature of controllers is to delay screen updates until the application has finished making changes rather than trying to update each pixel at the instant it changes. This saves considerable overhead and can improve response time for the user; however, the application may need to inform the controller when screen updates are needed, and this further complicates life for the application programmer.

Programming with a GUI Framework

GUI programming is a specialized skill, because the frameworks are complex and the tools to exploit the frameworks take time to learn. One framework could easily have hundreds of widgets, each with dozens of methods. Full documentation of these frameworks, let alone accurately maintaining this documentation in the face of new versions and improvements to the frameworks, is not common. Mastering a framework is time-consuming and best done by implementing applications, experimenting with widgets, reading texts, participating in online discussions about the framework, and plenty of debugging. This chapter barely scratches the surface of one GUI. The Tk framework is poorly explained in the Python documentation, so it would probably be better to explore another framework for serious applications. Nonetheless, the Tk examples in the rest of the chapter do illustrate the organizing principles of GUI programming.

Because GUI frameworks can be hard to learn, and because there remains some demand for GUI applications, software engineers have created tools that help programmers write applications. The most important of these is the IDE (*Integrated Development Environment*), which combines smart editing of program text, debugging (the ability to run a program one step at a time or have it pause at certain statements, and to inspect variables during the run), and searching through documentation while the programs are being written. Professional IDEs like Visual Studio or Eclipse give the programmer instant access to lists of methods available for an object and the parameters of a method. All the programmer need do is start typing and the IDE will attempt, like a spelling corrector, to complete the current typing to something in the programming language or in a library. After connecting a GUI framework's library of classes to the IDE, the programmer does not have to recall the exact names of methods or parameters, since the IDE will supply these in a list for selection.

Another tool to assist developers is an *application generator*. The idea of an application generator is to provide a library of templates for applications. The templates include widgets and some basic fragments of programs and class constructors. Usually, application generators are launched as online applications which resemble drawing programs or presentation creators. The programmer selects widgets from a toolbar, drags them onto the screen, sizes and positions them. Various other operations and pull-down options customize the widgets, even allowing for the naming of variables and event handlers to be associated with the widgets. Finally, the tool can emit source programming language statements to run the application. Typically, the programs generated by such a tool are incomplete: they lack the application-specific needs of reading files, accessing a database, communicating over a network, or whatever else the application will need. However, the programs generated may be the "skeleton" of a completed program. It can save considerable time to use an application generator to get some crude form of the desired application, and then use an IDE to edit the generated code and complete the job.

The Tk GUI

The Tk GUI framework was introduced in the 1980s as a rudimentary tool that simplified application programming for the Unix X-window system. Since then, Tk has been adapted to many other windowing systems. Though Tk is powerful enough for some impressive applications (the turtle drawing system of Chapter 24 is based on Tk), it has been eclipsed by more modern frameworks. The purpose of this chapter *is not* a comprehensive introduction to Tk; the examples that follow just show some of the organizing principles explained earlier in action.

The examples are organized around a few widgets to show different styles of display and interaction. The first two examples show Tk directly, whereas the remaining examples use another Python module Tix, which introduces some convenient higher level widgets built from the basic Tk widgets. All of the examples are expressed using Python2, though adapting them to Python3 could easily be done by renaming the module names.

Adding, Removing, and Changing Widgets

To begin the process of working with widgets, a "root window" has to be created; Tk is a class, so Tk() creates an object representing the root window. The root window is also considered to be a widget, and additional widgets are put into the root window. For all the widgets to be added to the root window, the process has essentially two steps.

(1) First, there is a class for the widget, and an instance (object) is created for that widget. A typical widget creation statement is

```
buttonref = Button(container)
```

where `container` is either the root window object or a reference to some other widget that will contain the `Button` instance. The new `Button` object then has `buttonref` as the variable to reference it.

(2) Second, the newly created widget is "packed" using the `pack()` method:

```
buttonref.pack()
```

The `pack()` method makes the widget visible and put into an appropriate place on the window.

Changing a widget (text, style, what it does when clicked) is done by invoking the `configure()` method and supplying keyword arguments to `configure()`. To remove a widget, use the `destroy()` method. If the `destroy()` method is used on the root window, then the entire window is closed.

Frame and Label

Our first Tk GUI program shows a label without any provision for interaction. The `Label` widget is used only to show some text, typically a title or some directions for the user. Program statements are annotated with ①–⑨ for explanatory notes below. The widget and window shown by the program appears to the right of the code.

```
① from Tkinter import *
② class MyApplication(Frame):
       def buildMyWidgets(self):
③          forshow = Label(self,
              text="Just for Show")
④          forshow.pack()
⑤    def __init__(self,master):
          Frame.__init__(self,master)
          self.pack()
⑥          self.buildMyWidgets()
⑦ root = Tk()
   Tobject = MyApplication(root)
⑧ Tobject.mainloop()
⑨ root.destroy()
```

Notes:

① The `Tkinter` module (renamed to `tkinter` in Python3) here is imported using `from` to get simpler names of widgets; later examples use the `import` statement and longer names.

⑦ This is the first statement of the script to run (previous statements only define classes and methods). The `Tk()` creates an object and a window on the screen associated with that object: it is sometimes called a *root window, parent window*, or emphmaster window, since additional GUI widgets will be considered children or slaves of this window. This example does not show it, but applications can have multiple root windows.

② The `MyApplication` class is a subclass of `Tk`'s `Frame`, a container widget. In this very simple program, there is not much geometry to calculate, because the container will have only a label widget. The main reason to introduce `MyApplication` is to show how setup of additional widgets within the frame can be put into the object's constructor method. The statement following ⑦ creates an instance of `MyApplication`; notice that the new frame object is created using the root window as an argument to the constructor. This is the general rule for `Tk` widgets: the first argument to the constructor names the parent widget, which is the root window.

⑤ defines the constructor. The thing to observe here is that, for the `MyApplication` class to be a properly working container with geometry management, the constructor for `Frame` has to be invoked. The first line following ⑤ does that, explicitly calling the `__init__` method of the parent class. The next line of the constructor calls the `pack()` method, which is the standard call that a widget uses to tell a geometry manager to place the widget in the parent widget. Here, the statement tells `Tk` that the newly created frame should be placed in the root window.

⑥ uses another method to put the label widget into the frame. There is no advantage for this small example putting this into a new `buildMyWidgets` method, however, this is typical of GUI application programming.

③ builds a `Label` widget, one of many in the `Tk` catalog of widgets. The single argument to constructing the label object turns out to be the frame (`MyApplication`) that will contain the new label. There is also a keyword argument, `text`, which provides a string used in setting up the `Label` widget. One has to find in some documentation, a textbook, or copy from other `Tk` examples that the `Label` widget has a `text` argument. Many other arguments are possible, depending on the kind of widget. The choices for these arguments can be changed later using a `configure()` method, if needed.

④ is a `pack()` on the new `Label` widget, requesting placement inside the `Frame`, which has previously been placed within the root window. Thus, after ④ finishes, there is a parent-child-grandchild relationship between the root window, `Frame`, and `Label` widget.

⑧ kicks off the interactive cycle. The `mainloop()` method runs indefinitely, waiting for user events and invoking handlers. Usually, the application will eventually use a `destroy()` method on the root window, to finish the application and return from the `mainloop()` method. The statement ⑨ shows how to use the `destroy()` method, but actually it is a bug to place the `destroy()` here: it should instead be called within a handler (which this example neglects to define).

Buttons

To the previous example for the Label widget, we add here a Button widget. This time the Frame contains two widgets, Label and Button. The pack() methods therefore have been tuned for widget placement: the Label widget is placed on top, the Button on the bottom of the frame. Right of the code, shown below, are two versions of what the users see. The uppermost version shows the window before the user moves the mouse over the button, and the lower version shows that the button turns yellow when the mouse is over the button (you likely cannot see the color difference on the black/white rendered page of the book). This is a standard cue to the user that the button would like to be clicked. The Button widget has some handy arguments controlling the normal background color and the "active" background color, shown in the method setting up the widgets.

```
from Tkinter import *
import sys
class MyApplication(Frame):
    def quit(self,event):
        sys.exit(0)
    def buildMyWidgets(self):
        forshow = Label(self,text="Just for Show")
        forshow.pack(side="top")
        forinput = Button(self,text="Click Here")
        forinput.configure(background="beige",
                    activebackground="yellow")
        forinput.bind("<Button-1>",self.quit)
        forinput.pack(side="bottom")
    def __init__(self,master):
        Frame.__init__(self,master)
        self.pack()
        self.buildMyWidgets()
root = Tk()
Tobject = MyApplication(root)
Tobject.mainloop()
```

The bind() method associates a widget with an event handler. The first argument to bind() is a string that names the kind of event that the named handler expects. Options for this argument include

> <Button-1>, <Button-2>, <Button-3>, <Key>, <Enter>, <Leave>, <Return>,
> <Home>, <Up>, <F3>, <ButtonRelease-1>, <DoubleButton-1>

and many others. The handler defined for this example, the quit() method, expects a single[1] argument, the event parameter, which is an object with information about the event (location of the mouse and some other data). The example shows another way that the Python program could end the GUI: instead of using the destroy() method to remove the root window, the program just calls verb—sys.exit()— which ends the entire program immediately.

Playing Around

The examples here are not advisable to copy, but are sometimes used as a preliminary demonstration. It is interesting at least one time to see Tix/Tk done interactively:

```
>>> import Tix
>>> r = Tix.Tk()
```

---

[1]Remember, the self parameter is present in every method definition, and does not really count as an argument given by the method's caller.

```
>>> f = Tix.Frame(r)
>>> f.pack()
>>> b1 = Tix.Button(f,text="one")
>>> b1.pack()
>>> b2 = Tix.Button(f,text="two")
>>> b2.pack()
>>> b3 = Tix.Button(f,text="three")
>>> b3.pack(side="right")
>>> b4 = Tix.Button(f,text="four")
>>> b4.pack(side="left")
>>> b2.destroy()
>>> b1.destroy()
>>> f.destroy()
>>> r.destroy()
```

Done interactively, you can see the window appear, grow, and shrink as the buttons are packed and destroyed. Another attractive example is this script, using the `Grid` layout instead of `Frame`:

```
from Tix import *
r = Tk()
f = Grid(r)
f.pack()
for i in range(8):
  for j in range(8):
    b = Button(f,text=str(i)+str(j))
    if i==j:
        b.configure(background="lightblue")
    b.grid(row=i,column=j)
```

This produces a square array of buttons, colored on the diagonal. If the above is put into a script `grid.py`, then the shell command `python -i grid.py` brings up the window (the `-i` on the command is needed to keep Python up and running after the script finishes, so that the window remains on the screen).

Assorted Tk/Tix Widgets

The rest of the chapter shows selected widgets available in Tk/Tix modules. These are presented mainly to show binding and interaction in Python.

Tix Meter Widget

The example here does not follow the pattern of earlier examples or later ones. It avoids using a `mainloop()` method, since interaction with the GUI is not intended. The program imports the `Tix` module, which goes on to import Tk internally. The `Tix` module acts as a *wrapper* for Tk. The notion of a *wrapper* is similar to the idea of inheriting or extending a class in an object-oriented design. The `Tix` module provides nearly all the widgets that Tk does, and adds many more new widgets that simplify application design. Thus, `Tix` "wraps" Tk into a new package with extra features. For Python3, the name is changed from `Tix` to `tkinter.tix`.

The `Meter` widget is familiar to users as a "progress bar" for a lengthy, time-consuming operation. It informs the user of a percentage (usually percent complete on an operation), and this is periodically updated as the application makes progress. To the right of the code below there is an example of how the `Meter` widget appears.

```
import time, Tix
def runMeter():
  root = Tix.Tk()
  progressbar = Tix.Meter(root,value=0.0)
  progressbar.pack()
  root.update_idletasks()
  for i in range(31):
    time.sleep(0.5)
    progressbar.configure(value=i/30.0)
    root.update_idletasks()
  time.sleep(2)
  root.update_idletasks()
  root.destroy()
while True:
  text = raw_input("stop or go: ")
  if text.startswith("stop"):
    break
  runMeter()
```

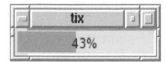

The code above does not run the `mainloop()` method for user interaction. The program starts with a `while` loop, which asks the user for a string, and in the body of the loop either `break`s out or invokes `runMeter()`, defined earlier. The `runMeter()` function creates a root window, places a `Meter` widget in the root window, and then loops (slowly) to update the meter. The `update_idletasks()` method counters the "lazy" way that Tk changes widgets on the screen (recall that operation of the GUI controller is asynchronous, and may delay showing changes to widgets). The `update_idletasks()` ensures that a new value for the `runMeter` will be shown. After the loop finishes, at the end of `runMeter()`, the root window is destroyed.

The Entry Widget

The `Entry` widget is for user input of one line of text. The example below shows the code; there is no image because the widget's display is quite elementary.

```
import sys, Tix
class MyApplication(Tix.Frame):
    def quit(self,event):
        sys.exit(0)
    def whatentered(self,event):
        text = self.entrywidget.get()
        print("Entered: '{0}'".format(text))
    def buildMyWidgets(self):
        forquit = Tix.Button(self,text="Quit")
        forquit.configure(background="beige",
                          activebackground="yellow")
        forquit.bind("<Button-1>",self.quit)
        forquit.pack(side="right")
        forentry = Tix.Entry(self,
                        background="palegreen",
                        width=64)
        forentry.pack(side="left")
        forentry.bind("<Return>",self.whatentered)
        self.entrywidget = forentry
    def __init__(self, master=None):
        Tix.Frame.__init__(self,master)
        self.pack()
        self.buildMyWidgets()
root = Tix.Tk()
Tobject = MyApplication(master=root)
Tobject.master.title("Entry Demo")
Tobject.mainloop()
```

The example binds the `Entry` widget to the event of a user pressing the "Enter" key, denoted by the string `<Return>`. Within the handler `whatentered()`, the code needs a reference to the `Entry` widget, however, no reference is passed directly as an argument—only a reference to a containing widget, the `MyApplication` object, passed as `self` (the other parameter `event` is an object that has information about the cursor location and type of event). The problem is thus how to get a reference to the `Entry` widget when only the container widget is known. This is solved simply by inventing a new attribute, adding that to the container widget (the `self.entrywidget = forentry` statement), and then using that later in the handler. The `get()` method is used in the handler to obtain the string that the user entered and print it.

Tix Control Widget

The `Control` widget lets a user raise or lower a numeric value in predefined steps to set some value of meaning to an application. The `Control` widget in the example is packed along with a `Label` and a `Button` (copied from the earlier example) into a `Frame` container.

```
import sys, Tix
class PrivateStuff():
    pass
class MyApplication(Tix.Frame):
    def quit(self,event):
        sys.exit(0)
    def showvalue(self,event):
        print self.privatestuff.R.get()
    def buildMyWidgets(self):
        forshow = Tix.Label(self,text="value selection")
        forshow.pack(side="top")
        forinput = Tix.Button(self,text="Quit")
        forinput.configure(background="beige",
                        activebackground="yellow")
        forinput.bind("<Button-1>",self.quit)
        forinput.pack(side="right")
        self.privatestuff.R = Tix.IntVar()
        self.privatestuff.R.set(3)
        forvalue = Tix.Control(self,label="Value",
                    variable = self.privatestuff.R,
                    min=-5,max=5,step=1)
        forvalue.pack(side="bottom")
        forvalue.bind("<Leave>",self.showvalue)
    def __init__(self, master=None):
        Tix.Frame.__init__(self,master)
        self.pack()
        self.privatestuff = PrivateStuff()
        self.buildMyWidgets()
rootwindow = Tix.Tk()
Tobject = MyApplication(master=rootwindow)
Tobject.master.title("Control Widget")
Tobject.mainloop()
```

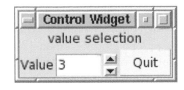

The code for this example illustrates another feature of Tk. In addition to widget classes, Tk (and `Tix` by extension) provides a wrapper for immutable types. The `StringVar` and `IntVar` classes wrap `string` and `int` types, respectively, with `set()` and `get()` methods. The reason for such classes is that an application may wish to manipulate a value used within a widget and have that value automatically appear on the screen without having to invoke `update_idletasks()` or otherwise reconfigure widgets. When a value in a widget is represented with a `StringVar` or an `IntVar`, either side (normal application code or the controller, on behalf of a user event) can change the value and it will instantly be available to the other side.

The binding for the `Control` widget is set to invoke the `showvalue()` method each time the mouse leaves the area occupied by the `Control` widget. For this example, the `showvalue()` method prints the current value for the widget. However, there is a technical problem: how can the `showvalue()` method know this value? The only arguments to `showvalue()` are `self` and `event` objects, which neither are the desired value nor a reference to it. There are two ways to solve this problem. First, it is possible to use the `global` statement and then define global variables that will be known within the method; this is generally not good practice in object oriented design. A better solution is to make the value, or a reference to the value, an attribute of the widget. This technique was used earlier for the `Entry` widget as a way to "remember" a reference to a widget in the container object. In this program, the `self` argument to `showvalue()` is specified to be the `MyApplication` object at the time `bind()` is called. Thus, `showvalue()` can easily refer to any frame attribute (because `MyApplication` is a subclass of `Frame`). The trick is therefore to add a new attribute to `MyApplication` which refers to the value set in the `Control` widget. The body of `showvalue()` can use this new attribute. One caution is to make sure that the new attribute really is new: it should not be, by accident, some attribute which is already in the `Frame` class or any other ancestor (remember, this is object-oriented design where classes inherit attributes from ancestor classes). The program above uses a name unlikely to be in the Tk or Tix modules, namely `privatestuff`. Furthermore, we let the new `privatestuff` attribute be of an object reference to which any number of other attributes can be added without fear of collision with an existing name in Tk or Tix. While these precautions are more extreme than the example merits, they illustrate the flexibility of object-oriented design in using a GUI framework.

Tix ComboBox

The `ComboBox` is a fancier sort of widget from the `Tix` module. It combines labels, pull-down selection, scrollable list, text entry, and buttons. The `ComboBox` widget is inspired by a similar widget from the Microsoft Windows catalog of widgets. It should be no surprise that the setup for this widget has many methods and arguments, so an example is rather lengthy. The code is shown on the next page, but we do not explain the details. The `PrivateStuff` class is used here to contain attributes for month and year, as `StringVar` objects; a practical application would access their values in the handlers.

(ComboBox example on next page.)

```
import sys, Tix
class PrivateStuff():
    pass
class MyApplication(Tix.Frame):
    def selmonth(self,event):
        print "month selected"
    def selyear(self,event):
        print "year selected"
    def ok(self):
        sys.exit(0)
    def buildMyWidgets(self):
        self.privatestuff.month = Tix.StringVar()
        self.privatestuff.year = Tix.StringVar()
        self.privatestuff.month.set("Jan")
        self.privatestuff.year.set("2010")
        a = Tix.ComboBox(self,
          label="Month: ", dropdown=True,
          command=self.selmonth, editable=False,
          variable=self.privatestuff.month)
        b = Tix.ComboBox(self,
          label="Year: ", dropdown=False,
          command=self.selyear, editable=True,
          variable=self.privatestuff.year)
        a.pack(side="top", anchor="w")
        b.pack(side="top", anchor="w")
        monthlist = "Jan Feb Mar Apr May Jun"
        monthlist += " Jul Aug Sep Oct Dec"
        for m in monthlist.split():
            a.insert(Tix.END,m)
        for y in range(10):
            b.insert(Tix.END,str(2005+y))
        box = Tix.ButtonBox(self, orientation="horizontal")
        box.add('ok', text='Ok',
            underline=0, width=6,
            command=self.ok)
        box.add('cancel', text='Cancel',
            underline=0, width=6,
            command=self.ok)
        box.pack(side="bottom",fill="both")
        self.pack(side="top",fill="both",expand=True)
    def __init__(self, master=None):
        Tix.Frame.__init__(self,master)
        self.configure(border=True,relief="raised")
        self.pack()
        self.privatestuff = PrivateStuff()
        self.buildMyWidgets()
rootwindow = Tix.Tk()
Tobject = MyApplication(master=rootwindow)
Tobject.master.title("ComboBox Widget")
Tobject.mainloop()
```

File Selection Widget

Applications that use files may ask the user for the location of the file (name and directory). This is often done interactively by browsing for the file, clicking on icons or names to navigate through folders until the file is located. The widget is shown below, followed by the Python code. There are several widgets for file selection in Tk/Tix; this example uses the ExFileSelectDialog widget. The starting widget in the code is a simple frame with a label and a button; clicking on this button pops up the file selection widget. Thus, the button widget is bound to a handler (selectfile), which creates a ExFileSelectDialog widget. As with other complex widgets, this one is composed of many other, more basic widgets. The code uses a Tix method for retrieving a subwidget: the statement

```
fsbox = dialog.subwidget("fsbox")
```

extracts a reference to a ComboBox subwidget of the file selection dialog widget to customize its features. The popup() method of the file selection widget causes Tk's controller to bring up the dialog on the screen, asking the user for a file name. The image below shows the result where the dialog appears while the original label/button remains on the screen. After the user locates a file and clicks Ok, the showfile handler is given the selected file name (it will be a fully qualified name, including directory names). The example saves the name as an attribute, though nothing further is done with it.

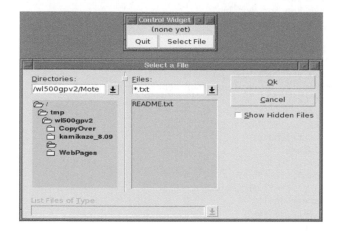

```
import sys, Tix
class PrivateStuff():
    pass
class MyApplication(Tix.Frame):
    def showfile(self,chosenfile):
        self.privatestuff.Fname.set( chosenfile )
    def quit(self,event):
        sys.exit(0)
    def selectfile(self,event):
        dialog = Tix.ExFileSelectDialog(self,
                    title="Select a File",
                    command=self.showfile)
        fsbox = dialog.subwidget("fsbox")
        fsbox.config(pattern="*.txt")
        dialog.popup()

    def buildMyWidgets(self):
        self.privatestuff.Fname = Tix.StringVar()
        self.privatestuff.Fname.set( "(none yet)" )
        forshow = Tix.Label(self,textvariable=self.privatestuff.Fname)
```

```
            forshow.pack(side="top")
            forexit = Tix.Button(self,text="Quit")
            forexit.configure(background="beige",
                              activebackground="yellow")
            forexit.bind("<Button-1>",self.quit)
            forexit.pack(side="left")
            forsel = Tix.Button(self,text="Select File")
            forsel.configure(background="beige",
                              activebackground="yellow")
            forsel.bind("<Button-1>",self.selectfile)
            forsel.pack(side="right")
        def __init__(self, master=None):
            Tix.Frame.__init__(self,master)
            self.pack()
            self.privatestuff = PrivateStuff()
            self.buildMyWidgets()
    rootwindow = Tix.Tk()
    Tobject = MyApplication(master=rootwindow)
    Tobject.master.title("Control Widget")
    Tobject.mainloop()
```

Scrollable List Widget

Tix's `ScrolledListBox` widget can show a
list of items too lengthy for display in the window. Scrollbars let the user move the view of
items. The widget allows individual items or
a range of items to be selected; clicking, dou-
bleclicking, and a few other events can trigger
actions in handler methods. Within the object
representing the widget, there are methods to
insert items and delete items. The example
shown to the right reads a file for the items to
show, each item being a line from the file (a
string).

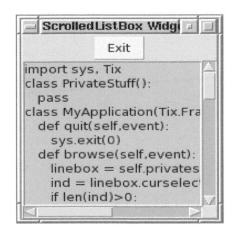

```
import sys, Tix
class PrivateStuff():
   pass
class MyApplication(Tix.Frame):
   def quit(self,event):
      sys.exit(0)
   def browse(self,event):
      linebox = self.privatestuff.LB
      ind = linebox.curselection()
      if len(ind)>0:
         print "Clicked on", linebox.get(ind[0])
   def buildMyWidgets(self):
      box = Tix.ScrolledListBox(self,
            scrollbar="auto")
      box.pack(side="bottom", anchor="e",fill="both")
      listbox = box.subwidget("listbox")
      try:
        f = open("demo7.py")
        for line in f:
          listbox.insert("end",line[:-1])
        f.close()
      except:
        listbox.insert("end","failed to open file")
      #listbox.configure(width=60)
      listbox.bind("<ButtonRelease-1>",self.browse)
      self.privatestuff.LB = listbox
      forquit = Tix.Button(self,text="Exit")
      forquit.configure(background="beige",
                        activebackground="yellow")
      forquit.bind("<Button-1>",self.quit)
      forquit.pack(side="top")

   def __init__(self, master=None):
      Tix.Frame.__init__(self,master)
      self.configure(border=True,relief="raised")
      self.configure(width="10c",height="12c")
      self.pack()
      self.privatestuff = PrivateStuff()
      self.buildMyWidgets()

rootwindow = Tix.Tk()
Tobject = MyApplication(master=rootwindow)
Tobject.master.title("ScrolledListBox Widget")
Tobject.mainloop()
```

The items for display and selection are associated with a subwidget of the `ScrolledListBox`, the `listbox` subwidget. For convenience, the program retains a reference to the `listbox` as an attribute,

```
self.privatestuff.LB = listbox
```

The code shows only two method calls for the `listbox` items. Adding items to the list is done by the method call

```
listbox.insert("end",line[:-1])
```

The `insert(index,text)` method has two arguments, the index for a place to insert the item (zero for start of the list) and a string, which is the item to insert. The first argument can also be `"end"` to insert an item at the end of the current list. Since lines are read from the file in first-to-last order, it makes sense to insert each at the end of the list. The reason to omit the last character of the line (i.e., using `line[:-1]`) is for display, because the `listbox` will not display a newline (`\n`) nicely. The other `listbox` methods occur in a handler. The method `curselection()` returns a list of indices of the `listbox` items that were selected by the user. Selection of multiple items has not been enabled for this `listbox`, so the list will have a single item. The `get(index)` method returns an item at the specified index. Another method, not used in this program, is the `delete(index)` method for removing a specified item from the `listbox`.

Scrollable Text Widget

The `Tix` widget for scrollable text is `ScrolledText`. This widget could be the basis for a text editor, since the widget allows a user to highlight and select text that spans lines, or select a small number of characters, such as a word in a sentence. The example follows with no explanation; the reason to show it is mainly to contrast this widget with the previous `ScrolledListBox` widget.

```
import sys, Tix
class PrivateStuff():
    pass
class MyApplication(Tix.Frame):
    def quit(self,event):
        sys.exit(0)
    def buildMyWidgets(self):
        box = Tix.ScrolledText(self,
                scrollbar="auto")
        box.pack(side="bottom", anchor="e",fill="both")
        try:
          f = open("bookdemo8.py")
          for line in f:
            box.text.insert("end",line)
          f.close()
        except:
          box.text.insert("end","failed to open file")
        forquit = Tix.Button(self,text="Exit")
        forquit.configure(background="beige",
                          activebackground="yellow")
        forquit.bind("<Button-1>",self.quit)
        forquit.pack(side="top")
    def __init__(self, master=None):
        Tix.Frame.__init__(self,master)
        self.configure(border=True,relief="raised")
        self.configure(width="10c",height="12c")
        self.pack()
        self.privatestuff = PrivateStuff()
        self.buildMyWidgets()
rootwindow = Tix.Tk()
```

```
Tobject = MyApplication(master=rootwindow)
Tobject.master.title("ScrolledText Widget")
Tobject.mainloop()
```

Canvas Widget

The Tk/Tix modules have widgets for images and for drawing. The Canvas widget has
methods for drawing lines, upon which applications like turtle can be built. The example
below, shown without explanation, uses the Canvas widget to plot a sine wave.

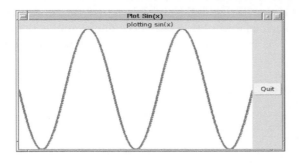

```
import sys, math, Tkinter, Tix

class MyApplication(Tix.Frame):
    def quit(self,event):
        sys.exit(0)
    def plot(self,canvas):
        canvas.delete(Tkinter.ALL)
        canvasX = canvas.winfo_width()
        canvasY = canvas.winfo_height()
        canvas.create_rectangle(0,0,
                    canvasX,canvasY,
                    fill="white")
        sinwave = [ ]
        span = 5*math.pi / 1000
        for i in range(1000):
            sinwave.append( (float(i), math.sin(i*span)) )
        plotCoords = [ ]
        oldx = oldy = None
        for x,y in sinwave:
            newy = (y+1.0)*(canvasY/2.0)
            newx = x*(canvasX/1000.0)
            if oldx != None:
                line = canvas.create_line(oldx,oldy,newx,newy)
                canvas.itemconfig(line,fill="magenta",width=4)
            oldx, oldy = newx, newy

    def buildMyWidgets(self):
        forshow = Tix.Label(self,text="plotting sin(x)")
        forshow.configure(padx="2i")
        forshow.pack(side="top")
        forinput = Tix.Button(self,text="Quit")
        forinput.configure(background="beige",
                        activebackground="yellow")
        forinput.bind("<Button-1>",self.quit)
        forinput.pack(side="right")
        fordrawing = Tix.Canvas(self)
        fordrawing.pack(side="bottom",
                    fill="both",
                    expand=True)
```

```
                self.update_idletasks()
                self.plot(fordrawing)

        def __init__(self, master=None):
            Tix.Frame.__init__(self,master) # initialize parent class first
            self.pack()
            self.buildMyWidgets()

rootwindow = Tix.Tk()
Tobject = MyApplication(master=rootwindow)
Tobject.master.title("Plot Sin(x)")
Tobject.mainloop()
```

Terminology Review

This chapter introduced the jargon in GUI frameworks related to object-oriented design. Widgets are the reusable components of GUI applications. Container widgets host the on-screen widgets, and are packed into the root window or a parent window by a geometry manager. Widgets can be bound to event handlers, which are invoked by the GUI controller as driven by user inputs. IDEs and application generators can reduce development time for applications using a GUI framework.

Exercises

(1) A *random walk* is a simulation of a particle that moves randomly. The idea can be illustrated simply with a coin and a ruler. The ruler is 12 inches long, with tick marks at 1, 2, ..., 11 inch positions. The coin is placed initially between the 5 and 6 inch marks. Now, repeatedly, the following is done: pick up the coin and toss it. If it comes up heads, move the coin one inch to the right of where it was; if it comes up tails, move the coin one inch to the left. This process repeats until the coin is off of the ruler. This problem is to simulate a random walk showing the position using the `Meter` widget. Write a GUI application that uses `Tix` and the `Meter` widget to show the steps of the random walk. You may wish to experiment with the timing of the steps (using `time.sleep()` so that the steps of the random walk are visible.

(2) Write an application with at least six `Button` objects. The application is to a primitive game of guessing which button "wins" the game. Bind each of the buttons to an event handler so that nonwinning buttons cause some message, perhaps a hint, to be displayed. It is easy to use `print` to display such a hint, but you may wish to be more ambitious and write the message into some widget. For example, you could use a `Label` widget to show the message: the method `mylab.config(text=S)` changes the text on the label object `mylab` (which you have to create and pack first) to the contents of string S. Another idea would be to change the title on the root window.

Part IV

Appendices

Chapter 30:   Advanced Topics

> *You are in a maze of twisty little passages, all alike.*
> — Colossal Cave Adventure
> (game by Will Crowther, circa 1977)

There is much more to Python and to the community of software developers using Python than previous chapters might suggest. Our aim throughout the book has been to emphasize computing concepts, rather than cover the Python language in every detail. Thus, this chapter is a sampling of some advanced topics with interesting computing ideas.

Of the advanced topics in Python and its infrastructure, there are two major themes and many small features. The first major theme is found in *decorations*, which express higher-level patterns in the spirit of Chapters 14 and 27. The second big theme is so-called "Python magic," which exposes many internal methods and attributes of the Python platform, enabling customization and playing tricks with the language. Except for highly specialized cases where extreme efficiency or some peculiar flexibility is required, one should avoid these "magic" features. However, from the computing view, looking at the internals of the platform is quite interesting.

Decorators

Many consider automation techniques to be key notions in reducing the cost of software engineering. Most automation rests on expressing repetitive aspects of programming in abstract ways and providing tools or language features that capture frequently repeated patterns. One of the oldest ideas goes back to assembly language programming, when *macros* were invented. A *macro processor* is one that takes source code as input and produces better or more elaborate source code as output. For example, using a "macro language" one may be able to define one-line expression that turns into the equivalent of a `while` loop with a `break` statement; a programmer could then concisely write code using macros that turns into much larger programs in a target language, be it machine language, C, and so forth. The problem with macro programming is that it is *too powerful*: using macros can introduce mistakes that are hard to find and tends to confuse code.

Modern practice tends to avoid macro programming in favor of more structured and comprehensible techniques. One example is the use of *wrappers*. Suppose we would like to have some subset $\mathcal{T}$ of the functions in a program do some bookkeeping by adding to a global counter each time one of these functions is evaluated. The direct approach to implementing this would be to manually insert extra statements into each function in $\mathcal{T}$. Imagine, however, that our programming language has some facility to replace each call to $f(args)$, for any $f \in \mathcal{T}$, by a call to a new function `fcount(f, args)`, where the code for `fcount` takes care of adding to a global counter and also invoking $f(args)$. The function `fcount` is called a *wrapper*, as if it "wraps" around the function call to f (wrappers can do some computing before calling f and also some computing after f returns).

Wrappers are just one example of a larger theme of *program transformation*. What is useful, yet constrained enough to be principled and reasonable, is a language facility to add statements or mutate code in ways that constrain what is done to be understandable. Such transformed code could be functions, classes, methods, or other units of program construction (as opposed to macros, which may not respect the units of program construction).

Python's answer to program transformation is the *decorator* feature. In terms of the fcount example on the previous page, a Python decorator could be the code shown to the right. The @fcount statement just before the definition of function foo is essentially a transformation directive to Python. This statement tells Python to invoke fcount(foo): the function foo is the argument to fcount. When we look at what fcount does, we see that foo is input, but another function, newFunction, is what is returned. The net effect of this is that every place in the program that appears to call foo actually calls the transformed version of foo. When the script runs, it prints 25, 49, 81, and 3. The first three numbers are printed by the (transformed) foo, and the number 3 is the count of

```
global FCount
FCount = 0

def fcount(originalFunction):
  def newFunction(*args):
    global FCount
    FCount += 1
    originalFunction(*args)
  return newFunction

@fcount  # decorator
def foo(x):
  print x*x

foo(5)
foo(7)
foo(9)
print FCount
```

how many times foo has been called. What the example does not show is that the @fcount statement could as well be put before other function definitions, so they would also be counted in the FCount total. It is even possible to have multiple decorator statements precede a function, class, or method definition; this means that a definition can have several transformations. Decorators can also have parameters in addition to the functions being transformed to tailor the transformation.

Python Magic

At the highest level of software development, tool construction becomes important. One becomes interested in more than solving a particular problem, hoping to generalize the solution so that it can solve other problems. In a sense, a computer language like Python is such a tool. Experience has shown that choices made in the design of a particular language are not universally the best ones for particular problems. Sometimes, we would like to revisit how a language works, perhaps tweaking the design to make life easier. More than most languages, Python actually accommodates customization. This kind of customization is rarely helpful to beginners (and some would argue that these features are not worth the obscurity they encourage), however, many of the customization techniques reveal design choices of Python and computing languages more generally.

First, we consider the *introspective* capabilities of Python, that is, how a program can inspect its own structure, the structure of classes, objects, and so forth. The inspect module has methods to go through all the attributes of modules, classes, objects, and more. When function calls "stack up" due to recursion or just by a series of calls, inspect also has methods to examine the "frame records" of a stack of calls, which can further be examined to see the local and global variable values at each point. Python's parser and ast modules make it possible to inspect the internal objects representing a program. This kind of detailed look at the structure of how data is represented in Python is needed for implementing *foreign function* interfaces (using the ctypes library) to code written in a nonPython language.

Most of the "magic" customization relates to Python's type, class, and object-oriented facilities. Recall that the __init__ method is automatically invoked when a new instance of a class is created. There are many other methods automatically invoked when objects are created, mutated, and deleted. Further, all of Python's operators (+, *, /, etc.) are secretly methods with names __add__, __mul__, and so on. It is possible to define a new type, write the methods corresponding to operators, and have instances of the new type allow syntax such as `A + B`, which invokes `__add__` in the intuitive way. Really advanced magic methods even permit the definition of functions that create new types, change attributes of modules, and more.

One interesting customization, also a feature of languages Java and C#, is the Python `property` attribute feature. Roughly put, `property` is a function used in the definition of a class which establishes so-called *getter*, *setter*, and *deleter* methods for a named attribute of objects in the class. When a property is established for an object D with attribute m, then an assignment `D.m = 2` turns into a method call to the setter method for D. The setter method can do extra checking, prevent any assignment, add to counters, or any other action we might like.

Platforms and Virtual Machines

The standard Python is built upon a virtual machine: the Python code is first compiled into byte code, which is then interpreted by a virtual machine. This way of doing things can be much slower than how truly compiled code, written in C or machine language, runs on computing hardware. For really efficient program execution, needed when problem size or data scale is enormous, Python is probably not the best choice. Similarly, to take advantage of parallel computing hardware or intense graphical processing, Python's standard concurrency modules `threading` and `multiprocessing` might not be adequate.

Several projects have built alternative virtual machines that either optimize how Python runs or add new features not in the standard distribution. One example of this is `Jython`, which translates Python's byte code to a form that can run on the Java Virtual Machine. The significance of this development is that all of Java's data structures and methods are available through Python; applications can be written in a mixture of Python and Java. The `PyPy` project takes another approach. Instead of interpreting bytecode, the goal is to compile the bytecode yet further into optimized machine code; in some cases the result can run 10 times faster than standard Python. Other, less mature, projects aim to use Python in smartphone, tablet, or embedded computing platforms.

Scripts as Commands

Under Linux or other Unix-like systems, a Python script can have a special first line comment, typically of the form "`#!/usr/bin/env python`" or perhaps "`#!/usr/bin/python`"—this is a comment in Python because the first character is #. When the file containing the script is given *executable* permission, say with a command such as `chmod +x prog.py`, and if the search path for commands has been set up to include the directory containing `prog.py`, then you can use `prog.py` as a command. Better yet, rename `prog.py` to a simpler name, like `prog`. Then, at a shell command line, a command `prog one two` will run the Python script, where "`one two`" are parameters to the script, available via the `sys.args` mechanism described in Chapter 28. You can build your own command environment, even to the point where one script calls another (see the `subprocess` example in Chapter 27), the scripts read and write files, go through directories, databases, and invoke other tools that have command-line syntax.

Trivia

There are many curious points of syntax and operation not mentioned in this book. Though these are inessential, it is likely you will encounter them if you explore Python further. A few of these are listed here:

- It is possible to use single-line "compound statements" in Python. For example, the following is valid Python syntax:

```
if x<y:  a = x;  print(y);  b = y
```

  Two features shown in this example are (*i*) when the body of the if would be a single line, it can be placed after the colon on the same line (rather than indented as a block). Also (*ii*) the semicolon (;) makes it possible to put more than one statement on a line, though there are restrictions on doing so. Some programmers with experience in programming Java or C, where ending statements with a semicolon is the norm, continue to put a semicolon at the end of statements in Python. Accidentally, this often works. The semicolon binding, above, has priority over the colon: if x<y evaluates to False, then the assignment to b will not occur (because it is considered to be part of the body of the if).

- Compound statements are applicable to def, for, while, and other statements, so long as the body is a single line. For example, "for x in range(10): E.append(x)" is a legal statement.

- The full syntax for try ...except includes else and finally statements. The for and while statements also can have else clauses.

- Though it is not advisable for beginners, one often sees statements like "while L:" where L is a list that is depleted by the body of the loop. This plays on the trick that all empty containers (string, list, dictionary, tuple) are treated as False in Python's evaluation for conditions.

- The single underscore (_) is a variable referring to the last evaluated result. To observe this, in an interactive Python session, enter some expression; then enter the single underscore to see what is shown in response.

- repr(x) and `x` are equivalent. (you may have to search for the back-leaning single quote on the keyboard to use this).

- Python allows new classes to inherit from the built-in types, int, list, str, etc.

- Functions, like objects, can be given attributes (try f.x = 1 for some function f); however, the "self" mechanism for objects has no meaning for these attributes. Of course, f.__doc__ is the attribute referring to the docstring of the function f.

- The int() function can also convert bases, e.g., int("284",9) converts using base 9 instead of base 10.

Chapter 31:   Solutions to ☆-Exercises

Chapter 8

(4) There are many possible answers. This one illustrates how the newline (\n) character works along with operators * to repeat and + to concatenate.

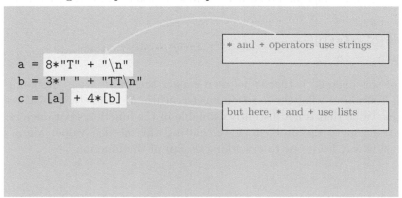

If you try this, you may observe that the **print** adds an extra newline. To prevent that extra newline, one can either add an extra comma to the **print** command or make a slightly different c, which does not have a newline as the final item's character.

Chapter 9

(4) There are two roots of the quadratic,

$$\frac{-b + \sqrt{b^2 - 4ac}}{2a} \quad \text{and} \quad \frac{-b - \sqrt{b^2 - 4ac}}{2a}$$

Although one can write a function for each, it is simpler to write one function that returns the two roots as a pair—but only simpler if we streamline the notation first. Let's rewrite the two roots like this:

$$
\begin{aligned}
m &= \frac{\sqrt{b^2 - 4ac}}{2a} \\
n &= \frac{-b}{2a} \\
roots &= (m + n, m - n)
\end{aligned}
$$

Now it is straightforward to define `quadroot(a,b,c)`

```
def quadroot(a,b,c):
    d = (b**2 - 4*a*c)**0.5
    m = d/(2*a)
    n = -b/(2*a)
    roots = (m+n,m-n)
    return roots
```

The lesson of this exercise is that a bit of planning can simplify function design. In particular, if we find that a particular expression or part of an expression is used more than once, then consider defining a name for that expression. The remainder of the calculation is then simpler.

(5) What operator returns `True` or `False` depending on whether a string `r` is contained in parameter `s`? The comparison "`r in s`" does the job. Therefore, the last line of the function can be something like

```
return (r in s)
```

All that remains is to let `r` be the concatenation of the first and last character from `s`; the first character is `s[0]`, and the last character is `s[-1]`. The concatenation we need is `s[0]+s[-1]`, which puts together the first and last character as a new string.

```
def foo(s):
    r = s[0]+s[-1]
    return (r in s)
```

The lesson of this exercise is that it helps to *reason backwards* when designing functions. Think first about what the function has to return. Most likely, what is returned will need some value that is not instantly available in the function's parameters. Then turn your attention to the problem of calculating this needed value. Many times, reasoning in this way leads one to a working design of the function.

Chapter 10

(2) This problem has a simple solution which illustrates a technique that should be in everyone's toolbox. Problems that involve comparison, or testing some property of a parameter, are often solved by *conversion*. The idea is to first "convert" a function argument to a form that makes the problem simpler to solve. A solution to (2) is this function definition:

```
def IsUpper(val,upval):
    y = val.upper()
    return (y == upval)
```

In this definition, the first line of the body defines `y` to be the uppercase conversion of parameter `val`. The solution is then simple: `y == upval` is the desired result.

Most people first see the idea of conversion for testing a property when they learn about fractions. Mathematically, there is the question

$$\frac{1455}{9603} \overset{?}{=} \frac{505}{3333}$$

The answer is found by converting the two fractions to ones with common denominators, then comparing. Similar ideas of conversion are valuable problem-solving techniques in computing.

The `IsUpper` problem inspires a simple test of whether a string is all uppercase characters or not:

```
def allupper(val):
    y = val.upper()
    return (val == y)
```

The `allupper` function returns `True` only if the conversion of the argument to uppercase does nothing: that is, after conversion, you get the same thing as the original argument. The same idea can be illustrated with a function to test whether a number is zero or not:

```
def iszero(x):
  return ((-x)==x)
```

(in practice, the simpler x==0 would be better, but this definition is just to make the point about conversion).

(6) Given was the definition:

```
def multicat(prefix=(1,2),value,suffix=(9))
  a = prefix + value
   b = a + suffix
  return
```

This definition has two syntax errors and one design flaw:

1. the colon (:) is missing from the function head;
2. the second line of the body is indented one extra space;
3. the **return** statement does not give a value to return—it should have been **return** b so that the caller of **multicat** will get the concatenated result. A **return** statement with no value is a legitimate Python, because not all functions return results (some functions, for example, just print something). Python will not complain that this is an error, but the program is likely to encounter a bug because of this mistake.

Chapter 11

(6) When run using Python3, the result is this:

```
Testing
value = 3.0
value = 1.7320508075688772
value = 2.2795070569547775
1.509803648477105
value = -1.0
done
None
```

There are several points this exercise emphasizes:

*   A function can both print something and calculate a result to be returned. The value returned by **selpow** needs to be printed, but also the first line in **selpow**'s body causes Python to print something, as a *side effect* of calling **selpow**.

*   Do you see the final "None" in what is printed? This is explained by the fact that **selpow** does not **return** anything when none of the **if**-cases evaluate to **True**. So, when **value** is -1.0 the function **selpow** prints value = 1.0, and prints done, but no **return** statement is applicable—so "**print selpow(-1.0)**" prints None, as explained in Chapter 10.

*   The earlier part of the output is relatively straightforward. In order to evaluate **selpow(selpow(selpow(3.0)))**, Python has to first calculate the result of **selpow(3.0)**, then use that as the argument to **selpow**, and repeat this once more to finish.

(7) This problem shows the difference between "inclusive or" and "exclusive or," sometimes called *either-or*. In specialty of logic (either mathematical or philosophical), when we say that "*a* or *b* is *true*," it could well be the case that both *a* and *b* are *true*. This is Python's definition of the `or` operator. So the version of `aei` with `return (u or v or w)` uses inclusive or, and thus returns `True` for `aei("invalidate")`. What about the other version of `aei`, is this exclusive or? To be an exclusive or, we would need that *only one* of the three vowels ("a," "e," "i") is contained in the argument. A helpful way to understand the first version of `aei` is to draw a flowchart (in fact, this function has to be so confusingly written that we are almost *forced* to make a flowchart to understand it!).

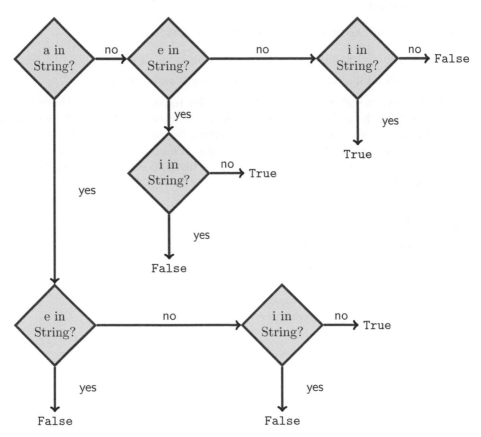

How confusing this `aei` is! Is there no better way to make a test of exclusive or? One source of confusion is the "negative" testing, using code like `'a' not in String`. Reading from the flowchart, the `aei` function could have been written differently. Consider this:

```
def aei(String):
    if 'a' in String:
        if 'e' in String:
            return False
        else:
            return not ('i' in String)
    else:
```

```
        if 'e' in String:
          return not ('i' in String)
        else:
          return ('i' in String)
```

This looks perhaps less confusing, but it is still a mess. A much simpler way to write aei that tests for the exclusive-or containment of the three letters is the following:

```
    def aei(String):
      if ('a' in String) and ('e' not in String) and ('i' not in String):
        return True
      elif ('e' in String) and ('a' not in String) and ('i' not in String):
        return True
      elif ('i' in String) and ('a' not in String) and ('e' not in String):
        return True
      else:
        return False
```

The lesson of this exercise is that it is a good idea to *avoid nested if* code in programs, because they can be confusing. This type of confusion leads to mistakes. Most times one sees statements like

```
    if A:
      if B:
```

it would be better to have "if A and B" instead.

This simplified aei above is a great improvement, but still somewhat unsatisfying, because it has a kind of repetitious style. A common trick for implementing test of "exclusive or" uses *counting*.

```
    def aei(String):
      return ( 'a' in String,
               'e' in String,
               'i' in String ).count(True) == 1
```

This definition returns True precisely when one (not zero, not two, not three) of the three vowels is contained in the string argument.

Chapter 12

(3) The problem states that we may assume the argument String satisfies len(String)==3*n* for some number *n*. Knowing the value of *n* will be useful because slicing specifies the length of a slice, as the chapter explains: String[i:i+*n*] is a slice of length *n* (provided that i+*n* does not go past the end of String). How can *n* be calculated? The expression len(String)/3 does the job (even if *n* is zero, this works). The three parts of trisect's result are left, middle, and right; each of these is a string of length *n*. Putting these observations together suggests this definition:

```
    def trisect(String):
      n = len(String)/3
      left = String[0:0+n]
      middle = String[0+n:0+n+n]
      right = String[0+n+n:]
      return (left,middle,right)
```

Notice that `middle` starts where `left` ends: the value `0+n` is `n`, meaning that `left` includes all the characters *up to but not including* `n`. That is convenient, because it is just the place where `middle` starts. To emphasize this pattern also works for ending `middle` and beginning `right`, the code above expresses the second "splitting place" as `0+n+n`.

(5) The behavior of `fsub` is different for the part before the period and the part after the period. A good first step is to split the argument of `fsub` into the part before the period and remainder. Here is a function doing that:

```
def twoparts(String):
    place = String.index('.')
    part1 = String[:place]
    part2 = String[place:]
    return (part1,part2)
```

The rest of the work is to use the `replace` method changing `"o"` into the empty string (which effectively removes all o-letters) and again use `replace` changing `"y"` into `"ia."`

```
def fsub(String):
    part1, part2 = twoparts(String)
    newpart1 = part1.replace("o",'')
    newpart2 = part2.replace("y",'ia')
    return newpart1 + newpart2
```

The function `fsub` can be written more compactly, in a single function (instead of first defining `twoparts`). One advantage, for beginners, of defining `twoparts` is that it can be written and tested interactively as a first step. Once we know `twoparts` is correct, then we can try extending the program by writing `fsub`. This style of software development is a slow-but-steady way of making progress. A second advantage is that when a function has many lines that each contribute some small progress toward the result, it is easy to add some `print` statements during debugging to see what is going on in case the function does not work as expected. Once we know that all the technical things are working, a more compact definition can be attempted:

```
def fsub(String):
    place = String.index('.')
    return String[:place].replace("o",'') + String[place:].replace("y",'ia')
```

Chapter 13

(3) The problem is equivalent to asking the question, *are all items in P vowels?* The reason to look at the problem this way is to realize that "all" is in the problem statement. This naturally suggests we use the `all` function: it must be `all(itemv(P))` where `itemv(P)` returns a sequence of booleans (`True` and `False`) for each letter in P. For example,

```
itemv("aaed")   ➜   [True, True, True, False]
```

is what we expect `itemv` to do. What is a list comprehension expression that does what `itemv` needs to do? To test whether a letter is a vowel is straightforward: `letter in "aeiou"` is the simplest (or, if you prefer, `letter in "aeiouyAEIOUY"` for sake of completeness). The list comprehension is thus:

```
def allvowels(P):
  vowels = "aeiou"
  itemv = [ (letter in vowels) for letter in P ]
  return all(itemv)
```

Looking at the above, it may seem confusing to see "in" appear twice, with different meanings for Python: the first "in" is a comparison operator, testing whether a single character `letter` contains `vowels`; the second "in" is part of the syntax of list comprehension—it says where the `letter` comes from, one `letter` for each item in P. Some professional programmers would not be satisfied with this definition because it will encounter an error if P is not a string. Instead, they might prefer this definition:

```
def allvowels(P):
  vowels = "aeiou"
  if type(P) != type(vowels):
    return False
  itemv = [ (letter in vowels) for letter in P ]
  return all(itemv)
```

Python has other ways to deal with type-checking, complaining about arguments being inappropriate types, and more—later chapters introduce other techniques for this.

(4) How many positive integers smaller than 100,000 are divisible by both 11 and 13? The idea is nearly the same as used for question (3), but instead of "all" we use "count," totaling over a sequence of True and False values. It is handy to make a function `et(n)` returning True or returning False, depending on whether n satisfies both divisibility tests. Here is a definition of `et(n)`:

```
et = lambda n: n%11==0 and n%13==0
```

The problem's solution now just counts a list comprehension of all the `et(n)` values for n between 0 and 99,999 (smaller than 100,000).

```
[ et(n) for n in range(0,100000) ].count(True)
```

(6) When confronted with a problem dealing with nested lists (a list whose items are lists), it is helpful to look at some concrete cases. Instead of working on `column(p,M)`, ask the simpler question, what is the first column (column 0) of M? We know that M is supposed to be a matrix, which is an arrangement of numbers we describe by rows and columns—each number in the matrix is at an intersection of a row and column. In Python, a matrix like M is represented by a list, namely a list of the *rows* of M, shown horizontally in the problem statement's example. Simple list comprehension [row for row in M] is nothing more than M itself: it is only a list of the rows. What we need for the first *column* is to get `row[0]` for each row. Thus,

```
[ row[0] for row in M ]
```

is the first column of M. But the problem is to get a particular column, the one indexed by p. The solution is to *generalize* from 0 to a parameter p. So, for the definition we have

```
def column(p,M):
  return [ row[p] for row in M ]
```

Though this exercise is simple (and the function definition is short), there is an important lesson here: as a problem-solving technique, it can be very helpful to first try a solution with a particular value rather than a parameter (0 rather than p, above); once we understand how it works with a particular value, try to generalize what you have done by using the parameter.

Chapter 19

(8) The essential trick of the solution is to realize that `A[i]` is found either in the left or the right half of sequence A. As a first step, let's see how simple expressions can tell us which half of A contains `A[i]`. If we can do that, then we can use recursion to repeat the same problem but on the left or right half of A. Using splitting, the left half of A is `A[0:len(A)/2]`; the right half of A is `A[len(A)/2:]`. What if `len(A)` is odd? Try an example, say A being `"abcdefg."` Then `len(A)/2` is 3, so the left "half" is `A[0:3]`, or `"abc,"` and the right "half" is `A[3:]`, or `"defg."`

Proceeding on the question of locating `A[i]`, observe that the comparison `i<len(A)/2` evaluates to `True` if `A[i]` is in the left half of A. Now we can try a recursive definition—which will turn out to be incorrect, but easy to repair:

```
def whittle(A,i):
  half = len(A)/2
  if i<half:
    answer = whittle(A[0:half],i)
    return answer
  else:
    answer = whittle(A[half:],i)
    return answer
```

While it expresses the right idea, there are a couple of bugs with this definition. First, when does recursion ever stop? We need to have a check at the start of the function for a "base case," that is, a situation where no recursion is needed. If `len(A)` is 1 and i is zero, we can skip any recursion and just return `A[0]`.

```
def whittle(A,i):
  half = len(A)/2
  if len(A)==1:
    return A[0]
  elif i<half:
    answer = whittle(A[0:half],i)
    return answer
  else:
    answer = whittle(A[half:],i)
    return answer
```

The remaining "bug" for this definition is what happens when `A[i]` is in the right half of A. The bug is that i is the index with respect to the original sequence A, but we are asking to solve `whittle` on a sequence (the right half) whose length is smaller than i. For example, consider `whittle("abcdefg",5)`—which would trigger the recursive call `whittle("defg",5)`. See the flaw?

To overcome this flaw, the recursive call to `whittle` needs to adjust the second argument: it needs to "skip over" the first half of A, which is sensible since we know that `A[i]` is not in the first half. So, instead of using `i` as the argument, we can use `i-half`.

```
def whittle(A,i):
    half = len(A)/2
    print ("***",A,i)
    if len(A)==1:
        return A[0]
    elif i<half:
        answer = whittle(A[0:half],i)
        return answer
    else:
        answer = whittle(A[half:],i-half)
        return answer
```

Above, a debugging `print` statement has been added to the function. If this definition seems unclear, try using this definition of `whittle` for some examples and observe what is displayed. An example:

```
>>> whittle("abcdefghijklmnop",12)
('***', 'abcdefghijklmnop', 12)
('***', 'ijklmnop', 4)
('***', 'mnop', 0)
('***', 'mn', 0)
('***', 'm', 0)
m
```

(10) This is the sort of problem that highlights the almost mysterious attraction of recursion. With relatively few statements in a program, the search for a solution is described.

```
def factor(N):
    if N == 0:
        return (0,0)
    if N < 5:
        return (None,None)
    a,b = factor(N-5)
    if a != None:
        return (a+1,b)
    a,b = factor(N-8)
    if b != None:
        return (a,b+1)
    return (None,None)
```

The body of `factor` begins with "base cases," which are the easy (and exceptional) values of `N` that do not need recursion. These are `N` being zero, which has an easy answer, and positive `N` less than 5, which has no answer. The body of `factor` then potentially tries two different recursive calls, `factor(N-5)` and `factor(N-8)`; either of these provides an answer to the problem. If both of these attempts fail, the final line of the function returns a value indicating that the search failed.

Most experienced computer scientists look upon such a function with suspicion. The function turns out to be inefficient; for instance, it always uses subtraction of 5 or 8 whereas there could be a test in the function for `N` being divisible by 5 or 8. Another more serious question is, does this function always work? Maybe there is some value like 10341 and even though $5x + 8y = 10341$ for some (x, y), `factor(10341)` would return `(None,None)`. Is there some way to know whether or not this recursive search always does the job of finding factors? Yes, there is a way to reason about this, which is standard in computer science.

Divide the possibilities for `N` into two groups, the small numbers (say, less than 20) and the remaining group of large numbers. We can verify that `factor(N)` works for small numbers just by trying them all and manually checking that the answer is correct. For the large numbers, it was previously observed that if `factor(N)` does have a solution `(x,y)`, then either `factor(N-5)` or `factor(N-8)` will be enough to calculate the answer. So, provided `factor(M)` is a correctly working function for all the values of `M` smaller than `N`, the recursive search method used by `factor(N)` will be correct. Note, however, that `factor(N)` might depend on `factor(N-5)`, which in turn might depend on `factor((N-5)-8)` (by recursion), and so forth. Each deeper level of recursion will be trying the search on a smaller value for its argument, trusting that the deeper search has a correct result. Does this kind of searching go on forever? Eventually, the search argument will be one of the small numbers, which will have been verified at the beginning of the reasoning process. This is because, with a subtraction of 5 or 8, a big number cannot "skip over" the small numbers and get to a negative number. Thus, a chain of trust is established, starting from `N`, then `N-5`, then `(N-5)-8` (or however the search turns out) and so on, down to a small number. By this reasoning, we can trust the pair `(x,y)` that `factor(N)` returns. But will `factor(N)` incorrectly return `(None,None)` when in fact there is a solution? Looking at the body of `factor(N)` we see that it tries `factor(N-8)` whenever `factor(N-5)` fails; so the function does search all possibilities for a chain of trust down to the small numbers before giving up and returning `(None,None)`. Put another way, if there is such a chain, `factor(N)` will either find that chain, or find another satisfactory chain that produces a correct answer.

Chapter 32:   Reference Tables

This appendix is for quick lookup of selected features of Python, assuming that you are already familiar with the concepts, but may have forgotten a syntax feature. If you are online, you might want to look at `http://www.python.org/doc/QuickRef.html` for a more complete quick reference. Some of the material in this chapter is not explained in earlier chapters.

Python Operators (in order of precedence, highest to lowest)

Operator	Explanation
f(args...)	function invocation
x[index:index]	slicing
x[index]	subscript (lookup)
x.attribute	object attribute reference
**	exponentiation (raising to a power)
~x	bit flip
+x, -x	positive, negative
*, /, //, %	multiplication, division, remainder
+, -	addition, subtraction
<<, >>	left, right bit shifting
&	bit "and" operation
^	bit "xor" operation
|	bit "or" operation
<, <=, >, >=, <>, !=, ==	comparison operators
is, is not	reference comparison
in, not in	membership
not x	logical negation
and	logical conjunct
or	logical disjunct

Note: X < Y < Z is equivalent to X < Y and Y < Z.

Formatting

A special operator, for Python2 only, is the format (%) operator, which takes a string on the left side, and a variable or tuple on the right side; it produces a new string by substituting, converting, and formatting as directed by the left-side string.

In the left-side string can be formatting codes (%c, %s, %i, %d, %u, %x, %e, %f, %g and others) and one can also specify precision for floating point conversion. Examples:

```
a = '%s has %03d quote types' % ('Python', 2)
a ==> 'Python has 002 quote types'
```

There is also a fancier way to use format with a dictionary:

```
a = '%(lang)s has %(c)03d quote types' % {
    'c':2, 'lang':'Python}
```

For recent Python2 versions and for Python3, use the `format()` method on strings, e.g.,

```
a = '{0} has {1:03d} quote types'.format('Python',2)
a ==> 'Python has 002 quote types'
```

or with keywords,

```
a = '{lang}s has %val:03d quote types'.format(
        lang="Python", val=2)
```

or with a dictionary,

```
b = {'lang':"Python", 'val':2}
a = '{lang}s has %val:03d quote types'.format(**b)
```

Decorators

The "@" symbol precedes decorator directives. Example:

```
def hello(CODE):
  print "Hello World"
  return CODE

@hello
def foo(x):
  print x*x

foo(5)
```

The runtime output from `foo(5)` are the two lines `Hello World` and 25.

Reserved Words in Python

and	as	assert	break	class
continue	def	del	elif	else
exec	finally	for	from	global
if	import	in	is	lambda
not	or	pass	print	raise
return	try	with	while	yield

Many other special words are part of Python's type system, including `bool`, `int`, `float`, `list`, `dict`, `set`, `file`; the list above is just a list of keywords that are the verbs, so to speak, in program statements.

Assignment Statement

A single = assigns to variables. An assignment statement can assign to multiple variables and unpack tuples and sequences. Examples:

```
x = 2*r[5]    # assign to x
a,b,c = ('e',1.1,0)
m,r = "hello", "goodbye"
a,b,c,d = "word"
x,y = range(100)[45:47]
m,r = r,m     # swap r and m values
a = b = c = 2   # make 'em all 2
```

An assignment can also be augmented with an operator:

```
e += 1  # equivalent to  e = e + 1
e *= 2  # equivalent to  e = e * 2
```

Statements

Illegal Symbols (but allowed within data or quoted strings): $?

Multiline Statements: Normally, a Python language statement is a single line of text. Exceptions: the \ character, when the last character on a line, can continue the statement to the next line—*this is not recommended, and may not work on all systems.* Within any matched pair of parenthesis, including (), [], {}, the statement can continue over many lines until the matching parenthesis is found. Triple-quoted strings can span multiple lines.

Comments: Comments start with # and continue to end of line.

`pass` is the do-nothing statement.

`del` removes a variable, a slice of a list, item in dictionary, an attribute of an object, etc.

`print` writes to the console; it puts a newline at the end (Python2: unless you end the statement with a comma; in Python3 `print` is a function).

`exec` takes a string and interprets the string as a Python statement (not in Python3).

Semicolons can be used to put multiple statements on one line, provided they are "simple statements" (see Python documentation).

Name and Type Syntax

Variable, Class, Function, and Other Names: The pattern allowed is sequence of alphabetic characters (that is, letters a–z, A–Z) and may also include underscore symbols (_); numbers (0–9) can appear within the name, but not as the first character. Generally, names that begin with two underscores are special Python names.

Strings: Three ways of defining strings:

```
"a string"
'another string'
'''a string containing embedded newlines,
and quote (') marks, can be
delimited with triple quotes.'''
```

There are more advanced types of strings in Python2 (sometimes you might see something like `r'Unistring'`) for more general (nonEnglish) usage.

Meta-Characters in Strings:

```
\n Newline      \\ Backslash (\)
\' Single quote (')   \" Double quote (")
\r Carriage Return (CR)
\b Backspace (BS)    \t Tab (TAB)
```

Octal and Hexadecimal Notations:

```
octal: 0177, 01777777777777777777L
hex: 0xFF, 0xFFFFFFFFFFFFFFFFL
```

Tuple Syntax: Tuple of length 0, 1, 2, etc.: () (1,) (1,2) (parentheses are optional if length is greater than zero).

List Syntax: List of length 0, 1, 2, etc.: [] [1] [1,2]

Set Syntax: set([]), set([2,9]), set("abc"), {2,9}.

Dictionary Syntax:
Dictionary of length 0, 1, 2, etc.: {}, {1:'first'}, {1:'first', 'next':'second'}

Slicing, Indexing, Lookup

```
X = (0,1,2,3,4,5,6,7)  # define X for examples below
X[3] ==> 3
X[-1] ==> 7
X[2:4] ==> (2,3)
X[1:] ==> (1,2,3,4,5,6,7)
X[:3] ==> (0,1,2)
X[:] ==> (0,1,2,3,4,5,6,7) # makes a copy of the sequence
X[::-1] ==> (7,6,5,4,3,2,1,0)
```

Slicing and numeric subscripting can use negative numbers to count leftward, from the end, rather than rightward, from the beginning of the sequence. For dictionary indexing,

```
R = { 1:True, (2,3):"Pair", 3.14159:"Pecan Pie" }
R[1] ==> True
R[(2,3)] ==> 'Pair'
R[0] ==> Error - not in dictionary
```

Special Values

None: None is used as the default return value on functions. Input that evaluates to None does not echo/print when running Python interactively.

Logical Constants: True and False are the results of comparison, and can be used in assignments. In logical expressions, the following act the same as False: the special value None, the number zero, an empty sequence ([]) or empty dictionary ({}). All other values put into logical expressions act the same as True.

Built-In Functions and Manipulators

Built-In Numeric Functions:

```
abs(x)              absolute value of x
int(x)              x converted to integer
float(x)            x converted to floating point
divmod(x,y)         the tuple (x/y, x%y)
pow(x,y)            x to the power y
range(start [,end [, step]])
                    use range for a sequence of integers
chr(i)              return character for ASCII code i
ord(c)              return ASCII code for character c
```

Functions for Sequence Types: These work on lists, tuples, and strings.

```
len(s)              length of s
min(s)              smallest item of s
max(s)              largest item of s
sum(s)              add up items in s
x in s              True if an item of s
                    is equal to x, else False
x not in s          False if an item of s
                    is equal to x, else True
s + t               the concatenation of s and t
s * n, n * s        n copies of s concatenated
s[i]                i'th item of s, origin 0
s[i:j]              slice of s from i to j
```

Operators on Lists: These operators can *change* a list:

```
s[i] = x            item i of s is replaced by x
s[i:j] = t          replace slice of s from i to j
del s[i:j]          delete slice (same as s[i:j] = [])
s.append(x)         add x to end of s
s.count(x)          number of i's for which s[i] == x
s.index(x)          smallest i such that s[i] == x1)
s.insert(i, x)      item i becomes x,
                    old item i is now at i+1, etc
s.remove(x)         same as del s[s.index(x)]
s.pop(i)            remove item at index i and return it
s.reverse()         reverses the items of s (in place)
s.sort()            sorts the list (in place)
```

Note: The built-in *functions* reversed() and sorted() do not change their argument: each returns a new list, in reversed or sorted order.

Operators on Dictionaries

```
len(a)          the number of items in a
a[k]            the item of a with key k
a[k] = x        set a[k] to x
del a[k]        remove a[k] from a
a.items()       list of (key, value) pairs
a.keys()        a's list of keys
a.values()      a's list of values
a.has_key(k)    True if a has key k,
                else False
k in a          same as a.has_key(k)
```

Operators on Sets

```
len(s)          number of elements of s
x in s          test if x is in set s
s <= t          ask if s is a subset of t
s | t           union of sets s and t
s & t           intersection of sets s and t
s - t           new set, remove elements
                of set t from set s
s.copy()        create a new copy of s
s.add(e)        add element e to s
s.discard(e)    remove element e from s
s.clear()       makes s empty
s.pop()         return (and remove) some
                element from s
```

Type Conversion: You can create lists, dictionaries, sets, integers, floating numbers (and more) by putting what you want as the argument of a function that has the type's name. For instance, to return a list, based on set s: `list(s)`; to get a floating type from an integer: `float(3)`; to create a dictionary, supply a list of pairs: `dict( [('a',2),('b',3)] )`.

Compact Notation to Create Lists

Create interesting lists using Python's *list comprehension* syntax. Here are a few examples:

[2**i for i in range(10)] creates [1,2,4,8,16,32,64,128,256,512].

["->"+e for e in "abcd"] creates ['->a','->b','->c','->d'].

[(i,j) for i in range(10) for j in range(3)] generates a list of 30 pairs, with every combination from the two ranges.

[x for x in myDictionary if x not in yourDictionary] generates a list of items in myDictionary that are not in yourDictionary (the example illustrates how if can be combined with for to generate a list).

Other Comprehensions

{ k:k*k for k in range(8) } creates dictionary mapping numbers to their squares.
(i*i for i in range(8)) creates a generator of squares.

Zip. The built-in function *zip* creates a new list of pairs from two given lists: zip("abc", range(3))' returns [('a',0),('b',1),('c',2)]; zip(*m) returns an unzip operation.

Higher-Order List Operations

Python gives you some "higher order" methods of using lists, called filter, map, and reduce.

```
filter( myfunc, myseq )
```

has two arguments: the first, myfunc, must be a function that returns a bool (that is, True or False), and myfunc must take a single argument, which is of the same type as elements of sequence myseq. The result is a new sequence consisting of all elements of myseq where myfunc returned True. For instance,

```
def foo(x):
   if x != 'a': return True
filter(foo,"abracadabra") ==> 'brcdbr'
```

map creates a new sequence consisting of applying the first argument, a function, to each element of the second argument, a sequence:

```
map(ord,"ASCII") ==> [65, 83, 67, 73, 73]
```

reduce takes a function of two arguments, and successively evaluates the function iteratively through a sequence. A classic example is this:

```
def add(x,y):
   return x+y
reduce(add,[3,9,20,5]) ==> 37
```

Of course, sum([3,9,20,5]) does the same thing, but using reduce you can use the "pattern" of adding all the elements of a sequence for more general functions than just addition.

Files

A "file object" is created with `open("someFileName")` (other forms of `open` specify whether to read the file or write it, where the file is located, and more). If `f` is a file object, these are standard operators:

```
f.close(x)          close file f.
f.flush(x)          flush file's internal buffer.
f.read(k)           return string
                    (next k bytes from file f).
f.read()            read all of f, return as string.
f.readline()        read one entire line from file
f.readlines()       read all of f with readline()
                    (and return list of lines read).
f.write(str)        write str to file f.
f.writelines(list)  write list of strings to file.
```

Control Flow

`if` statement:

```
if 5>3:
  print("hello")
  x = 20
```

`if` with `else`:

```
if 5>3:
  print("hello")
  x = 20
else:
  x = 0
  print("bye")
```

There is also a way to chain multiple tests (a "many-way" `if` statement) using the `elif` keyword.

The `while` statement:

```
x = 19
while x>0:
  print('-')
  x = x - 1
print('.')
```

Note: Rarely used, it is also possible to follow the `while` statement with `else`, which gets executed when the loop ends. Within a `while` loop, the `continue` statement causes the next iteration of the loop to start immediately; the `break` statement terminates the loop immediately (and skips over any `else` part, if there is one).

The `for` statement:

```
e = range(3,23)
for i in e:
  print(50-i)
```

The `continue`, `break`, and `else` statements can also be used in `for` loops. The `return` statement: the `return` statement immediately exits a function; if there is a value to the right of `return`, then that value is the result of the function invocation.

Exception Statements. The keywords `try`, `except`, `finally`, and `raise` are used to alter control flow using exceptions; this is a more advanced topic than this brief appendix covers.

Library Statements

`import` copies a module from a library or from a file. Example:

```
import sys
print(sys.argv)
```

Note: The names of things inside the imported module have a "qualified" or "hierarchical" way of referring to them. The `from` statement copies from within a module, allowing the names to be accessed directly:

```
from sys import *
print(argv)
```

Function Invocation and Definition

`function(arguments)` invokes a function; depending on the function definition, the arguments may include keywords with assignments, for example:

```
f(7,term=True)
```

The function *head* (where you define the function) can specify keyword *default values*, which say what values to use if the function's caller does not provide these keyword arguments. If a keyword default value is a mutable object, such as a list, then that default value can actually be changed by one call, and persist for later calls (this is a tricky behavior of Python).

The syntax `function(*myargs)` in a function's head allows *function* to be called with any number of arguments; then `myargs` will be a tuple, consisting of the arguments supplied by `function`'s caller. The same syntax, `function(*someargs)`, when used by the caller of `function`, means that `someargs` is a sequence, which should be converted to a tuple used for the list of arguments to `function`. The syntax `function(**myargs)` in a function head presumes that `myargs` is a dictionary, with strings as keys, so that the keys can be used as keyword arguments. The syntax can use both styles, for example, `function(*a,**b)` would allow positional arguments first, then keyword arguments.

The **def** statement defines a function, declaring its arguments (which can include keyword parameters and their defaults),

```
def myfun(x,y):
    print("myfun called with", x, y)
    if x>y:
        return x-y
    else:
        return y-x
```

Lambda Expressions:

It is possible to define very simple functions in a one-line expression: `f = lambda x: 2*x` defines `f` the same as a longer definition

```
def f(x):
    return 2*x
```

Using a lambda expression can make programs more concise:

```
reduce((lambda x,y: x+y),[3,9,20,5])
```

Class Definition and Object Creation

The **class** statement defines a class, which establishes the pattern for future objects that will be created for this class.

```
class MyClass():
    def __init__(self):
        self.pos = 0
    def move(self,t):
        self.pos = self.pos + t
```

A fancier form of the class statement allows you to define a class in terms of another class, which is the idea of *inheritance*. To create an object (also called an *instance* of the class), an example would be:

```
x = MyClass()    # create a new instance
x.move(3)        # invoke the move method on x
print(x.pos)     # will print 3
```

Aliasing

Two variables can refer to the same object; conversely, different instances of the same class can have different values:

```
x = MyClass()
z = MyClass()
y = x
x.move(15)
print(y.pos)    # will print 15
print(x is y)   # will print True
print(x is z)   # will print False
print(z.pos)    # will print 0
```

Note: Lists are essentially objects of a "list" class, so aliasing occurs with lists (this is a frequent difficulty for beginning Python programmers). The following example illustrates how aliasing can be confusing—you change the object using one variable name, and all the other variables referring to the same object also get changed.

```
a = [1,2,3,4,[True,False],5]
b = a
b[0:4] = []     # replace a slice of b
print(a)        # will print [[True,False],5]
```

Dictionaries are also objects; all objects are *mutable* types, whereas strings, tuples, booleans, and numbers are *immutable*, so these do not suffer from alias situations. Use the `is` operator to test whether two variables are aliases.

Inside Python

DocStrings. If the first line of a Python program (or function) is a string, then that is called the "documentation string" of the program (or function).

Introspection. There are built-in functions to ask Python about the type of a variable, list of defined variables, list of functions, the documentation string, and many other things.

```
vars()    returns a dictionary of names
dir()     returns keys of vars()
locals()  dictionary of local names
globals() dictionary of global names
__doc__   the DocString
type(x)   returns the type of name x
isinstance(x,T) True if x is of type T
id(x)     internal key of name x
x is y    True if id(x)==id(y)
```

Index